THE HEARSTS

FAMILY AND EMPIRE—
THE LATER YEARS

Lindsay Chaney
Michael Cieply

SIMON AND SCHUSTER
NEW YORK

Copyright © 1981 by Lindsay Chaney and Michael Cieply
All rights reserved
including the right of reproduction
in whole or in part in any form
Published by Simon and Schuster
A Division of Gulf & Western Corporation
Simon & Schuster Building
Rockefeller Center
1230 Avenue of the Americas
New York, New York 10020

SIMON AND SCHUSTER and colophon are trademarks of Simon & Schuster
Designed by Eve Kirch
Photo editor: Vincent Virga
Manufactured in the United States of America

1   3   5   7   9   10   8   6   4   2

Library of Congress Cataloging in Publication Data

Chaney, Lindsay, date.
The Hearsts : family and empire—the later years.
Bibliography: p.
Includes index.
1.   Hearst, William Randolph, 1863–1951.   2.   Journalists—United States—Biography.   3.   Hearst family.
4.   Hearst Corporation.   I.   Cieply, Michael, 1951–
joint author.   II.   Title.
PN4874.H4C47   070.5′092′2 [B]   80–23623

ISBN 0-671-24765-4

*The authors would like to express their appreciation to the following for permission
to publish or reprint material from copyrighted or other controlled sources.*

Mrs. George Randolph Hearst, Sr., for excerpts from letters by her late husband,
George Randolph Hearst, Sr.

Joanne Hearst, for excerpts from letters by her late father, John R. Hearst.

(Continued on page 411)

ACKNOWLEDGMENTS

THIS BOOK BEGAN WITH the authors' curiosity about a subject that was almost too familiar, and yet remained tantalizingly unexplored. By 1976, when we first conceived of writing about the Hearsts, the family name had become a watchword for the times; to mention the word "Hearst" was to conjure images of wealth and influence, of manipulation, rebellion, violence and guilt. Yet no one seemed to really know who they were, this family that had fallen into the maelstrom. "William Randolph Hearst, is that Patty's father?" people asked. "How much money do they really have?" "Is Patty really a newspaper heiress?"

We, too, wondered about the Hearsts—about how they, of all people, had become the symbol of inherited wealth in America. So we began delving into the family's past, first through the standard printed sources, and then through the magnificent collection of family documents that are housed in the Bancroft Library of the University of California.

The first stages of our story unfolded in the Bancroft, where the Phoebe Apperson Hearst, George Hearst, William Randolph Hearst, Millicent Hearst, William Randolph Hearst, Jr., John Francis Neylan and Edmond Coblentz collections provided a rare firsthand view of the family legacy. Few of these letters and documents were available to previous biographers, and we owe a special debt of gratitude to Bancroft

Director James Hart not only for guiding us to them, but for granting us access to several collections that are as yet uncatalogued.

Other manuscript collections that later proved useful include the Peck family papers in the Huntington Library in Pasadena; the Marion Davies–Hedda Hopper correspondence in the library of the Academy of Motion Picture Arts and Sciences; the W.R. Hearst–Marion Davies correspondence (private collection); the Columbia University Oral History Series (in which a number of interviews deal with Hearst's early newspaper and political careers); and the John Hearst papers (private collection). A special thanks is due to William Robertson, of the Los Angeles County Federation of Labor, who provided access to files of that organization dealing with the strike at the Los Angeles *Herald-Examiner*, and helped arrange interviews with other area labor leaders. The clipping files in New York's Lincoln Center library were most helpful in documenting Millicent Hearst's stage career, while the Special Collections Department at the University of California, Los Angeles, contained a complete file of leaflets published by unions during the Los Angeles strike.

For the balance of the material on which this book is based, we are indebted to the many people who shared their time, their thoughts, and, in some cases, their friendship with us.

Many of the Hearsts were both generous with their help and surprisingly candid in their observations about the family. Bill Hearst, Jack and Phoebe Cooke, Joanne Hearst and her husband, Walter Lawrence, John Hearst, Jr., and Mrs. George Randolph Hearst, Jr., all spent long hours remembering and explaining their family's history. Randy Hearst, George Hearst, Jr., Austin and Denise Hearst, Will and Nan Hearst, and Bernie Shaw provided us with eminently useful material. Patricia Hearst Shaw was gracious enough to share one of her visiting days in the federal correctional facility at Pleasanton; for that favor we thank her.

While declining to divulge precise financial information, corporate executives John Miller and Frank Bennack were nonetheless willing to talk freely about the company, and to arrange a number of interviews with key Hearst personnel. This represented a clean—and, we are sure, salutary—break with the policy of silence that prevailed during the years of the Berlin regime.

Reg Murphy managed to find time for the authors on several occasions when he obviously had no time to spare.

Among the other Hearst friends, employees and—sometimes, at least
—opponents who provided us with interviews are Charles Bates, Gregson
Bautzer, Ed Bell, Honey Berlin, Richard Berlin, Jr., Donald Biggs,
Virginia Blight, Gene Block, Greg Braxton, Seward Brisbane, Helen
Gurley Brown, Herb Caen, Tim Cahill, Joe Camillieri, Edward H. Clark,
Jr., Dorothy Chandler, Steve Cook, Buster Collier, Stevie Collier, Wes
Davis, Newton Drury, Ted Dumke, Peggy Fears, Lynette Fromme, Bud
Furillo, Charles Gould, Faith Grant, Terence Hallinan, Howard Handel-
man, Ted Harbert, John Harris, Julian Hart, Nieson Himmel, Jean
Howard, Harry Huberth, Bernie Hughes, Tony Ingrassia, Woodrow
Irwin, Tom Kennington, Theodore Kheel, Larry Kramer, Archie
Lamedeer, Anne Shirley Lederer, Lynn Ludlow, Donald McLaughlin, Ray
Mann, George Martinez, Arthur Mejia, Jr., Anne Miller, Harrison Mit-
nick, Ed Montgomery, Mike Moore, Dave Neuwirth, Jack O'Connell,
Harriet Parsons, Sal Perotta, Bert Powers, Raul Ramirez, George Rascoe,
Mabel Reed, Michael Rogers, Malcolm Roop, Denise Ross, Charles
Rowland, Bob Rupert, Adela Rogers St. Johns, Bernard Silbert, Joe
Kingsbury Smith, Kevin Starr, Howard Strickling, John Sullivan, Ted
Thackrey, Jr., Trish Tobin, John Barr Tompkins, Alice Brisbane Tooker,
Bill Torrence, Agnes Underwood, Reg Vaughn, Diana Vreeland, Emily
Smith Warner, James Wechsler, Steven Weed, Jann Wenner and George
Woods.

Several writers and researchers stole time from their own projects to
lend us their help. We remember especially Chris Cooke, Mack Eastham,
Lacey Fosburgh, Bob Gottlieb, Robert Griffith, Fred Guiles, Rosemary
Kent, June McMullen, Kenneth Marx, Dave Oshinsky, Carla Rapoport,
Roger Rapoport, W. A. Swanberg and Ken Turan.

We received professional help beyond the call of duty from Paul
Borden and Jim Kantor at the Bancroft Library. David Eisen, of the
Newspaper Guild, was both helpful and encouraging. John Callinan, of
the Los Angeles County Clerk's office, steered us through the red tape
surrounding the Hearst probate file. Without Robert Sturhahn's legal
expertise, we might never have deciphered the William Randolph Hearst
will.

Any book must bring with it a roster of personal debts. In our case,
we know that we can acknowledge but never repay: James Vann and
Paul Robinson, two friends who counseled courage and cheer throughout;
Arlene Nieman, whose confidence was greater than our own; Terry

Pristin, whose uncommon good sense and advice were a continual inspiration; William Abrahams, whose enthusiasm launched the project; John Dodds, our editor, whose excitement brought it to life; Mary Cieply, for her valuable help in arranging interviews; Andrew Juhasz, for his support and always incisive criticism; and finally, Nancy Kuriloff, who helped us through the inevitable crisis.

CONTENTS

Contents

Photo section follows page 160

THE FAMILY
and
THE EMPIRE

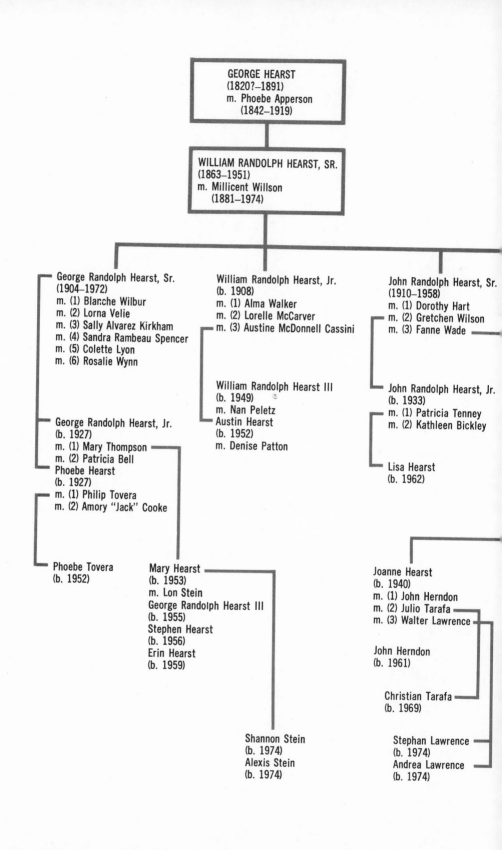

THE FAMILY

Randolph Apperson Hearst
(b. 1915)
m. Catherine Campbell

David Whitmire Hearst
(b. 1915)
m. Hope Chandler

Catherine Hearst
(b. 1939)
Virginia Hearst
(b. 1949)
Patricia Hearst
(b. 1954)
m. Bernard Shaw
Anne Hearst
(b. 1955)
Victoria Hearst
(b. 1956)

Millicent Hearst
(b. 1939)
m. Raouf Baoudjakdji
David Whitmire Hearst, Jr.
(b. 1944)

Anita Baoudjakdji
(b. 1964)
Cherif Baoudjakdji
(b. 1967)
Samia Baoudjakdji
(b. 1969)

William Randolph Hearst II
(b. 1942)
m. (1) Jennifer Gooch
m. (2) Julie Harris

Debra Hearst
(b. 1950)
m. (1) Dale Woodard
m. (2) Gary Gallagher

Jason Hearst
(b. 1972)

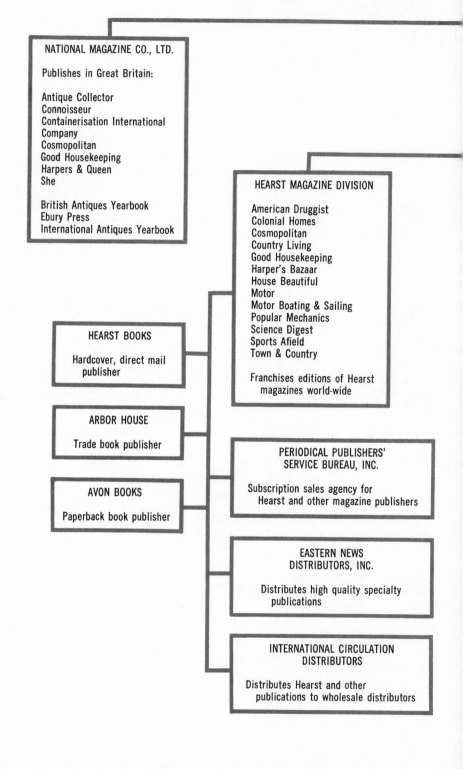

NATIONAL MAGAZINE CO., LTD.

Publishes in Great Britain:

Antique Collector
Connoisseur
Containerisation International
Company
Cosmopolitan
Good Housekeeping
Harpers & Queen
She

British Antiques Yearbook
Ebury Press
International Antiques Yearbook

HEARST MAGAZINE DIVISION

American Druggist
Colonial Homes
Cosmopolitan
Country Living
Good Housekeeping
Harper's Bazaar
House Beautiful
Motor
Motor Boating & Sailing
Popular Mechanics
Science Digest
Sports Afield
Town & Country

Franchises editions of Hearst
magazines world-wide

HEARST BOOKS

Hardcover, direct mail
publisher

ARBOR HOUSE

Trade book publisher

AVON BOOKS

Paperback book publisher

**PERIODICAL PUBLISHERS'
SERVICE BUREAU, INC.**

Subscription sales agency for
Hearst and other magazine publishers

**EASTERN NEWS
DISTRIBUTORS, INC.**

Distributes high quality specialty
publications

**INTERNATIONAL CIRCULATION
DISTRIBUTORS**

Distributes Hearst and other
publications to wholesale distributors

THE HEARST CORPORATION

Corporate offices
Management service department
Intercompany clearing agent

Holds:
New York City real estate
Art objects and antiques
warehoused in New York and San Simeon

KING FEATURES SYNDICATE

Newspaper feature service

PUCK—THE COMIC WEEKLY

Sunday color comic section

HEARST NEWSPAPER DIVISION

Albany Knickerbocker News Union-Star (p.m.)
Albany Times-Union (a.m.)
Baltimore News American (p.m.)
Boston Herald American (a.m.)
Edwardsville [Ill.] Intelligencer (p.m.)
Huron [Mich.] Daily Tribune (p.m.)
Los Angeles Herald-Examiner (p.m.)
Midland [Mich.] Daily News (p.m.)
Midland [Tex.] Reporter-Telegram (p.m.)
Plainview [Tex.] Daily Herald (p.m.)
Seattle Post-Intelligencer (a.m.)

San Francisco Newspaper Printing Co.
(50% interest)
San Francisco Examiner (p.m.)
Sunday Examiner & Chronicle

HEARST BROADCASTING DIVISION

Television
WBAL, Baltimore
WISN, Milwaukee
WTAE, Pittsburgh

Radio
WBAL (am)
WIYY (fm)   Baltimore
WISN (am)
WLPX (fm)   Milwaukee
WTAE (am)
WXKX (fm)   Pittsburgh
WAPA (am)   San Juan,
Puerto Rico

SUNICAL LAND & LIVESTOCK DIVISION

Manages timberland and ranch operations at:
Jack Ranch, Cholame, Ca. (65,000 acres)
Piedra Blanca Ranch, San Simeon, Ca. (80,000 acres)
Wyntoon, McCloud, Ca. (70,000 acres)

PEJEPSCOT PAPER DIVISION

Produces specialty papers
Manages timberlands in Washington
Co., Me., and New Brunswick, Canada (100,000 acres)

SOUTHWEST FOREST INDUSTRIES, INC.
(17% interest)

Diversified forest products company
with headquarters in Phoenix, Ariz.

SAN LUIS MINING CO.
(25% interest)

Operates gold and silver
mine in Durango, Mex.

BOOK ONE

THE LEGACY

Chapter 1

"Forget his faults..."

It was a driving sense of urgency that swept Richard Berlin into 1007 North Beverly Drive, Los Angeles. The time was midmorning on Tuesday, August 14, 1951. The man, who looked more than usually strained and self-important, was the fifty-seven-year-old president of the Hearst Corporation. And the occasion was the death of William Randolph Hearst.

Hearst had died just twenty minutes before the executive's arrival, succumbing to what the attending physician, Dr. Myron Prinzmetal, called "a series of cerebral-vascular accidents"—that is, a brain hemorrhage. Berlin, who for nearly four years had known that Hearst's grasp on life was precarious, can hardly have been surprised by his employer's final collapse at the age of eighty-eight. But he was nevertheless convinced that this was a critical moment. For Richard Berlin realized that there is much at stake on the manner of a great man's passing; and he was determined that Hearst's death should be arranged to the best advantage of those who would be left to succeed him.

To that end, the executive's first task was to quickly remove the body from the pink stucco mansion on North Beverly—the house belonged to Marion Davies, Hearst's mistress of thirty years; as Berlin viewed the matter, it was wholly inappropriate that a man who prided himself on publishing newspapers "for the NICEST KIND OF PEOPLE, the great middle class," should die in the home of a woman other than his wife. As it happened, the rescue of Hearst's remains was easily accomplished. Arriving on the scene, Berlin found Miss Davies tranquilized into oblivion, and thus in no condition to object when he told her gathered retainers: "You're all working for me now." Under his direction, the body was whisked off to Pierce Brothers, a Beverly Hills undertaker that had been put on notice several years before, while Marion was left to awaken in an empty house. Later, still in shock, she would sob to reporters:

> He was gone. I asked where he was and the nurse said he was dead. His body was gone, *whoosh*, like that. I didn't even know whether he was dead when they took him. Old W.R. was gone, the boys were gone. I was alone. They didn't even let me say good-bye. Do you realize what they did? They stole a possession of mine. He belonged to me. I loved him for thirty-two years and now he was gone. Yes, I couldn't even say good-bye.

Marion was not to have her private farewell, or a public one either for that matter. She spoke with the publisher's son Bill on the telephone that night, but when she asked where the funeral was to be held, he pointedly refused to tell her.

Berlin, meanwhile, was busy assembling the Hearst family for a final display of solidarity. After dispatching attorney Henry McKay to file the press lord's will for probate (the document was submitted before Judge Newcomb Condee within hours of Hearst's death so that, as McKay said, "there would be no break in the continuity of his far-flung operation"), the executive began combing Los Angeles for four of the five sons— George; William Randolph junior; Randolph; and David—who had gathered in the city to be present at the patriarch's end. None of the boys was in the house when their father died, but a quickly contrived press release—which carefully avoided any mention of Marion—announced that they, along with Berlin and fellow executive Martin Huberth, had been at Hearst's bedside when he expired.

By late that afternoon, Berlin had managed to collect the four and to load them, with their father's hastily embalmed corpse, aboard a Hearst Corporation plane. In accordance with a long-standing plan, the group was then flown north to San Francisco (passing over San Simeon, the pilot dipped his wings in salute), where the fifth son, John, waited, and where arrangements had been made to complete the family circle. There, in the interest of propriety, William Randolph Hearst was at last to be reconciled with his wife, the boys' mother, Millicent.

It was a reconciliation that Hearst would not have relished. The old sybarite, who had been estranged from Millicent Hearst, nee Willson, for three long decades, had made no secret of the fact that he wanted a divorce on almost any terms his wife would care to name. In his determination to dissolve their bond he had not only hired a battery of detectives to dog her steps, but had mobilized his newspapers in a highly uncharacteristic campaign for liberalized divorce legislation. But Millicent, a New York showgirl who had become a society matron on the solid foundation of Hearst's name and money, would never consent to a voluntary divorce (she stood firm behind the shield of her Catholicism), and took special pains to avoid the sort of impropriety that might have given her husband his freedom.

Apparently Hearst's wife had some qualms of her own about this final meeting, which she privately referred to as "my ordeal." There is a story—especially favored among Marion's friends—that the plane bringing her and John and her sister Anita to San Francisco was struck by a bolt of lightning en route. Turning pale, the widow gripped the seat and gasped, "I'm being punished!" Yet it seemed that long-time Hearst associate John Francis Neylan offered the best advice when he told her, "Forget his faults; they were bound to be big ones. Notwithstanding them he was an amazing figure and towered over the little fry who are playing with American newspapers."

Deciding that she was willing to forgive and forget if her husband would do the same, Millicent hustled off to a suite of rooms at the Fairmont, while the old man was installed across Nob Hill in the towering gloom of Grace Cathedral.

It was early Wednesday morning when Hearst was laid out in the Cathedral's Chapel of Grace, which was a small-scale replica of the Parisian church of Saint Chapelle, bathed in a deep-blue light emanating from beyond the delicate webwork of its mock-Gothic windows. Attendants draped the body in a scarf of roses sent by the family and surrounded it with flags and yellow mums, while an honor guard from the American Legion, the VFW, the police, and the firemen took their positions around the casket. The cathedral's great Ghiberti doors were then thrown open to the few odd members of the public who might want to pay some kind of tribute to the old publisher who had kept himself locked away from prying eyes for the last several decades.

In the beginning, there seemed to be little interest in the man; on the first day tiny knots of onlookers, six or eight at a time, collected outside the church and were escorted in groups to the chapel. But as the word spread through the city that William Randolph Hearst was at last exposed to public view, the crowd began to swell. By the second morning the original trickle of visitors had become a long file, stretching out of the church and down California Street, as thousands of San Franciscans turned out to steal a parting glimpse at the gaunt old corpse. Apparently it was a spontaneous demonstration of the impression Hearst had left on the minds of not one generation, but two or even three. The *Examiner* chose to call it a "tribute" and was delighted to report that "there were those who were well dressed and others of obviously lesser means, and wounded veterans and youths who wore their country's discharge emblem, and each with marked sincerity passed the casket and walked slowly out of the chapel." But the motley army of gawkers almost certainly had more to do with curiosity than with reverence. Hearst had achieved the status of a legend; with his monstrous reputation for both good and ill, he had swollen in the popular imagination to almost mythic proportions, and it seemed clear to all but the *Examiner* that those who came were there less to admire than to wonder.

The Hearst family is reticent about how they spent those two days while the crowds filed by. One friend remembers peering from the dining room of the nearby Pacific Union Club to see a fat and doleful George wandering about; he hailed the eldest son to offer his condolences, and was invited out to a bar. And a long-time Hearst newsman who slipped into the cathedral just before the service for his first glance at a man he had dealt with scores of times by phone and telegraph recalls that he ran into the second son, Bill, in the church; he was sitting alone and silent, obviously lost in a deep reverie. But for the most part, the Hearsts were more elusive. The clan gathered in Millicent's suite, and spent two days —in the words of one who was there—"talking family." They asked themselves questions: Would it be different now with the old man gone? How far could they trust the people he had left in charge? Whom, for that matter, had he left in charge? And every so often, someone would go to the window to pull back a curtain and mumble the question that for the moment weighed heaviest of all—"I wonder if she's coming."

Marion did not come, nor did hundreds of her Hollywood friends, who were already abuzz with talk about what one of them still calls "the worst piece of bitchery the world has ever seen."

So at least for the morning of August 17, a cool and overcast Friday, the Hearsts were a family united. The loyal sons flanked their grieving mother at the service, filling the first two pews on the left, while hordes of solemn dignitaries and the empire's aristocracy lined the church on the right. The presiding clergyman, a stiff and unctuous Bishop Karl Morgan Block, droned through the Psalms—46th, 121st and 130th—while the Cathedral Men's Chorus bellowed Dvorak's "Twenty-Third Psalm" and Ferdinand de la Tombelli's "My Lord and Saviour." Hearst was never a religious man (he had faithfully sent Sunday guests at San Simeon to church in the village while he remained at home, presumably communing with gods of his own), but the prelate made the best of his subject's less than doctrinaire brand of piety, by embellishing the service with a reading of Hearst's own "Song of the River." The poem, much publicized by his papers, seemed to indicate a vague belief in reincarnation with its lines that ran:

> *The river ran its allotted span*
> *Till it reached the silent sea.*
> *Then the water harked back to the mountaintop*
> *To begin its course once more.*
> *So we shall run the course begun*
> *Till we reach the silent shore,*
> *Then revisit earth in a pure rebirth*
> *From the heart of the virgin snow.*

Yet whatever Hearst had lacked in dogmatic rigor, he had surely made up in patriotic fervor. So it was fitting that the most striking feature of the service—barring, perhaps, the flag of red, white and blue carnations presented by the staff of the San Francisco *Examiner*—should be a list of honorary pallbearers that included such national luminaries as Herbert Hoover, Douglas MacArthur, Earl Warren, Bernard Baruch, Arthur Hays Sulzberger, Roy Howard and Colonel Robert R. McCormick. Without doubt Hearst would have approved of MacArthur and Hoover; he referred to the general as one of the greatest Americans since Valley Forge, and he always maintained great respect for the Presidency, although, in point of fact, he had believed Hoover to be a fat and fatuous failure and had taken considerable pains to warn the public against his wholly un-American ways. One wonders, however, whether Berlin and his confederates had not succumbed to an excess of zeal in arranging to have the Chief carried to his grave, however figuratively, by a pair of old competitors. Hearst could not have been happy knowing that he would be buried by men like Chicago *Tribune* publisher McCormick, who had beaten him repeatedly on his own mass-circulation turf, and Howard, about whom he had been feeling uneasy since 1932, when one of his United Press reporters called at the ranch to commit the unthinkable sin of asking Hearst whether he was dead yet! (The query prompted a wire: "Now Roy stop this damned nonsense. I have never been sick in my life nor dead either. Moreover, if you want to participate in a little light humor I will bet you ten thousand dollars that I attend your funeral.")

But it was probably Berlin's precise intention that old antagonisms should be forgotten in the moment of death. And so William Randolph Hearst was borne away on the shoulders of presidents, generals, governors, mayors, rival press lords, and well-connected financiers—friend and foe alike—to be placed in the family vault at the Cypress Law Cemetery in the San Francisco suburb of Colma, where he found his final rest.

Magnificent as it was, of course, the stately service was by no means the only assistance Hearst received in treading the path to immortality. The Hearst organization was well aware that a great man must be greatly mourned—and it happened that no one was so admirably equipped for the task as the organization itself. Determined to make America feel its loss, the vast Hearst publicity machine unlimbered, sparing none of the devices it had developed in sixty-four years in the business, as it set out to bemoan its founder's death.

The papers had hung fire for a moment, checked in their early editions by Hearst's insistence that they not preset his obituaries. But when at last they found their voice, they compensated for the delay with an outburst of lamentation that was nothing short of Biblical in its vehemence. Weeping and gnashing its teeth under a 172-point banner, the flagship New York *Journal-American* set the pace with its eulogistic lead: "The world has lost a colossus . . . such a man as he, who became a legend within his lifetime, we shall not see again." From Los Angeles, James Padgitt of the International News Service, the Hearst wire, reported that citizens "stood in stunned silence in realization of their loss," while in San Francisco, the morning *Examiner,* "Monarch of the Dailies," asserted its rights as Hearst's premier paper by devoting the entire front page to a somber, black-bordered portrait of the press lord. Reviewing his career, the *Examiner* decided that the only question posterity would face regarding William Randolph Hearst was: "How could one man in one lifetime have established so huge a reservoir of good will?"

Hearst columnists vied with one another for days in assessing the damage inflicted on the Republic by Hearst's death. The injury they described was so great that artist Burris Jenkins felt compelled to portray the Statue of Liberty not just in mourning, but swooning on the verge of total collapse. Gene Fowler did some quick arithmetic and discovered that his boss had been "eyewitness to almost precisely one half of our nation's existence." Marveling at the staying power that had "kept him in the ring" decade after decade, he eulogized that "his refusal to accept the ill-conceived and cowardly slogans of political office boys posing as statesmen or to veil the truth from the American public sometimes invited adverse criticism that would have crushed a lesser mortal." But it was editorialist Merryle Stanley Rukeyser who reached for the limit in the chain's official "Farewell to the Chief." Rukeyser shamelessly declared that it was no one other than Hearst—"decades ahead of routine politicians and professional liberals"—who had "set down the specifications for the future promise of American life." Before the week was out, millions of Hearst readers must surely have doubted that the nation would survive the blow.

If the wailing was meant to drown out the voices of detractors who might use the occasion for a last jab at a fallen giant, it was, as usual, a case of overkill. Negative judgments were remarkably few. Certainly *Time,* playing the conscientious journalist, noted that Hearst, after inventing the techniques of modern newspaper communication, "had often misused those techniques to sensationalize journalism, to seduce its public, and debauch its practitioners." The iconoclastic A. J. Liebling wrote in *The New Yorker* that Hearst's principal contribution to the art had been "to demonstrate that a man without previous newspaper experience could, by using money like a heavy club, do what he wanted in the newspaper business except when comparable wealth opposed him." London's *News Chronicle* called him a "wicked old reactionary" who had used his papers "to oppose all that was liberal and progressive." And *Christian Century,* in a fit of moral fervor, claimed for Hearst that "his papers bred a race of journalistic mercenaries who took his money as sufficient recompense for the denials of decency and truth he constantly exacted from them."

But on the whole, the reviews were respectful and, where necessary, forgiving. Hearst's most bitter opponents—Al Smith, Franklin Roosevelt, William McKinley, Joseph Pulitzer, Mark Hanna, Collis Huntington, John D. Rockefeller and Leland Stanford, to name only a few—had long since preceded him to the grave. And the greatest of his sins—the demagoguery of his political campaigns, the ruthlessness of his sometimes bloody circulation battles, the supreme irresponsibility of his efforts to ignite a war with Spain—roused little indignation from a generation that could no longer remember the *Maine*.

Chapter 2

The Legend

(1)

HE BEGAN with a single paper, a "miserable little sheet" called the *Examiner*, which ran to as many as eight pages and stretched the truth considerably when it claimed a paid circulation of 23,914. It was neither the biggest, nor the best, nor the most respected journal in San Francisco. In fact, Hearst himself said it furnished "the crowning absurdity of illustrated journalism," and accused it of reportage "so detestable that it would render the death of the writer justifiable homicide." But, at the age of twenty-three, he had set his heart on owning it.

His father, George, a California mining baron who had purchased the paper as part of a political deal that eventually put him in the United States Senate, tried to persuade his son that getting involved with the *Examiner* "was the very worst thing he could do." He offered to put the boy in charge of a million-acre ranch in Mexico, or to let him take over his share of the great Homestake mine in the Black Hills of South Dakota. But Will Hearst replied that "I have begun to have a strange fondness for our little paper—a tenderness like unto that which a mother feels for her puny or deformed offspring. I should hate to see it die after it has battled so long and so nobly for its existence." Possessed by what he called that "very common weakness"—the conviction that he could run a newspaper successfully—he pleaded, he cajoled, and then finally he insisted, until his father had no choice but to surrender the *Examiner*, along with an open account for the first two years.

William Randolph Hearst became proprietor of the San Francisco *Examiner* on March 4, 1887. Within one short week, he had christened his puny offspring the "Monarch of the Dailies," proclaiming it, by royal fiat, to be "THE LARGEST, BRIGHTEST AND BEST NEWSPAPER ON THE PACIFIC COAST." And within four short years, he had made it so. With an intensity that was almost frightening to those who knew him, he had launched into the paper, breaking it down piece by piece—discarding old habits, old type, old personnel, with reckless abandon—and then building it up again, not according to a vision of his own, but in the image of the one newspaper he truly admired, the raucous and mighty New York *World* of Joseph Pulitzer. Like the *World*, the *Examiner* screamed in headlines that broke through column rules: "HUNGRY, FRANTIC FLAMES LEAPING HIGHER, HIGHER, WITH DESPERATE DESIRE," ran the standard fare. Like the *World*, the *Examiner* stopped at nothing in its zeal to create a sensation. At the behest of its frantic young publisher, the paper sent trainloads of artists and writers flying through the night to scoop its rivals on a story as routine as a hotel fire; it dispatched its reporters to traipse through the hills in quest of grizzly bears and gun-slinging fugitives; it escorted Sarah Bernhardt on a tour of the city's opium dens and lofted young lovers above the bay in balloons, where they were married by airsick clergymen, all for the sake of a few column inches.

Like the *World*, too, the *Examiner* flourished. Not that the paper ever made money—on the contrary, it devoured the family's gold dollars at the rate of some twenty thousand per month, and was to cost the Senator a solid million before he finally saw fit to lock up his accounts. But no one could doubt that the Monarch was growing in stature. Its enemies were forced to take notice of the boy editor they had smugly dismissed as a flash in the pan. Hearst knew he had passed a milestone when he could gleefully inform his father that "the *Call* is crazy at us and comes out every morning with an editorial against us, but we like that. It advertises us." And the news-hungry public could scarcely resist the attraction of a paper that promised to pack all the "tragedies and romance of life" into each and every edition. Even before the first year had ended, Hearst was pleased to note that "the great and good people of California want the *Examiner*. They don't want it very bad; they don't want it much harder than at the rate of thirty additional copies a day, but in time this will count. If we can manage to keep ahead we will have in a year from now thirty to thirty-two thousand subscribers." In the second year, the reborn *Examiner* could claim some 40,000 paying customers, and by 1891, when its daily circulation reached a grand total of 57,352, the Monarch of the Dailies had indeed become the biggest paper on the Pacific slope.

But even before he had conquered his native city, Hearst was beginning to flirt with a scheme that was grander and a great deal more volatile than the rescue of a beleaguered little Western journal. From the first he had worked with an eye trained on Pulitzer, the immigrant Jew whose frenetic energy, coupled with a wide streak of genius and an almost rabid determination "to root out public abuses and expose evildoers," had made him the nation's most formidable publisher. Hearst knew that Pulitzer's grip on New York was unchallenged. With a circulation that topped half a million, his *World*, three times the size of its nearest competitor, commanded fierce loyalty among the teeming masses, who looked to the paper not just for news, but for solace, for guidance, and— above all—for protection from the predatory "interests" that it managed to expose, edition after edition and day after day. But Hearst also knew something else: by 1890, Joseph Pulitzer, the man who had invented the yellow journal, was showing the signs of age. His nerves, always fragile, were fast becoming unraveled. He was living for the most part in Europe by then, away from his readers and away from the men who made his paper hum. And, what was still more telling, he was exhibiting just enough caution, for the first time in his life, to leave him vulnerable before a younger Turk—like William Randolph Hearst.

Hearst was twenty-seven years old when the rumblings of ambition began to sound. It was in 1890, the year before his father's death that he first warned his mother, Phoebe, "I am getting so that I'm not afraid of Pulitzer even . . . but I do wish this town were bigger or that the *Examiner* were in New York." The next year he made his initial move on the metropolis. In the course of a month-long foray to the East (during which he was pleased to report that "there is a great deal of gossip in newspaper row about my being here and I meet with all sorts of rumors"), he managed to talk with "every newspaperman in New York." He considered a partnership with the old Pulitzer ally, John Cockerill; he bargained for the dying *Recorder* with its tobacco-king owner, James Duke; and he spent a full night pumping Ballard Smith, managing editor of the *World*, for the tiniest scrap of information about his distant employer. But not until four years later was he able to persuade his mother, who had since fallen heir to the Senator's fortune, to part with the cash that he would need for his venture. In August of 1895, the woman at last sold her interest in her husband's last bonanza, the Anaconda mine of Montana, for $7.5 million;* and on October 7 of that year her son, who received the proceeds from the sale as his patrimony, became the owner of his second paper, a modest daily (circulation 77,000) called the New York *Journal*.

It was in New York that the legend was born. He was always an outsider there, always the stranger who had come from the West with his Stetson hat and his father's mining millions to take the city by storm. Even as late as 1906—when he had already been to Congress for Manhattan's Eleventh District and was claiming to be the rightful mayor of New York (after having been narrowly beaten by Tammany's John McClellan in a scandal-ridden contest)—the local reviews would brand him a "Man of Mystery," while the more sophisticated wags continued to debate whether Hearst was only an enigma or perhaps an out-and-out myth.

And yet, from the day he arrived, in the early fall of 1895, he had done a great deal to make himself known, if not quite loved, by those who watched his enterprise grow. Certainly he had lost no time in announcing himself to the city's publishers. When he took over the *Journal*, he doubled its size, while slashing its price to a penny—and within months two lesser competitors, the *Advertiser* and the *Press*, were dead. Nor did he neglect to pay a special homage to the ailing Joseph

---

* In the course of his own phenomenal career, George Hearst, a rough, uneducated pioneer from Missouri, amassed a spectacular hoard of mineral claims. Hearst was one of the men who opened Nevada's Comstock Lode in 1860. Later, in partnership with the San Francisco entrepreneurs James Haggin and Lloyd Tevis, he developed the Ontario silver mine in Utah and the Homestake gold mine in South Dakota, along with hundreds of smaller claims in Mexico, Canada, and the American West. The Anaconda mine, which Hearst and his partners acquired in 1881, was to become the world's greatest producer of copper ore in the years after Phoebe sold her shares.

Pulitzer. Working from a redwood-lined office in Pulitzer's own building (which was leased as a New York bureau for the *Examiner*), he made a point of recruiting the very cream of his idol's staff as the core of his rapidly gathering legion.

With the help of the crew he had stolen from Pulitzer, Hearst soon made the *Journal* a Jekyll and Hyde, a force for good and a force for evil bound up in a single one-penny sheet. Backed by his fortune and his almost unfathomable zeal for reform, the paper established itself as a crusader without equal in an age when the muckraking press had at last come into its own. It was the *Journal* that first fought Consolidated Gas, forcing the giant combine—by means of violent front-page assaults and more than a thousand separate court injunctions—to roll back its scandalous rates to the legally mandated limit. The *Journal* exposed Ramapo Water, the paper corporation that, with the help of Mayor Grant, might well have made off with some $200 million from the public coffers. It defended the overworked women in the sweatshops of New Jersey; it campaigned for decent wages and the ten-hour day; it pressed for expansion of the public schools, and saved forty miles of the city's streets from devastation by the Nassau Railroad. When the Eastern press joined ranks against the rising tide of Populism in 1896, the *Journal* —alone among the New York dailies—took up the cudgels for William Jennings Bryan and for silver. And when twenty miners were shot by the sheriff's men in the bloody coal fields of Luzerne County, Pennsylvania, the *Journal*—again alone—took its stand not against the "striking anarchists" who haunted most of the established Eastern press, but against the overfed mining barons who, said Hearst, made strikes and violence inevitable.

No less formidable a figure than Lincoln Steffens paid tribute to the *Journal*'s crusades, when he wrote, "Mr. Hearst has waged as many good fights as any reformer I know. There isn't room even for a list of the good things Mr. Hearst has done or tried to do." But with that much said, Steffens could only add, "There isn't room either for a list of the bad, the small things he has done; the scandals he has published, the individuals he has made to suffer beyond their deserts. He has sent his reporters slumming among the rich; he has pandered to the curiosity about the vice and wickedness of wealth. His papers 'appealed to the people'; yes, to their 'best interest,' and to their worst." Indeed the *Journal* pandered. The men who made the paper for Hearst were never so happy as when a violent rape or a wanton stag party gave them the chance to let their instincts for the "tragedies and romance of life" run wild. Editors like the urbane Arthur Brisbane were perfectly capable of producing a paper that they didn't think fit for consumption in their own homes. "I remember that Papa would tear up the magazine section each Sunday before he allowed the paper in the house," one of Brisbane's daughters recalled. And more than a few of the *Journal*'s staff believed that their greatest coup was not the Ramapo Water fight, but their discovery in the Hudson of a sodden torso—armless, legless, and headless—that was displayed before several thousand shocked *Journal* readers until finally the murderer was identified, by a *Journal* man, of course, and duly executed.

But what truly staggered observers like Steffens, and E. L. Godkin, and even the redoubtable Mark Twain (a sometime contributor who once called Hearst's paper the "calamity of calamities") was the uninhibited drive with which the *Journal* pursued its ends. The paper was soon behaving like a sovereign state, a separate little kingdom on the isle of Manhattan, complete with a law of its own and a *Realpolitik* as ruthless as that of any nation in Europe. It first flexed its muscle in 1896, when it usurped the prerogatives of the city's Democratic machine. Opening its own Democratic party headquarters, the *Journal* took over the William Jennings Bryan Presidential campaign in New York. By 1897, it was laying plans for an expeditionary force to free Dreyfus from Devil's Island, and that same year it boldly dispatched its "commissioner," James Creelman, to the Royal Court in Madrid with an unconditional demand for the liberation of Cuba. In 1898, it was the *Journal*, a full three months in advance of the United States government, that declared the nation at war with Spain; though Congress would debate until well into April, the *Journal* was busy from February 15, the day the *Maine* went down, fighting the "Spanish butchers" with its imaginary regiments of cowboys, Indians, and heavyweight champs. And when the victorious fleet returned that August from what William Randolph Hearst, in conference with his minions, was inclined to call "our war," it was the *Journal* again that granted New York a holiday. The paper closed down the city's great retailers—Macy's, Lord and Taylor's, and the rest—simply by ordering its advertisers to join in the paper's victory celebration.

Not incidentally, of course, the *Journal*'s exuberance had finally beaten Pulitzer. By the time his war was over, the Westerner had driven the circulation of his paper—now divided into separate morning and evening publications—to the unprecedented peak of 1,250,000. In the three years since he had come to the city a virtual stranger, Hearst had made his name a daily habit among hundreds of thousands of laboring people who believed that he understood their plight. He had perfected the formulas of mass appeal; he had learned to command the loyalties that had once belonged to his rival; and—what seemed rather more troubling to those for whom he remained more than ever a mystery—he had touched the levers of national power.

The newspaper chain grew with Hearst's ambitions, thriving and multiplying almost unchecked, until finally it had become a force in nearly a dozen major cities. From New York he had pushed on to Chicago, where he traded favors with the Democrats in the summer of 1900. In exchange for giving a voice to the party in the heart of the Midwest (this fourth paper, the *American,* was rushed to production in time for the second great Bryan campaign), he was granted his first political sinecure, the presidency of the National Association of Democratic Clubs. Next he came to Los Angeles in 1903 as a powerful friend of labor. In mid-December of that year, the city's unions greeted his second *Examiner* with not just a rousing parade, but an advance list of some 50,000 eager subscribers. And by the time he reached Boston (with another paper called the *American*) in March of the following year, he had already been mentioned, by the Tammany men, as a serious contender for the Presidency.

Certainly, the papers became no better as he reached from city to city, adding Atlanta, Milwaukee and Washington to the chain by the end of the First World War. It was the magazine *World's Work* that summed up their tawdry and only too uniform appeal when it noted in 1906 that

These Hearst newspapers do not circulate among the most highly educated of the wealthy or the fashionable people of the cities wherein they are located. They sell for a cent, are printed in ink of various colors and with headlines of circus poster type. Their illustrations are fanciful and often sensational. The largest space is given to tragedies, to murders by women or on account of women, to elopements, to scandals and exaggerated descriptions of happenings in that class of society whose notoriety or wealth is best known.

But whatever their multicolored failings might be, the Hearst papers held fast to their primary virtue, loyalty to the man who owned them. Through the rising crescendo of his restless drive for office—as he ran twice for Congress, twice for mayor, and once for the governorship of New York, while angling so often for a Presidential nomination, that the wags finally dubbed him "William Also-ran-dolph Hearst"—the chain served with unflagging devotion as his private political machine. Cartoonists impaled his opponents without mercy. Circulation men pressed into ghettos and factory towns, to spread his word through the pockets of discontent. Reporters staffed his campaign offices, and when the heat was on—as in the bitter mayoralty race of 1905—they put their cameras and pads aside while they stumped from door to door for the candidate Hearst. For editors in the growing constellation of Hearst cities, the political angle had become second nature.

There may have been some on the papers who knew even then that his ambitions were corrupting them—turning them into the tools of an "interest," just as surely as the agents who did the work of Rockefeller, Hanna or Morgan. James Creelman, a *Journal* reporter who was wounded in Cuba and survived to run errands for Congressman Hearst, sounded an early note of regret when he wrote for *Pearson's*, in September 1906: "At first Mr. Hearst's New York paper was bright, enterprising, full of clever pictures and striking cartoons, saucy, but without malice or ruffianism. It caught the fancy of the crowd and won friends. Its raw and abusive politics were developed later on." Brisbane too had his private fits of conscience—he would tell his children that his columns in praise of Hearst were "trash." And Ambrose Bierce, who been with Hearst since the year he took over the *Examiner*, finally stalked off to other employment when he was pressured to join the rising fury of promotion. "I don't like the job of chained bulldog," he snapped in a letter to Hearst, "to be let loose only to tear the panties off the boys who throw rocks at you."

But for most, the fevered campaigns only served to cement a bond, a special *esprit*, that would endure when the wild political aspirations of Citizen Hearst had long been dead. When his payroll had swollen to more than four thousand, there were few among his employees who could claim to really know him. The rumpled and ink-stained proprietor who would emerge from the *Journal*'s composing room, usually in full evening dress, after putting the paper to bed had since given way to a loftier figure, a man who was familiar only to the handful who were summoned to his councils in his palatial apartment on Riverside Drive. But the sense of personal fealty had never waned. Even as he became more remote from the printers, the rewrite men, the copyreaders, and the front-line editors who fought his battles, they began to speak proudly of something they called the "Hearst Service," and to exhibit a peculiar reverence for their enigmatic Chief.

(2)

Hearst's empire grew until, in October of 1935, the editors of *Fortune* magazine could write with only slight exaggeration that:

> Mr. Hearst does not merely own newspapers. He owns magazines, radio stations, ranches, and New York City hotels. He owns mines and a warehouse full of antiques. He hires 31,000 men and women for $57,000,000 a year, and he has working for him nearly a hundred executives who earn $25,000 or more. Living literally like a king, he has probably been the nation's No. 1 spender even surpassing Mr. Ford with his schoolhouses and Mr. Mellon with his paintings. He is certainly the world's No. 1 collector of objets d'art, specializing in armor, tapestry, and furniture of any period he fancies. At heart a medievalist, he keeps his ear to the ground in a hundred local political issues, in all the major national ones. His correspondents cover the earth; he has acquaintances everywhere and invites them wholesale to his palaces. And all this is his, and he runs it.

When he died fifteen years later, Hearst still ruled that empire, though by then it had grown old and eccentric, like a wealthy dowager who has passed her prime.

Considered as a fortune alone, his legacy ranked among the greatest that the country had seen. With assets that were valued between two hundred and four hundred million dollars (uncertainty reigned because there were so many unknown quantities—forested acres that were barely accessible, crated castles that might never find buyers, antiques and artifacts in quantities so vast that they could scarcely be offered for sale without depressing the market), it was smaller, perhaps, than the Rockefeller Trusts or the portfolios of the quietly thriving Mellon clan. But in its way, the Hearst fortune was far more imposing. For its millions were not spread through the financial establishment, but were concentrated instead in a single great enterprise, a family business that dwarfed all but its nearest rival, the automotive kingdom of Henry Ford.

Since 1941, the assets had been vested in the Hearst Corporation. This was a holding company for the empire, a fief that controlled a score of units—Hearst Consolidated, Hearst Enterprises, Hearst Publishing Company, Hearst Metrotone News, and Hearst Magazines were the major components—and was in turn controlled by the holder of its one hundred shares of voting stock. The Corporation was very private: only one division (namely, Hearst Consolidated, with its half dozen newspapers) used public money, because Hearst could never be satisfied with something that was not his own without reservation. And, even in 1951, its reach was almost staggering. For in spite of the dark years at the end of the 1930s—when the empire had once come close to total collapse and the newsmagazines had written smugly of a "Sunset at San Simeon"—the Hearst Corporation held fast to not only the grandest estates in the West, but a communications network that remained the most powerful in the world.

In 1951, much of the old domain, the expanse of Western lands that had once belonged to George and Phoebe Hearst, was still intact. Indeed, the northern Sierra estate of Wyntoon had only grown larger in the years since 1903, when Phoebe had first been charmed by the hunting lodge of her attorney, Charles Wheeler. She had solicited his consent to build a "modest home," the total value of which, according to their written agreement, was not to exceed $10,000. Yet Phoebe, in her indomitable way, had proceeded to construct a five-tiered château (designed by her protégés Bernard Maybeck and Julia Morgan) that cost something more than ten times that limit. Wheeler was sufficiently appalled at the incursion to sell her the land, a parcel on the headwaters of the McCloud near Shasta. And in 1929, when the château burned to the ground, her son took it over for a retreat of his own. He replaced the castle with a Bavarian village, four gingerbread houses that were painted with murals by Willy Pogany, and year after year, he expanded his holdings, until finally the estate sprawled over some 67,000 acres, most of them densely covered with fir, in the mountains of Shasta and Siskiyou Counties.

Babicora, another vast holding in the Mexican state of Chihuahua, had declined only a little since the 1880s, when George Hearst acquired its million-plus acres—from ranchers who were all but worn out in their battles with Geronimo—for the bargain price of twenty cents each. There had been one expropriation in 1935, when the Mexican government—under the agrarian laws that limited holdings to 100,000 acres each—had seized 175,000 acres of the best farming land, and another in 1940, when the family was forced to part with a second 117,000-acre block. But lobbying and bribes had saved the rest; and so in 1951, the ranch remained what it had been for fifty years past, a richly productive estate ruled by the exacting agents of the absentee Señor Hearst. The land was high and arid, watered in places by artesian wells, and divided almost in two by a rugged spur of the Sierra Madre. Some of it was covered with marketable timber, and some of the arable land was let out to be worked by bean- and corn-growing Mexican tenants, because, as an early overseer named M. F. Taylor had once assured Phoebe, the tenant farms cost very little to start, and the Mexicans would return their share to the Hearsts by trading with the company store. But most of the plains were reserved for Hearst's cattle. His herds of prize Shorthorns and Herefords numbered in the tens of thousands, with hundreds of vaqueros to tend them. They were counted among the finest stock in Mexico—indeed, men had died to defend them in the days of Carranza and Villa—and in the fall of 1951, they fetched premium prices in the markets of El Paso, just as they had done every year since the family had taken the land.

In that same year, San Simeon was already a spectral palace. It had always been a lonely place—even in the brightest of years, the castle lights were smothered in gray coastal fog, and the trainloads of Hollywood charm did little to dispel the gloom of remote San Simeon Bay. But the gloom had deepened appreciably since the spring of 1947, when Hearst finally deserted the hill, leaving only a skeleton housekeeping crew to inhabit his manor. For a while the unceasing construction went on. After thirty-two years, workmen were still trying to balance the lopsided Casa Grande with a new recreation wing on the northern side. And sometimes the household would brighten to unfounded rumors that the old man was about to return. But there were no more parties, no more grand feasts in the tapestry-hung refectory. The vacant palace was opened only for an occasional visit by the sons, who came with their wives to "honeymoon" in the Cardinal Richelieu bed, or for the periodic corporate conclaves that were convened on the hill even when Hearst was no longer there to preside.

Apart from the castle itself, however, there was still a great deal of vitality at San Simeon—and, for all that anyone knew, a wealth of potential that had never been tapped. Out on "the ranch" (as the surrounding property had been called since 1865, when Senator George Hearst bought the old Piedra Blanca estate as a breeding ground for his horses), the rhythm of a thriving cattle operation was disturbed only slightly by the meandering of zebras and mountain goats that had broken loose from the hilltop menagerie. The pear orchards were still producing fruit for the canning plant that packed them under Hearst's own label. More frequently, too, now that the lord of the manor had left, the corporate agents were beginning to appear with their surveying gear and electronic divining rods, to mull over what might become of a tract that included thirty miles of the California coast and more than eighty thousand acres of unspoiled land.

The media empire too had managed to survive the man who created it, though there had been a time, almost fifteen years before, when those who knew the business best were prepared to agree with the historian Charles A. Beard, who declared in March 1936, that "despite all the uproar he has made and all the power he wields, [Hearst] is a colossal failure and now holds in his hands the dust and ashes of defeat."

That disaster should finally have found him was hardly surprising, for all through the thirties he had continued to buy and to build without check, almost as if the Depression itself, which he dismissed as a "wonderful opportunity to invest," was a problem for beings less lofty than himself. When his mother's fortune was exhausted—he had liquidated the last of the family mining stock by 1932—he simply turned to the sources at hand, pressing his papers to provide the cash not only for further construction at San Simeon, but for his communication empire's phenomenal growth. The demands he placed on his business managers were almost beyond belief. He had them send heavy cash payments of $50,000 or more to his accounts each month, and he insisted that they meet the personal bills that came home to the various *Examiners* and *Americans*. When even that failed to sate his need for ready money, a darker, more ruthless Hearst would sometimes dispatch his collectors (the most feared of whom was the gangster Max Annenberg) to terrorize his own management and to empty the tills of papers that couldn't keep pace.

It was an ominous sign that his fiscal habits did not improve when he first turned to public financing. Though the Hearst Consolidated shares were marketed in 1933 as a Depression-proof investment for the man-in-the-street ("IN THE AUTUMN OF LIFE, FREE FROM ALL WORRIES, I INVESTED WISELY IN HEARST 7% SHARES: YOU CAN DO THE SAME," read the ads), Hearst treated the common man's money as his own. His worst offense was his habit of draining away the Consolidated capital with the inflated charges of his "upstream companies," the news, feature and advertising bureaus. Nor did it bode well that he took loans from the New York banking establishment—a total of $126 million, all of it personally guaranteed—even while excoriating his creditors in signed columns that read: "America's banking system has been the most reckless, the most unreliable, the most unethical in the world. . . . It has been the come-on, and no bunco game on Broadway or the Bowery has robbed the trusting yap more relentlessly than these great banking houses and their affiliates."

In the end, it was the banking establishment that put a halt to the fiscal riot. In 1936 the cash had run short. There was a panic late in the year when the Canadian papermakers demanded payment of long-overdue bills, and then another in the early months of 1937, when the SEC denied a Hearst application to issue $35,000,000 in debentures. By June, a consortium of seventeen banks, led by Chase National and the implacable Winthrop Aldrich, had stepped in to impose a trustee.

Adela Rogers St. Johns remembered the wave of shock that rolled through the organization as reporters and editors learned that, at the bankers' behest, the management of the empire had been vested in Clarence J. Shearn, a man who had once served as Hearst's own political agent. "The idea of Mr. Hearst as a bankrupt—*Mr. Hearst?*" she wrote, some thirty years later. "If J. D. Rockefeller, Sr., had been down to his last dime or Henry Ford to his last cylinder, we wouldn't have been more incredulous. Also we were furious. How dared they?" Yet they had dared—and those in the service who believed that the creditors meant not to rehabilitate but to destroy him may not have been far wrong. The Napoleonic Shearn, acting on instructions from Aldrich, was ruthless in his economies. Within two years, "the miserable little wretch" (as Jack Neylan called him) had sold seven radio stations, and either sold or dismantled six daily papers, beginning with Hearst's flagship, the New York *American.* (Eight more papers were to follow later.) He closed the Universal News Service and ended the production of feature films, while among the executives he conducted a reign of terror, reducing the salaries of some by half, and marking others for extinction on a hit list maintained by the renegade Hearst accountant, Frej Hagelberg.

At times, it seemed that Shearn was inclined to hold very little of Hearst's world together. Although without success, he begged Harry Chandler to foreclose on a $600,000 mortgage that the latter had acquired (without Hearst's knowledge) on the castle at San Simeon and at one point was on the verge of selling the entire stable of profitable Hearst magazines for a bargain-basement price.

That Hearst escaped annihilation in the hands of the ambitious trustee (who by 1940 had invaded the editorial side with a ban on anti-British pieces, because they might offend Canadian creditors) was due in part to the wartime boom. The fever of government spending, $300 million a day by 1942, sent the rump organization roaring into the black even before Japan had surrendered.

But there was also much truth to the theory, advanced with vigor by Hearst partisans, that, when the cards were counted, "the only man who saved Hearst was William Randolph Hearst." Though he was well over seventy when his empire began to crumble, the old press lord refused to believe that the dream had come to an end. With his majesty scarcely diminished, he remained in his retreat at Wyntoon through the years of the crisis, dictating orders to papers that only occasionally failed to respond and, unknown to the bankers, directing a quiet guerrilla war against the alien force that had invaded his institution. It was Hearst who rescued the best of his own antiques by sending an undercover agent to bid at a forced sale of his property at Christie's. Likewise, it was Hearst who instigated stockholders' suits against his own newspaper company (through the ostensibly retired John Francis Neylan), in order to harass the Shearn-appointed board of directors.

In April of 1945, when Shearn and his minions had at last been dismissed, Neylan told Hearst of his wonder that "any man in his late seventies could stand the mental and physical strain inherent in the struggle to overcome the damage done by the coterie which had visions of empire." But more wonderful still was the fact that even while the organization had been reduced by 40 percent from its peak of a decade before, it remained what its own promotion men called it—"the mightiest publishing venture the world has ever known." In the last years of his fantastic career, Hearst, the unfettered autocrat, ruled once more over sixteen newspapers, all of them big urban dailies, with a combined circulation of more than five million. He presided over the greatest features service in the business (King Features, with its fifty-two million readers) and the world's most widely read magazine (the *American Weekly*, circulation 9,927,000). He had radio stations in Pittsburgh, Milwaukee and Baltimore, with television applications pending for each of those cities. His INS was as scrappy as ever; on the Korean front it scored beat after beat on the better-staffed but always less-spirited AP. His Metrotone Newsreels still ground on. His own superstars—Walter Winchell, Louella Parsons, Chic Young—usually outshone their nearest competitors. And the eight magazines that had survived the Shearn regime—*Good Housekeeping, Harper's Bazaar,* and *Cosmopolitan* among them—were hauling in revenue at the gratifying rate of some $50,000,000 a year.

Chapter 3

The Family

(1)

MILLICENT HEARST? To Diana Vreeland she was nothing less than a blaze of glory. "My God, she was remarkable . . . a dream . . . like a chandelier," gushed the breathless first lady of *Vogue*. "Millicent Hearst wore emerald shoulder straps—no one has ever worn emerald shoulder straps. She was too delicious . . . always warm, always laughing. Her skin was perfect, her eyes very, very gay, and she had lots and lots of beaus. A woman that attractive will always have beaus. But marry them? Why should she? Why should she ever want to be anything but Mrs. William Randolph Hearst?"

She was gaiety, grandeur, and something like the dowager queen of a world that used to be called Café Society. When her husband died she was already seventy, but to most of her friends she seemed to be as young as she thought she was. She still had the laugh, the peculiar rising trill, that tickled Cole Porter, and she had never lost the impish sense of humor that delighted acquaintances who expected a more sober matron. John and Emily Warner were only the latest in a long line of socialites to discover her surprising streak of whimsy; when they called on Millicent at her new home in the Hamptons and asked what she had planned in the way of décor, she sighed, with mock resignation at the hard demands of being a Hearst, "I suppose we shall have to do this one Louis the Limit. . . ." That same sense of fun bubbled up in the adventures she shared with her sidekick, the gnomish Elsa Maxwell. Through the thirties, the forties, and the fifties as well, they were two "Merry Widows" (one married and one decidedly not) who lived in a whirl of parties that usually ended with a madcap prank—as when Millie and Elsa posed the grandes dames of New York for a formal portrait in fake mustachios—or with the pair of them slung over a grand piano, singing "bum doggerel" in the company of a few good friends like Jack Hammond, Flo Ziegfeld and Billie Burke.

It was also true that at seventy, Mrs. Hearst enjoyed a rare kind of eminence. As the legitimate queen in a dynasty that ranked with America's richest, she had come to regard herself as a personage no less exalted than the titled friends—the Duke of Windsor, King Paul of Greece, King Alfonso of Spain—who graced her special occasions. Apparently she never once doubted that to be Mrs. William Randolph Hearst was reason enough to live in a castle, as she did for many years, at Sands Point on Long Island. Neither did the great lady hesitate to match tiaras and ermine (at a Hearst-sponsored opera benefit) with the reigning Greek Queen Frederika, nor even to decline proposals of marriage from nobles as grand as Britain's Prince Andrew and Lord Castlerosse.

And yet, the beginnings had been considerably less proud.

Millicent Veronica Willson was sixteen when she first met Hearst. She was a dancer then—a doe-eyed, Gibson-girl beauty in a troupe called the "Merry Maidens," who in 1897 were playing bit parts in Edward Rice's *The Girl from Paris*, six nights and two matinees a week, at the Herald Square Theater on Broadway. She and her sister Anita, another member of the troupe, were cast as the "bicycle girls," Edith and Violet. They weren't exactly in the chorus—Millicent would always insist on that. But as the reviewers (who were enthusiastic) recorded it, they did little more than to run through a few lively steps while providing a backdrop of dimples and lace for the comic star Louis Mann and his temperamental wife, Clara Lipman.

To their credit, the Willson sisters could lay claim to good stage lineage. Their father, an old vaudevillian who billed himself as "George Leslie," had made his reputation as an eccentric dancer on the South-

western circuit. He styled his act after that of an English team called
the Majiltons. And though he was never as acrobatic as the amazing
Majiltons, who astounded their audiences with their head-high kicks and
wrenching back-flips, Willson made up for his lack of agility by indulging in special effects; wearing skin-tight trousers, a tall white hat, and
a bright plaid jacket, he clattered a couple of canes in time to a pair of
clogs attached to his heels, as he worked his way through a series of
comic steps like the Mobile Duck, the mule in the sand, and the *pasa
ma la*. According to one reminiscent theater owner, quoted by the
Morning Telegraph in 1908, "George Leslie did not have an original act
and was not by any means one of the best of the many eccentric dancers
who appeared on the vaudeville stage, but he had one merit that appealed in those days. He was always ready to go on when he got his
music cue, and was always sober."

Millicent, the younger of the two Willson girls, had a story of her
own about her first encounter with Hearst. Many years later, when a
reporter asked how she had come to know her proprietor-prince, she
replied with a fairy tale, an impossible dream that began with a courtly
stranger who appeared backstage at the Herald Square. "When he asked
me to go out with him," she recalled:

> my mother was against it. We were carefully supervised in those days
> and I recall she said, "Who *is* he? Some young fellow from out West
> somewhere, isn't he?" She insisted Anita had to come or I couldn't go.
> Well, he took us down to the *Journal*—the New York *Journal*—we'd
> hardly heard of it, and he showed us over it, all over it. I hadn't the
> foggiest notion what we were doing, walking miles on rough boards in
> thin, high-heeled evening slippers, and I thought my feet would kill me.
> Of course this wasn't our idea of a good time. We wanted to go to
> Sherry's or Bustanoby's. More than that Anita kept whispering to me,
> "We're going to get thrown out of here, Milly, the way he behaves you'd
> think he owned it"; It wasn't until our next trip that I found out he
> did—own it, I mean. I told Anita and at first she wouldn't believe me.
> She said, "He's like all Westerners. All big brag strutting around as
> though they owned the earth." But . . . I guess I must have fallen in
> love with him at once, he asked me to marry him two weeks later, and
> I said yes right away.

The truth, of course, was never as simple as the idyl that Millicent
remembered. One suspects that the Misses Willson *had* heard of the
Journal—after all, New York's most vociferous daily had honored them

with a smashing review that January—and they may well have known that their gallant stranger (who was in fact a lonely man of thirty-four) enjoyed some reputation as a stage-door predator. Not only was Hearst a familiar figure in the haunts of Broadway, but that same January his moral stature had been questioned in no less conspicuous a forum than the United States Congress. There, on January 8, 1897, California's Grove Johnson had risen to brand the publisher "a debauchee . . . tattooed with sin . . . licentious in his tastes, regal in his dissipations, unfit to associate with pure women or decent men." Not to mention the fact that Lady Hearst's courtship endured for something closer to seven years than to the two weeks of her dimly romantic memory.

There were some who said that Hearst kept both Willson girls, and perhaps he did, for the three of them, arm-in-arm-in-arm, became one of the sights that livened Manhattan through those waning years of the nineteenth century. In the beginning he would simply appear at the theater, to whisk them away for dinner at Delmonico's or Sherry's, followed by a midnight session in the composing room of his *Journal*, where the ladies would yawn and stamp while he tore apart the next day's front page to accommodate his late-breaking whims. Later, there were favors, especially for Millie. He furnished his sixteen-year-old companion with a hansom cab, complete with coachman and milk-white charger, and when the *Morning Telegraph* conducted a poll to find the most popular girl in New York, he stooped to the blatant flattery of stuffing the ballot box in her favor. Apparently, too, he helped the girls to retire. In 1898, they worked their last show—a musical farce called *The Telephone Girl*, again starring Louis Mann—before withdrawing to the quiet of a new Gramercy Park home, courtesy of their suitor. But their farewell was nothing compared with the finale that Hearst arranged for their father. In that same year he had Tony Pastor book a special engagement for the retiring George Leslie, who earned a standing ovation (according to the *Journal* man who was assigned to give the event a column and a half) by closing his last act with the supreme effort, a death-defying backward flip.

Not until five years later, in 1903, did Hearst and Millicent marry— and even then some gossips suggested that the wedding took place less because the publisher wanted a family than because he needed one. Politics had come roaring into his life in the wake of the Spanish-American War, and with his new obsession had come the first signs of uneasiness over his casual relationship with the Willsons. There had always been talk—from the beginning, New York was abuzz with rumors about orgies in his Lexington Avenue home and wild parties on his yacht, the *Vamoose*, not to mention the mistress, an Irish girl named Tessie Powers, whom he had once kept in San Francisco. But not until the gossip threatened to cross his plans, which only that year had begun to focus on the Presidency, did he consider the advantages of marriage.

The ceremony was modest. It took place on April 28 in Grace Episcopal Church in New York, with Bishop Henry Codman Potter presiding and Hearst's friend Orrin Peck doing service as the best man. The honeymoon was rather more elaborate. To celebrate their long-delayed union, Hearst took his bride and all her kin on a jaunt through Europe and England, then on to Mexico for a tour of the Hearst lands, and finally to California, where they met his aging mother, who had yet to be convinced that a raft of in-laws who were not just dancers but Irish and Catholic might indeed be an asset to her family. Phoebe was gracious enough to stage a second ceremony for the newly wed couple, to make up for the one she had declined to attend in New York.

And only then did they turn to the business of forging a dynasty. Their family life began in the Lexington Avenue house, where, for the time being, they kept a ménage that was modest enough to let Hearst devote his money to the papers and to the Party. Millicent did domestic work, and she cultivated her distant mother-in-law with a flood of endearments, sent by the United States Mail. Though it would be years before she succeeded in penetrating Phoebe's reserve (she long addressed her with careful formality as "My Dear Mrs. Hearst"), Millicent found that the letters, in which she kept the old woman posted on intimate details of life with her son, were an effective means of easing herself into the family. But if anything was to guarantee her precarious status as a Hearst, it was surely the haste with which Millicent presented her eager husband with a son and heir. Only a little less than a year after the wedding, on April 10, 1904, she gave birth to a fat and healthy George Randolph Hearst.

The event provoked an unexpected display of paternal instinct on the part of the proud father. Despite the rigors of his schedule (he was then, in addition to running the papers, serving his first term in Congress), Hearst found time to spoil George horribly. During the summer months of 1904, he hovered about the house, tending to mother and son with a degree of care he usually reserved for the front page of his final editions. At one point Millicent was bemused by her husband's fevered attempts to mitigate the effects of a heat wave by rigging a form of primitive air conditioning for the baby. Hearst sallied forth into the streets of New York, returning with five electric fans and eight large buckets of ice, which he used to turn the nursery into a refrigerated warehouse. But, as Millicent recalled, Will became so hot carrying the ice upstairs and fussing with the fans that he raised the thermometer several degrees. Conceding failure, the anxious father gave up and moved his fledgling family to the somewhat breezier fourteenth floor of the Netherlands Hotel for the duration of the summer.

Millicent quickly discovered, however, that in return for the worried attention and the security she enjoyed as Hearst's wife, she was expected to pay a heavy price. In the years of her casual relationship with Hearst, she had always been kept in the background, away from the publicity that engulfed him; now, however, both she and young "Buster" were thrust forward and pressed into hard service as a political family. At every opportunity, Millicent and her child were displayed prominently in the pages of the *Journal* and the *American*, as living proof that William Randolph Hearst was indeed normal and fit to hold high office. The two made the dreary rounds of stump speeches and dedications until they became figures almost as familiar in New York City as Hearst himself. In 1906, after Hearst, with his Presidential ambitions intact, had captured the Democratic gubernatorial nomination, the family widened their range to include the entire state, which they toured in the private campaign car "Reva," striking poses and shaking hands in time-honored political tradition. When her husband was called on to address the massive rallies in Madison Square Garden (a work for which he was ill-equipped because of his high-pitched voice and his aversion to large crowds), Millicent was expected to offer her support, sharing the platform beside him.

When in the fall of 1905 the family was moved into a grand thirty-room flat in the Clarendon Apartments, overlooking the Hudson from Riverside Drive, Millicent began to enjoy some of the amenities she expected of a man as wealthy as Hearst; but at the same time, it was clear that the domestic idyl which she and her husband had played out on Lexington Avenue was over. To the endless political whirl were added the special strains of life as a newspaper wife. After long days on the political circuit, Hearst fell into the habit of spending equally long nights at the papers, seldom returning before 3 A.M. And when he did happen to be at home, the husband found little enough time for lavishing attention on his wife and son, for the apartment was flooded with a steady stream of editors and financial operatives, all in quest of guidance. Describing the frantic routine at the Clarendon, Millicent complained that the telephone began ringing before she and Will could get dressed. People trooped through the apartment all day long, so that the Hearsts never saw sun and rarely managed a breath of fresh air. The harried wife tried to insist on at least a touch of normalcy, but to no avail. To Phoebe she had to report that Will was working very hard, even while in bed, but she could not stop him.

Millicent had, of course, been prepared for a certain degree of trouble when she married Hearst; she knew that he was a relentlessly driven man, and that, in exchange for what she hoped to gain, she would have to accommodate herself to his drives. But as the demands on her became increasingly tiresome and began to encroach on her own scheme of social advancement, she became alarmed. Her occasional fits of pique hardened into angry resentment at the neglect and the exploitation that had become her lot.

To her mother-in-law, with whom she was beginning to share a genuine rapport, Millicent described the sources of her growing discontent. She had been worn down by the endless rounds of railroad travel, making political appearances and entertaining advertisers and civic leaders who could do the family any good in cities as widely separate as Boston, Chicago and Atlanta. As she complained to Phoebe from a Washington hotel in 1906, for the last two months she and Will had been living on trains, going from Washington to New York and from New York to Boston and back again, and she wished they could settle down somewhere for a few days and just keep still. She didn't see any signs of it. She knew too well that they would rush around on the trains until it was time to rush over on the steamer, and then they would rush around in an automobile until they were due to come home again.

Life with Hearst was maddeningly irregular. When Phoebe once asked about her plans for the summer, she could only gasp in exasperation that they never had any plans. Will thought he would do one thing one day and another thing another day, and when the time finally came they didn't do either but something entirely different. She never knew until the last minute whether they would go abroad or out west or take a trip to Canada. And when they were able to settle into the Clarendon for a few weeks, it seemed that the apartment was kept in a perpetual state of crisis by a constant file of party hacks and newspaper executives marching through the door. During the final stretch of the 1907 mayoral race, an exhausted Millicent described the chaos. There was a campaign on and a panic, and Will was in both, she said. There he was trying to learn his speech in time to go to six meetings, while Jerome and Willie Chandler were trying to arrest him for criminal libel and Edward Clark was explaining how Wall Street was collapsing and how they would all be broke in the morning.

Millicent's persistent complaints did nothing to alienate the aging Phoebe; instead they became a bond between the two, and, even, the basis of an alliance that would do much to decide the future of the Hearst family. Phoebe had been too long afflicted by her son's irregularities to feel anything but sympathy for her persecuted daughter-in-law. Surrendering her reserve, she encouraged a warmer relationship between them—by 1908, after years of formality, the two had finally become "Mama" and "Millie."

What's more, Phoebe recognized certain qualities in Millicent that were sadly lacking in her son, the most important among them being a strong instinct for propriety and status, and a growing sense of pride in the name of Hearst. Delighted to discover hope where she had expected none, Phoebe Hearst adopted her daughter-in-law as a social protégée. During the visits to Pleasanton (some 30 miles southeast of San Francisco where Phoebe kept an estate of her own, the magnificent Hacienda del Pozo de Verona), she worked to smooth the rough edges left by a vaudeville upbringing and to acquaint her willing pupil with the social graces. She introduced her to the Rockefellers, Vanderbilts and Belmonts, whom she considered proper associates for the Hearsts. And she listened gladly as Millicent recorded milestones in the course of her social development, reporting faithfully on an encounter with Lady Warwick in Paris, a luncheon with Sir Thomas Lipton in London, or an introduction to William Gillett, the English Society Leader.

What proved decisive, though, in allying Phoebe and Millicent against their common source of torment was the children. Somehow, in spite of the peculiar rigors and uncertainties of her life, Millicent managed to bear four more sons in the course of a decade—William Randolph junior was born in 1908, and John Randolph in 1909, while the twins, Randolph Apperson and Elbert Willson, arrived in 1915.

Both women vested a great deal of hope in the boys, whom they expected not only to maintain the family's expanding wealth, but perhaps to restore something of the prestige and moral credit that had been squandered by their father. By tacit agreement, Millicent and Phoebe shared the children on almost equal terms. All were sent within months of their birth for extended visits with Phoebe—by August 1905, for instance, George had already been left in California for several months, and the twins spent nearly nine months of their first year in the company of their grandmother. The arrangement persisted as long as Phoebe lived, with the boys spending at least half of every year at the Hacienda, which they came to consider more their home than the Clarendon. Millicent was, of course, pained at the long absences; she complained of her loneliness in her letters west, telling her mother-in-law how she longed for the children, how she felt as if she hadn't seen them for a year and was dreaming of them, hoping they were having a beautiful time. But she also recognized the separations as a price worth paying for the added strength they lent her liaison with Phoebe.

Moreover, both Millicent and Phoebe seem to have agreed that it would be best for the boys to be raised at a distance from their father. For her part, Phoebe had become increasingly embittered toward her son as the years rolled on; disappointed at the discredit he had brought her, and resentful of his continued demands for money, she shifted her attention to Millicent and the children, hoping to instill in them before she died something of the family vision that failed so dismally to take hold in her son. Sensing that he had been usurped, Hearst admonished his mother, only half in jest, that she ought to send *him* an occasional letter. Phoebe poured out her heart to Millie, but to Will she sent only a few short notes, telling him how dreadfully wicked he was—and that theme, he thought, should be worth some very long letters indeed.

Millicent, on the other hand, had her own reasons for thinking her sons better off away from their father. Certainly she feared for their health —George had contracted several serious afflictions during his travels as an infant, among them a lingering case of malaria. And she was plagued by an awful dread that they might somehow become a target for her husband's myriad enemies—dogged by premonitions of a kidnapping, she had the boys watched by bodyguards throughout their childhood. At the same time, however, it is clear that she felt Hearst to be a negative influence on the boys: she disliked and distrusted the company his dealings brought into the Clarendon, she deplored his failure to discipline his sons (whom she firmly believed to be in need of "an occasional cuff on the ear"), and she suspected that he did not provide the kind of model they needed to build a "manly" character. In fact, when George, William and John were old enough to begin their education, she made a point of sending them off to military schools (Manlius in upstate New York and the Hitchcock Academy in San Rafael, California) where they would room away from home, and where the discipline could be expected to "stiffen their spines."

Perhaps not the least of Millicent's reasons for wanting the boys away from New York was the fact that by the time the youngest were born their father had begun to stray. Millicent increasingly felt her marriage threatened by the newspapers and the endless political campaigns, and she was genuinely alarmed to see her husband so often bedridden from exhaustion, but continuing nevertheless to work and worry. Tensions were only aggravated, however, when she began to nag, insisting that he slow down and even dropping hints about his abandoning politics entirely. One can imagine Hearst's reaction when, on the day *before* the polling in the 1909 mayoralty race, she had the temerity to tell a rival newspaper that his political career was over. "No," she told a reporter who had elbowed past Hearst and into the Clarendon, "Mr. Hearst will not run again." Inevitably, her husband responded to the pressure by spending still less time at the Clarendon. Eventually he resumed his old habit of frequenting the Broadway theaters and clubs in the company of such notorious stage-door Johnnies as his friend and fellow publisher Paul Block. According to some sources, he engaged in a number of brief affairs.

And finally, in 1915, he discovered another dancer in another show.

Hearst first encountered Marion Davies in the chorus of *Stop! Look! Listen!*, a Charles B. Dillingham production, which was scored by Irving Berlin. He was fifty-two and married for twelve years; she was eighteen, blond and beautiful, and she stuttered badly—in the next year's *Follies*, Ziegfeld gave her one line and she muffed it. Raised in Brooklyn as Marion Cecilia Douras, she remained many of the things Millicent had ceased to be in a decade of married life. Raucous and improper, she retained the edge of vulgarity that was an inevitable product of life on the stage. She was part of a vaudeville family (her sisters Reine and Ethel were dancers, though her father was a not quite successful barrister), and while she was as interested as the next chorine in the subject of money, she had no particular respect for "wealthy boors." Marion was fresh, insecure and funny; and after some initial hesitation—she adored her "W.R." All in all, Hearst was captivated. He saw her often on stage and off, and by 1917 he had her enrolled in the Empire School of Acting and on the payroll.

While his mother lived, Hearst never dared to broach the topic of divorce. Painfully aware of the alliance between Phoebe and Millicent, and chronically in need of cash to support his expanding operations, he could scarcely afford to jeopardize the considerable legacy he stood to gain by remaining in the good graces of the aging widow. But when Phoebe died in April of 1919, leaving her son an estate valued at eleven million dollars, his restless urges began to grow increasingly obvious. His commitment to Marion had snowballed almost beyond control. After seeing her in her first film, a comedy called *Runaway, Romany,* which was financed by Block and directed by her future brother-in-law George Lederer, Hearst became obsessed with the idea of making her a star. He not only signed her as the centerpiece of his Cosmopolitan Productions, but, in 1920, named her president of the company. He hovered over Marion on the movie lot at his Harlem River studio, and consorted freely with her in Palm Beach and Los Angeles. And by 1922, he had conceived the idea of marrying her.

Though he might have expected resistance, the wayward husband can hardly have been prepared for the reaction he faced when he approached his wife to request her cooperation in divorce proceedings. Thoroughly outraged, Millicent flatly and unconditionally refused to hear of it. She had struck her roots deep in family territory, and she had no intention of being dislodged. Possibly she had a great deal to say about her five sons, not to mention the years she had invested in Hearst's largely fruitless political campaigns, and the many calls she had paid in Hearst cities for the good of the papers. What is certain is that she knew how to make her point felt: before her temper had cooled or her cowed husband had found time to recover his composure, Millicent Hearst drove off to Tiffany's. There—in view of a dumbfounded Cole

Porter, who chanced to observe the event—she selected the most expensive pearl necklace in New York, and very casually told the clerk, "I'll take the string with me. Send the bill to my husband's office."

Reflecting years later on the confrontation with her husband, Millicent mused, "I was awfully angry, but I got over it a long, long time ago." If she did indeed get over the affair (friend Elsa Maxwell insisted that "it cast a pall over her entire life"), it was principally by staking out her ground and keeping a jealous watch over her prerogatives as Hearst's wife. The couple agreed that they would continue to observe the formalities of marriage. Hearst was free to let his affections lie where they may, but he was to spend a substantial amount of time at the Clarendon, providing the semblance of a home until the boys were grown. Millicent would attend his political functions as before; he in turn would preside at her fund-raising affairs and social occasions of high formality.

The spurned wife was careful never to let her husband forget that she had earned an honest stake in the Hearst fortune by virtue of her long exertions, and that she intended to be treated with respect where business was concerned. Millicent retained access to her husband's accounts, on which she drew freely to maintain herself and the boys and to support the various charities in which she had taken an interest (the most prominent among these being her own pet project, the Free Milk Fund for Babies, Inc.). Traveling the globe at her husband's expense, she entertained lavishly in Paris; she visited with Mussolini and the exiled Spanish King Alfonso XIII in Italy; and she developed such warm relations with several British aristocrats that there was talk of her marrying a title. When Hearst moved into his palace at San Simeon, after the last of the boys had been sent off to school, Millicent even saw to it that she was provided with a castle of her own; in 1931, her husband purchased for her use a mansion with drawbridge and moat, once the property of Mrs. O. H. P. Belmont, at Sands Point on Long Island. Moreover, Millicent Hearst retained a strong proprietary sense toward what she still referred to as "our papers." She felt free, for instance, to call the *Mirror* with suggestions for boosting circulation long after her husband had broken with her, and she maintained her own, independent contacts within the organization. Through men like attorney John Francis Neylan and future corporate president Richard Berlin, she kept close watch on both editorial developments and the state of the family's finances. With Neylan she shared an especially warm friendship, based partly on their Irish background and partly on their mutual addiction to little conspiracies. The attorney, then the number-two man in the empire, supplied Millicent with regular written reports on the conduct of internal affairs; and when she responded with an occasional request for editorial action, or even an order to disperse company funds, he was glad to comply.

(2)

There was a touch of pathos about the five Hearst sons, something hopelessly sad in the way they were always less than they wanted to be, but could never quite grasp the initiative and the drive that they lacked. One of their boyhood tutors, Newton Drury, would remember that George, the oldest of the five, "had an attention span of about three-quarters of an hour."

"I'd teach him and his cousins for about that long in the morning," lamented Drury, recalling his tour of duty with the family at Wyntoon. "Then we'd wind up out on the McCloud River, fishing for the rest of the day. He used to tell me, 'Awww, I can't learn anything anyway. I'm a dummy.' I'd say, 'George, I don't ever want to hear you talk that way about yourself. You're not a dummy.' But you know something—I think he was right."

The boys themselves could be brutally frank about their own failings. It was Bill who once confessed that "We never did a goddamned thing. We never worked because we never had to. Believe me, if I ever got a reputation for anything at all, it was only because the rest of them were even worse. It got to the point where they held a parade if one of the Hearst boys bothered to get up in the morning." And the stammering George could babble for hours about what he planned to do "when Pop was gone." But when he was drunk enough, the point would come when he could only stop and stutter, "F-f-face it, I'm s-s-stupid. I'll never be what he was." Certainly all of them knew that their father, who admonished them a thousand times about the hazards of being a rich man's son, had expected something more of them. On offering his third son, John, his first job, he had written, "I want you to accomplish something and prove what is in you, for my satisfaction and for my guidance in allotting my properties. . . . It is better to be a successful workingman than a busted playboy. It is better to work and like it, at the head of your own properties, than it is to look for a small job somewhere that you cannot get and cannot fill." As for the twins, they were no more than sixteen when they received the same warning. "You have had a good time at Palm Beach and we try to give you a good time as often as possible," he wrote to the two at Lawrenceville:

> But you cannot always be merely having a good time, and your mother and I expect something more of you than to be playboys. This is not a good period in the world's history for playboys. Things are too serious. Situations are too dangerous, and I want you two boys, who are now getting to be men, to begin to take a man's view of life. You will have to work, and work hard. You might as well be learning how to work now. You have got to get an education that will make you able to take care of yourselves. No one knows whether you will inherit anything or not; but if you are not able to make money, you will not be able to keep money. If you are not trained for the contest that is ahead of you, you are likely to bring up in the rear of the procession.

And yet no one knew better than those same five sons how much their father had done to make them what they were.

To his sons he was a distant figure, a towering old man who lived in a world that sometimes had a place for them and sometimes didn't, depending on his mood and the needs of the particular moment. The older boys—George, William and John—would remember him as an erratic father. "He could be wonderful, absolutely wonderful when we were together," recalled Bill. "But we were together maybe a fifth of the time." In fact, they were together when he needed them. A thousand times in 1905, when he wanted desperately to beat the Tammany machine that slandered him badly in opposing his bid to be mayor, he was photographed holding Baby George, a decided political asset, on his knee. In the heat of the campaign one reporter called on the candidate at home and was astonished to find him stretched on a bed beside his infant son, "holding a milk bottle at which the child tugged vigorously," and looking every inch the family man. "Now and then the baby would utter a loud squall," wrote the enchanted James Creelman, "whereat Mr. Hearst would kick up his heels delightedly and cry, 'Extra! Extra! Extra edition!' " They were together, too, in 1922, when he needed to appease his conscience. It was in May of that year that he packed his wife and three eldest sons aboard the *Aquitania* for a European excursion (his first in ten years) that was supposed to make up for his persistent neglect, and was spoiled only slightly when he weakened, just three days out to sea, and wired a plea for Miss Davies to meet him in London.

But far more often, they were kept at arm's length by a father whose obsessions left him no time for the business of raising a family. It was Bill who explained how the Clarendon, the enormous brownstone on Riverside Drive where the brood spent their earliest years, was split into two separate realms. "The top floors—Nine, Ten, Eleven and Twelve— belonged to Pop," he remembered when the old man had long been gone:

> Oh, it was tremendous. He had a big ballroom up there, and armor— it was supposed to be the biggest collection in the world, I guess—and offices on the tenth floor where the politicians, guys like Jimmy Walker and whatshisname, Pop's Mayor . . . Red Mike Hylan . . . used to come a-courtin'. He and Mom each had a suite. They used to face each other, I think, right across the big hall.
>
> But us kids, we had our own place. We had our apartments down- stairs with Mom's folks, and Gus and Mamie Mayer—those were her cousins—and the maids, and the governesses, and the bodyguards and all that. I suppose we were allowed up past the tenth floor around once a week. You know, Sundays and holidays. That was about it.

The sons had Sundays and holidays to visit their father in the cavernous halls where he had already begun to assemble the collections that would furnish San Simeon. And during the long summers, when they made their yearly migration to their grandmother's Hacienda, they saw him not at all, for Hearst came to the ranch only rarely, and when he came at all it was less for the sake of the boys than to settle accounts with his mother, who still controlled the family's wealth.

To the tolerant William, who could worship his "Pop" even while conceding his failings, it seemed clear that the family had simply come too late. "The papers were already his children," he once theorized. "They were his first love, and nobody was ever gonna change that." But John, a year younger and much the feistier of the two, took a harder view of his father's ambivalence toward the boys' existence. The middle son believed not only that the younger boys were wholly unwanted, but that the senior Hearst had ordered Draconian measures to ensure that John, for one, would never arrive. In a scrawled fragment called "Achilles Was a Heel" (it was the beginning of a memoir that, typically, would never be finished), John described what he knew of his own precarious origins:

From what I can gather my advent into this world was a mistake—
well, not altogether a mistake, but rather an accident. I was the third
son born to an Episcopalian father and a Catholic mother.

We, the sons, arrived at rather irregular intervals but often enough
to worry my father, whom, I gather, didn't believe things were cheaper
by the dozen. From other information gleaned from the horse's mouth,
shall we say, I was the object of a purge that would have made Hitler
look like a schoolboy. Needless to say, I hung on with all the tenaciousness
of a fetus of Scotch-Irish heritage. I've never found out, or rather never
asked, who condemned me to the sewage disposal system of the City of
New York, but I have a sneaking hunch that it was dear old Dad.

Perhaps it was true that "dear old Dad" never intended to have all of
the family that he fathered. Or perhaps what he never really wanted—
and what he never would have—was a family bold enough to challenge
him or strong enough to take his place.

For it may have been more than simple neglect that confused the
boys and kept them from becoming the powerful heirs they might have
been. Surely they felt the subtle antagonism, the current of repressed
hostility, which their father had never quite managed to hide. It might
be concealed in oceans of sentiment—a gesture as slight as a mildly
filial note from John could move him to tears, and prompt him to tell
Millicent that, well, "they had a good mother anyway." But they knew
only too well that something was wrong in the way he discouraged them,
one and all, from finishing school. He himself had attended for only
three years before failing Harvard—and so none of the boys were going
to have more. George lasted a year at Berkeley, and Bill lasted two, while
John dropped out of Oglethorpe, Randy out of Harvard, and David out
of Yale—a record that Bill, at least half bewildered, explained by claiming that

> the old man wanted it that way! Hell, I was doing great in school.
> I *wanted* to finish. But I came back to New York between terms one
> year, I think it was 1928, and he talked me out of going back! He said,
> "Don't worry about finishing. You don't need it. You're an intelligent
> person. You can read and write. If you stay there any longer you're
> wasting your time."

Then, too, they must have wondered why he so persistently undermined
his own advice on the dangers of wealth by indulging their whims and
showering them with the things that could only do them harm. He
might well warn the twins to buckle down at Lawrenceville. But they

had only to count the weeks before he would weaken their fledgling resolve to do better with a peculiar enticement: "Why don't you close up that school and come West?" he would write. "We have a pool here, and it doesn't cost anything to keep it open. I am afraid you are studying too hard, especially David." He forgave their transgressions with a favorite Brisbanality. "It takes a good mind to resist education," he quoted the editor, when he would probably have done better to carry out his empty threats of summer school. And even while he advised his sons about the sorry fate of playboys, he continued to pay for the cars, the horses, the speedboats, and the aeroplanes that threatened to keep them from ever being anything else.

There were those who sensed that he was ruining the boys. Millicent—who had taken it on herself to place them in military schools, where she hoped that the discipline would "stiffen their spines"—put it as sweetly as possible in writing to Jack Neylan. She said that when she got through bringing up her five specimens she would write an article about how she did it, and Mr. Hearst could write another on how he undid all her discipline by giving them everything they wanted. Marion Davies was more direct. Convinced that Hearst was playing with the future of his family, she needled him about the way he treated the boys and sometimes she provoked bitter arguments over his refusal to take them in hand.

On one occasion, when she was worried about Jack, who at sixteen was rebellious and often in trouble, Marion accused him of letting the boys go because "people who are divorced are always too soft with their kids, they have a guilty conscience."

"But I am not divorced, and I do not have a guilty conscience," Hearst snapped back. And the truth was that, whatever the state of his conscience, he seemed to know precisely what he wanted where the boys were concerned. For as they came to an age when they faced the choices that governed their future, the five sons found, each of them in turn, that the decisions had all been made. They would work inside the family business, in positions of their father's choosing, because Pop wanted them there, and because—as he was known to remind them when he felt the urge to be severe—they were hardly good enough to earn on their own what he proposed to give them.

It was important to Hearst, perhaps as proof that he had, after all, spawned a dynasty, that the sons find a place in his empire. He made a great show of having them trained the way he had learned the business, by working their way through every department, from the pressroom to the publisher's office, on one of his big-city dailies. And as quickly as they mastered the slangy jargon of Hearstdom, he pushed them into jobs where they would be as conspicuous as possible. George was no more than twenty-five when he was installed as publisher of the San Francisco *Examiner*. At twenty-eight William became president of the New York *American*. John was a manager at *Cosmopolitan*, and the twins, at a tender age, became associate publishers in San Francisco and Los Angeles.

But Hearst and his sons and everyone who belonged to the inner circle of the empire knew how little those positions really meant. Whether it was because he doubted their ability—or because, as so many of his top men always suspected, he feared to cultivate a rival—the old man saw to it that none of the boys ever shared in the authority he held over the family's vast enterprise. As one of the sons themselves would put it, "To tell the truth, what he did was to set us up with a desk, a title, a good salary—and that was about it."

At his express command, each of the scions worked directly in the shadow of a powerful executive like Jack Neylan, Edmond Coblentz or Dick Berlin. In the beginning it was called an "educational" arrangement —the sons would have tutors, the best in the business, to reveal the *tao* of ruling a newspaper kingdom. But in time the five discovered that their tutelage was meant to be permanent, that however grand their titles might be, their father would persist in issuing his orders through men who were supposedly their subordinates. He simply ignored pleas like that of the befuddled Bill, who once implored him—"I am responsible for this paper [the *Journal-American*], but I can't very well be if you are communicating your suggestions or orders through half a dozen other people without my knowledge. This may seem like a trivial matter to you, but really, Pop, it is very important if you want me to function as I should function. At least apprise me of the things you clear through other people."

Apparently, Hearst seldom bothered to tell the boys of decisions that went over, and under, and around them. But at the same time, he never failed to remind them of how miserably they performed in the jobs they held at his pleasure. George he rebuked for the failings of the *Examiner*, though, according to legend, the son's authority on the paper was so slight that he was sometimes mistaken for a copyboy and asked to run errands (which, very obligingly, he did) in the halls of his own building.

Hearst realized—or should have realized—that he more than anyone was responsible for the way the "Monarch" was run. He had hand-picked the management of the paper, and he relayed his editorial notions almost daily by wire and phone. And yet, when the circulation figures began to slip, he was only too quick to snap at his ineffectual eldest. He told him to get the executives Mr. Lindner, Mr. Boone and Mr. Nourse into conference and to warn them that the *Examiner* was being edited in a very amateurish fashion. Even though Hearst was running the paper, he demanded that George, the hapless George, enforce the empire's rules and regulations and produce a dignified and conservative sheet, warning all the while that the boy would have no excuse if he failed.

For John it was much the same. Though his "mentor," Dick Berlin, showed no inclination to share the fiefdom he had made of the Hearst magazines, the middle son was nonetheless blamed for his own impotence by a father who claimed that he could do in one day what took John three months, and who only stated the obvious when he complained that John's contribution to the company was hardly sufficient to justify his salary.

But it was Bill, the namesake, who suffered most from the edge of contempt that poisoned his father's seeming solicitude for the boys. Bill Hearst was the eager son—the one who believed in his father and in the family, and who wanted more than anything to help lead the papers into a stable future. At the age of sixteen he had written his Pop, "I'll tell you what my ambition is. It is to be able to help you in your business, to be capable to do my part, and then some. I have tried to prepare myself in my school work with subjects that would help me in journalism, such as all the History and English I can get. I read a good deal, as you know, and I try to pick out useful books. You may think I am just saying this to please you, but it really is the truth." Later he proved his commitment by struggling through the nightmare of financial collapse. When his father was too tired or too deeply involved with his visions to fight for the empire on his own, it was Bill who stepped in to defend the interests of the family. He served as a liaison between the old man and his executives; he bitterly opposed Shearn's plan to sell the magazines to raise cash; and—what may have been the hardest of all—he worked, against his father's wishes, to set up the department-store sale of antiques that helped clear the way for the papers' survival.

That was enough to make him the heir apparent. "There was nothing very dramatic," says Bill. "I think he once wrote a letter to Martin Huberth, you know, evaluating us boys, and I guess he conceded that I was reasonably able. Later he made me Vice-Chairman of the editorial board. It didn't mean anything as long as he was Chairman. But it was supposed to be a sign."

The appointment was a sign that Bill was favored. But the heir knew as well as the others that no amount of effort would ever disarm his father or break down the tension that ran between the press lord and his sons. The more energy Bill poured into the *Journal-American*, the more likely he was to draw angry fire from Pop. "New York is about the only important Sunday paper which is not doing well," the old man would write. "In fact, New York is really going backwards. Please get busy and report on what you think should be done about this serious matter." But if Bill proposed a plan to cut overhead by combining production facilities with the *Mirror*, he could be sure that Hearst senior would embarrass him by warning the chain's publishers: "W. R. Hearst, Jr., spoke to me about the desirability of having more cooperation between the two Hearst papers in the same town . . . This is likely to develop into a fundamental mistake." If Bill was so bold as to suggest that a section on the Republican convention might reap an advertising bonanza, his father would accuse him of selling his principles.

And if Bill asked a favor as small as a job on the *Journal* for his wife, Lorelle, he was dismissed with an ugly thrust. His father complained that he was placing all the boys; he wouldn't pad his payrolls with their wives as well.

(3)

The future was, at best, an ambiguous promise.

All through his waning decades, when his health was uncertain and his finances worse than precarious, Hearst had been silent about the people and the properties that would survive him. The old Hearst adviser John Hanes believes that he may have had a will in those years; Hanes vaguely remembers an ancient, desk-drawer document that had been drafted before there was an empire, perhaps even before there was a family to consider. But others were less sure that he had even that. In

1933, when Hearst had already turned seventy, Jack Neylan—the self-proclaimed second in command—found himself sounding in vain for the least clue to the old man's intentions. "In the event that you should be disabled or your airplane should become temperamental, as airplanes have," he wrote, with all the tact at his command, "it seems inevitable that because of the relationship between us I would be confronted with the duty of acting as a trustee, with all the obligations which that implies; and I confess if I were confronted with that duty today I would probably worry myself to death in six months over whether I was acting conscientiously in accordance with your wishes."

Apparently, though, Hearst had no wishes, for his only reply was an oblique refusal to face the question. "Of course, anybody is likely to be hit by a cyclone at any time, from the age of one to the age of eighty," he philosophized. "But I am in good health, with no weaknesses of consequence as far as I know. As far as the airplane is concerned, do not worry about that. The way I use it, it is as safe as a train, and maybe safer than an automobile; because no reckless driver is likely to run into me. We never go up except in fine weather, and we never take undue risks of any kind."

Ten years later—when there was still no plan, and scarcely a hint that he had considered his approaching death—the executives began to prod him more vigorously. It was in February of 1944 that a cabal led by Berlin confronted Hearst with a threat. As Frej Hagelberg reported the incident, the group, which included the accountant Tom Smith and the newspaper manager G. O. Markuson, met the publisher at Wyntoon, where they warned him that unless he drafted a careful will, he could expect the papers to be taken over "by some wealthy red, such as Marshall Field." The next month, Neylan, now retired, brought him figures to show that estate taxes might take as much as three quarters of his fortune; if the estate were assumed to be worth $70 million, he said, the taxes would approach some $53 million. And to that, according to the notes of his conference, he added a warning: "The chances of liquidating fifty-three million dollars in assets to pay tax would be slim and the heirs *might get zero.*"

But apparently Johnny Hanes was the one who finally moved him. Hanes was himself a man of family, a tobacco heir of the Carolina persuasion whose reverence for Hearst stood second only to his abiding sense of propriety. Hanes knew the sons. He knew the fortune. And by

1944 he believed that he knew the aging publisher well enough to understand why he had refused to draft a will.

Some thirty years later, he would recall, in his muted, deep-South drawl:

> I admired that man greatly—I want you to realize that. I have never known anyone even remotely like him. But to tell you the truth, I was appalled when I saw what he was about to do to the boys—I mean the way he was gonna leave 'em without a dime.
>
> Well, I suppose I didn't have any choice but to go out there and tell him some things that his own people never would. I said, "It's not right. Frankly, I am shocked at the way you're treating your family. Whatever you might think about them or anything else, you're not gonna leave 'em out in the cold this way."
>
> Oh, he was mad when I told him that, he didn't say a word. But in the end he knew I was right. He finally said, "All right, Johnny, perhaps you'd better get to work on a will."

The Last Will and Testament of William Randolph Hearst was a massive document, a spectacular production that wholly belied the old man's reluctance to see it drafted or to watch his own fantastic career come trailing to an end. Three years in the making, it was begun in the wake of Hanes's angry sermon, and finished only when Hearst had reached eighty-four, in the spring of 1947. It was 125 pages in length— the longest will ever filed in California—and it disposed of more than $57 million, another Golden State record. It incorporated not only the conscientious efforts of John Hanes, but the legal talent of Henry MacKay, the financial wizardry of Arthur Graustein and Oscar Lawler, and the organizational cunning of Dick Berlin. It virtually restructured the Hearst Corporation, rebuilding the whole around a capitalization scheme and a charitable trust that have been called the "creation of a tax genius." It preserved the fortune; it calmed the nerves of worried executives; and it provided a blueprint for the future of an institution that would broadcast and publish under the Hearst name even when its founder had long been dead.

Yet, for all that, the will did curiously little to serve the family that Johnny Hanes had hoped to protect.

For his long-estranged wife, Hearst left nothing more than she might have taken by raiding his estate with a battery of attorneys and an arm-load of community-property law. There was a simple bequest for

Millicent V. Hearst, $7.5 million in cash and nonvoting Hearst Corporation shares, conditioned only on her accepting the terms of the will.

For the sons, he left considerably less. Under the terms of his testament, Hearst saw to it that the boys, and their descendants after them, would share in the family fortune only to the extent of their participation in the newspaper business. This he achieved leaving them no more than a modest direct inheritance: a total of thirty thousand shares of preferred stock and one hundred shares of common stock were placed in trust for the sons. With the cumulative annual dividend on the preferred set at no more than five dollars per share, this meant, in effect, that none of the boys would enjoy more than $30,000 per year in assured income—hardly enough to maintain the standard of living to which all five had been accustomed since birth. At the same time, however, it was understood that if they remained at work on the papers, the boys would continue to be paid disproportionately high salaries, and would enjoy special privileges with regard to property (like Wyntoon and San Simeon) that officially belonged to the corporation. The arrangement followed the advice of Neylan, who in 1944 had laid down the principle, "Retention of control is just as important as dollars left to heirs. Probably salary income may exceed in amount the principal of any practicable bequest."

But it was hardly the miserly financial arrangement, the pauper's share in a century-old fortune, that made the will an embarrassment to the Hearsts. The money was largely a matter of taxes; with the bulk of its assets invested in charity (through the vehicle of the newly formed Hearst and William Randolph Hearst Foundations), the estate would be safe, at least, from the hungry coffers of the Internal Revenue Bureau.

Taxes, however, had nothing to do with the hard terms that the old man had chosen to place on the one thing that mattered, the right to control the Hearst Corporation, and with it, the family empire. Under Article Two of his ironclad will, Hearst placed the critical one hundred shares of voting stock in trust for the benefit of the family. And under Article Fourteen, he put the trust under the power not of his sons and heirs, but of an administrative board that was cunningly divided in two. On the one side, there would be five family members—at first the boys, and later their chosen descendants. On the other side, there would be not five, but six of the Hearst executives. The first of these nonfamily trustees—Martin Huberth, Dick Berlin and Henry MacKay, along with three newspapermen, Hap Kern, Richard Carrington and Bill Baskervill

—were named in the will. Their successors, said Hearst, must be chosen from the ranks of the business, with the single proviso that "they be no issue of mine."

To one son, at least, the implications of his father's strange testament were clear. Bill remembers that his brother Randy first heard of the conditions that had been placed on his heritage in September of that same year, 1947:

> My God, was he upset. He had just come back from the service when somebody showed him that thing, and he could hardly believe it.
>
> Well, Randy—all puffed up with the wings on his chest and all the authority of the United States Army—said, "That's it. We've put up with a hell of a lot, but we're not gonna take this." I guess he flew right out to Beverly Hills, Pop was staying at M.D.'s by then, and marched up to the bedroom and told him he was gonna have to change it.
>
> You know what the old man did? He sat down and wrote up a codicil right there. Damned if he didn't *add* two more trustees—to the other side.

Chapter 4

The Woman

(1)

MARION WAS DRUNK the night before Hearst died. The death watch had begun a week earlier, and by Sunday, August 13, her house was full of people. Berlin had showed up early in the week, accompanied by Martin Huberth and Jake Gortatowsky; all three, who were staying in the guesthouse below, had spent considerable time hovering over the Chief, to what end no one in the household was quite sure. Bill had come soon afterward, followed by all the other sons but John, who remained with Millicent in New York. A number of Marion's friends and relatives, among them her nephew, the screenwriter Charles Lederer, joined the crowd that had already been swollen by nearly a dozen nurses, secretaries and household workers. Inevitably, tensions had been building throughout the week. The executives had cordoned off Hearst, installing strange nurses, and pushing Marion into the background. She insisted that they were killing him with the rush of activity—"There were blazing lights in the hall, and everybody was talking at the top of their lungs. He had no chance to rest. I was furious; I went out and asked them to go downstairs." But no one listened, and by Sunday night she was drinking heavily, and looking in vain for support.

The greatest blow that night was delivered by the Hearst boys. Marion had never had a serious fight with any of them in the past. But now that the sons had come to await their father's death, they suddenly seemed cold and distant, and were unwilling to treat her with more than a minimum of respect. George was still a friend, but of the others Marion complained, "They turned on me like vipers." The decisive moment between herself and the sons came sometime after midnight, just a few hours before Hearst's passing. Marion came down from her bedroom, reeking of Scotch, to find Bill and David sitting in Hearst's study. She asked the boys about their father's condition, and one of them—those who overheard it were never sure which—shouted back, "Why should you care, you whore!" With that the dam had burst. There followed what Marion called a "brutal" exchange, in which the two accused her of putting herself between Hearst and the business, and of trying to run the papers. Marion later recalled scraps of the argument:

> David said to me, "You trying to run the papers?"
> I said, "No."
> He said, "Who ordered that?" He showed me the third page of the Los Angeles *Examiner*, where there was a story about a children's party at the Mocambo (a nightclub on Sunset Boulevard).
> I said, "Your father ordered it."
> "I don't believe it. You're trying to run the papers."
> "Look—I don't want to run the papers, for God's sake. All I am is a messenger boy. W. R. orders a thing, and I have to telephone it. If you have any objections, go in and talk to your father."

The boys badgered her still further. They wanted to know what she intended by her interference, and why Hearst's secretaries couldn't call in the changes. It was Bill who cut the exchange short by telling her, "I think you've gone a little bit too far."

Shaken to the core by the attack, Marion was lulled to sleep only with the help of a strong shot of barbiturate administered without consent by her physician, Dr. Eliot Corday. When she awoke the next afternoon, she was virtually alone. Hearst had died at nine-thirty that morning—attended only by his faithful dachshund—and Berlin had cleared the house by noon. Marion's nephew, who had been present the night before, returned before the body was gone. Berlin had told him, "You're not wanted here. . . . Don't go into Mr. Hearst's room." To which Lederer replied, "I'll go anywhere I damn please in this house." Waking his aunt, Lederer found her groggy and delirious. She seemed to slip into a mild state of shock on hearing of her lover's death. She sat for a long time in her darkened room, hugging her dog and singing, "Little old lady in a big red room, Little old lady in a big red room." In her less coherent moments, she talked about murder, telling Lederer that she had been slipped a sedative the night before as part of a conspiracy between the executives and Hearst's doctors.

Of the family, only George ever returned to offer his condolences, though Bill called that night to "explain" what had happened. Apparently it was Millicent, determined to avoid a confrontation over the casket of her husband, who had decided that Marion would not attend the funeral. For, as the mistress recalled of her conversation with Bill, "I asked him when the services would be. I said, 'Look, you wouldn't let me say goodbye to him. At least you can tell me when the services will be, so I can pray for him down here.' He said that the whole thing was up to his mother. I found out about the funeral by reading the paper the next morning." In all probability, she had not learned of the plans by reading a Hearst paper, because someone had stopped delivery of the *Examiner* and the *Herald-Express* before plans for the services were announced. But by then it scarcely mattered, for Marion had come to agree that nothing would be gained by treating the press to the spectacle of two bereaved mates weeping over Hearst's remains. For Millicent, however, she had one short message. To a mutual friend, she whispered: "Please tell Mrs. Hearst not to forget to wear her widow's weeds."

The publisher and his pet had begun without illusions: they had only intended to use each other, and neither believed that they would ever have more than a fleeting, half-regretted affair. Marion had been eighteen when the two met, but she was worldly enough to know what Hearst wanted. As early as their second encounter (which occurred at a party, their first having taken place at a late-night dinner, with Paul Block escorting Marion, and Hearst in the company of Justine Johnstone, another stunning member of the cast of *Stop! Look! Listen!*), the restless publisher had cornered the chorine in a bedroom. There he had pressed a bejeweled Tiffany watch into her palm, stating with all of his usual authority "I'd like to see you soon." When Marion lost the watch within a week, he sent another. And not much later, he was indeed seeing her —intimately and often. Marion had been warned by other girls in the chorus to be wary of Hearst, who was, they told her, "a wolf in sheep's clothing." But she loved the gifts that he lavished on her—and she thought it great fun to play her own part to the hilt. On the first few evenings they enjoyed together, Marion, who was young enough to be Hearst's daughter, made her gratitude felt by crawling into his lap, ruffling his hair, and calling him "Daddy." By sometime in 1916, the two were spending their nights in a studio apartment that Hearst maintained for his rendezvous in the Beaux Arts Building, conveniently near the headquarters of his New York *American*.

Hearst knew the rules of the game even better than Marion. She was not, after all, his first affair. And yet, almost in spite of himself, he began to feel wildly possessive of his young chorine. He attended the theater every night without fail during Marion's run in the *Follies*. He would spirit her away for intimate dinners after the show, and try as best he could to ward off Block and other competitors. Against all sense, he began to take her pet names seriously. He was delighted to think of himself as Marion's "Pops" (though he more often felt like "Desperate Desmond" or "Lonesome George," especially when she insisted on the prerogative of seeing other men). And by the time the show had ended, he had even installed a special operator at the *American*; her only duty was to know where Marion could be reached at any hour of the day.

If Hearst came to depend on Marion Davies in a way he never intended, the reasons may have been at least partly professional. When he first spotted Marion onstage, after all, the publisher was approaching the end of his second wind; having succeeded as a newspaper entrepreneur and failed resoundingly as a politician, he was, at the age of fifty-three, looking for some place to go. There was no challenge left in opening new papers. But something in Marion, the eternal ingenue, helped to rekindle his waning creative urge.

That Marion could give him a whole new career seems to have dawned on Hearst in a flash. On seeing the first screening of *Runaway, Romany*— a miserable melodrama about a rich girl kidnapped by gypsies, which was produced on a shoestring because Block, the film's backer, considered it doomed to failure—Hearst had turned to his young companion and declared, "Marion, I'm going to make you a star." He meant it. But what he forgot to add was that he also intended to make himself an impresario, a major power in the world of film, on the slender foundation of her theatrical talent.

Hearst had already begun to dabble in film. Before working with Marion he had produced a number of shorts as well as two lengthy serials, the *Mysteries of Myra* and the *Exploits of Elaine*, which were modeled on the far more successful *Perils of Pauline*. Once he had his starlet, however, he was prepared to move into motion pictures on a grand scale. Even before *Runaway, Romany* was released (in December 1917) he had rented studio space in Sulzer's Harlem River Park Casino, and had begun to organize Cosmopolitan Productions around the figure of Marion Davies. Marion, of course, was hardly ready to support a major production company. She had led a moderately successful stage career, working in perhaps a half dozen major shows, and she enjoyed some celebrity around New York, owing largely to Hearst's having featured her in the *American* as a "star" of the 1916 Follies. But not only had she never held a major role; because of her charmingly incurable stutter, she had never been given more than a single line in any of the productions!

But Hearst was undaunted by his Galatea's obvious flaws. While Cosmopolitan was being set up, he put Marion through the paces. He pushed her through the Empire School of Acting, providing coaches to work day and night on her stammer, and arranging, too, for a badly needed dose of general education. Surely it was a monument to his determination that by the spring of 1918, the thirty episodes of *Beatrice Fairfax*, with Marion in the starring role, were ready for release by Pathé.

When audiences failed to respond to Marion as Beatrice, Hearst scarcely seemed to notice. Assuming that sooner or later the public would catch up (it never really did), he outfitted his protégé with all the trappings of stardom even before her talent had a chance to blossom. He gave her still more cash and credit for expanding her wardrobe, and then he moved both her and her family into a palatial town house on Riverside Drive, less than two blocks from the Hearst apartment at the Clarendon. Hearst stuffed her new quarters with antiques and saw to it that she had a fine book-lined sitting room, where she could receive correspondents from the fan magazines (who were forced to take notice by vigorous plugs in the *Journal* and the *American*). By May of 1918, when her first full feature—a tale of "humiliation and heartbreak" called *Cecilia of the Pink Roses*—was ready for release, the publicity had risen to fever pitch. Theaters were sprayed with attar of roses and New York was lined with billboards, while the *American*, calling the film a "masterpiece," assured the public that "there were few dry eyes at the Rivoli Theater yesterday when the vision of Marion Davies faded on the screen."

Certainly Hearst needed Marion on the screen (though possibly not as much as he thought he did, since most of her films were resounding failures). But even without the motion pictures, the publisher was driven by a deep, almost daemonic desire to possess her. More than anyone he had ever known, his starlet had the power to tap the oceans of sentiment that were locked inside of him. When the two of them were apart, he pined for her like a lovesick swain. If he had to spend even a day with Millicent, he would never fail to shower his lover with flowers and soulful telegrams, and snatches of romantic verse from his own pen. In Marion's favorite ode, Hearst sighed:

> *Oh the night is blue and the stars are bright*
> *Like the eyes of the girl of whom I write.*
> *And the day is a glimmer of golden light*
> *Like the locks of the girl of whom I write.*
> *And the skies are soft and the clouds are white*
> *Like the limbs of the girl of whom I write.*
> *But no beauty of earth is so fair a sight*
> *As the girl who lies by my side at night.*

When he finally swept her off to his California retreats, Hearst seemed to find a new lease on life in Marion's spirit. It was hardly surprising, for irrepressible vitality was, after all, the very stuff of Marion Davies' existence. She was a prankster and a wag, who could trade sly jokes, obscene or otherwise, with the best, and she always surrounded herself with a panoply of wits, wonders, and people on the make. Two and three times a week she gave great dinners at her Santa Monica house, where as many as 2,800 lockers had been installed for the use of visitors who might want to go for a swim. To San Simeon she invited whole trainloads of weekend guests, usually including the entire cast of whatever film she happened to be doing, to fill the four houses and to help disperse the chill that seemed always to grip the cavernous halls. The people who came were the best and the brightest of Hollywood—the endless roster of names included Harlow, Gable, Cooper, Pickford, Chaplin, Valentino, Lombard, Thalberg, Shearer, Mayer, Hecht, Mankiewicz, and more. All seemed to be her friends, and all helped her to keep Hearst from sliding back into the chronic loneliness, the Germanic melancholia that dwelled on the dark side of his character. Indeed, if Hearst depended on Marion in his sixties and seventies, it was because he was living on her energy as much as his own.

So Marion gave him life, at least thirty years of it. But she was never to have the one thing she craved in return. For more than anything, Marion Davies desired normality. She wanted, almost desperately, to be her lover's wife, or, if that was impossible, at least to be accepted as a part of his family.

Millicent, however, would never allow it.

Any sense of good will between Millicent and Marion was out of the question; in fact, the two had nothing to do with each other, partly because the wife's pride stood between them, and partly because Hearst, as a rule, was careful to keep the women apart. Sometimes, of course, they would have their encounters—some of them so close that one can only wonder whether Hearst felt some unspoken, perhaps unconscious, desire to provoke a confrontation. According to Marion, the two actually met, sometime in the spring of 1916. As the story goes, Marion was enjoying a vacation at Vizcaya, James Deering's Miami mansion, when Hearst and Millicent came down on one of their periodic visits to the resort. Out bicycling with a friend, the young showgirl—already deeply involved with the publisher—was shocked to see his maroon Cadillac bearing down upon them. Swerving into the curb, she fell; the car stopped; and to her dismay, Hearst, after asking innocently, "May I help with this accident?" had his chauffeur put the bicycle in the trunk while he escorted Marion to the vehicle. There she shared the back seat with a very reserved Millicent, all the way to a local clinic.

On her side, Millicent eventually arrived at a sort of grudging tolerance of her rival. Though she usually denied Marion the dignity of a name (the lover was always "that woman" or "that harlot" to Millicent), the wife was sometimes curious about the woman who had taken her place. Often she asked their mutual friends, of whom there were many, "What is she like?" Or "What does he call her?" (This last question would provoke an answer that never satisfied Millicent: "Well, I guess, he calls her Marion.")

But Marion could never mention Millicent without making a show of her bitterness. She called Hearst's wife "The Black Widow." She ranted about her social pretensions and supposed religious scruples, and blamed her for spending too much of Hearst's cash. Perhaps unfairly, she also held Millicent *solely* responsible for Hearst's failure to obtain a divorce. Marion was convinced that Hearst had exhausted every means at his command in his attempt to dissolve his marriage. Possibly he had. But people who knew him well found him much less uncomfortable with his ambiguous situation than was Marion. As late as 1940, when Hearst and his wife had been estranged for almost twenty years, one family friend recalled hearing the husband plead over the telephone: "Just give me a little more time, Millie, and I'll get this whole thing worked out."

With the boys, at least, Marion seemed to enjoy a certain rapport—once they were permitted anywhere near her. Apparently it was George who first broke his father's prohibition on visits to the ranch. Some time in the late twenties he came, unannounced, with his own wife, to meet the woman who had been with his father for almost a decade. Marion recalled the awkward moment when Hearst first spotted his son:

> Well, George and Blanche were in the dining room when W. R. walked in with me, and George tried to smile. W. R. said, "What are you doing here? When you come, you should notify me beforehand. And get up and say 'How do you do?'" That was the way it went. It was a delightful life. I was embarrassed all the time.

Of course, the sons were too old to substitute for the children she never had, but she enjoyed their company, and she insisted, despite the embarrassment of all concerned, that they be allowed to pay calls at San Simeon even when she was on hand. As she later said, "I guess Mr. Hearst didn't want them there, but I felt it was their due, that they should see their father. And I felt that I was in the way of that. But W. R. didn't feel that way at all. If they wanted to see him, they had to come to San Simeon and, inevitably, bump into me. It was too bad it had to happen that way. . . ." For the most part, the boys seemed to return her good will. They picked up the habit of calling her "Daisy," a nickname bestowed by her friend Connie Talmadge, and found her a good-natured pal, always game for a prank, and sometimes even willing to bait Pop for the sake of fun—something they never quite managed on their own.

Marion got along famously with Bill and John in 1934, when they entertained each other on a European tour by scheming to subvert Hearst's ban on alcohol, whether by cheating at a winetasting (where

Bill got drunk by crawling through an empty vat) or by passing a drink in a Coke bottle, under the old man's nose. But George was her favorite. Marion felt sorry for the oldest son because he seemed to be held in low esteem by the rest of the family; as she put it, "Most of the family thought he was null and void, but he was not. He always was very kind, and I always regarded him as my best friend among all of W. R.'s boys." The special bond between the two may have owed something to the fact that both stuttered, that both felt insecure and seemed always to be at a disadvantage where the rest were concerned. At the same time, too, Marion never forgot that George was the first to accept her; eternally grateful for his having taken the initiative in coming to the ranch, she flew full in the face of family opinion to insist that "George was the oldest and the smartest. He was the first one to be nice to me—and so he was in."

Still, it was impossible to ignore the ugly tension that lay just beneath the suface between Marion and her lover's sons. She felt it, and so did they. The boys were too close to Millicent not to resent the hold gained over their father by a woman who was scarcely older than themselves. And they were too acutely aware of Marion as a constant embarrassment to accept her as a normal part of Pop's life, however much they might sometimes enjoy her company. Even when the affair was common knowledge—as certainly it was after the release of *Citizen Kane,* if not before—the boys continued to think of it as something to be suppressed, something to be kept out of the columns and if at all possible, out of the family history. It was characteristic of their attitude toward the woman that she would be their first concern when the round of biographies began not long after Hearst's death. In 1953, when John Winkler requested cooperation in assembling his *New Appraisal* of Hearst's life, Bill, as family spokesman, was to write: "I shall be glad to cooperate, but I think we should have assurances that the book will meet with our approval. In other words, I do not wish to be a party in any way to something that would drag in Marion to the point where it would be embarrassing to Mom."

Unfortunately, Marion made it all too easy for those who were intent on "dragging her into it," on making her an embarrassment to Hearst and his family. Despite her public image as a second Mary Pickford (Hearst refused even to let her trade kisses on the screen), Marion Davies was no saint; at best, she was a sort of fallen angel, whose personal indiscretions kept her lover tottering on the brink of major scandal. It was well known in the film community that Marion was a disastrous drinker. Contrary to all of Hearst's rules, she kept a bottle of Scotch or gin cooling in the toilet tank at San Simeon. When she was feeling "blue," she went on devastating binges, and by the time Cosmopolitan had joined forces with Warners in the late thirties, she was often unable to work for days at a time. That Marion should have turned to alcohol is hardly surprising. It was not just an occupational hazard in Hollywood, but her special defense against a way of life that grew no more comfortable as the years passed. On several occasions Hearst tried to break her of the habit; but Marion rebelled, insisting that she had no intention of being "cured." Nor did Hearst ever manage to put a stop to his mistress' sexual adventures. Marion continued to have "small affairs," sometimes with characters as well known as Dick Powell or Charlie Chaplin, and her conduct, if not exactly notorious, nonetheless took its toll on the family. There were persistent rumors of illegitimate children, and one of the more troublesome variations had it that David and Randy (who, as people liked to comment, "looked just like her") were actually her sons. This was patently absurd, the boys having been born some months before Hearst had met the second showgirl in his life. But it may well be that not all of the gossip was as groundless—on at least one occasion Marion was able to tell a member of her family, whose friend was troubled by an unwanted pregnancy, "Go see Doctor Jackson.* He took care of all of mine."

To the family's dismay, open scandal did sometimes erupt, with the talk about Marion spilling over into the headlines. The first open breach of propriety occurred in June of 1922, when, at a New York party given in Marion's honor by her sister Reine, a friend named Oscar Hirsch had drunk too much bootleg liquor and wound up in a scuffle with his wife over a pistol he was carrying. Hirsch was shot, superficially, in the neck; and Marion woke the next morning to hear the newsboys shouting "Read all about the Marion Davies murder!" For the moment the Hearst name was kept out of the papers, but competitors like the *Daily News*, the *Herald*, and the *Telegram* used the incident to give the publisher an indirect clubbing. For days they riveted their attention on his mistress— turning her denials of having been at the party into confessions of guilt,

* Fictitious name.

and running stories that went as far as to say, "Woman shoots husband because of jealousy of Marion Davies." Finally an exasperated Hearst, against his own principles, began urging Marion to sue.

Marion chose to ride out the crisis. But a bare two years later there was trouble of a more serious kind when film director Thomas Ince died in ambiguous circumstances aboard Hearst's 210-foot steam yacht, the *Oneida*. After a hasty inquest, the coroner attributed Ince's death to "acute indigestion." But the public would have it otherwise. In a round of speculation that began in the Los Angeles papers and the New York *Daily News*, Ince was said to have been shot by Hearst, who, as the story went, was in a jealous rage over the director's romantic entanglement with Marion. Even Hearst was shaken by the uproar that followed the rumors—shaken enough to abandon his mistress for almost half a year, beating a retreat back to the family, with whom he stayed until the spring of 1925.

No less ominous than Marion's knack for attracting dangerous publicity, was the distrust she was by then beginning to arouse among another set of Hearst intimates, the businessmen. That there was no love lost between the actress and Hearst's business associates had been plain from the beginning. Most of the executives kept their distance from Marion, perhaps out of respect for Millicent, perhaps simply as a sign of their uneasiness over the trouble she repeatedly caused the Chief. Many could hardly even bring themselves to mention her by name; in executive circles, Marion Davies was usually "M. D.," or, more formally, "Marion Douras."

It is easy to understand the men's suspicion of a woman who had quickly worked her way into the confidence of a boss whom most of them found barely approachable. While they quailed before the grueling executive sessions, where Hearst would grill them man by man, prodding for their weaknesses, Marion would bully and nag him, sometimes daring —in public—to *tell* him what to do. One small incident that occurred in 1925 did much to convince Hearst's staff that Marion was fast becoming a force that would have to be taken seriously. The exchange was at a dinner party in Beverly Hills; Marion was the hostess, and a battery of newspaper executives were numbered among the guests. At one point during the evening, Marion decided that the newspapermen were hovering too close around her host. And as Charlie Chaplin, who was present, described what ensued:

About fifty of us were standing about while Hearst, looking saturnine, was seated in a high-backed chair surrounded by his editorial staff. Marion, gowned ala Madame Récamier, reclined on a settee, looking radiantly beautiful, but growing more taciturn as Hearst continued his business. Suddenly she shouted indignantly, "Hey! You!"

Hearst looked up. "Are you referring to me?" he said.

"Yes, you! Come here!" she answered, keeping her large blue orbs on him. His staff backed away and the room hardened into silence.

Hearst's eyes narrowed as he sat sphinxlike, his scowl growing darker, his lips disappearing into a thin line as his fingers tapped nervously on the arm of his thronelike chair, undecided whether to burst into fury or not. I felt like reaching for my hat. But suddenly he stood up. "Well, I suppose I shall have to go," he said, oafishly hobbling over to her. "And what does my lady want?"

"Do your business downtown," said Marion disdainfully. "Not in my house. My guests are waiting for a drink, so hurry up and get them one."

He fetched the drinks while the nervous executives looked on, silent and appalled. Many of them wondered, no doubt, how long it would be before Marion brought that commandeering tone to bear on matters that were properly their concern, perhaps planting a word with Hearst that would spell the end of their careers. Already she had begun to voice opinions about a number of Hearst's associates. She carried on a running battle with Arthur Brisbane, of whom she said, "A. B. was a big crook, incidentally, but W. R. liked him." Though she was touched by Hearst's grief at the editor's death in 1936, it would probably not be going too far to say that one of her fondest memories was the sight of A. B. stretched out in his coffin with an encyclopedia propped in his hand. She remarked in wonder, "He even died reading a book." Nor did the woman have any use for Clarence Shearn, the New York attorney who was in charge of Hearst's political dealings. Marion may have held a grudge against Shearn because of the way he had kept her romance at the backstairs level for so many years, so that she wouldn't have the chance to wreak still more damage on Hearst's already battered political career. At any rate, she freely warned Hearst that Shearn (whom she called Napoleon, because he scratched his chest) was "a little bit vicious," and probably harbored secret intentions against his boss. But this was nothing compared to the animosity she felt for Neylan, "the great, wonderful Holy Roman Catholic, John Francis Neylan, the biggest crook that God ever created." Marion knew that Neylan was close to Millicent, and that he strongly disapproved of her relationship with Hearst. Neylan, who was indeed a devout Roman Catholic, made a point of avoiding all contact with Marion; usually he refused even to visit San Simeon when she was there. Marion reciprocated his ill will many times over. She called him a "black Irishman who was jealous of anybody he thought was a little more powerful than himself." And she tried, in vain, to convince Hearst that his lieutenant was conspiring to destroy him. According to Marion, Neylan had betrayed his true color to her friend Frances Marion as early as the middle twenties. As she insisted,

> Frances Marion knew him very well. She told me that one time he had come up to San Simeon and went over and hid in House B or C and didn't appear for four or five days. He used to go on awful benders.
> She said she was there one night when he was loaded. He staggered into the living room and said, "Where is Hearst?"
> Frances said, "I don't know where Mr. Hearst is. I always refer to him as Mr. Hearst, because I worked for him a long time and I have great respect for him."
> He said, "I call him Hearst."
> She told him he was drunk and should go to bed. And he said, "I'll get that son-of-a-bitch if it kills me." Frances Marion asked why. He said, "Because I've always hated his guts."

For the most part, Hearst seemed to discount Marion's ravings—neither Brisbane, nor Neylan, nor Shearn was ever called to account on her recommendation. But that was little comfort to the men who watched him lavishing more and more of his resources on Marion and her career. In their terms, money and attention were power, and Marion Davies was clearly receiving more than her share of both.

According to one time-honored story, an acquaintance of Hearst once assured him, "There's money in the movies."

"Yes, mine," he shot back.

It was something more than a joke. For Marion Davies' film career was a costly enterprise that never returned as much as it took out of the corporate coffers. The reasons were many, and most could be traced back to Hearst. He insisted on paying Marion a scandalously high salary throughout the years that she worked for Cosmopolitan. Some supposed that he wanted her to stay one step ahead of Mary Pickford—whatever his motives, he made her his highest-paid employee, giving her $100,000 annually as the company's president, and supplementing that with another $10,000 per week whenever she was working on a picture.

After Marion's salary, Cosmopolitan was burdened by enormous production costs, which were inflated by Hearst's preference for costume spec-
taculars, and his fetish for authenticity. (Often he insisted on using his
own priceless antiques for the settings.) But it was Marion's laissez-faire
attitude toward the films that did most to keep the company in the red.
The actress thought nothing of burning up $5,000 to $10,000 a day by
clowning on the set, ruining takes by appearing with a tooth blacked out
or a pillow stuffed under her dress. And even when she was working, she
wasn't working very hard. At half a million dollars a year, her daily
routine was a prima donna's dream:

> Sometimes I would get to the set around eleven. Sometimes ten—
> sometimes noon. Then at luncheon we had banquets at the bungalow,
> and we'd sit around and talk about things. We wouldn't talk about
> pictures.
>
> We would get back on the set around three, do a scene or so, and
> then have tea about four-thirty. They would blow the whistle at five, and
> everybody'd whisk off. So we'd only get a few scenes done all day.
>
> But W. R. didn't worry about the budget. He'd even call the set
> about a quarter to five and say it was time to quit. He'd be lonesome.
> He'd say, "You've been working all day"—not knowing we'd done only
> one scene.

But if Marion was ruining Hearst, it was also Marion who came flying
to the rescue when finally the empire crumbled under the combined
weight of the movies, the extravagant houses, and the great Depression.
Marion learned one morning early in 1937 that the crisis had hit. Bill
had appeared at the Santa Monica house, and insisted that she waken
his father. He said that the "empire was crashing," and that Hearst
would have to go east immediately, if he were to salvage anything from
the banks. No one asked for her help. But while Bill and his father
prepared to embark for New York, Marion summoned her financial
manager, Edgar Hatrick, and had him begin a crash liquidation of her
stocks and real estate. By the time the train left that evening, Marion
was able to present Hearst with a certified check for a million dollars. A
million dollars was hardly enough to secure the Hearst enterprise; but at a
critical moment, it did help to stave off foreclosure by the Canadian
banks that handled Hearst's newsprint contracts. Millicent, who consented to having her allowance cut, closed down the Clarendon and
moved into her Long Island palace. But Marion did much more.
Scrabbling to collect badly needed dollars, she sold her jewelry and

joined with her sisters in turning over a trust fund that had been set aside for her grandmother. Pooling her own "petty cash" with some money she managed to borrow from her friend Babs Rockefeller, she finally raised a second million.

Hearst was deeply touched by her help, which he realized was more than a gesture—certainly Marion had done as much as anyone to salvage his fortune at a time when all of it might well have been lost had it not been possible to keep the creditors at bay. But Marion's relations with his sons and advisers were scarcely improved by her efforts. In fact, Bill, Berlin and Tom White (who was then president of the Hearst Corporation), had counseled against accepting her money. When Hearst finally took it in spite of their advice they insisted that she be given collateral, in the form of the two Boston papers.

Marion, who wanted no collateral—and who knew as well that the papers were notorious losers—saw the offer for the insult that it was. She accepted, but she continued to tell Hearst that "he had enemies in his camp," that he had "put his faith in people who had no faith." She was convinced that the financial debacle was the result of a conspiracy engineered by Neylan, and she was not entirely sure that Berlin and Bill didn't belong in the enemies' camp. She pounded away repeatedly on the theme of betrayal, giving voice to her theory that Hearst had been "sold down the river by the people he had placed great faith in." Marion insisted that the New York executives had been accumulating bank loans on purpose, hoping to force the aging Hearst into relinquishing control of the enterprise. But they hadn't counted on her. "They weren't smart," she said. "They didn't figure on me at all. They thought I was just a nonentity, a dullard, a stupid who sits in the corner with a dunce cap."

Whether Hearst ever really accepted Marion's claim that he had been betrayed by friends and family is uncertain. But there were signs toward the end that he had begun to believe it. In the last fifteen years of his life, he began to repose extraordinary trust in Marion. There was no longer any question about whether she was entitled to express opinions about business; she did, and he listened. He often consulted her at length about the papers, and when he received important calls from New York and Los Angeles, he made a point of telling her, "Please stay. I would like for you to hear this." Marion, who claimed to have a one-track mind, said that she paid no attention to politicians, politics or society. But Hearst kept her as closely informed on topics of importance as he could, and when she displayed a spark of interest in people or events, he was quick to respond, "Let me get you a good book on that." Despite her disclaimers, Marion picked up a great deal of inside information. She was up to date on the publisher's intention of starting a tabloid in Los Angeles, and claimed to know for a fact that he was a secret partner in the *L.A. Daily News;* she was aware that the New York *Mirror* and the Chicago *Herald-American* were regarded as the biggest disappointments in the chain; she took part in the controversy over installing color presses and rotogravure equipment; and she gained a workable, though no doubt distorted, sense of the strengths and weaknesses of the executives. She knew at any rate whom Hearst relied upon, and whom he didn't—and so finally the more savvy Hearstlings came to realize that they were reporting not only to the Chief but to Marion. They began to address duplicate copies of their memoranda to her, under the cover of cordial notes that urged her to use her influence with "Mr. Hearst."

After twenty years and more, the two had grown together, as man and wife often will, until finally they seemed to have been welded into a unit. Sometimes, indeed, it seemed as if the aging Hearst was indifferent to everything but Marion, and those moods deepened in the years after he had written his will, when she finally brought him down from San Simeon to end his days in Los Angeles. When Hearst's health slipped into a serious decline in 1946, Marion had found him the pink stucco house on North Beverly, where he could live in relative seclusion (since it was set back on an eight-acre lot), and still be near his battery of physicians. Bringing him down the hill for the last time, she had said, "We'll come back, W. R., you'll see." He only shook his head and cried, knowing that he would never go back. During the four years he had yet to live, there were no more parties, and the loneliness that had dogged him all his life began to consume his existence. He was usually lucid, and he still paid a great deal of attention to the papers, calling his Los Angeles editors daily, or, more and more often, having Marion do it for him. His sons visited occasionally. And sometimes he would still receive guests, like Howard Hughes, who often came just to sit in the old man's presence, or Louis B. Mayer, who dropped by once in a great while to talk about old times. But there was no hiding the fact that he felt alone and deserted. When his last new secretary, Richard Stanley, came to the house to meet him, he told the fledgling assistant, "Young man, when you die, if you can count your friends on the fingers of two hands, you'll be fortunate."

Surely Hearst was thinking of the many people who had filled his life but were no longer on hand to share the end of it. Phoebe had been dead some thirty years, and his father, George, more than fifty. The few men whom he had been able to call his friends—men like Brisbane, and his childhood companions Jack Follansbee and Orrin Peck—were gone as well. To be sure, all the boys were alive, but they had become increasingly distant with the years; and Millicent he had scarcely spoken with for more than a decade. The closest approach his wife had made since the financial crisis was a visit she paid to his Bronx warehouse in 1941. She had wanted to look over his possessions, and perhaps to search for some fleeting sense of intimacy with the man who had drifted beyond recovery; never really able to understand her lost husband, she mused to a warehouse employee, "How could one man buy all these things? I think he went out and bought things whenever he was worried."

Only Marion had been constant to the end, and only Marion seemed to understand whatever it was that made him tick. Yet of all the people who had ever been close to him, Marion alone seemed to have no future without him. Hearst knew that once he was gone, the precarious triangle he had built around himself, his mistress, and his wife would crumble. That in itself was inevitable; but what he feared was that Marion would be badly hurt when finally the collapse occurred. Presumably he felt no anxiety for her financial security, for Marion had not only recovered her million dollars, but had garnered her gifts and earnings into a small financial empire of her own. By 1950, she was said to be the wealthiest woman in Hollywood, holding real estate and Hearst Corporation shares valued at something in excess of ten million dollars. But emotional security she had none. Though she had been Hearst's de facto wife for decades, it remained true that without him she had no real place in the circle that had revolved around himself and the papers. As Hearst confided to one of his late visitors, he was very much afraid that Marion would be "pushed around," and perhaps pushed out altogether, unless he could find some way to guarantee her a continued stake in the empire.

Not until ten months before his passing did Hearst finally decide what that stake would be. In October 1950 he called Charles Lederer, who from childhood had been close to Hearst, and asked him to come up to the house on Beverly. There he told Lederer of his fears, adding that he believed someone had been tampering with his will. He informed the nephew that he intended to create a trust arrangement which would assure that Marion would be treated with "courtesy" once he had died, and he asked Lederer to hire an attorney to assist in the work—someone who had no connection with the Hearst enterprise, or any other publishing firm.

Lederer hired Gregson Bautzer, a Los Angeles attorney recommended by his friends. And together, the two joined Hearst in preparing a trust agreement that was simple, but devastating in its effect. Under its terms, the voting rights to Hearst's 170,000 shares of preferred and 100,000 shares of common stock in the Hearst Corporation were to be pooled with Marion's own 30,000 shares. Marion herself was to act as voting trustee for the entire bloc. She would hold the power of life and death over all corporate directors and employees; she would enjoy the same authority that Hearst had exercised over ultimate decisions, both financial and editorial; in fact, for all practical purposes, she would control the 200-million-dollar fortune that had—after much travail—found its way down from the Comstock Lode to the present. Whether Hearst fully intended that Marion should wield her authority is open to question— but he was clearly willing to run the risk that she might, in order to secure her future. On November 5, he signed the paper, and ordered a member of his staff to deposit the shares with his bank.

For almost two weeks after Hearst's death, Marion and her advisers held their counsel. They watched as the great and near-great filed by to pay their respects to her fallen lover, and they listened carefully to the din that was being raised in the Hearst press. No doubt they took special note of the press releases in which MacKay revealed details of the will— the attorney repeatedly stressed that Hearst had left the bulk of his assets to charity, and he made a point of emphasizing the trust he had reposed in his sons and executives. Berlin even broke his habit of editorial silence to tell the Hearst readers that "He [Hearst] took great pride in training his top executives in the most painstaking manner so that he could rely on them to carry on after his death with uninterrupted continuity the policies and ideas for which he fought throughout his life."

Most of all, though, Marion waited for word from the family. Probably she would never have resorted to her secret agreement had she received even a gesture of conciliation from Millicent or the boys. She was not a vindictive woman; indeed, she could scarcely afford to be, so many were the slights she had suffered over her talent (which was not negligible, though it never measured up to her publicity), and over her life together with Hearst. But neither was she someone to overlook a snub. And clearly she had been something worse than snubbed in the weeks since Hearst's death. In fact, she had been written off without a word of sympathy; she had been warned to stay away from the papers; worst of all, she had been called a whore, and then treated like one, by people whom she had come to regard as something more than friends, if not exactly family. The truth was that the Hearsts had left her no choice but to play her hand to the end. If nothing else, her dignity was at stake.

John Hanes, always a friend to Marion, remembers that she called him, very late and very drunk, in the first days after the funeral—"She told me, 'Johnny, I've got control of the whole Hearst empire. I've got a paper here that's worth millions, and I'm sending Charlie to New York tonight to show you.'" At first Hanes didn't understand—he had done well by Marion in the forties, when the business was first restructured, had gone out of his way to endow her with shares and with real estate, so that she would never be left at the mercy of the family or the executives. That night he calmed her, and talked her into sending him a copy of the document, without her nephew Charlie.

Hanes was stunned when the paper arrived, and his own attorney pronounced it not just valid, but airtight. According to his best recollection,

> My man told me, "She's the king. She can wipe the slate clean if she wants to."
> So I called her back, and I told her, Marion, don't do it. If he wanted you to have more money, he'd have given you more money. You know that.
> And then I took that paper over to Bill Hearst. I told him, Bill, you've got some trouble on your hands and if you're smart you're going to settle up, because the lawyers tell me she can make it stick.

Apparently, Marion Davies was in no mood to wait any longer. She broke her public silence about the agreement on August 26. As was her habit, she leaked the news through a gossip columnist, though in this instance she was careful to avoid Louella Parsons, who belonged, body and soul, to the organization. Instead, Hedda Hopper, another old friend, was asked to announce the existence of a document "giving complete control of all Hearst enterprises to Miss Marion Davies, the late publisher's friend and confidante."

In the storm that followed, only the barest outlines of the struggle between Marion and the Hearsts were visible through the screen of flack that was quickly thrown up by each. Besieged by the press in the wake of Hopper's bombshell, the family chose to call the agreement a phantom. Speaking as special administrators for the Hearst estate, Randy and MacKay told reporters, "This so-called agreement . . . was never executed and for this and many other reasons has no more effect than if it never existed." But when Bautzer tersely replied, "The document will speak for itself when filed," they must have given some hard thought to the words that had—and hadn't—been exchanged in the two weeks past. Marion had insisted for the benefit of the correspondent from *Time* that she "would do anything to avoid hurting the boys. After all, they're half of W. R." But they knew only too well that she had been deeply wounded by the exchange with Bill and David, and that she possessed the resources to press her case as far as she chose to take it. That she might choose to take it all the way—if for no other reason than stubborn loyalty to Hearst—was a frightening possibility. But that it *was* a possibility became clear when she told the gathering reporters, "I'm not the fighting type, but I don't believe in disregarding W. R.'s wishes. He had a reason for having the agreement drawn up. He thought I was the one who understood best what his policies and principles were and that I could see to it that his ideas were carried out . . . Gosh, I thought I'd have a peaceful time in my old age. Now look at the spot I'm in."

When people began asking Marion what she would do with the papers—and she came back with answers, mentioning the possibility of firing Westbrook Pegler and easing up on Eleanor Roosevelt, a woman whom she greatly admired—the boys dismissed any thought they may have had of stonewalling their onetime pal. After talking with Bautzer, they conceded that Marion had a case and sat down to serious negotiation.

The bargaining was rough and sometimes vicious. The Hearst attorneys pointed to technical deficiencies in Marion's paper, arguing that it was unenforceable because it carried no effective date, and because the shares had never been deposited with the bank, in accordance with Hearst's instructions. More obliquely, however, they made it clear that if the matter came to trial, they wouldn't hesitate to raise questions about Marion's competence; they knew enough about her drinking to make her vulnerable to public attack, and they sensed how she would feel about newsphotos showing her on her way to court supported by nurses, as almost certainly she would be, since she suffered badly from "rubber legs." (There were stories, too, that Marion had abused the old man, that she had sometimes come to him drunk and threatened "to cut off his balls" unless he gave her things she wanted. Perhaps it was only servants' talk or the family's own bitterness become real; but the Hearsts made it known that they had those tales, and that they could use them if they had to.) Bautzer and the East Coast attorneys who supported him came back with a promise to tie up the Hearst estate indefinitely, unless Marion were granted substantial concessions by the family. But what really gave teeth to his threat was the assurance that he had witnesses, many of the members of Marion's domestic staff, who would testify not only to Hearst's intention of providing for his mistress, but to the deepening lack of faith he had felt in his sons and associates.

Had the dispute ever found its way into court, the family would have been torn apart. In addition to seeing the details of Hearst's affair with Marion placed in the public record (along with depositions on their own behavior since his death), the boys would probably have been forced to cast doubt on the old man's mental competence, in order to impugn the agreement. It would have been a spectacle, a public airing of the family closets, with all the skeletons on open display—and it might well have occurred had Millicent not stepped in to prevent it.

That Millicent should have held the trump in dealing with Marion was ironic enough, considering the pains Hearst had taken to shut his wife out of the empire. But what crowned the irony was the fact that she found her high card in a simple expression of gratitude that Hearst had dedicated to Marion in his will.

Marion had been mentioned only once in the will. In the first codicil, which was executed on August 15, 1947, he had parted through the legal terminology long enough to include an expression of gratitude to "my loyal friend MISS MARION DOURAS, who came to my aid during the great depression with a million dollars of her own money, thereby doing much to save myself and my Institution from financial disaster." He sought to acknowledge, if not exactly repay, the favor by leaving Marion the mansion on North Beverly, where both of them were living at the time. But according to Marion's attorney, A. Lawrence Mitchell, Hearst altered his plan in June of 1948, instead presenting the house to Marion as a gift (though he remained the owner of record, so that, officially, at least, he was to die in his own home). In consequence, the codicil, with its tender avowal of thanks, was later revoked.

The Hearst attorneys, however, now believed they had found a way to use that same codicil *against* Marion.

Their intended maneuver turned on the nature of California's community-property law.

Under its terms, all the earnings attributable to a husband's effort during the years of a marriage were community property, of which the wife was entitled to half. Ordinarily, of course, Millicent might have been hard-pressed to show how much of Hearst's fortune was rightly hers, since he had already been fantastically wealthy when they married. But Hearst, in leaving the Beverly house to Marion, had succumbed to sentiment; he had admitted that in 1937, when Marion came to his aid, he had been destitute. The cards were on the table. The Hearst attorneys told Bautzer that Millicent would press a community-property claim to everything accumulated since that date. And when she did, she would also reclaim half of everything that Hearst had given to Marion.

The thrust hit home. Even if Millicent's claim had not held, Marion would have found the title to her own property clouded for years.

Realizing that she had more to lose than to gain by going to court, the actress broke the deadlock by agreeing to a settlement which, in effect, left her nothing but her dignity. Under the agreement hammered out by Bautzer and MacKay, Marion Davies was to be paid a cash consideration of exactly $1. But what was far more important to her, in return for dropping her claims she was accorded a formal promise that her status as a member of the Hearst corporate family would be carefully protected. The agreement made her an "editorial consultant and adviser," entitled to the same "courtesies" that were enjoyed by the rest of the executive fraternity. Presumably this meant not only that her daily papers would be delivered again (they were), but that she would have the right to use corporate property, including the houses and planes, and would be free to place stories in the papers when she wanted to boost a favorite charity or a friend's career. Apparently, it was all she had ever really wanted; like Millicent before her, Marion had refused to be written out of the magic circle just because her link with the center was broken.

The settlement was announced on October 30, under the usual billowing cloud of public-relations prose. Reporters were told that there had never been a problem, and that all problems had been settled peaceably. The press release said:

> Despite numerous stories that have been printed since the late Mr. Hearst's death indicating dissension between Miss Davies, the voting trustees now serving as such and the Hearst estate, there has in fact been no conflict between them and all questions to their respective interests have been subject to amicable discussion and have been amicably resolved.

The announcement went on to add that Marion had "every faith in the intentions and abilities of Mr. Hearst's sons and the other directors and executives of the Hearst enterprises to insure the continuity of Mr. Hearst's editorial policies."

But Marion said it better on her own. The night the agreement was signed, she wept, and then sighed through her tears, "Thank God, it's all over."

(2)

The day the voting-trust agreement was announced, Marion began drinking heavily again. The next day she and Horace G. Brown of Virginia arrived in Las Vegas at three in the morning, drunk. They went to a twenty-four-hour wedding-license bureau, where they obtained the necessary legal papers. Marion told the license clerk she was forty-five, although she was in fact fifty-four. Brown was forty-six. The couple then headed for the El Rancho hotel, where the ceremony was performed by Justice of the Peace James Dower, with an El Rancho staff member serving as best man. The small wedding party also included Ken Frogley, publicity director of the Las Vegas Chamber of Commerce.

Photographers caught up with the couple as they prepared to emplane for a honeymoon in Palm Springs, following a night of drinking at the El Rancho café. The pictures that appeared in papers across the country and the newsmagazines were less than flattering—Marion was hung over, overweight, wearing dark glasses and frowzy in pants and a shirt.

Marion told the reporters that Horace was "Mr. Hearst's cousin," a story that reportedly left Hearst "associates" in Los Angeles in shock, but some papers reported it as fact, because Brown did bear an uncanny resemblance to W. R., being of the same large-bone stature, with narrow-set blue eyes.

When asked about the agreement she had just signed with the Hearst Corporation, Marion waved her hand airily and replied, "Just call me a dollar-a-year man. I'll still have control of the editorial policy and entertainment pages." Someone at Hearst choked on that last statement, because the next day Marion issued a careful denial, saying she had been misquoted and directed attention to the wording of the official settlement announcement.

Brown—divorced in 1947 from his second wife, Grace Tibbett, who had been previously married to opera star Lawrence Tibbett—had met Marion during the war years. At one time, he had been in the Military Sea Transport Service, and he insisted on being called "Captain Brown." There was doubt in some quarters that Brown had actually been a captain —one Davies household employee insisted that Brown had been "a third mate on a ship that carried cement between Okinawa and Japan." Nonetheless, most people accorded him the captain title. Brown had three children by his first wife, Virginia, who was killed in a car accident when Horace failed to make a hairpin curve on a mountain road.

While Hearst was alive, Brown, who hit it off with the old man, had been a frequent visitor at the Beverly Drive house for Sunday suppers and cribbage games with the aging press lord.

Marion's life with Horace was never dull—friends said he appealed to her "taste for the outrageous"—but neither was it particularly pleasant. From the beginning, the couple had two or three serious fights a month, which ended with one or the other packing up and leaving. The separations were always followed by reconciliations, but it often seemed that the latest breakup would be the final one.

A frequently reenacted scenario would be Marion taking off her wedding ring and heaving it out the door, screaming at Brown that it was all over between them. The servants, however, quickly learned that they should keep a careful eye on where the ring landed, because the next day Marion would want it back.

Most of Marion's friends found Brown crude and vulgar, while the household staff found him temperamental, demanding and condescending. The staff especially disliked Brown's continued carping that they were paid too much—he often told them that back in Virginia he could "hire a whole staff of niggers for twenty-five cents an hour." The staff retaliated in preparing mint juleps, which Brown insisted on drinking as befit his image of himself as a Southern gentleman. The mint for the drink came from a small patch outside the back kitchen door. The staff made it a standard practice to water Marion's dog on the mint patch— and the mints then went straight into Horace's drink.

Many of Horace's antics were a source of household amusement, such as the time, in the wee hours of the morning, when Horace, thoroughly drunk, was driving his motor scooter down Sunset Boulevard and thought he spotted a burglar in a closed liquor store. For some reason, Brown was deathly afraid of burglars. He also considered liquor stores a vital national resource, so—doing his patriotic duty—he called the police. The gendarmes arrived to discover that the "burglar" was a cardboard "Schwepps man," a mixed drink proffered in his hand. Far from being embarrassed by the incident, Brown was inspired. To discourage burglars at the Beverly house, he obtained his own "Schwepps man" and placed it on the bedroom balcony, where any potential burglar coming up the driveway would see it and be warded off.

On another occasion, Brown attempted a bit of environmental engineering and discovered that goldfish, bullfrogs and oysters were not compatible neighbors. It started with a sparkling clear ornamental pool on the Beverly mansion grounds that was stocked with 10-inch goldfish and kept immaculately clean. Brown, who had grown up where he could hear bullfrogs croaking in the night, thought it would be a nice touch to have some bullfrogs around the house. So, he brought in a load of dirt to cover the bottom of the pool and added the frogs. The bullfrogs thrived and nightly produced a rousing chorus of frog sounds. The goldfish, unaccustomed to the muddy waters, died. Then Brown decided to make another improvement, which was to make the water salty and raise oysters. It must have been the salt that killed all the bullfrogs, and the oysters did not do well either.

Another of Brown's pets was a monkey that he named "Junior" and allowed free run of the house. At one dinner party Junior defecated on comedian Red Skelton. That was the last time Skelton visited the Davies-Brown household. Marion also did not like the monkey, having a dreadful fear that it would somehow get tangled in her hair.

Within a few months after their marriage, Marion's fights with

Horace had become so serious that she began "contemplating divorce in a very serious way," as she told her friend, gossip columnist Hedda Hopper, in May 1952. Hedda encouraged her to "get rid of" her husband, as it had been her opinion that he was in the marriage just for the money. Marion had one of her lawyers, Bernard Silbert, draw up the divorce papers, but later changed her mind about filing. The same thing happened often enough—Marion wanted a divorce, then changed her mind— that Silbert finally prepared a stack of divorce papers, leaving only the date blank and sent them up to the Beverly house; from then on, whenever she felt like divorcing Horace, Marion only had to fill in the date. Silbert actually filed for Marion's divorce on three occasions, but the suits were later withdrawn.

Marion got nationwide publicity again in November of 1952; and again it was the type of scandal-edged publicity that the Hearsts tried so hard to avoid, but which had a tendency to dog them nevertheless. This time, it wasn't really Marion's fault at all.

Marion was dining at Romanoff's Restaurant in Beverly Hills with Horace, Kay Spreckels, New York art dealer Messmore Kendall and his wife when, shortly after 10 P.M., Bill Hearst wandered in looking for his friend Mike Romanoff. Marion, spotting Bill, wondered wistfully whether he resented her. Horace decided to find out, and sent the waiters' captain with a message inviting Hearst junior to join their group for a drink. Bill replied, no thanks, he was too tired and was going home. Bill later told a reporter that he wanted "nothing to do with that gal anymore. I had it too long while Father was alive. Besides, Mother is in town and it would have been murder."

Bill left the restaurant, but Horace followed him outside, insisting that he join their party for a drink. Again, Bill refused. "That's no way to treat my wife," Brown protested. "Your brother George doesn't feel that way about her."

"I'm not interested in your so-called wife," Bill shot back. Horace later said at that point, he had no choice but to take a swing at Bill, which he did. Hearst blocked the punch; Horace took another swing and Bill decked him. The parking lot attendant, recognizing Brown, rushed over and thrust himself in front of Hearst, shouting "don't hurt that man." Horace got up and persisted, "Forget this whole thing and come in and have a drink." But Bill was adamant. "Nope," he replied, and he continued on his way.

The incident received full coverage in the daily press and news weeklies.

Horace wasn't bothered by the fact that he had been knocked down by a man at least twenty pounds lighter than himself, but for months afterward he bemoaned the fact that in the scuffle he had lost a valuable cat's-eye ring, which he said had been pulled off his finger while he was down on the ground.

If Horace was obnoxious, belligerent, given to temper tantrums (he once purposely smashed up an MG that Marion had given him after an argument with her) and just plain crude, he nonetheless filled an important need in her life.

"He put some excitement in her life, some variety, some spice," said Anne Lederer, wife of Marion's nephew Charles Lederer. "Without Horace, she could have been a very lonely old woman."

Indeed, even with Horace to liven things up, as the 1950s wore on, Marion became lonely enough. She was getting old, but did not do so gracefully. She persisted in believing she was a beautiful woman, although she had become overweight and pot-bellied, and when she went out in public, wore rubber bands to stretch out wrinkles on her face. A group of hangers-on and sycophants who stopped in frequently at the Beverly house constantly reassured her that she "hadn't changed a bit," since her acting days.

But it was more than growing old that contributed to Marion's loneliness and depression. She was the richest woman in Hollywood, but she was out of touch with the times; she belonged to a different age—an age that had seen its golden years a quarter of a century earlier. Even the biggest Hollywood stars of the 1950s did not have household staffs of thirty or more. And it was a different Hollywood now. Names like Billie Dove, Eleanor Boardman, Corinne Griffith—all well-known in the '20s and '30s—meant nothing to the average movie-goer of the day. Nor, for that matter, did the name Marion Davies. Marion's last movie, after all, had been in 1937; there was a whole generation that had never seen her name on a theater marquee.

Once in a while, an old fan would recognize her on the street and say, "You're Marion Davies, aren't you?" Marion would happily acknowledge that it was so, and the encounter would keep her spirits up for a week.

Public recognition was something Marion loved, and she received it to a degree through her charities and investments. The Marion Davies Children's Clinic, which she had supported in West Los Angeles since 1927, was annexed to the UCLA Medical Center and housed in a new wing, for which Marion donated the $2-million construction cost.

Marion always enjoyed a dramatic gesture. At a fund-raising luncheon for the Jewish Home for the Aged, Marion leaped to her feet and pledged $25,000 for installation of a new elevator. Afterward, however, she told her secretary, Tom Kennington, to get her out of the donation. Kennington consulted her attorney, but in the end they decided to honor the pledge.

There was something more than dramatics in the way Marion pledged a donation for the Los Angeles Music Center, the pet project of Dorothy "Buff" Chandler, wife of Los Angeles *Times* publisher Norman Chandler.

The Chandlers had been guests of Hearst and Marion at San Simeon, and being so acquainted, Marion seemed a likely prospect to become a "founder" of the Music Center. Mrs. Chandler sent her a pledge card and subsequently she and her husband were invited to the Beverly house for tea to discuss a donation.

Mrs. Chandler recalled that Marion and Brown and some other members of Marion's family were there and "everyone sat around talking for a while. Then, Marion leaned over and whispered to me to leave in a few minutes and meet her in the ladies powder room." Marion immediately excused herself and left the room, and after a few minutes, Mrs. Chandler did likewise.

Upon entering the powder room, Mrs. Chandler found Marion with two men, whom she did not recognize. The men, who had entered by a back stairway so as not to be seen by anyone else in the house, were introduced as Marion's business consultants, who were there to witness the pledge.

After mentioning how kind Buff had been to her at San Simeon, Marion pledged $25,000 and the two men signed the card as witnesses. The men then left by the back stairway and Mrs. Chandler never saw them again. Marion cautioned Buff not to mention the pledge to anyone in the other room, especially "Captain Brown"—the implication was that Brown would object to her giving away so much money.

Mrs. Chandler never knew that Marion afterward told Horace that she had pledged $100,000. But Marion then proceeded to try to back out of the pledge and at the time she died, had paid only part of the $25,000. The whole pledge and more eventually were collected from Marion's estate—her executors gave Mrs. Chandler jewelry to satisfy the pledge. When assessed, along with what Marion had already paid, it brought her total contribution to the Music Center to $39,000.

There was extensive media coverage when sixty-one workmen installed the aluminum sheathing on the Marion Davies Building—a $9-million, twenty-two-story office building on Park Avenue at 57th Street—in one day. The media also took notice when Marion put up another New York office structure named the Douras Building in honor of her father, the judge, and when she bought the well-known Desert Inn resort hotel in Palm Springs.

Marion passed up the opportunity to invest in a Texas warehouse, because there seemed to be no possible publicity value. "You can't have a Marion Davies Warehouse," she told her accountant.

Even if her investment philosophy was motivated by publicity value, it worked well. Marion had a canny instinctive business sense—she particularly liked real estate—and also received sound financial advice. During the decade after Hearst died, her net worth doubled from ten million to more than twenty million dollars.

It was a good thing too, because Marion was supporting several dozen people, some of them in lavish style. To begin with, her household staff numbered about thirty. There were Horace and his three sons, and her sister Rose. Rose was an especially heavy liability—her liquor bill ran $1,000 a month and total expenses came to $4,500 or $5,000 a month, according to Marion's secretary. In addition, Marion contributed heavily to the support of her niece Pat and her husband, Arthur Lake, an actor who gained fame playing Dagwood in the television and movie series *Blondie.*

Marion also gave large amounts of money to George Hearst, the only Hearst son who remained on friendly terms with her after W. R.'s death.

Her health, unfortunately, was not as sound as her financial condition. Her drinking problem, which began in the 1930s, was still with her. It was all the more of a problem because Marion refused to recognize that she was a victim of alcohol. To her, drinking was as natural as breathing, and she genuinely could not understand people who did not imbibe. She went so far as to change business-management firms when her first one sent around a counselor who happened to be a teetotaler.

"That goddamned Presbyterian," as Marion scornfully called him, just didn't seem normal to her.

In 1956, Marion suffered a minor stroke, a poignant reminder of her own mortality. The next year, Louis B. Mayer died, and the obituaries called it the end of an era. Marion realized it was *her* era that was ending. Within a few months, her old friends Norma Talmadge and Harry Crocker also died. "There aren't many of us left," Marion remarked sadly to Mary Pickford at Crocker's funeral.

In February 1959, a potentially malignant growth was discovered in Marion's jaw in the wake of a tooth extraction. Her doctors urged her to undergo surgery to have the growth removed. Marion, unable to bear the thought of being even slightly disfigured, flatly refused. She consulted other doctors and underwent cobalt treatment, which was unsuccessful in halting the spread of the cancer. She attempted several other remedies, including having platinum plugs implanted in her mouth. But nothing worked, and her health slowly deteriorated.

A bright spot in Marion's last years was provided by a close relationship with the Kennedy family. Marion first met Joseph Kennedy in the 1920s when he was in the film-making business and a frequent guest at San Simeon. The two developed a warm friendship that continued through the years. Marion and Horace were guests at the 1953 weddings of Eunice Kennedy to Sargent Shriver, and John F. Kennedy to Jacqueline Bouvier. Marion turned her Beverly house over to the newly wed John and Jackie Kennedy for their honeymoon. The following year, she was a guest at Patricia Kennedy's wedding to the actor Peter Lawford.

In 1960, Marion turned her house over to Joe Kennedy to use as a "headquarters" during the Democratic party convention, held in Los Angeles. That fall, she opened her house for several fund-raising events on behalf of John Kennedy. To her friends, it seemed unusual that Marion, who had urged the nomination of General MacArthur in 1948, who was deathly afraid of Communists and who had been an avid supporter of Joseph McCarthy, was now so enthusiastically backing the liberal Kennedy. Of course, Marion had no particular fascination with Kennedy's political philosophy, to her he was simply the son of an old friend making a run for the all-American boyhood dream—to be President of the United States—and she wanted to help in any way she could. When Kennedy was elected, by the narrowest of margins, Marion vowed she would see him inaugurated "if it's the last thing I do."

At the swearing-in ceremonies, Marion and Horace were honored guests, standing just behind the Kennedy family. The Kennedys also saw to it that she and Horace were given the Presidential Suite at Washington's Sheraton-Park Hotel.

That spring, with Marion in need of ever heavier sedation to dull the constant pain, Joe Kennedy called her doctors and learned there was nothing more they could do for her. He then arranged for three cancer specialists—two from New York and one from Illinois—to fly out to the Coast to examine her. They operated on her and for a while it was thought the surgery was successful. But Marion then broke her leg while attempting to walk, and her condition afterward steadily deteriorated. She died on a Friday night, September 22, 1961, surrounded by her close family— Horace, her sister Rose, nephew Charlie Lederer and niece Pat Lake.

No one from the Hearst family attended the funeral, although George had originally been named as a pallbearer. When his brothers learned of his plans they let him know in no uncertain terms that his presence at the funeral would be a potential embarrassment to the family, a definite embarrassment to their mother, and if he still went through with the whole thing, they would "cut him off without a penny." Suitably cowed, George stayed away.

BOOK TWO

THE DARK YEARS

Chapter 1

"Imagine me . . ."

(1)

SOMETIMES DICK BERLIN had to pinch himself to make sure it wasn't all a dream. "Imagine me, a little guy from Omaha, Nebraska, running the whole damned show!" he would marvel.

A lot of people thought that Richard Berlin was a remarkable man, although perhaps none thought him so remarkable as he thought himself. Berlin was fond of telling people that he was the one who held the Hearst Corporation together during its big financial crisis of the late 1930s and early 1940s. He was responsible for piloting the world's biggest communications empire through the treacherous shoals of paper-company creditors clamoring for payment, cold-hearted bankers threatening to call in notes, and capricious government investigators making noises about deceptive advertising. Yes, he liked to say, if it hadn't been for him, there likely would be no Hearst Corporation today.

Berlin was president of the Hearst Corporation, a position he had obtained through loyalty to the interests of W. R. Hearst and long years of hard work. By September 1951 he had been working for Hearst thirty-two years and had been president of the corporation for the past eleven years. Berlin greatly admired W. R. Hearst—in fact, idolized him—and if there was one thing he would have liked that was forever out of his grasp, it was to be a Hearst, a son of William Randolph Hearst. And it was such a shame, he thought, because he would have been a much better son than any of W. R.'s five real sons, none of whom worked as hard, cared about the Hearst Corporation as much or were as smart as Dick Berlin.

Berlin had risen through the ranks of the Hearst Corporation, aided to no small extent by what even his enemies—who were many—conceded was a flair, bordering on genius, for office politics. He had a fine sense of who was gaining power and influence and who was losing it and what it took to cajole, flatter, bully or threaten enough people to accomplish whatever task was at hand. Of course, that sense had served him well under the regime of the old press lord, who allowed—and even encouraged—the vicious infighting for which his organization was known, because he knew that men who fought and feared each other would never rise to challenge himself. And now, three decades into his career, that same sense was telling Berlin that Bill Hearst, the second son and namesake of William Randolph Hearst, Sr., was on the verge of becoming a serious threat. Something would have to be done, and quickly.

Richard Emmett Berlin was born January 18, 1894, in Omaha, Nebraska, the middle child in a family that included one older and one younger sister. His father was in the meat-packing business and, shortly after Berlin graduated from South Omaha High School in 1913, moved the family to Oakland, California, where he set up business as a meat distributor.

The elder Berlin died on Christmas Eve, 1915, of a brain hemorrhage, causing a certain amount of financial strain for the family. Berlin at the time was working as a messenger for a San Francisco brokerage house.

In later years, Berlin frequently told people that his family had been extremely poor. "I think he would have liked to claim he was born in a log cabin," noted his son, Richard junior. Ted Harbert, the son of Berlin's sister Ruth, said that to the best of his knowledge, the family was pretty much in the middle-class economic bracket.

Sensing that there was opportunity in the Navy, especially opportunity to avoid being drafted into the Army, Berlin enlisted in 1917. He took his training at Great Lakes Naval Station, where he qualified as a radio operator, which carried an officer's commission, and he was then assigned to the U.S.S. *Ryndam*, ferrying troops from New York to France.

Opportunity knocked one Saturday afternoon late in 1918 when the captain of the *Ryndam* informed Lieutenant Berlin that Mrs. William Randolph Hearst was having a party that evening and had requested the presence of six young officers from the *Ryndam*. The captain's invitation was in the nature of an order, so Berlin reluctantly canceled a date he had lined up for the evening and along with the other officers showed up at the Hearsts' Riverside Drive apartment.

Young Lieutenant Berlin made a very favorable impression on Mrs. Hearst that evening, charming her with his unusual combination of gentlemanly courtesy and youthful enthusiasm. She invited him to several more parties. Shortly before he was scheduled to be discharged from the Navy, Millicent asked Berlin what he planned to do when he returned to civilian life. Return to California and get a job, he replied, explaining that he had to support his mother and sisters.

Nonsense, Millicent insisted. Her husband's organization could get him a fine job right here in New York City. She told him to look up Joe Moore, who was in charge of the Hearst magazines.

The first thing Berlin did, upon being discharged from the service, was call on Joe Moore. He learned, somewhat to his dismay, that Millicent had been in the habit of telling any number of young men who struck her fancy for one reason or another that her husband would give them a job. So Moore was not overly impressed with the former Navy lieutenant who showed up with a referral from the boss's wife. Moore put Berlin to work selling magazine subscriptions door-to-door, no doubt thinking that like dozens of Millicent referrals before him, the stocky twenty-five-year-old ex-serviceman would last a few months or maybe a year at most.

Berlin attacked his new job with enthusiasm. Loaded with an abundance of Irish charm, good-looking and fast-talking, he proved admirably equipped for the task at hand. Moore quickly decided that Berlin's selling ability could be more profitably put to use peddling advertising, and he gave him a position on the staff of *Motor Boating* magazine. Berlin quickly proved himself as adept at talking businessmen into buying space as he had been at talking housewives into buying the magazines. His efforts caught the eye of Hearst himself when he sold a six-page spread to Horace Dodge; it was the largest single ad *Motor Boating* had ever carried. After asking Moore who had sold the ad and being told "it was one of the young Navy officers your wife sent over, a fellow named Dick Berlin," Hearst sent a congratulatory note and encouraged Berlin to "keep up the good work, you could have a great future with this organization."

But it was going to take more than mere conscientious work to have a great future in the Hearst organization, as Berlin must have realized fast. More so than in most companies, the Hearst organization was a jungle of office politics. This was a situation largely fostered by Hearst himself, who paid fantastic salaries to his top men—more money than they could ever get anywhere else, and they knew it. At his whim, Hearst could cut any of them off, which they also knew and which inevitably instilled in them a kind of groveling attitude that Hearst seemed to enjoy. Hearst then exacerbated the problem by frequent shuffling of his top executives from one position to another or into newly created positions. It was not always clear whether these moves were promotions or demotions or neither—a situation that in turn kept middle-level managers in a constant state of panic, trying to figure out who among the top men was rising and who was falling, so they could then build the appropriate alliances.

All executives felt obliged to keep an eye on one another and vigorously defend themselves against any criticism that could possibly be construed as an attack on their professional ability or loyalty to Hearst's interests. Even such a commonplace matter as editing an article could produce an angry exchange of memos, as when editorial writer Edwin J. Clapp, of the Los Angeles *Examiner,* took umbrage at deletions in one of his columns made by editorial page editor John Gray and felt compelled to send a three-page single-spaced letter to publisher G. G. Young, defending his original article point by point, and concluding with the threat that he would not have John Gray tampering arbitrarily with his editorials and spreading the word that he was careless with his facts. For good measure, Clapp sent a copy of his letter to J. W. Willicombe, Hearst's personal secretary, with an added note to the effect that there was no need to bring the matter to the chief's attention, unless Gray brought it up first.

An atmosphere of intrigue, petty jealousies, vying for favor and watching one's backside made its impression on the young Berlin, who moved steadily through a series of advertising and management positions within the magazine group, while honing his skills as an office politician.

In a decade-long rise through the magazine ranks, Berlin developed a valuable ally in Millicent Hearst, whom he continued to cultivate assiduously. After getting the job as a door-to-door salesman, Berlin dropped Mrs. Hearst a note, thanking her profusely for her role in securing the position. When he was promoted to advertising salesman, he again sent her a card expressing his gratitude for her confidence in his ability. Whether it was landing a big account or getting a minor promotion, Berlin made sure that Millicent knew about it, and he managed to make it seem like the credit should go to her for having the foresight to have him hired in the first place.

The flattery, attention and professions of gratitude did not go unnoticed by Millicent, who responded by occasionally inviting the young man to her parties and dinners. The fact of his attendance at these affairs was carefully noted by his immediate superiors and co-workers; the quiet word was out in the Hearst magazine jungle that young Berlin had some kind of "in" with the Chief. It was a rumor Berlin did nothing to squelch.

Berlin's credentials as a heavyweight in the Hearst organization were firmly and dramatically established in the spring of 1931, when, in a coup that stunned the magazine world, he compelled the resignation of Ray Long as editor of *Cosmopolitan* magazine. News reports at the time merely announced in straightforward fashion that Long planned to leave his post as editor of *Cosmopolitan*, editor in chief of all Hearst magazines and president of International Magazine Company, which was the Hearst magazine group. The story for public consumption was that Long, who had taken over *Cosmopolitan* in 1918 after a quick rise through a series of newspaper and magazine editorships, was resigning to become chairman of the board of Richard R. Smith, Inc., a small publishing house that he had helped to start eighteen months earlier. However, insiders knew that Long did not leave his $185,000-a-year post voluntarily, but had lost out in a showdown with Berlin, who the previous December had been named executive vice-president and general manager of the Hearst magazines.

News of Long's forced departure sent a wave of fear through the other magazine editors and signaled the start of what one of them called "an office reign of terror." They all knew that the small, dapper Long had been a favorite of Hearst, one of the highest-paid magazine editors of all time, and one of the few executives who routinely contradicted and argued with the boss and got away with it. Long was known for bringing big-name authors to the pages of *Cosmopolitan*. It was Long who got John Masefield's first work, "The Wanderer," after he was named Poet Laureate of England. Another Long publishing scoop was printing Calvin Coolidge's autobiography in 1929. No one had seemed more firmly ensconced than Long, and every other magazine executive immediately got the message: no one's job could be taken for granted.

What irritated Berlin about Long was that Long was a "star." He was a literary celebrity; a regular at the Algonquin "Round Table." He gave speeches; he thrived on publicity; his name was always in the publishing trade journals. All this indicated to Berlin that Long was more interested in being Ray Long than in working for the interests of William Randolph Hearst. And Berlin, ever conscious of waste and inefficiency, figured there were about twenty people on the Hearst payroll whose only function was to flatter Ray Long.

From his position as general manager of the Hearst magazines, Berlin began to encroach on the prerogatives formerly reserved to Long as president of the International Magazine Company. In a typical Hearst executive arrangement, there were no clear lines of authority between the general manager and the president of the magazine company, so the struggle between Long and Berlin became an all-out test of wills. The patient, calculating, always-polite Berlin turned out to be much better suited for what promised to be a protracted struggle than flamboyant, restless and temperamental Long. Berlin's subtle undercutting of Long's authority was cloaked in the ostensible purpose of budget-tightening—curbs on spending for big-name writers, stricter accountability for expense-account reimbursements, a freeze on hiring for secretarial positions; budget-cutting measures that made good business sense in a Depression year, but inconvenienced Long, who was not used to being inconvenienced. Furthermore, these were matters that Long felt should rightly be decided by himself. However, when Long protested to Hearst over Berlin's meddling in what he considered his bailiwick, it only served to reinforce Berlin's contention that Long was thinking of himself first and did not really have Hearst's interests at heart. Berlin also helped spread the word among Hearst's general management that Long was "losing his mind."

Long decided that either he or Berlin would have to go. Whether he ever presented such an ultimatum to Hearst is unknown, but it quickly became clear that Hearst was not going to get rid of Berlin. For Long, there was only one other choice—in July he submitted his resignation, effective that October when his contract expired.

Long's career plummeted after leaving Hearst. One year later, on the verge of a nervous breakdown, he left with his secretary for a year-long sojourn in the South Seas. Meanwhile, his publishing company was thrown into bankruptcy. On his return to the United States, he worked in the script departments of three motion-picture firms, then took a brief stab at editing *Photoplay* magazine. On July 9, 1935, depressed and nearly broke, he poked a rifle barrel into his mouth and pulled the trigger. His obituary made page one of *The New York Times.*

Long was replaced as editor of *Cosmopolitan* and president of the International Magazine Company by Harry Payne Burton, a former editor of *McCall's*, but real administrative control of the magazines lay with Berlin.

People who knew him in the early 1930s invariably describe Berlin as a "hard worker" and "serious." Ruddy-faced and slightly nervous—he had a habit of fidgeting with his fingers while listening or thinking—he nonetheless never lost his salesman's charm, prompting the frequent observation that "he always makes a terrific impression when you meet him."

Actress Jean Howard, who dated Berlin during that period, remembered him as being earnest and polite, but always a little grim. "I never associated Dick Berlin with any of the fun in New York," she said. He also struck her as being a calculating man, an assessment echoed by other acquaintances, who also used such adjectives—with a touch of admiration —as "scheming" and "conniving."

Berlin was involved in brief romantic encounters with several top New York models of that decade. Years later he would remark that all of those affairs came to an end when the model made it to the cover of *Cosmopolitan* magazine.

But Berlin's primary love was his work. Perhaps wisely, he stayed away from the editorial side of the magazines and stuck with what he knew best—selling advertising and making money. He regularly put in twelve-hour days at the office, then went out at night with advertisers and potential clients. Entertaining business acquaintances, became—and would remain for the rest of his career—his primary social activity.

Under Berlin's guidance, the Hearst magazines in the United States (which were operated as a separate unit from the British magazines) turned in healthy profits year after year. Although every year some of the magazines lost money—*Cosmopolitan,* for example, showed an $867,000 loss in 1932 and did not turn the corner until 1935, when it posted a $75,000 profit—the group as a whole made average yearly profits of more than two million dollars from 1931 through 1940.

It was in 1939—the dark year when the empire was tottering—that Dick Berlin survived the only serious threat to his own position in the Hearst organization when the *Pictorial Review* collapsed. With a circulation of three million, it was the largest magazine ever to fold in the United States. And it had been Berlin's baby.

A top woman's magazine in the 1920s, *Pictorial Review* began slipping during the Depression and was in rocky financial straits when Berlin, acting as an agent for Hearst, bought it from George S. Fowler in 1934. Berlin's plan was to use some of the two million dollars that the Hearst magazines were earning by then to aggressively promote *Pictorial Review.* Unfortunately, other Hearst properties were in need of the magazines' ready cash, and very little in the way of a promotion campaign could be mounted. The moribund magazine limped along, losing money steadily, until the Hearst Conservation Committee decided to let it die.

Because of its size, *Pictorial Review*'s collapse was painfully spectacular and fueled the rumors, already widespread, that the entire organization was about to go under. At this point, Joseph Kennedy stepped in with his offer of $14 million for the whole magazine unit. Clarence Shearn, the reigning power, wanted to accept. Berlin was outraged. The magazines would earn $2.5 million that year, and *Good Housekeeping* alone was worth $5 million by itself, he argued. Nonetheless, the New York banks were adamant about getting some money, quickly, Shearn replied. Interest and penalty payments were mounting. Hearst needed a quick $7 million to pay off notes, and then maybe—just maybe—they could pull through. That was ridiculous, Berlin answered. If they sold the magazines, they would lose their biggest money-maker. The company would go under for sure.

To buy a few weeks' time, Berlin traveled to Chicago to plead with Johnnie Cuneo, who did most of the printing for the Hearst magazines, to defer payment on the Hearst account yet again. Then, the company could use precious cash to placate the New York bankers a bit longer.

Cuneo agreed to give Hearst more time, and—on an inspiration that salvaged his friend's career—he suggested that Berlin talk to A. P. Giannini, president of the Bank of Italy.

"How am I going to meet him?" Berlin asked.

"Well," Cuneo replied, "he happens to be taking the Overland Limited to San Francisco tonight, from the LaSalle Street station. Why don't you get a ticket to San Francisco and be on the platform when the train is ready to leave. I'll be there with Giannini, and I'll say 'Why Dick Berlin, what are you doing here?' Then you say 'I'm going to visit my mother in Oakland.' "

Berlin was willing to try anything. "Remember," Cuneo said. "He likes families, and doesn't like New York. Be sure to say your *mother* in *Oakland.*"

After being introduced to Berlin, the San Francisco banker invited him to his drawing car. Over a glass of wine, Giannini commented that Hearst didn't seem to be doing well.

"That's right," Berlin said dejectedly. "We're having problems. The New York banks are killing us."

"A good California boy should not be in the hands of those thieves," Giannini answered.

"Mr. Giannini," Berlin said. "Do you have any suggestions for me?"

"Come over to my office the day after we get back," said the banker. "And we'll see what we can do."

The result was that Giannini lent Hearst eight million dollars, saving the magazines from the clutches of Joe Kennedy, and at the same time giving Berlin's standing in the Hearst organization a sharp boost upward. Berlin never forgave Kennedy for what he considered an unethical attempt to take advantage of the Hearst Corporation's confused financial circumstances.

One of Berlin's particular talents that made him valuable to the Hearst organization was that through a vast network of contacts he had built up over the years, plus an aptitude in the area, he was a man who could get things done—little things that might involve indelicate subjects or gray areas of legality or ethics. One such incident occurred in late 1939, when it became known in the publishing business that a manuscript about Charlie Chaplin—written jointly by Gertrude Von Ulm and Chaplin's valet, Kono—was being circulated to book publishers. The manuscript contained details of an affair between Chaplin and Marion Davies, and mentioned Hearst in an uncomplimentary manner, things certain to cause Hearst acute embarrassment. Berlin was able to shepherd the manuscript away from big New York publishers to the small Caxton Press of Caldwell, Idaho. Once that was done he convinced its editors to allow Hearst reporter Percy Waxman to do a rewrite—which, Berlin happily reported to Hearst in January of 1940, eliminated all references that the chief might have found objectionable. When the book came out later that year, Waxman also reviewed it for the Hearst press.

The year 1940 turned out to be crucial in the Hearst organization's battle to pull itself away from the chasm of bankruptcy, and the man of the year was Richard Berlin.

By 1940, Winthrop Aldrich decided that Shearn did not have the empire on the road to recovery, and sent for another watchdog—John Hanes, who was then the head of the Internal Revenue Bureau under Roosevelt. Berlin went down to Washington to discuss the job with Hanes.

Berlin also had it in mind that Hanes might be helpful with income-tax problems the Hearst organization was having at the time. However, when Berlin suggested that they talk about Hearst tax difficulties before the Treasury Under Secretary left his government post, Hanes cut him short, pointing to a sign above his desk: "I'll do anything you ask, provided it would look good on the front page of the New York Times." Berlin dropped the subject, but was favorably impressed with Hanes's apparently scrupulous honesty. In addition, he was not expecting a large salary for his efforts, his credentials as a financial manager were impeccable and he had a good reputation and rapport with the New York banking community.

Hanes began working for Hearst in July, just a few weeks after Berlin was quietly promoted to president of the Hearst Corporation. And for the next four years, the two quietly joined forces against Shearn, and against the debt that held the institution in thrall.

The most urgent matter was a group of Canadian papermakers who were pressing for payment of some ten million dollars in past debts. Hanes and Berlin called a meeting of all the papermakers—they needed the grand ballroom of the Ritz in Montreal to accommodate everyone. One by one, Berlin and Hanes took the creditors aside and showed them the figures. Hearst, the largest user of newsprint in the world, owed every Canadian paper manufacturer money. Every single one. Berlin gave it to them bluntly: If the papermakers forced Hearst into bankruptcy, they could get ten cents on the dollar of the money owed them, and they would lose their biggest customer. If they would readjust terms, together with all the creditors, they would get their money in five years.

The papermakers were skeptical, and angry. They never realized that Hearst *couldn't* pay his debts. Berlin's scheme to spread the debt across forty years on the books, get new financing—it all sounded like a shell game.

Berlin, though, had one more card up his sleeve; Morris Wilson, president of the Royal Bank of Canada was a personal friend. And more importantly, the Royal Bank of Canada held notes from many of the paper companies. Wilson stood behind Berlin and insisted that Hearst be given time.

The papermakers reluctantly agreed to a one-year moratorium on collection of their back debt, on the condition that all current newsprint purchases be paid for in cash, and that their own people would monitor all Hearst financial activities. Actually, they had little choice. Hanes later claimed that Hearst had the entire Canadian paper industry on the verge of collapse.

Berlin was pleased with the Canadian arrangement. It bought time, and he confidently wrote Hearst that with smart trading he could take the Canadians out of the picture by offering them 50 to 75 cents on the dollar.

But there were still troubles ahead. Although the biggest financial liability of the Hearst organization—W. R. Hearst—had been effectively curbed, Hanes was unable to get the massive bank refinancing he needed to put the organization on an even keel. By and large the bankers, especially those who had already loaned Hearst money, were unwilling to advance more credit. Those who were willing to loan money, advanced relatively small amounts.

For Berlin, it was a hectic time; Hearst Consolidated stockholders were up in arms and filing lawsuits; the Federal Trade Commission charged *Good Housekeeping* with misleading advertising in connection with the magazine's Seal of Approval; the organization was negotiating with the Army to sell 154,000 acres of land, part of the San Simeon ranch, for $2 million; more newspapers had to be closed; and then, there were the ever-present Canadians, scrutinizing and questioning every disbursement.

Because the cooperation of Morris Wilson was so important, Berlin was especially careful to keep on his good side. One of Wilson's daughters was an aspiring actress, and Berlin spent hours on the telephone trying to get her a part in some New York production. "Just let her carry a spear across the stage," he would plead to his friends in the theater.

On top of everything, old W. R.—feeling considerably constrained by his $100,000-a-year allowance—was badgering Berlin to get him more money. "Dick," he wrote. "I want some more salary. We paid Brisbane $260,000 a year and while I am willing to take a HALF cut from $500,000 I do not think it is a positive reflection not to pay me as much as Brisbane got."

Berlin could only reply that he was "thoroughly sympathetic with your request," but noted that it was unlikely that the Canadians would approve more money as only a few days earlier they had been giving Martin Huberth a hard time about some charges and were "scrutinizing disbursements very closely."

Berlin, a former Hearst executive said, "was holding the empire together with spit," but it seemed only a matter of time before everything would go, unless something drastic happened.

Something drastic did happen. The United States entered World War II, an entanglement that Hearst had been inveighing against for years. Ironically it was that war that kept the company afloat. Wages were controlled, and because of a paper shortage, advertising space was at a premium. Business boomed, and the organization was able to settle its debts. There was a bit of unpleasantness with Shearn, who was convinced to give up his trusteeship only under threat of a federal lawsuit. In 1945, Hanes, who decided that his job was done, resigned as Chairman of the Finance Committee with a parting word of advice to Hearst: "Don't let anybody talk you into buying anything at 10 percent down."

In the middle of the financial crisis, Berlin at the age of forty-four, married for the first and only time in his life. His bride, on December 21, 1938, was Muriel Johnson, a New York socialite who went by the nickname "Honey." Berlin and Honey met the previous May at the White Plains country home of Emil Mosbacher, a real-estate broker who was a business acquaintance of Honey's father.

Honey, a popular twenty-two-year-old blond, was being courted by a platoon of wealthy young men, or rather, young men whose fathers were wealthy. Among her beaus was Randy Hearst. Honey said she was immediately attracted to Berlin because he was older, serious and hardworking, unlike the "playboy" types she usually dated who were always getting drunk and engaging in other frivolous activities.

After the wedding, Honey and Berlin flew to Oakland, where she met his mother and sisters. Then it was down to San Simeon for a New Year's Day dinner at the Hearst Castle.

Walking toward their places at the table in the great hall, a thoroughly nervous Honey whispered to her husband, asking what she should talk about with Mr. Hearst.

"Talk about anything you like," he replied. "You can talk about needlepoint and he'll be interested."

Honey sat next to Hearst at the dinner, and recalls having a delightful conversation with the publisher. After dinner, Hearst turned to Berlin and asked what his immediate plans were. Berlin replied that he had work to do and was going back to New York. Hearst was taken aback, and insisted that Berlin and his new wife take a month off for a honeymoon. In fact, Hearst ordered them to take a month off, and he had just the place for them to go—Hawaii. Without wondering whether Berlin or Honey even wanted to see Hawaii, Hearst immediately arranged for steamship passage and hotel accommodations in Honolulu. Since it was on the orders of his boss, Berlin felt an obligation to go, but he didn't like Honolulu much.

Back in New York after their honeymoon, the Berlins moved into a luxury apartment at 834 Fifth Avenue that had previously been occupied by Jack Hearst.

Honey quickly found that her husband's life revolved around his business more than she had realized. Their standard social evening involved entertaining advertisers, whom Honey found boring. After Berlin was put in charge of straightening out the corporation's financial affairs, they started entertaining bankers, a group that Honey found more boring than advertisers.

A typical evening would begin with dinner, then progress to a round of the clubs, usually ending at the Stork Club. The drinking would begin with martinis, move to Scotch, then champagne and finish with beer. Many evenings, Berlin would bring his business cronies home at three in the morning, and they would drink for another couple of hours.

But no matter how much he had drunk the night before, or how late he had stayed up, Berlin would be up, full of pep and ready to face a new day at 7 A.M., a remarkable display of resilience that never failed to amaze his wife. On the rare occasions when he experienced a hangover, his cure was a morning bowl of pepper pot soup.

Honey was always a bit skeptical of her husband's claim that these evenings included serious business discussions—as nearly as she could tell, most of the business talk consisted of the men "telling each other how smart they were."

Berlin, however, knew that socializing was critical in developing business and advertising contacts. His theory of publishing success held that advertising was a commodity difficult to define, which was purchased not so much on the basis of worth as on the basis of good will, good fellowship and access to the right people at the right time.

Throughout his life Berlin cultivated contacts that might help the Hearst Corporation. He had a voracious memory for anniversaries, birthdays, and other occasions that would warrant sending a small gift or a congratulatory note. Every Christmas he sent a necktie to each member of Congress he had met personally or had occasion to deal with for one reason or another. In the 1940s, this meant six hundred ties every year. Berlin was forever reminding Hearst to send a note or make mention in his column of someone who had helped the Hearst organization at one time or might help them in the future. While the Canadian paper creditors were hovering over the organization, Berlin suggested that the newspapers might create some good will with the Canadians by publicizing a "Vacation in Canada" campaign then being mounted by the Voluntary Tourist Committee of Montreal. Hearst accepted the suggestion.

Although Berlin generally stayed away from the editorial side of both newspapers and the magazines, he may have entertained a secret ambition to be a writer or a news executive. In 1945 he went along with a group of journalists invited by General Dwight Eisenhower to tour German concentration camps, and he wrote a book about the tour entitled *Flight Over Occupied Germany*. He had the book published privately and gave copies to friends as gifts. About the same time he installed an Associated Press teletype in his bedroom and took an avid interest in reading the news wire every evening. Honey quickly tired of the ceaseless racket and insisted he get the machine out of the house. He put it in a soundproof room adjacent to his office in the Hearst Building.

For the most part, however, Berlin limited his incursions into journalism to occasional suggestions about the newspapers. While Hearst was alive, if Berlin had something particularly critical to say, he would disguise the criticism as coming from an unnamed source, as when he passed along to Hearst a memo from a young associate editor at Cosmopolitan regarding the newspaper Sunday supplement, *American Weekly*.

The memo scathingly castigated *American Weekly's* 1915 makeup and the poor quality of the fiction, which the memo writer said was not merely servant girl fiction, but the worst servant girl fiction imaginable. The writer also commented on what must have been the world's worst artwork at the world's lowest prices, and concluded by saying that week after week the *American Weekly* screamed, "Cheap, Cheap, Cheap."

Berlin noted that he was not endorsing the criticism, merely submitting it to Hearst as an interesting comment.

Hearst's reply came in an angry memo. He did not think one of the young associate editors of *Cosmopolitan* was competent to run the *American Weekly* or to criticize those who were being paid good Hearst money to run it. What's more, the *American Weekly* was not cheap, cheap, cheap—it was popular, popular, popular, and Hearst suggested that the "young associate," if he ever wanted to become the chief, had better tend to his own assignments.

Hearst may have seen through Berlin's ruse, because following a long tirade about the associate editor's obvious lack of intelligence, perception, respect for authority, etc., there was an unsubtle jab at the *Pictorial Review*, obviously something of a sore spot with Berlin. He pointed out that, to him at least, the memo looked more like a communication from the editor of the *Pictorial Review*, that late, lamented prize failure, than from anyone who had sense enough to produce *Cosmopolitan*. Naturally, thought Hearst, Dick Berlin would not endorse such shallow criticism.

The Berlins' first child, a daughter they named Bridget, was born soon after their marriage. Berlin desperately wanted a son, and when a second daughter was born two years later, he went ahead and named her

Richie Emmett Berlin anyway. By the time a third daughter, Christina, was born in 1947, Berlin resigned himself to raising a family of all girls.

However, in June 1951, Honey Berlin gave birth to a baby boy at Leroy Sanitarium in New York City. Berlin was ecstatic. He hovered around the hospital, constantly demanding reassurance from the doctors that his wife and son were doing well. Harvey Firestone threw a party for him at the Stork Club. The strain and excitement quickly proved too much for the proud father, and he had to be hospitalized for two days in order to recuperate.

His children were always something of a problem for Berlin, and he sometimes jokingly complained that one of his biggest frustrations in life was that he couldn't run his family the same way he ran the Hearst Corporation.

None of the daughters did well in school, and all apparently developed psychological problems of varying magnitudes. Berlin was especially anxious that his son and namesake do well at Choate, the exclusive prep school. But again, he was doomed to disappointment. Neither threats— "Boy, if you don't shape up at Choate, I'm going to kick your ass into the Marine Corps"—nor homespun platitudes—"as they say in the parlance of golf, put your ass in every shot"—had much effect on Richard, who was pretty much of an average student.

Richard did well enough, nonetheless, to get into Dartmouth, where Berlin counseled the lad to study economics, a field that would provide "practical insight into the world of high finance and big business." Berlin foresaw his son then going on to get a law degree or an MBA. Richard, however, had plans of his own, or perhaps no plans of his own, but at any rate decided to major in art history—a field that, Berlin grumbled, had no relevance to the "real world."

But if Berlin was a bit disappointed in his children, he nonetheless was extremely protective of them and displayed a continuing affection that was genuine, if sometimes awkward. When the children were small, Berlin insisted on tucking them into bed and saying goodnight, a ritual common enough among adoring fathers, except that he was rarely home at the children's bedtime, being usually engaged in serious business drinking. Upon arriving home—a typical hour would be 3 A.M.—he would wake up the children one by one, hug them and tell them how much he loved them, and then, depending on his degree of sobriety, and other unaccountable factors, either burst into tears and cry, or deliver a fatherly lecture on how to become a success in life, with himself as a model. These little talks tended to heavily emphasize his accomplishments; his favorite topic was how he saved the Hearst Corporation during the pre-World War II financial crisis. His next-favorite theme was his humble origins, which seemed to become more and more humble as time went on. His first job with Hearst, as he told it, paid $40 a week. Later it went down to $30 a week, then $25 a week, and along the line he began supporting his mother and two sisters.

Berlin's love for his family was also manifested by an intense concern for their physical safety. On one occasion, Richard was roughed up by a neighborhood bully, an event that alarmed Berlin to the extent that he took a day off from work to personally hunt down the bully and deliver a stern lecture, the substance of which is unknown, but presumably it dealt in some way with the morality of physical violence. An ever-present worry was that his family would become the target of a kidnaping, a possibility that Berlin worked to minimize by insisting that no one in the family court publicity. He issued a standing order that the Hearst press never print a picture of his wife or children, and stories were allowed only if the family members did something genuinely "newsworthy"—his yardstick of newsworthiness was something the Hearst press would cover if it were done by a member of the Rockefeller family. Berlin also kept publicity about himself to the minimum required in connection with accepting or giving awards, announcements of corporate matters, service with various civic organizations and other perfunctory obligations that go with being the head of a large corporation. He was acutely uncomfortable about giving speeches, and he avoided them as much as possible.

While he had a reputation as an elegant dresser, Berlin's sartorial splendor was due entirely to his wife's good taste in clothing, not his own. Honey ordered his suits from the exclusive London tailors Kilgore, French and Stanbury. She picked out his shirts and ties and laid out his clothes each morning when he went to work. If left to his own devices Berlin inevitably ended up wearing such combinations as checked trousers, a madras shirt and a plaid jacket. As a close friend noted on one such occasion, "He looked like a neon sign." To avoid such embarrassments when Berlin went away from home for a few days, Honey would supervise packing his clothes and include a note specifying which shirt, pants and jacket to wear each day.

In regard to his personal life style, Berlin was basically a man of very simple tastes. In spite of a salary as president of the Hearst Corporation that made him one of the country's highest-paid executives, Berlin had a very thrifty streak in him and enjoyed sending away for mail-order underwear offers that included a free belt with each dozen pairs.

He was also very big on saving money. Richard recalls that he would give each of his children an allowance, then "practically chase us to the bank and watch us deposit it in our account."

Saving money was almost an obsession with Berlin, both in personal and corporate matters. One of his favorite sayings was, "There's gonna be another depression, just wait and see."

But of all his personal habits, the one that served him best was a tremendous will power. Berlin had an iron will that he could focus into a single-minded pursuit of a specific goal. Anything that was humanly possible, that relied on his own effort and he wanted to do, got done. A two-pack-a-day smoker for many years, Berlin's doctor advised him to cut down in 1955. He walked out of the doctor's office and never smoked another cigarette in his life. When weight started to become a problem—for years he weighed 186 pounds, but then gradually started gaining until he was up to 210—Berlin asked his doctor how much weight he should lose. The doctor said about twenty-five pounds. Within eight weeks Berlin had lost thirty pounds, and he has maintained that weight ever since.

It was this type of personal discipline that made Berlin a formidable corporate jungle fighter.

Chapter 2

Young Bill

(1)

"I don't need a title. My father gave me one when I was born." No one had to tell Bill Hearst the value of a name. It was his greatest asset—William Randolph Hearst, Jr. He flaunted it as one might an expensive diamond ring, and it certainly was more valuable than any ordinary piece of jewelry.

Which is not to say that Bill was exactly haughty or imperious. Most people found him to be a congenial, down-to-earth individual. Trying to describe him as frankly as he could, the long-time Hearstling Harry Bull once said: "Bill is kindly, bumbly in appearance, tall, puffy and pop-eyed with balding, slightly crinkly sandy hair. He pays little attention to clothes. Dresses like a newspaperman: sloppy. I've never heard anyone speak highly of his ability nor badly of him as a man. . . ."

Bull might have added that the heir possessed a boyish charm and an easy grin, and that almost everyone at Hearst called him "Young Bill," even when he was well over forty and balding and fighting hard to make a place for himself in the empire that belonged to his ghost-ridden family.

Maybe Bill was really too affable ever to make that birthright his own. In his own paper, the *Journal-American*, Westbrook Pegler dared to call him "a tenacious optimist who seems unable to entertain suspicions of ulterior intent against whatever weight of evidence." Pegler, who thought Bill soft-headed, added with more than a trace of malice that "a guilty man couldn't ask for a gentler juror or give himself a better break than Bill would." Certainly the stories about his phenomenal good nature were legion. Joseph Pulitzer II, for one, liked to recall what happened when he met Hearst junior at a banquet, one of the thousands of dreary affairs that publishers' sons learn to tolerate at a tender age. A wag decided to strike a few sparks by reminding the two that young Joe Pulitzer, in an earlier day, had once leveled Bill's father with a wild left hook in the office of the St. Louis *Post-Dispatch*. "Hey, that's okay," beamed Hearst. "A couple of times I wanted to take a poke at the old man myself."

Walter Howey, for his part, thought that Bill's charm and bluff good will were great assets. "Bill is a real newspaperman, a real editor and publisher," said Howey. "He has a genius for bringing two people with conflicting viewpoints together. He works hard and never complains about anything. He's got a quick mind, and gets along well with everybody."

It may have been true that Bill had talent; as Howey noted, his very geniality made him a newsman, born and bred. But from the beginning, Young Bill had never been sure what position he had, or could ever expect to have, in the great institution his father had built. When he first came to the business, early in the summer of 1928, there had been no commitments, no grandiose promises, and precious little in the way of paternal advice. "Pop said I was supposed to 'represent the name in New York.' That was it," said Bill. "Maybe I never figured out exactly what that meant, but I tried to take it seriously. He fixed me up with a big apartment in the Ritz and a pretty good salary. And he said, please stay outta trouble. So what the hell, I packed up and got started . . ." He took his first job on the *American*, as a cub reporter on the City Hall beat, because he wanted to learn the business "like Pop—from the inside out and from the bottom up." And within three short years, he found himself sitting at the president's desk.

According to Hearst junior,

It was all too fast. Way too fast. It was a mistake and I think Pop knew it, because he went slower with the twins. I was upstairs, in management, before I knew what a newspaper was all about—and some of those editors had been around from the day Pop bought the place. There was bound to be trouble.

But if anything saved me, I guess it was Cobbie. When I came in off the street—I'd been reporting for a couple of years—old Cobbie sat me down and said, more or less, "You might be the president around here, but lots of people are going to stay out of your way because you're a kid, and maybe because of your name." He said, there's no use setting up an office of your own, because if you do, nobody will ever set foot inside it.

So we dragged my desk over into his office—he must have been publisher at the time—and we set it up facing his. He said, "You sit here. And keep your eyes open."

Bill watched and listened, and maybe he learned as Edmond Coblentz (whom the Washington *Post* publisher Eugene Meyer identified as "another one of those queer Hearst people with good minds and unstable character") not only ran the paper, but placated the power in distant San Simeon and kept up a running patter on the idiosyncrasies of the Hearst institution.

Apparently Cobbie was devoted to Bill. He taught him to think of himself as an heir, and he was careful, even when he was handling all of the paper's essential business, to preserve an aura of authority around the person of his young protégé. Decisions already made were presented for the considered approval of William Randolph Hearst, Jr. "Every scrap of paper that came to his desk was channeled over mine," said Bill.

But Bill Hearst never ran the *American*, down to the day, in June of 1937, when it was collapsed at the behest of the bankers. And when he emerged that year as publisher of the newly formed *Journal-American*, he found that he was wedged between two men—executive editor Bill Curley and general manager Tom White—who had much less regard than Cobbie for the interests of the boss's son.

"That's where I sat until the war," said Bill. "I was down on South Street, nursing an ulcer and worrying myself to death. When they started the draft, I was classified something like 4-B—exempt, essential industry. But I never felt especially essential. Finally it was Mom who said 'Why don't you just pack up and go, for God's sake. You'll hate yourself if you don't.' "

His father, who had no use for the war, objected. In an audience at Wyntoon, he warned Bill that, if he went overseas, the British would use their wiles "to charm him off his American pedestal." But for once Hearst junior stood fast. He petitioned the draft board for a change of status, and by February of 1943, had been reclassified 1-A. By August, he was boarding a troopship at Norfolk, bound for Algiers with his own commission as a war correspondent for the *Journal-American*.

Bill never claimed heroics in the theaters of war. He was the first to admit that he saw more of the generals (like his friends Omar Bradley, Red O'Hare, Pete Crisada and George Patton) than of the dog-faced GIs at the front. But for Bill it was an education nonetheless, to find himself standing on his own, five thousand miles from Pop at Wyntoon, in the middle of the debacle that would finally put an end to his father's much simpler world. Bill did a tour of North Africa in the wake of the desert war, and after a brief return to the States, he assigned himself, in March 1944, to cover the invasion of Italy. He followed the action from Naples to Anzio—moving with the Army, cultivating generals, visiting the mad, Catch-22 airfields, where half-deranged men launched their B-24 raids on Ploesti and the German bases in southern France.

Just before the breakout at Monte Cassino, Bill headed for Algiers, and then on to England.

"Actually, I was bumped in Algiers," he remembered. "This was just before D-Day, though nobody knew it at the time. The gate was already closed and I couldn't get in. God knows, I didn't want to stay in Africa, so I wired Beaverbrook, and he got me on a courier plane to London." Hearst junior arrived in London on June 4. Two days later, the invasion erupted in Normandy, and by the end of the week, Bill too was in France, with the First Army at Grandchamps under Omar Bradley.

There were memorable experiences for Bill Hearst in Europe. When his father taunted him for writing about bombing raids without having flown one, the correspondent arranged to go up with a B-26. According to Bill, "It was a terrible mess. The bombs hung up, so we jerked them off manually, on top of some poor bastards in the middle of France." At one point, he and his sometime partner, the UP's Ed Beatty drew fire when they wandered too close to the enemy lines in central France; the next day Beatty returned to the spot, alone, and was captured.

Back in London for a spell of R and R at Claridge's, Bill took up with the son of another famous father, Elliot Roosevelt, who was then attached to a photo-reconnaisance unit in the Army air corps. Bill and Elliot became "the best of friends" before Hearst junior pressed on again to Paris, on the heels of the Allied armies. But the publisher's son was less than happy when his second wife, Lorelle, later showed up in London (having wangled press credentials of her own from the *Journal-American*), and Roosevelt decided to entertain her for two weeks before sending her on to the front. "Her war experience was with the good-looking guys in Elliot's unit," groaned Bill. Eventually, though, Roosevelt did his buddy the favor of flying Lorelle to Paris, where, she said, she intended to "cover fashions."

From Paris, Bill filed his own first story on the Liberation just two days after the Allies secured the city: typically, it was a hopelessly muddled tale about how he had gone shopping for "the fancy ties Pop likes." Harry Bull summed up the reaction back at the *Journal* when he roared, "Now who gives a damn!" Some weeks later, Bill raised eyebrows in New York again when he penned a remarkable dispatch that read: "Inasmuch as these shows are pretty similar, plus the fact that we had seen two already, added to which I had been working with the Ninth Air Force for some time, and, while it was not exactly an old story, it was beginning to wear a little." *Editor and Publisher* was intrigued enough to cable and ask what the report meant. But the *Journal-American's* top correspondent was too amiable to do more than reply, "I don't know how it happened . . . Maybe that's the way I wrote it."

Maybe Bill was sorry that it ended. Germany's collapse found him back in New York, recuperating from an infection he had contracted in Belgium and chafing to begin his third tour of duty. Reluctantly, he returned instead to the executive offices. But he was determined to see that some things at Hearst would never be the same.

The quiet revolution began at San Simeon. When his father welcomed him home from the war with a homily on the evil of spending American dollars to reconstruct Europe, Bill replied with a sermon of his own: "I told him, look Pop. If you're as anti-commie as you say you are, then you've got a problem here. Are you gonna stand back and watch while they take over Europe? I guess I'd seen enough to know that his old line about Europe might have worked with the League of Nations, but it wasn't gonna work any more. Of course, he never believed it."

Once back in New York, Bill started building toward the day when he might come into his own. He recruited a personal aide-de-camp, an "idea man" named Frank Conniff, who was a Democrat and a liberal, and who had once written speeches for Harry Truman. Bill liked to claim that the two of them had a "Brisbane-Hearst" relationship. "Frank taught me that the Democratic party was not full of evil-doers," he declared, "and that it had both a left and a right wing. Frank was also the first one to inform me that the ADA was not a Communist front." The pair were soon plotting a program of change for the papers. Somewhat sporadically, they also began to produce a front-page column under Bill's by-line, in order to remind the reading public that there was another, and younger, Hearst waiting in the wings.

But what Bill forgot to reckon with as he and Conniff began drawing up their plans for the papers was the fact that his claim to authority at Hearst was still, at best, unclear. Later, he would admit that he had been naïve—he had relied on his name; he had assumed too easily that he would fall heir to the organization when his father died. "I didn't know anything about office politics," he would explain. "When Pop was alive, all he had to do was lift his little finger and he got what he wanted. I just assumed that was the way it was done."

Yet within weeks of his father's funeral, he already found himself face to face with a challenge. This first board-room skirmish was a shadow affair, a contest that passed almost unnoticed by all except the two principals—Bill and Dick Berlin.

The field of battle was the Editorial Board of the newspapers, a committee of seven top news executives (including Bill, Randy and Coblentz) that had been formed in the old man's dotage to begin the inevitable shift in power. The issue was the office of chairman. While he lived, Hearst senior was titular head of the Board. And when he died, Hearst junior—who as vice-chairman, had long presided at its sessions—expected to step into his father's shoes.

"Pop never said it," contended Bill, "and while he was alive the position didn't mean much, because he was still in charge as Editor-in-Chief. But I took my title, Vice-Chairman, as a sign that he wanted me to have the papers. Everyone knew that."

Omniscient *Time* apparently knew it. Working on leads that came from Conniff, the magazine, on August 27, 1951, reported that Bill was the number-one power at Hearst, and that he was planning to renovate the newspaper chain. "Those closest to young Hearst," said the weekly,

> predict that he will soon drop such Hearstian acts as antivivisection campaigns, try to get a note of restraint into editorials. Young Bill has a tough job; the Hearst chain, long faltering, was saved mainly by the lush advertising of World War II and the ensuing boom, plus stringent

economies. Most of the top brass is now 60 or over, and new blood is needed in the top command. In Hearst shops, the talk is that young Bill will want some changes made.

But even as the magazines sat on the stands, Dick Berlin prepared to advance a pawn. According to Bill's rendition of the affair,

> Conniff was the one who told me that Dick was scheming. Somehow he got wind of the story that Berlin had told Bill Baskervill [a trustee and the editor of the Baltimore *News-Post*] that everything was "set"—he [Baskervill] was gonna take over as Chairman. I told him, no, Frank, this time you've got it wrong. Dick knows that place is mine. Conniff was a pretty smart guy, though. He said go ahead. Find out for yourself.

So Bill went to the top news executives one by one. And one by one, they told him that the story was true—Berlin had informally arranged the appointment with a quorum of the corporate directors. "Still, I could hardly believe it," said Bill. "I finally went to Baskervill, to tell him how I felt, and how I knew Pop felt, about the family and about the chain. He was so upset when I talked with him, he actually cried. Dick had told him that he'd checked it with *everyone* . . ."

Bill, of course, was gracious. Berlin was impassive. And Baskervill withdrew.

(2)

That Bill Hearst and Joe McCarthy should find each other was probably ordained by the gods of history. Bill's father, of course, had been among the first Americans to raise the specter of an advancing "red menace." As his papers never tired of repeating, Hearst had been "telling the American people the lowdown about the gangsterism in the Soviet Union popularly described as Communism" long before they had been prepared to accept his message. And McCarthy himself was no stranger to Hearst junior when, on February 9, 1950, he stepped into the limelight at Wheeling, West Virginia, holding what he alleged was a list of 205 State Department employees "that were known to the Secretary of State as being members of the Communist Party and who, nevertheless, are still working and shaping policy in the State Department."

His three-year Congressional career had been less than distinguished.

To most of the Washington press (who had voted him the nation's worst Senator in 1949), he was known only for his idiosyncratic defense of Nazi war criminals who had massacred some 150 American prisoners at Malmedy.

But to Bill Hearst, Joe was already a friend.

According to Bill's best recollection, it was in 1947 that his third wife, Austine, first introduced him to the junior Senator from Wisconsin. Austine, known as "Bootsie" to her friends, was a stunningly beautiful Southern girl, the daughter of Army Major Austin McDonnell, who had retired to Warrenton, Virginia, in the heart of fox-hunt country. In 1940, at the age of twenty, she married Igor Cassini, a society columnist on Cissy Patterson's Washington *Times-Herald*. When Cassini was drafted in 1943, Bootsie—by then a Patterson favorite—took over his column and continued it until 1953. Upon returning from the war in 1945, Cassini was hired as a gossip writer for Hearst's New York *Journal-American*, where he penned his column under the Cholly Knickerbocker pseudonym. With Cassini working in New York and Bootsie in Washington, their marriage began to wane, and Bootsie started dating other men, including Bill Hearst, Jack Kennedy, and a lonely Washington neophyte, Joe McCarthy.

In July of 1948, Bill and Bootsie were delighted to have McCarthy as a guest at their wedding. There they introduced him to Dick Berlin, who shared the Senator's Irish heritage, political leanings and fondness for booze. Soon Dick and Joe were friends. Berlin often entertained McCarthy at his Fifth Avenue apartment (where he saw that he became acquainted with not only columnist George Sokolsky, but Millicent Hearst and General Douglas MacArthur), and occasionally invited the Senator to spend an interlude at his hunting lodge in Murray Bay, Canada, ninety miles down river from Quebec.

So it was hardly surprising that McCarthy thought of Hearst when, in the wake of his Wheeling address, Democratic Senators Herbert Lehman and Scott Lucas began pressing him to produce the names of his 205 subversives. This was Bill's own version of what followed:

> Joe gave us a call not too long after the speech. And you know what— he didn't have a damned thing on that list. Nothing.
>
> He said, "My God, I'm in a jam . . . I shot my mouth off. So what am I gonna do now?"
>
> Well, I guess we fixed him up with a few good reporters . . .

Bill is vague, perhaps genuinely uncertain, about the help that McCarthy culled from Hearst that year. He says that he doesn't remember the reporters' names, or what they did for Joe, or why they were willing to work for a man who was apparently little more than a self-confessed fraud.

Possibly, then, Hearst junior has forgotten the little band of antired zealots who made their nest at the *Journal-American,* where he reigned as publisher and where he maintained his principal office. And possibly he has forgotten too what his own assistant—the formidable red-baiter, Joseph Brown Matthews—did to launch the McCarthy crusade.

J. B. Matthews was the True Believer, a man who had devoted his life to the Cause and who felt nothing but contempt, said one of his Hearst confreres, for "the Johnny-come-lately anti-Communist who plunges into battle with no knowledge of the enemy he is up against." His own past, of course, had been madly erratic. As a young man he was devoted to the Word of God: ordained to the Methodist clergy at twenty, he sailed for Java, where he evangelized the natives and dedicated his energies to a Malaysian translation of the Protestant hymnal. On returning to the United States, however, Matthews succumbed to the lure of Socialism. He renounced the cloth; he took a "red card" from the Socialist Party; and—to his everlasting shame—he emerged as a leading Depression-era radical, active by his own count in more than twenty-eight "Communist fronts." Apparently the firebrand Matthews was renowned for the rousing pitch of his rhetoric. Describing the reaction to one of his speeches, at a Communist Party rally in Madison Square Garden, the *Daily Worker* said: "It seemed that the very steel girders that arched across the roof would bend from the ear-splitting cheers that went up." The best-remembered of his oratorical efforts was a 1935 address before the Friends of the Soviet Union in Detroit, in which he roundly denounced the reactionary foreign policy of one William Randolph Hearst. By 1938, at the age of forty-four, Matthews had undergone yet another conversion, this time abandoning Marxist ideology to become one of the nation's most ardent anti-Communists. Driven by remorse, he atoned for his revolutionary indiscretions by serving first as the star witness before Martin Dies's House Committee on Un-American Activities, where he implicated hundreds of former associates, and then, from 1938 to 1945, as both Chief Researcher for the Dies investigation, and Interrogator and Chief Investigator for the Illinois Commission on Seditious Activities.

When Dies dismantled his investigative apparatus after the war, "Doc" Matthews moved on to Hearst, bringing with him an array of committee records that included a copy of the celebrated "Appendix 9," an unpublished listing of some 100,000 individuals allegedly associated with various Communist fronts. Matthews, who was designated an assistant to the publisher of the *Journal-American*, was to function as a "consultant" on matters relating to subversive activities.

Matthews was to have more than his share of support from the *Journal*, for in the '40s the paper had attracted many of his ilk—so many that it was known as a halfway house for bitter, unhappy characters who had left their old socialist convictions behind. As James Wechsler of the rival New York *Post* once explained,

> There were dozens of sick and disillusioned people in the newspaper business in New York. People who'd been through the ringer with the Party and with the committee investigations of the '30s—who loved Joe Stalin, and then loved Joe McCarthy almost the same way.
>
> Sooner or later, most of them found their way to Hearst, usually to the *Journal-American*. No matter what kind of trouble they'd had, the *Journal* was glad to take them in, as long as they felt guilty enough and were willing to take it out on some of their old friends.

These were the core of Bill's "few good reporters," the men who were assigned to help Matthews and McCarthy. They included Howard Rushmore, a former Communist who had enlisted with Hearst in 1940, within a week after being fired by the *Daily Worker*; Larry Kerley, a former FBI agent who had monitored Party activities in the '30s and '40s; George Sokolsky, the conservative columnist, who had once considered Trotsky his bosom friend; and the newsmen Ray Richards and Kent Hunter, who had worked closely with Michigan Congressman George Dondero on the investigation of *Amerasia* magazine, a publication espousing Communist causes, which had come into possession of classified State Department documents.

The first task for the Hearst group, which functioned as a kind of technical staff for McCarthy and his chief researcher, Donald Surine, was to prepare McCarthy for the upcoming hearings before a Senate Foreign Relations subcommittee chaired by Maryland Senator Millard E. Tydings, which had been delegated to test McCarthy's allegations.

Working out of the *Journal-American* offices, Hearst headquarters and Matthews' Riverside Drive apartment, the Hearst staff set out to correlate McCarthy's random numbers (his list at first had 205, then 57 and then again 81 subversives on it) with some recognizable names. The raw material for their effort was provided by Matthews, who was considered to be something of an expert in the field of "names": in addition to the Dies Committee Appendix 9, he possessed an elaborately cross-indexed file, said to contain over 500,000 names, which he had, over the years, collected from the letterheads and programs presented by various "Communist front" organizations. McCarthy, who only a few weeks before had been hard-pressed to produce a single credible suspect, was plainly impressed with the resources of the Hearst consultant. Calling Matthews "a man who seemed to carry in his head millions of biographies," he was later moved to confess, "Whatever I have done, I owe to J.B.'s encyclopedic knowledge."

However, despite a heroic effort, the Hearst staff was no more successful than the Senator himself in discovering an actual Communist to satisfy the doubts of Tydings' skeptical committee, which opened the hearings on March 8. With his half million cards, Matthews could do no better than to place on the roster of suspects Dorothy Kenyon, a former New York Municipal Court judge, whose membership in a number of liberal organizations had left an ominous trail of references in his files. The feisty New York attorney—who had, in fact, never worked for the State Department and whose record of anti-Communist activism was considerably more impressive than McCarthy's own—effectively dismantled the Hearst-built case against her and called McCarthy "an unmitigated liar," a charge he did not attempt to refute.

For their part, Richards and Hunter attempted to make a case against Owen Lattimore through Emmanuel S. Larsen, one of three men originally indicted in the *Amerasia* affair five years earlier, and who was now apparently willing to divulge an insider's knowledge of Lattimore's subversive dealings. Larsen's testimony, however, basically boiled down to one fantastic story about an exchange of secret documents at a Lattimore backyard barbeque, and even that story was only through second- or third-hand information.

It was left to Sokolsky and Kerley to produce—or, rather, fail to produce—the most disappointing witness of all. After careful coaching by the Hearst men in New York, John J. Huber, an FBI informant known to Kerley from his days with the agency, was brought to Washington to seal Lattimore's fate by testifying that he had met the State Department

consultant at a 1946 party attended by known Communists in the home
of Frederick Vanderbilt Field. But on April 25, when the committee's
clerk called his name, Huber failed to respond. An embarrassed Kerley,
who had already delivered his introduction to an increasingly hostile committee, suggested that the absent Huber had probably been abducted by
"Communist thugs." The less romantic truth was that Huber, a decidedly
unstable individual, had on his arrival at the committee room taken one
look at the glaring Klieg lights that illuminated the witness stand, and
bolted for parts unknown.

The Tydings committee entered its majority report on July 17, 1950,
and in it condemned McCarthy's allegations as "the most nefarious
campaign of half-truths and untruths in the history of the republic." It
further observed that "for the first time in our history, we have seen the
totalitarian technique of the 'big lie' employed on a sustained basis."

The Hearst organization, choosing to view the document as a challenge to its own integrity, prepared a quick reply. On Wednesday, July 19,
the sixteen Hearst dailies proclaimed in one angry voice:

> The Tydings Committee's majority report on the McCarthy charges
> of Communist influence in the State Department is probably the most
> disgracefully partisan document ever to emanate from the Congress of the
> United States.
>
> As a public paper prepared in parlous times, it verges upon DIS-
> LOYALTY.

When Bill assumed the chairmanship of the Hearst editorial board in
September 1951, the organization had already developed a close working
relationship with McCarthy, who remained in the news through the
Tydings aftermath largely because the Hearst press kept him there. The
Hearst staff had an unfailing pipeline to the Senator—through Don
Surine, and later through Roy Cohn, McCarthy would telegraph items
about forthcoming targets to the handful of journalists who had done
the most to help him survive his hour of desperation. And the grateful
Hearstlings (like their Patterson counterparts) knew how to use their
scoops; with their unholy genius for spinning bad dreams, they turned
McCarthy's notorious half-truths into their own reckless, raging, ill-
informed stories about red infiltration and the betrayal of America.

Bill, for his part, approved of the McCarthy connection. When he was questioned about it—as he was, repeatedly, by fellow publisher Dorothy Schiff, who could never fathom his tolerance for the demagogue —he defended the commitment as a sound journalistic alliance. McCarthy was the hottest news of the day. Therefore Hearst was bound to cover him, and when he was right—which in Bill's book was always—the chain would lend him its editorial support.

Apparently, though, Bill never realized that the red monomania was destroying the papers even as he made his first faltering efforts to revive them. In 1951, when nothing could save the chain but a leader who was strong enough to restrain it, Hearst junior was talking about "the dispersal of power." Addressing his first major policy statement over the Hearst wire, he decreed an unprecedented degree of autonomy for Hearst editors and publishers, in effect, telling the men who ran the eighteen newspapers, for the first time in their institutional careers, to think for themselves. Henceforth, there would be a new emphasis on local coverage. "The first job for our newspapers now will be looking after their local communities," he declared. "Any place where we have been weak in that respect, we intend to be strong." Instead of relying on the frantic "must-go" editorials that had been wired almost daily from New York and San Simeon, local writers and editors were to generate their own ideas and campaigns. Material from headquarters was to be used with discretion by each of the editors. Even Bill's own "Publisher's Report," which was theoretically the cutting edge of Hearst policy, would from now on be subject to control at the local copy desks.

While Bill's motives were good, he was guilty of a disastrous miscalculation when he assumed that Hearst news executives, who had for so long subordinated their own professional judgment to that of a higher power, would develop the faculty of journalistic sense on a moment's notice. To decentralize editorial power and to demand local responsibility may have been theoretically ideal as correctives to the inversion of values that had occurred under his father's jealous administration. But practically speaking, it was only naïve to suppose that writers, reporters and editors who had never been permitted the luxury of professional independence—the very newsmen whom *Christian Century* had labeled "a race of journalistic mercenaries" and whom Westbrook Pegler (who ought to have known) had called "some of the worst bums in the business"—would, if only given their rein, become an instant credit to some dozen American communities.

In fact, the one mistake Bill's father had never made was to trust his own organization. Having created his journalistic Caliban, he was well aware of the lengths to which it might go if not carefully restrained. Admittedly, it was Hearst who had originally corrupted the papers. But at the same time, it was Hearst who had sensed better than anyone else that, if ever those papers were allowed to cross the fine line between partisanship and fanaticism, they would almost certainly destroy themselves. On many occasions, he had found it necessary to reel the papers in, warning that the editorials had become too partisan or the news columns too political. And at times, it had taken all of his formidable authority to pull his press up short once it had lunged. When, for instance, *Fortune* magazine published a review of his career which Hearst newsmen perceived to be critical of the Chief (although, in fact, it was written with his full cooperation), he had to insist three times that he did not intend massive retaliation against Luce before his editors eased their attack. Later, when his minions—presumably to please him—tried to destroy Roosevelt with their journalistic hatchets, Hearst virtually begged them to stop their violence. "We are nagging Roosevelt too annoyingly and ineffectively," he wired from San Simeon. "Nothing he says or does seems to please us. Let us discuss policies, and discuss them logically and temperately, not violently. That is, anyhow, the only way to CONVINCE people."

Under Bill Hearst's new regime, editors were apprised that henceforth there would be no official Hearst policy on McCarthy. "Play the story for what its worth," was the instruction from New York. What McCarthy was worth, of course, depended to a great extent on one's political persuasion, and by something more than chance, the vast majority of news executives on Hearst papers were rabid anti-Communists and McCarthy admirers.

In fact, the Hearst editors needed no cue, no special command, to exploit the Great Fear that had settled on the nation in those early years of the 1950s. They supported McCarthy and Velde and McCarran, and they did their best to invent schemes of their own for dealing with pinks and fellow travelers. Hearst editorialists, writing for the chain, promoted legislation to "resolve the problem of the Fifth Amendment." They excoriated the "anti-anti-Communists" (a double-hyphened breed that Bill himself placed "somewhere between the fellow traveler and the appeaser"). At the same time they clamored for the institution of widespread government wiretapping; and, at one point, they went so far as to propose the construction of detention centers, perhaps in a remote area of Wyoming, for the incarceration of Communists and their friends in the event of war with the Soviet Union.

Federal Bureau of Investigation chief J. Edgar Hoover, who was a close friend of Berlin and long-time Hearst editor Edmond Coblentz, was quick to detect themes that called for strong Hearst advocacy, and the Hearst newspapers were happy to oblige the FBI chief. Such chain-wide editorials as "The Real Danger" (not the Communists, said Hearst, but their liberal associates) and "Still Too Many" ("dupes and dopes") were direct results of Hoover suggestions.

As with any Hearst crusade, however, it was not on the editorial pages that the most effective efforts in behalf of McCarthyism were to be found. Rather, it was in the news columns, where the charges of investigators could be cast as accepted fact. Week after week, Hearst readers were given the lowdown on such developments as the sixty Communists or fellow travelers known to be monitoring American troop movements from the Army finance center in Missouri, the lately discovered Communist plan to establish a black Soviet Republic in the Southern United States, and a Soviet attempt to subvert 15,000 Eskimos. The identification of political opposition with disloyalty was carried to a high art in headlines. To choose a random example from hundreds: "Only Pinks in Washington Excited About Senator Nixon's Financial Trouble."

The Hearst newspapers took an active role in exposing subversives in their own communities. The Seattle *Post-Intelligencer*, under publisher C. B. Lindeman, organized its own "red squads" to keep files on local subversives. When the House Un-American Activities Committee visited Seattle in June of 1954, the paper turned its records over to Chairman Harold Velde, who praised the paper for its diligence. The California papers worked closely with Hearst intimate John Francis Neylan, who had become a regent of the University of California, in his attempt to impose a loyalty oath on University employees.

The *Journal-American*, of course, proved to be a hotbed of anti-Communist fervor. The paper's education reporter, Charles Rowland, was sent around to give talks in the schools, where he warned groups of youngsters that "things are going to be terrible" when McCarthy got his campaign in motion, and "anyone who's got anything at all to do with the party had better resign now, and save himself."

Howard Rushmore, once given carte blanche to ferret out subversives, proceeded with hysterical energy. He didn't have a committee, and he couldn't subpoena. But he did have the *Journal-American*, a tool that could be devastatingly effective. In one case, a New York teacher was exposed as having been affiliated with the Party sometime in the hazy past. The story broke in the early edition. Before the second edition hit the streets, the Board of Education had called the desk to report that the *Journal* could kill the story: the man had been safely expunged.

Rushmore's diligence even made some of his colleagues nervous. Rowland was surprised to return home after a night at the paper to be told by the doorman that Rushmore had been there, in the company of another grim-looking figure, supposedly from the FBI. The two had demanded to be let into Rowland's apartment. Once inside, they rifled the desk and scanned the bookshelves for evidence of subversive tendencies, telling the incredulous attendant they had reason to believe that Rowland was a Communist.

"For God's sake," Rowland said. "I was no Communist. I was giving talks in the schools for those people." He confronted Rushmore, who assured him everything was "okay"—the two had decided he was "clean." Rowland later learned other *Journal-American* employees had been subjected to clandestine loyalty checks.

The obsession with disloyalty spread beyond the newspapers themselves to poison the work of far too many Hearst columnists and feature writers. Igor "Cholly Knickerbocker" Cassini reveled in his own maladept barbs at the "rich parlor pinks, traitors to their class." Twenty years later, in his memoir *I'd Do It All Over Again*, he was still laughing: "Mrs. Cornelius Vanderbilt, the dowager queen of American society, received Andrei Gromyko for tea—Russian? English? Chinese? Indian? The incongruity was such it was irresistible. I called her the Red Duchess and predicted they were about to announce their engagement." Dorothy Kilgallen, with her overdeveloped sense of drama, suddenly discovered Communism running "like veins of marble" through the Mickey Jelke vice case, which she covered, interminably, for the *Journal-American*. "It seems unlikely—and even impossible," quivered the girl reporter in February of 1953, "that the District Attorney's office could have investigated the various witnesses as thoroughly as it must have done without becoming aware of the links between some of the paygirls of the Jelke orbit and subversives in our Federal Government."

To Louella Parsons, the First Lady of Hollywood, fell the awesome responsibility of patrolling the film community. Perhaps it was to prove her own loyalty that in September of 1952 she launched a cruel and gossip-ridden series on the decline and fall of her once-dear friend Charlie Chaplin. "I don't know when all this so-called un-American activity started with Charlie," she was at pains to explain. "In his early days he was charming, amusing and gracious, and, as far as I know, had no part in any alleged subversive groups." But the INS motion-picture editor explained that she, for one, had finished with the star "from that day in May 1946, when Chaplin and other fellow travelers were guests of honor aboard a Soviet ship anchored in the Long Beach, California, harbor." Charlie drank Russian champagne. He became acquainted with high Soviet officials and lent his name to a host of "red fronts." All of which left the unhappy Louella no choice but to declare:

> It is nothing short of insolence on his part to be talking about a new film. I can assure Charlie that real Americans will not pay to see him on the screen and add more dollars to the millions he has already collected in this country.

No one was ever sure what it took to move Walter Winchell, the frantic little bantam whose gossip column reached almost 40 million readers daily through the *Mirror* and the King Features Syndicate, into the McCarthy camp. Winchell had once been a Roosevelt man and had fought endlessly with Hearst senior for the right to run liberal plugs when no one else in the organization had dared to buck the Hearst party line. So, when his friend Drew Pearson heard Winchell air his first pro-McCarthy plug, on April 23, 1950, he could only note in bewilderment that "Walter really must think he's slipping." Others theorized that the columnist was blackmailed. His biographer, Bob Thomas, flatly stated that: "Whatever doubts Winchell may have had about getting behind McCarthy were resolved by a simple threat. The McCarthy forces informed Winchell that unless he fell into line he would be a forthcoming target for the junior senator from Wisconsin." But Herman Klurfeld, one of the ghosts who wrote many of Winchell's columns, believed that something more personal was involved. The reporter had been insulted by Harry Truman, he said—at a meeting with Roosevelt's sharp-tongued successor, he had proposed his pet scheme, a plan for a Presidential summit with Stalin, only to be dismissed with the jibe, "I don't kiss anybody's ass." Where Walter Winchell was concerned, that might indeed have worked a revolution.

According to Winchell's own account, he first met McCarthy through Richard Berlin. It may have been a calculated encounter, or perhaps it was simply by chance that Berlin brought his friend to the Stork Club early in 1952, at a time when Winchell was feeling low and bitter, and when McCarthy was still badly in need of allies. The three of them shared a cordial dinner, and that same night the columnist introduced the Senator to lawyer Roy Cohn—a "boy genius" who, he kept telling Berlin, should have been working for Hearst.

By the beginning of 1953, Joe McCarthy had his committee; Roy Cohn was in Washington, serving (side by side with Bobby Kennedy) as the inquisitor's counsel; and the "Bard of Broadway" found himself wired to the hottest news in the nation's capital. Long after the night ride had ended, Winchell would still crow about the scoops he had taken from his McCarthy connection. In his *WINCHELL Exclusive!* (a memoir dedicated to "all the skeletons in your closet and mine"), he gloried in the fact that "when the McCarthy Red Probe was the top-rated radio and teevee program, no newspaper man got more 'firsts' than I." He described his pipeline in clinical detail:

> Saturday nights (about 1 or 2:00 A.M.) I could always depend on Roy meeting me in the Cub Room. He never failed to bring a batch of memos—written in my style: brief, concise, punchy scoops. Then he would jot down a lot more at the table.
>
> After a snack Roy would go home. I would hasten to the New York *Mirror* and my typewriter to finish getting my Sunday night coast-to-coaster ready.
>
> The news about Washington—what the McCarthy Committee would do on the following day, names they would subpoena, who would testify, what McCarthy would charge—was made public via my newscast. The late Monday (and early Tuesday editions) invariably confirmed the beats.
>
> What a source! The opposition papers in New York and elsewhere called me a "McCarthy stooge," a McCarthyite, Roy Cohn's Svengali.

He was never embarrassed to stooge for McCarthy; the items were hot, the stakes were high, and the plain truth was that the epithets came easily to Walter Winchell. He was a vindictive man, a man who had more enemies than friends. He knew how to use the words that hurt. And even before he enlisted with Joe, he had begun to discover that

some words—words that had the right political slant—were never cut by
the libel attorneys who dogged his steps at Hearst.

Already in the fall of 1951 Winchell had been baiting his No. 1
Ingrate, the repatriate Josephine Baker, who had accepted his plugs for
her new nightclub act and then roused his columnistic wrath by claiming that she was refused service at the Stork Club because she was black.
Apparently it wasn't enough to say that Baker was wrong or perhaps
misguided (as she may have been, for there were legitimate questions
about whether she had in fact been slighted). Instead he tore her apart
in the column. He told 50 million readers that the dancer was not only
antiblack, anti-American, and anti-Semitic, but that she was hand-in-glove
with a Communist plot to discredit him; that she had conspired with
Paul Robeson to incite the riots at Peekskill; and that the Justice Department (which explicitly denied the charge) was compiling a file of her
subversive activities that would be used to keep her from reentering the
country if ever she left it again.

His own writers knew that the allegations were little more than para-
noiac ravings. But Hearst printed the libels uncut and sent them out on
the Syndicate, because they were in tune with the mood of the masses,
and because, as Winchell archly discerned, "When I exposed Reds (by
name!) for full columns . . . Mr. Berlin thought that was Just Peachy."

The observation was shrewd enough. Nobody moved to stop him
when he turned his sights on Barry Gray, the midnight mahatma on
WMCA who had mounted an airwave defense of Baker and who had
let Ed Sullivan (a Winchell archrival) use his radio forum to declare that
"Long before McCarthy came into the character-assassination racket,
Winchell was one of [its] originators . . . This small-time vaudeville
hoofer who never even got to the Palace . . . has developed into a small-
time Hitler . . . He has capitalized on the Big Lie." Winchell began
writing about "Borey Pink," the radio "disk jerk" who "so far hasn't
discussed the fact that he wrote for the *Daily Worker* under a nom de
Commie." He freely suggested that Gray was a Communist and he
reported—twelve times in three weeks—that Gray's sponsor, a Manhattan
restaurant called Chandler's, was a "gyp" joint run by gougers and thieves.
When Gray lined up celebrity guests for his program, Winchell warned
them off. Not much later, when Gray was beaten, twice, by thugs who
cornered him as he left his studio in the dead of the night, Winchell

managed a wicked laugh. Herman Klurfeld was pained to remember that after one of the attacks, "A *Journal-American* editor sent Winchell a photo of Gray's mashed face. Walter examined it and smiled. 'He never looked better.' "

But the worst of his slurs he reserved for the New York *Post*.

The feud, of course, was a personal matter—with Winchell it always was. The gossip had once been a friend to the people who ran the *Journal-American*'s chief rival. James Wechsler had once been Winchell's ally in plugging Roosevelt; in fact, when the two were both writing for the liberal *PM* (where the gossip, as Paul Revere II, would print political items that were too far to the left for Hearst), the *Post* editor had actually ghost-written attacks on the red-baiting Martin Dies, which Winchell, always in a hurry, was only too happy to use. The *Post*'s Broadway man, Leonard Lyons, was a Winchell protégé as well as the chairman of the columnist's pet charity, the Damon Runyon Cancer Fund. And even Dolly Schiff had won his affection by asking him, on several occasions, "Why don't you come over with us? Why work for those Hearst Fascists?"

It was the *Post* that decided to end the romance—partly because Winchell had sold his soul in the deal with McCarthy, and partly because by 1952 even his onetime admirers were beginning to believe that the gossip had become too big. "Those who are discreet enough to avoid any quarrels with him are permitted to live in peace," noted Wechsler in his memoir, the *Age of Suspicion*. "And those who violate his rules can expect to be set upon from behind in the journalistic dark alley known as 'Walter Winchell on Broadway.' . . . Whatever else might be said about him, it had to be acknowledged that Winchell had achieved a frightening power to bully and browbeat."

On January 7, 1952, the *Post* launched an exposé, a twenty-four-part series that described in grueling detail the education of a demagogue and a Broadway bully. The paper revealed the names of Winchell's ghosts. It laid bare the easy relationships he enjoyed with Frank Costello and the mobsters of Murder Inc. It maintained that he had never known the meaning of political principles—that he had been used by Roosevelt, and then by the friends of McCarthy, and that whatever side he was on, he had kept his politics at the level of the cheap scoop and the personal feud.

When the series had finally ended, Winchell (who was sufficiently shaken by the exposé to drop his column for a full three months), replied in character, if not exactly in kind. The gossip suddenly "discovered" what the better part of the New York press corps had known for years: that James Wechsler had once been not only a Communist, but a national committeeman for the Young Communist League at the age of twenty-two. And he decided to use that item to settle his score with the *Post.*

Winchell opened his last vendetta with what he liked to call "a straight left to the balls." In a full-column tirade that ran in the *Mirror* (though a great many out-of-town editors simply cut it), he denounced the New York "*Compost*" as a haven for most of the pinks and punks who infested the newspaper business. Then, in a frenzy, he lunged for Wechsler, the "son of a bitch" who, he told one of his assistants, was "trying to kill" him. On a television show that he had lately begun for ABC, Winchell fell into the habit of flashing a portrait of the editor, sandwiched between snapshots of wanted fugitives; Wechsler, he warned his audience, was in the habit of associating with known subversives like Gil Green and the ill-fated Julius and Ethel Rosenberg. For his column, he coined a dozen epithets that could only be read to mean that Wechsler was still in thrall to the Comintern. Week after week, in more than thirty columns, he dropped items, most of them mindlessly derogatory, about James "Jake Ivan" Wechsler, the Pinko-Stinko who saw to it that the "New York Pravda" hewed to the Party line.

A dozen years earlier—when Hearst senior had warned his editors to "Please edit Winchell very carefully, and leave out any dangerous or disagreeable paragraphs. Indeed leave out the whole column without hesitation, as I think he has gotten so careless that he is no longer of any particular value"—the wild innuendo might have been cut. But apparently neither Berlin nor Bill Hearst had any intention of curbing the assault.

On October 4, Dolly Schiff, who counted herself among Bill's friends and who seemed to be on amicable terms with Berlin, begged them to reduce the heat before the feud turned serious. In a column that was addressed directly to Bill, she calmly refuted the notion, advanced by Winchell, that she was a "former capitalist," and she tried to disarm his charges against Wechsler by reprinting a long and thoughtful discussion of the editor's political history, which had been written by Alicia Patterson for the *Bulletin of the American Newspaper Editors.* The only discernible response by Hearst came from the *Journal-American*; someone on the paper dispatched Howard Rushmore to Winchell with a new file of anti-*Post* material, while the Hearst admen gleefully launched a whispering campaign among retailers who might not have heard that the *Post* and its fellow-traveling editor had been tainted by charges of disloyalty.

"Finally it got so bad," said Wechsler in an interview many years later, "that we decided we had to call them. Walter was a very sick man by then, very bitter over a lot of things, and I thought he had to be stopped. Obviously we knew we were outgunned—we didn't have all those big Hearst papers with all that circulation behind us. So it looked like the only place for a showdown was open court." Late in December, Wechsler and the *Post* filed suit, for $1,525,000, against not just Winchell, but ABC, the Gruen Watch Company (his broadcast sponsor), the King Features Syndicate, and the Hearst Corporation.

(3)

Nineteen fifty-four was a dismal year for Hearst, a year pervaded by the awful sensation that the world of the old man's dream had at last begun to disintegrate.

The properties, of course, were still intact. Of the legacy Hearst left at his death, only the Babicora ranch had been sold (by Berlin, who in 1952 had ceded the 900,000-acre domain to the Mexican government in exchange for $2,000,000 in cash), and a major magazine, *Sports Afield*, had been added, by purchase, to the stable of Hearst monthlies.

But at the same time, an air of decay had already begun to settle in around the massive newspaper chain. The *American Weekly*, Hearst's antique Sunday supplement, was slowly dying for want of ads in spite of its almost ten-million circulation and a costly effort to modernize the Gray Lady with new features, a new format, and printing by rotogravure. Bill promoted the renovation almost as vigorously as his father, who stood by his old Hoe-Pancoast four-color presses, had resisted it. But the program had come ten years too late, and by 1952, when it was finally completed, nothing could recover the accounts that had fled to younger and slicker rivals like *This Week* and *Parade*. Elsewhere, too, there were bitterly discouraging signs that the great Hearst dailies had begun to lose their grip on the loyalties of some fifty million readers. For 1953, Hearst Consolidated, with its eleven newspapers, was forced to report that profits, which were "not as satisfactory as we had hoped," had dwindled to a modest $2 million. By 1954, there was a net $340,000 loss—which left the directors lamenting that the year had been bad "for the newspaper industry as a whole."

In fact, the newspaper industry was marching steadily ahead in those first five years of the decade—but Hearst decidedly was not. Between 1951 and 1955, the papers dropped a full 5 percent of their once solid circulation. For 1954 alone, the Consolidated block showed a loss of $1.5 million in circulation revenue and a 1.1 percent drop, across the board, in advertising linage. Apparently the readers were deserting Hearst, and the advertisers—who took some $4 million in accounts with them that year—were beginning to follow in droves.

Perhaps it was true, as the analysts said, that the malaise was a wholly predictable phenomenon. *Fortune* had long before explained that the Hearst managers were far too dependent on the whims of their Chief to function well without him. "Only one thing is certain," the magazine had proclaimed in 1935. "The Hearst empire will be difficult to hold together. Its diversity, its extraordinary aggregation of high-priced, ambitious, jealous executive talent, and, above all, its peculiar personal method of operation, all of these elements give the predicter pause. HEARST is Hearst himself, and is all-but impossible to imagine without him." *Time* had added that the executives were aging—"new blood is needed in the top command," advised the Luce writers—and more perceptive observers may have sensed even then that the papers were fighting demography. With the Levittown revolution already begun, the great urban base on which Hearst built his empire was crumbling before the exodus to the suburbs. As Bill was to put it much later, "We found out we were stuck with all the wrong markets. But when Pop started the papers, let's face it, he was looking for votes not for dollars."

Yet for all that, it was also true that if the papers were foundering, the fault was largely Bill's. For the hard fact was that, in 1954, too many Hearstlings had gone too far. And no one had been there to stop them.

The list of Bill's failures was an unhappy litany of good intentions gone hopelessly wrong.

In four years, for instance, he had been able to do nothing about Westbrook Pegler, though he knew all too well that the writer, who produced the most primitive of all the Hearst columns, was doing the papers irreversible damage.

There was no excuse for Westbrook Pegler. He was brutal and vile. "Poorly educated, nonintellectual, not even sophisticated, he found it easier to grapple with an enemy than with an idea," wrote Oliver Pilat, his most sympathetic biographer. And even the fact that some twelve million people read his column each day could never justify the things he said or the way his publishers egged him on. Long before he came to Hearst, Pegler had earned a reputation for verbal assaults that were too personal to be funny and, perhaps, too bitter to be the work of a man who was wholly sane. In fact, Pegler himself was strangely unashamed to admit that his column was spawned in a pool of hatred. In an astonishing journalistic confession, the writer once called it "odd that honesty and friendship both are held in such tender sentimental regard considering that both are so little patronized and that their opposites have by far the greater appeal." For his own part, he was willing to add that "my hates always occupied my mind much more actively and have given me greater spiritual satisfaction than my friendships."

In the course of his career as a political commentator—a career that began in 1933 on Roy Howard's *World-Telegram*—Pegler had written with relish that Franklin Roosevelt was a "feeble-minded *fuehrer*," and that his wife, "La Boca Grande," enjoyed the company of "queers." Harry Truman he called "thin-lipped, a hater, a bad man in any fight . . . malicious and unforgiving and not above offering you his hand to yank you off balance and work you over with a chair leg, pool cue, or something out of his pocket." Orson Welles was an "elf" (which in the jargon of the time meant homosexual). Heywood Broun was a "liar." And, according to Pegler, who advocated salutary hangings of union pickets, "the Reuthers had it coming."

In one of his better-remembered columns—written in 1940, when he was still secure in his niche at Scripps-Howard—Pegler labeled William Randolph Hearst not only a "never-to-be-adequately damned demagogue," but "an unprincipled rich man . . . [who] always found high-principled poor men to sell their principles for a few dirty dimes."

By late November 1944, however, Pegler was writing for the *Journal-American* and circulating his column through King. He paid the expected visit to San Simeon, where he did homage to an old man who thoroughly disliked him. Not surprisingly, though, he got along well with Dick Berlin, who sometimes urged him to plug Taft and McCarthy (Peg gladly complied) and who called the journalist a personal friend.

Berlin welcomed Pegler with an ironclad contract—in which Hearst agreed to pay for his libels—while King Features drowned him in torrents of attention. In 1944, the syndicate sponsored a testimonial at which a thousand guests (including Jimmy Walker, Roy Howard, and all the Hearst brass) chuckled while toastmaster Bugs Baer proclaimed that "if genius is an infinite capacity for taking pains—and giving them—then Pegler is a genius!" Later, in a spectacular *Editor and Publisher* ad, King credited no one other than "the courageous Westbrook Pegler" with having generated the great Republican ground swell of 1950.

Still, no amount of flattery or good will could change the fact that Westbrook Pegler was a negative force and a man who would finally cost Hearst more than his syndicate profits could ever repay.

Already in June of 1949, he was sowing his seeds of destruction when he accused Winchell of driving the luckless Defense Secretary James Forrestal to suicide with the "dirty aspersions" of his "malicious and untruthful gents'-room journalism." Winchell read the charge as a murder rap, and snapped back that Pegler was a "presstitute." And with that the two Hearst stars launched a bloody in-house vendetta, which, as Winchell once boasted, not even Berlin was able to settle. "Pegler and Winchell—at the time and for many years," wrote the gossip, "were not speaking to each other except in our columns. Not even Hearst monarch Richard E. Berlin or Roy Cohn could get me to shake hands with him. In fact, whenever Pegler came into the Stork Club, I took a walk—to some other late spot."

That feud had barely cooled to a steady simmer when, on November 29 of that year, Pegler loosed his bludgeon on still another "family friend." This time the victim was Quentin Reynolds, a journalistic star who had begun his phenomenal reportorial career with the INS and who remained on good terms with a roster of Hearst powers that included Barry Faris, Seymour Berkson, Bill Corum, Bob Considine, and even Dick Berlin. Pegler too had been Reynolds' friend. But when Reynolds accused the columnist of the "moral equivalent of murder" (for badgering Heywood Broun on his deathbed), Pegler responded with a column that "exposed" the ex-Hearstling as a nudist, a parasite, a Communist sympathizer, a war profiteer, an absentee war correspondent, and an ardent "interventionist" who, "though he was a giant and a bachelor, let several million kids about eighteen years old do the fighting."

Reynolds sued both Pegler and Hearst for libel. In the trial that followed, some five years later, the journalist provided a moving indictment not only of Pegler, but of the organization that had chosen to support him. Under questioning by Hearst attorney Charles Henry with regard to the question of malice, Reynolds, with rising emotion, struggled to explain his sense of betrayal. "Well, all I know," he said:

> is that Pegler made the bullets and the Hearst papers shot them. That is all I know. I don't know the meaning of malice in its legal sense.
>
> Until what to me was a pretty horrible answer which you made to our complaint, and I couldn't conceive of Hearst executives even implying their approval of this column written by Pegler, but in the answer which was signed by you as the representative of the corporations, I was horrified to find that in effect this was signed by these top executives of the Hearst organization whom I knew and who knew me and who knew better . . .
>
> That is what horrified me—that [it was endorsed by] men like Berlin, who knew better than to think I was this grotesque moral degenerate pictured by Mr. Pegler.

When Pegler got his own turn on the stand, he turned almost suicidal. Under oath and with his very integrity on trial, he displayed his bile by demeaning not only Generals MacArthur and Eisenhower (two heroes of the day who were invoked by Reynolds as character witnesses), but by impugning the reliability of his own employer. To reproduce just one in a long series of remarkable exchanges between Pegler and Reynolds' attorney, Louis Nizer:

> NIZER: Do you think Damon Runyon was a reliable reporter?
> PEGLER: No.
> NIZER: Do you think that he was an honorable man with integrity?
> PEGLER: No. . . .
> NIZER: Do you recall that this Exhibit 138—this is Louis Sobol's column. Do you consider him reliable?
> PEGLER: No.
> NIZER: Do you consider the fact that he writes for the New York Journal [-American] gives him any reliability in his statements?
> PEGLER: No.
> NIZER: Do you think that the appearance of Damon Runyon's article in the Hearst publication the Mirror gave it any sense of reliability?
> PEGLER: No.

It was hardly surprising that when the trial ended, in June of 1954, Quentin Reynolds was awarded $175,000 in punitive damages—one of the highest libel judgments ever granted in the history of the American courts.

To his credit, Bill, who personally detested Pegler, had made at least a halfhearted attempt to curb him even before the Reynolds case went to trial. He had his first confrontation with the writer in 1953. In that year, Pegler had smeared Bob Patterson, a former Defense Department official, by branding him a "renegade Republican who turned New Deal bureaucrat with a strong sympathy for the Communist treachery." Under severe pressure from Patterson's friends—among them Julius Ochs Adler of the *New York Times*'s ruling family—the Hearst chairman flatly ordered Pegler to "lay off." He personally apologized to Adler for the attack, which he said would not have gone through had he not been away in Mexico when it was printed. But he quickly discovered that the ranting columnist, who only redoubled his assault on Patterson, had no intention of respecting his authority.

That wretched scenario was replayed again in July, when Bill, at the express request of the Supreme Headquarters of the Allied Powers in Paris, told Pegler to drop his campaign of abuse against Irving Brown and Jay Lovestone, a pair of former Communists who were serving as "labor consultants" to American embassies in Europe. Pegler's only reply had been to conjure another column in which he insisted that the two were Communists still, and were working for "the Central Intelligence Agency, a mysterious American Gestapo [engaged in] dirty work . . . mysterious under-handed activities."

Bill would have done well to end that defiance, to begin cutting Pegler the way he should have been cut when Reynolds was libeled or when dozens of less well-defended victims were battered and bloodied by his merciless prose. Perhaps he had intended to do as much: reporter Oliver Pilat, has written that Bill tried to muzzle the columnist, but found himself blocked by fellow executives, who felt that Pegler should "be allowed a free voice," and possibly by editors who failed to enforce his call for sanity in the columns as well as the news. Bill himself has claimed that Berlin encouraged the writer's effrontery. "Dick was using Peg," he once explained, "and sometimes he used him to get at me. If I wanted the papers to plug for Ike, to give you just one example, Berlin asked Pegler to cut him down—to work the guns for Taft. There wasn't much I could do to stop it."

Presumably, too, there was nothing he could do to stop the wildly incongruous tribute that the organization offered to Pegler in the wake of the Reynolds verdict. On November 18, 1954, the directors of the

Banshees (a Hearst-sponsored tribe of newsmen and newsmen's friends, organized largely to promote the King writers) chose to name Westbrook Pegler "the outstanding reporter and columnist of the year." The award, betokened by a statuette called the Silver Lady, was presented at another great Waldorf testimonial. From the podium, Bob Hope quipped, "Even enemies read Pegler's column. Quentin Reynolds buys two papers every day—one for each birdcage. By the way, I met Quent recently on the way to the bank. . . ." At which Bill Hearst—like his executive confreres Ward Greene (of King), Jake Gortatowsky, Bill Curley and Dick Berlin, who were all in attendance—undoubtedly managed a hearty laugh.

There may have been a small victory for Bill and for sanity when Winchell (whom the publisher now remembers as "a small man . . . petty . . . a peephole journalist") was compelled to end his vendetta with Wechsler. The gossip was silenced when the *Post* filed suit; as he put it, "My Hearst employers told me to stop: 'We are now in litigation. Cut it out.' " He was stunned soon afterward to find that before the case could come to trial, someone, perhaps Bill himself, had undercut him by arranging a truce with Dorothy Schiff, who offered to drop her action if Winchell would apologize for his assault on her paper.

Winchell, who choked on retractions, resisted the deal for months. But apparently the powers at Hearst were beginning to sense what the Reynolds verdict had meant not only to the corporation, but to the nervous King subscribers, who could be sued individually for a columnist's libels.

Three years too late to prevent the damage that Winchell, like Pegler, had done to the company, Hearst executives Charles McCabe, Glen Neville, and Charles Henry were dispatched to present the columnist with a document that authorized the *Mirror* to state:

> Walter Winchell . . . never said or meant to say in the *Mirror* or over the air that the New York *Post*, or its publisher or Mr. James A. Wechsler, its editor, are Communists or sympathetic to Communism. If anything which Mr. Winchell said was so construed, he regrets and withdraws it.

The trio ("that double-cross cast," Winchell called them) explained that Hearst had concluded a separate peace with Schiff: she was dropping her suit against the corporation in return for a $30,000 settlement. Unless he signed the retraction, however, she intended to initiate a new action—

and this one would be designed, with Hearst help if need be, to hurt no one but Walter Winchell.

The gossip signed, as he said, "to keep my contract and bankroll intact." But he couldn't resist adding a postscript of his own. "I knew then," he spat in bitter recollection, "I would never again sign another deal with Hearst."

Winchell, at least, had capitulated. And yet, on balance, Bill had done little to change the papers or to replace the vision that had died with his father. Three years after the old man's passing, there had been no sweeping reforms, no improvement in the news columns, no visible change in the way the Hearst papers battered their enemies or plugged their friends. All the sixteen dailies still wore the ancient façade that young Will Hearst, with the help of George Pancoast, had devised in the 1890s. Page-one editorials and screaming banners still prevailed. Far too many editions were still peppered with grisly newsphotos of accident victims and the scattering of wicked little articles that were intended less to inform than to titillate.

One mark of the papers' inability to escape the past was the gloomy image of their founder that still haunted the top of the Hearst editorial pages each day. The photo, which had apparently been snapped in the middle thirties, was always captioned with a well-worn Hearstian exhortation on the virtues of free enterprise or the dangers lurking behind foreign entanglement. And beneath this shrine, the Hearst writers still hammered tirelessly at the same old themes. Antivivisectionism, that standing joke of the newspaper business, had gone by the way. But "Americanism" still graced the editorial repertoire, along with the age-old campaign for better roads (which had begun with the founding of Hearst's first magazine, *Motor*, in 1903) and, of course, the phobic warnings about the ubiquitous influence of domestic subversives.

Bill had once maintained that the crusades were over—that the "must go" editorials would be dropped, that the editors would be free to use their discretion, and that the papers would be pushed to serve their own communities as they had never done while Hearst senior was alive.

Inevitably, the promises had been coupled with a mouthful of corporate tough talk. "Those papers and people who have been doing a good job need have no qualms," Bill told the reporters from *Time*. "Those who haven't should unquestionably and rightfully have some qualms." Yet none of the measures, none of the talk had stopped the

Hearst press from crusading more violently than ever. Even in the waning months of 1954—when the Senate was preparing to censure Joe McCarthy, and when even Dwight Eisenhower was cracking to the Cabinet, "Have you heard the latest? McCarthyism is McCarthywasm!"—the Hearst machine was grinding along, unchecked in its anti-Communist fervor. In the fevered weeks before the censure vote (which was recorded on December 2), Hearst dispatched its Washington correspondent, Dave Sentner, on a desperate scramble for political dirt that could be used to stop anti-McCarthy Senators Ralph Flanders and Arthur Watkins. On November 30, Hearst, through the INS, reported that the Ten Million Americans Mobilizing For Justice had "gone way over the top" in its drive to put ten million names on an angry pro-McCarthy petition—when in fact the total number of signatures stood at precisely 1,000,816. And on December 3, when the battle was lost, Hearst (some of whose editors claimed a McCarthy victory because the charges against their hero had been whittled to just two counts of contempt and abuse toward the Senate) had nothing but bitter recriminations to offer the Senators who had finally ended the nightmare. "So the 'Get McCarthy' lobby has finally managed to drive a censure resolution through the Senate and we hope they're satisfied," began the chain's sour comment. "If they are— and we have a hunch their morning-after feeling is that of an anticlimactic hangover rather than the heady lift of achievement—they must be the only Americans to derive any comfort from the amazing performance of the Senate in the last few weeks."

Indeed, if anything had changed in those first three years of the new regime, it had only been Bill himself. In 1954, his friend Frank Conniff, virtually alone in the vast institution, was using his own *Journal-American* column to oppose the McCarthy madness. But Bill, the apostle of moderation, had lapsed into tones that were painfully reminiscent of his father. Succumbing to the momentum of the last Hearst crusade, the editorial chairman voiced his regret, in his column for October 24 of that year, that the only person who had been investigated in the twelve months past was Senator Joe McCarthy. Roundly excoriating the Republican leadership, who "threw away the Commies-in-Government issue," Bill blamed Dwight Eisenhower, his one-time ally, for selling out to the "Get-McCarthy faction" and for all but destroying the Grand Old Party.

That alone was an incredible charge to level at a man whose only crime had been excessive patience with a trigger-happy demagogue. But still more fantastic was Bill's wistful observation that "the noble experiment was over."

He was referring, of course, to the era of blacklists and unfettered congressional investigating committees. But he might as easily have been writing of his own faded dream—that of a newspaper empire reborn.

Chapter 3

Dynasty Manqué

(1)

To ANYONE who has heard the name, "San Simeon" means one thing—the Hearst Castle. Hearst himself never used the term "castle." Having spent more than $30 million on the project, he could afford to flaunt his modesty by calling it simply "the ranch." To the millions of tourists who have traipsed across its ancient Roman floors, gaped at the incredible art collections—some of it truly valuable tapestries and some of it virtual junk—or marveled at the simple enormity of the place, the castle has seemed a reflection of the Byzantine personality that built it. The castle and the man who made it surely are things that will never happen again.

But for the Hearst family, in the early 1950s, the years immediately following the patriarch's death, the castle was a sad reminder that so many things Hearst touched or affected had little or no importance, influence or even meaning, except as they related to him. The castle was one such thing. The Hearst family was another. It was a time when the futures of both the Hearst Castle and the Hearst family were in doubt. The castle found its role by 1958. It took the family much longer.

If any one location could be said to hold a special significance for the Hearst family, if there was any place remotely resembling an ancestral home, it had to be San Simeon. Ever since W. R.'s father, George Hearst, had bought the original 40,000 acres in 1865, San Simeon had been a favorite family refuge, a place in which to escape the cares and pressures of day-to-day living. George often made the 200-mile trip by horseback from San Francisco; once on his property, he would sometimes sit for hours on the hills, staring down at the shimmering San Simeon Bay, where a few dozen fishing boats bobbed serenely on the Pacific swells. Occasionally, George brought his son along on these excursions, and Young Will quickly developed a genuine fondness for the hilly, wild terrain. It wasn't until 1878, when George built a wharf on the bay, that his wife, Phoebe, came to visit, by steamer. Hearst raised cattle on the land, added more acreage, put up some modest buildings and eventually had a thriving ranch operation.

When W. R. had become publisher of the San Francisco *Examiner*, it became his habit to invite a boatload of friends down to San Simeon for a weekend of roughing it in the hills. One particular hill, a rise that provided a view of the bay on one side and a breathtaking panorama of the Santa Lucia mountains on the other, became a favorite camping and picnicking site. W. R.'s version of camping out was slightly less rugged than that of his father, who made do with building a campfire and unrolling a blanket beside it. When W. R. Hearst went camping at San Simeon, he usually brought along three tents, all with wooden floors, each divided into four bedrooms and a bath. Meals were served under a huge circus tent, which also served at night as a theater for showing movies, which would be projected on one of the canvas walls.

In early 1919, Hearst, who was then fifty-six, decided that he was getting a bit old to be sleeping in tents, and contacted architect Julia Morgan about designing some type of permanent structure—nothing too fancy—for his favorite hilltop location.

Walter Steilberg, an associate of Morgan's, recalled the day Hearst first proposed a structure at San Simeon. Steilberg, in an adjacent room, could clearly hear Hearst's high-pitched voice as he explained what he had in mind:

> The other day I was in Los Angeles, prowling around second-hand bookstores, as I often do, and I came upon this stack of books called Bungalow Books. Among them I saw this one which has a picture—this isn't what I want, but it gives you an idea of my thoughts about the thing, keeping it simple—of a Jappo-Swisso bungalow.

Within a few weeks (during which time his mother died leaving him the bulk of the family fortune) and before Miss Morgan could really begin designing a structure, Hearst had some further ideas for his bungalow—perhaps there should be some guest accommodations, and he would also like to be able to display his huge and growing art collection there. All of this called for something more elaborate than a bungalow.

The first of three guesthouses went up that year; in the next two years two more were constructed, and by that time, work on the main house—the Casa Grande—had begun. Work on the elaborate gardens and pools was also progressing. Construction involved a veritable army of workers, since all supplies had to be brought in by steamer, then hauled five miles up the hill. In addition to the inherent difficulties of massive construction in a remote location, the task was made more difficult by Hearst's maddeningly mercurial ideas about the building's design. Once, while inspecting construction on the Casa Grande with Miss Morgan, Hearst admired the mountain view and told her he wanted to have his living quarters right there. "But this is the roof, Mr. Hearst," Miss Morgan replied. "Then add another story and raise the roof higher," Hearst ordered. On another occasion he had a garden wall built and torn down six times before he was satisfied, with what turned out to be the first design. The workers hated Hearst. His offhand orders to tear down something they had just built with meticulous care were too much for the craftsmen to take. Whole crews sometimes quit en masse, and Hearst went through five construction foremen in ten years, even though he paid wages considerably above the going rate.

Hearst moved into the Casa Grande on Christmas Eve, 1925, but construction on the castle continued until the 1930s financial crisis forced a temporary halt to the building. Perhaps "building" is a misnomer inasmuch as it implies a certain amount of organization and direction that was totally lacking at San Simeon. "Tinkering" would be a more appropriate verb. Hearst loved to tinker with his castle, putting up or tearing down a wall, a room or a new wing, to accommodate newly acquired art treasures or simply because he had become bored with things the way they were.

Even the most jaded Hollywood sophisticate must have felt a quiver of anticipation upon answering the telephone and hearing the polite voice of Hearst's private secretary: "If you are free this weekend, Mr. Hearst would like to invite you to be his guest at San Simeon."

Those were the golden days of San Simeon. Every weekend, fifty to a hundred guests, most of them members of the movie colony and friends of Marion Davies, would be invited to the "ranch," to be pampered and indulged in any or all of the numerous diversions Hearst could provide— swimming, camping, horseback riding, tennis, picnicking or just plain relaxing in luxury—all at the publisher's expense. The royal treatment began Friday night when a special train left Glendale station, carrying the guests north to San Luis Obispo. En route, Hearst thoughtfully provided a band for entertainment and an open club car for nourishment. A fleet of limousines transported the guests from San Luis Obispo to La Cuesta Encantada ("The Enchanted Hill"), where each was assigned a personal maid or valet upon arrival. On the five-mile drive up the hill, the limousines would pass through the borders of the world's largest private zoo, where lions, bears, pumas and leopards roamed in uncaged splendor.

Hearst himself did not usually mingle with the guests, who were free to amuse themselves in whatever diversion struck their fancy during the day. The only required activity was the late dinner each evening, which Hearst would preside over as lord of the manor. The dinner was held in the castle's Great Hall, where the guests ate off sixteenth-century monastery tables. In keeping with the "ranch" spirit, however, there was no tablecloth; paper napkins were used and catsup was dispensed straight from the bottle. After dinner, Hearst usually showed a movie, often a major studio production that had not yet been released. The epic *Gone With the Wind* was screened at San Simeon six months before its formal première, December 14, 1939, in Atlanta. (Apparently he had overcome his prejudice against the film. Two years earlier, worried by the preponderance of British actors in the cast, he had felt compelled to ask Louella Parsons, "Will not Clark Gable—almost a lone American in this foreign galaxy—feel considerably out of place in such an array of foreign talent? Is he not likely to emerge from intimate association with this British cast with a monocle in his off eye and an Oxford accent on his Anglicized tongue? May he [not] be expected henceforth to call the ladies of his acquaintance 'my deah gel' and the gentlemen 'old top' eh what?")

The golden days wound down when the corporation teetered on the brink of bankruptcy at the end of the 1930s. Then, during World War II, Hearst abandoned San Simeon in favor of his Wyntoon retreat, fearing the Japanese might try to shell his castle in retaliation for the Hearst newspapers' anti-Oriental editorial stance.

He returned to his beloved San Simeon after the war, but within two years moved to Beverly Hills at the insistence of his doctors.

Hearst's grandson, Bunky, who had been living with his grandfather following the divorce of his parents, stayed on at the castle until the school year finished—one small twelve-year-old boy in a huge castle.

After Hearst died, his sons continued to use the castle for long weekends and summer vacations, sometimes staying a month or two at a time. Randy and his wife, Catherine, came with the children and liked to "honeymoon" in the Cloister; Bill and Bootsie preferred Hearst's own Gothic suite. Fun-loving George staked out the Doge Suite as his preserve, and everyone took to calling it "Chez George"; its noteworthy characteristic was that one could always be assured of getting a drink there.

But still, the castle was not a home. It had been built to William Randolph Hearst's own peculiar specifications. Its frequently garish combinations of architectural styles and antique furnishings were tailored to the tastes of just one man. For anyone except Hearst, it just wasn't a homey atmosphere. "Like growing up in a museum," was the way Bill recalled his younger days at San Simeon. Certainly none of Hearst's sons possessed the funds to keep up the castle, and even if Dick Berlin had been inclined to spend corporate money maintaining the castle for the family—which he decidedly was not—it is unlikely that any of the children would have wanted to make it their permanent residence. It was, after all, in a remote part of the state, two hundred miles from either Los Angeles or San Francisco. This was no hardship for someone like Hearst, who more or less saw the world, or at least all of it that mattered, revolving around himself, wherever he might be. But for less exalted beings—especially those, like his sons, who enjoyed the pleasures of cosmopolitan living—distance from any large city was a major handicap.

In his will, Hearst had expressed the desire that his castle be donated to the University of California as a memorial to his mother. The university regents, however, declined the gift, on the grounds that it would be prohibitively expensive to maintain.

The corporation then tried to sell the castle, attracting a parade of prospective buyers who came by to try it on for size. There was a Texas millionaire who envisioned a resort hotel; another Texas oilman thought he might like to live in the castle; a group of high-ranking army officers thought it would be nice as a western retreat for Pentagon brass, but despaired of getting the necessary congressional appropriation. The disadvantage in turning the palace into a resort was its remote location on the undeveloped coast. The enormous upkeep was an added burden. Property taxes alone were $40,000 a year.

When it seemed clear that no one would step forward to buy the castle, Dick Berlin, who was not disposed to maintaining a thirty-million-dollar weekend home for the Hearst family, as much as it might enhance their status as a bona fide dynasty, began casting about for suitable donees with the wherewithal to keep up the monument. The state of California seemed the most likely recipient, if only a convincing case could be made that the castle was a historical monument. Berlin approached Goodwin Knight, governor of California, and Knight turned the matter over to Newton Drury, chief of the state Division of Beaches and Parks, a position that placed him in charge of the state park system, which encompassed state historical monuments.

It was one of those lucky twists of fate that Drury was well disposed toward the Hearsts, since he had personal ties with the family that antedated William Randolph Hearst. Drury's father had known George Hearst in Virginia City and had later been a reporter on the San Francisco *Examiner*. His mother was a second cousin to Phoebe Hearst, and during Drury's days at the University of California, Phoebe had hired him to tutor the Hearst sons during summer vacations.

Drury, it turned out, was probably the only person in the State Parks system, or maybe even in the whole California state government, who was eager to preserve the San Simeon castle. From the beginning, he faced either ambivalence or outright hostility to the idea of the state taking it over. The Parks Commission, which had to approve the gift, was dubious. At one of the first Parks Commission meetings at which the gift was discussed, one of the members expressed grave reservations about a scheme to monumentalize William Randolph Hearst, and he sharply demanded to know what was so historic about the house Drury was proposing to have dedicated as a historical monument. Drury could only reply, "Well, for one thing, you can be sure it'll never happen again."

Drury eventually constructed a rather elaborate rationale for preserving the castle; according to his theory it was an architectural masterpiece, a geologic wonder, an uncatalogued museum and a link to the days of the gold rush, all rolled into one.

Still, there was resistance to the proposed gift, and much of it went beyond the strong suspicion that the state was getting a colossal white elephant. "There was, frankly, some resistance to the name William Randolph Hearst," Drury acknowledged. "He was not universally loved in California, you know."

Joe Knowland, chairman of the Parks Commission, and publisher of the Oakland *Tribune*, was one of those who did not love Hearst, although his opposition could have been tinged with professional jealousy. Nonetheless, he was in a position to make trouble, and at one point threatened to unleash his newspaper in an all-out war against the gift.

Even Drury had doubts, which he kept carefully concealed, regarding the charge that the castle was a "white elephant" being dumped on the state. He had confidently based his cost and revenue projections on the assumption that up to five hundred people per day would visit the castle, and pay $2 a head for adults and $1 for children. Whether the five-hundred figure was realistic could be questioned, and it was. Drury privately worried that it was a very real possibility the public would stay away—would find the drive too long or would boycott the castle in a show of disdain for Hearst.

While he was attempting to "sell" the castle to the Parks Commission and state legislature, Drury also faced initial resistance from the Hearst Corporation board, some of whose members wanted to hold out for a cash settlement. He eventually convinced them they would be lucky to find a willing taker for the property, let alone anyone who would pay for it.

Drury had to lobby the Parks Commission members one by one, but by May 1954 he had convinced them in principle to accept the castle as a gift, and the legislature passed a resolution authorizing the commission to proceed with details of the transfer. It took another three years of negotiation, however, before an agreement was reached on exactly how much land would go with the castle, how many antiques and other details. The final agreement transferred 123 acres of land at the top of the hill, which included the three guesthouses, the main house, and a large number of antiques, together with a 30-acre area at the base of the hill to be used as an assembly site and parking lot.

* * *

When the castle was opened to the public on June 2, 1958, it immediately became clear that public interest in the Hearst home was greater than anyone had expected. More than one thousand people showed up the first day—twice as many as could be accommodated. Drury had to quickly revise the tour schedule and hire additional guides to accommodate the larger crowds. On some days, as many as twelve hundred people were ushered through the antique-lined castle, but since tickets were on a first-come, first-served basis, many disappointed tourists were still turned away each day.

During the first six months of operation, the Hearst castle drew 160,000 visitors, and far from being the expensive white elephant its critics had contended it would be, the castle actually became the only money-making operation in the entire state parks system.

Although the castle had become state property, the Hearsts still retained a proprietary feeling toward the buildings, and continued in casual conversation to refer to "their" castle. When Bill Hearst decided he would still like to stay in the "A" guest house when he was in the area, Drury helped arrange it by making Bill part of an "advisory" committee on San Simeon, which carried the privilege of staying in the guest bungalow. Drury was mildly amazed that no one ever questioned Bill's right to the house, since it belonged to the state and was maintained at taxpayer expense. But by general agreement, "A" house was closed to the public and reserved for the Hearst family's exclusive use for twenty years.

The Hearsts were able to exert proprietary clout in one other minor accomplishment that was nonetheless notable in that it showed the degree to which Marion Davies discomfited the family. Guides at the castle were firmly instructed never to mention Marion Davies' name on the tours. While the guides could authoritatively answer questions about the antique chairs, medieval ceilings, valuable tapestries or the dimensions of the castle, their response to a tourist's query about "that actress who lived with Mr. Hearst," would be a sudden hearing loss. History, as dispensed by the state guides at the San Simeon Historical Monument, was effectively rewritten to exclude the woman who had shared Hearst's life for thirty years.

(2)

By 1961, the Hearsts were still a family living in the shadow of the patriarch, now dead ten years. It was a family nervous and uneasy about the past and uncertain about the future. They were still trying to live down the stigma—more imagined than real—of Hearst's open relationship with Marion. That problem was dealt with by pretending that Marion did not exist. The future was a big question mark. In the ten years since their father died, none of the five sons had gained a position of real power in the Hearst Corporation. Jack had died in 1958. David was forced out as publisher of the *Herald-Express* in 1960 in favor of George Hearst, Jr. George senior, perpetually broke, and never having taken much interest in the company, was an alcoholic. Randy too was a heavy drinker and involved in corporation business only to the extent of having a title and getting paid. The only son who was actively participating in a job was Bill, and he was involved in writing his column, not running the company.

The person who did more than anyone else to keep the Hearsts out of power in the company was Dick Berlin. His strategy in dealing with the family was to "throw them a fish or two," as one of Berlin's friends described it.

Berlin remembered that old W. R. a few years before his death, in discussing his sons had said: "Bill likes to travel; let him travel." Traveling was Bill's fish, and he was content. Bill became something of the Hearst Corporation's ambassador to the world. He gave speeches, traveled throughout the country and organized the Hearst Task Force, which traipsed around the globe interviewing international leaders. A Hearst Task Force interview with Soviet Union leaders won a Pulitzer Prize in 1956.

The other Hearst sons were given well-paying jobs with little responsibility; they were not encouraged to concern themselves with the operation of the business.

For several years, the Hearsts were satisfied with the arrangement. They had grown up under the thumb of their father, who never gave them real decision-making power in the corporation. They were willing to concede that the executives knew more about the business than they did, so it seemed right that the Old Guard should run things for the time being.

The empire mourns. (1) Hearst's flagship, the New York *Journal-American*.
(2) Liberty swoons in a Burris Jenkins cartoon. (3) George, Bill, David and
Millicent leave Grace Cathedral, August 17, 1951.

4

(4) The family united in the mid-1920s: the twins, David and Randy, stand in front of John, William Randolph, Sr., Millicent, George and Bill. (5) Mother and sons shortly after the patriarch's death.

6

7

(6) Marion reaped a fortune from her liaison with Hearst. Here she inspects the Davies Building during its construction on one of her valuable Park Avenue lots. (7) In a club with Horace. (8) Joe Kennedy was her friend. At the inauguration, Marion stood with the Kennedy family.

8

9

(9) Richard Berlin, Hearst's successor, in 1955.

10

11

(10) The "black Irishman," John Francis Neylan. (11) Berlin's protégé, John Miller, with printer Johnnie Cuneo.

(12) Randy Hearst on assignment with Edmond Coblentz (second from right). (13) A.P. Giannini (right), president of the Bank of Italy, lent the Hearsts eight million dollars in 1939. This backing prevented Joe Kennedy from taking over the magazines.

(14) The Hearst minions in 1937. Berlin stands second from right. The "Napoleonic" Clarence Shearn is seated to the left of Hearst.

(15-17) The Hearst stars: Louella Parsons, Igor "Cholly Knickerbocker" Cassini and Dorothy Kilgallen.

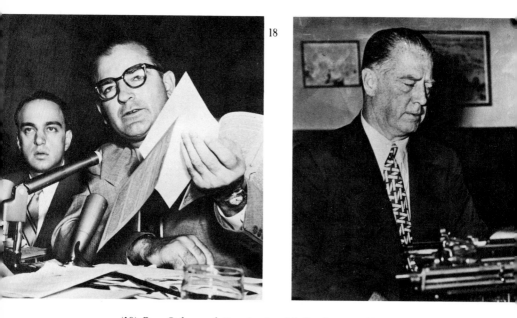

(18) Roy Cohn and Senator Joe McCarthy, two Hearst favorites.
(19) Westbrook Pegler. (20) Walter Winchell *was* the *Mirror*.

Hearst gave us the comics.

1

Hagar the Horrible

22

Blondie

Beetle Bailey

25

Popeye

Flash Gordon

26

(26) John and his Mercedes. Some considered him the brightest of the sons. (27) David (far left) and George and Randy (right) smile through another dedication. (28) Bill Hearst on the telephone, reporting from Berlin.

27

28

30

29

(29) John Hearst and his third wife, Fanne, on vacation in Palm Springs. (30) A beaming Bill Hearst and wife, Austine ("Bootsie"), in 1949 with new-born heir, William Randolph Hearst III. (31) John "Bunky" Hearst, Jr., logged several years as an award-winning photographer on the New York *Mirror* before it folded in 1963. (32) Hearst executives were happy to unload the Hearst Castle, which they considered a gigantic white elephant, onto the state of California. To almost everyone's surprise, it became a wildly successful tourist attraction from the first day it was opened to the public in 1958.

31

32

33

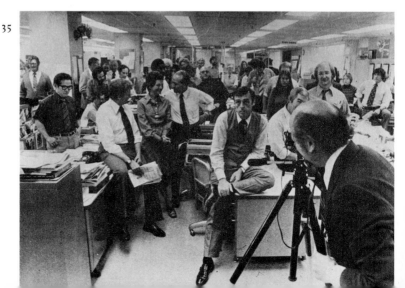

(33) Leonard Woodcock and Walter Reuther were among labor leaders from throughout the country who lent their support to *Herald-Examiner* strikers. (34) The strike became a *cause célèbre* among liberal Los Angeles citizens.

(35) Reg Murphy (seated on desk) was the subject of a lavish *New West* article shortly after taking over the helm of the San Francisco *Examiner*. An *Examiner* photographer snapped this picture of the *New West* photographer setting up a shot.

34

35

36   37   38

(36) That Cosmo Girl: Helen Gurley Brown. Spinning end-less variations on the theme that any girl can get her man, she transformed moribund *Cosmopolitan* into the biggest, splashiest success story in magazine publishing history. (37) San Francisco *Examiner* investigative reporter Lynn Ludlow worked with Willie Hearst on a 1976 series that probed water rights abuses by big agribusiness interests. (38) The new metropolitan editor, Frank Lalli, brought to his job a level of creativity and talent never before seen at the *Herald-Examiner.* (39) The Hearst Corporation pinned its hopes for reviving the *Herald-Examiner* on James G. Bellows, an editor of national stature with a reputation as a fixer of ailing newspapers.

39

(40) Bill Hearst traveled the world as the Hearst Corpora-tion's goodwill ambassador.

40

(41) Randy Hearst (center, facing camera), Rosalie Hearst (behind Randy), and George Hearst, Sr. (left, back to camera), participated in the Hearst Senate Youth Program.

(42) Unpretentious Bill Hearst could be comfortable discussing his tight shoes with President Kennedy.

43

44

(43) Phoebe Cooke, eldest grand-daughter of William Randolph Hearst, Sr., works tirelessly to uphold "Hearst traditions." (44) Randy Hearst and his wife, Catherine, hobnobbed with titled nobility, including the Duke and Duchess of Windsor.

(45) The grande dame of New York society, Millicent Hearst, didn't hesitate to match tiaras with Queen Frederika of Greece (left).

45

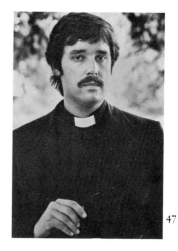

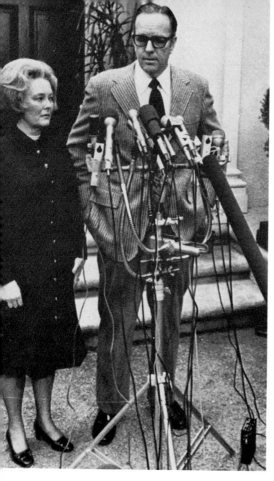

47

(46) Catherine and Randy Hearst had the press camped in their front yard for weeks after their daughter Patricia was kidnapped. (47) Young Episcopal priest Ted Dumke counseled Patty while she was in jail and later officiated at her wedding. (48) News-hound Ed Montgomery, who won the first Pulitzer Prize ever for a Hearst newspaper, in 1951, was chasing radicals in the 1960s, but found his sources had dried up by the time of the Hearst kidnapping.

49

(49) Patty's brother-in-law, Jay Bosworth, was an *Examiner* reporter when she was kid-napped.

(50) The vast food giveaway, one of the conditions for her release demanded by Patty's kidnappers, sparked confusion that led to rioting. (51) Randy Hearst grumbled when the San Francisco *Examiner* ran pictures of Patty following her capture in which she appeared vibrant and defiant and definitely not as brainwashed as he was sure she was.

(52) The staff at *Outside* magazine: (left to right) Mike Rogers, Virginia Team, Willie Hearst, Jack Ford and Terry McDonell. (53) The new Hearst team: (left to right) Gilbert Mauer, John Miller, Frank Bennack and Richard Deems.

And then, too, it was a comfortable life being a Hearst—high pay, good hours, lots of travel opportunities. Eventually, so all the Hearsts thought, the Old Guard would start bringing the family, at least those who were interested, into positions of real power in the corporation.

But Berlin thought differently. While the Hearsts were occupied being Hearsts, the adopted son was consolidating his hold on the corporation. By the late 1950s, the family sadly realized that Berlin had the trustees "in his pocket" and showed no sign of relinquishing any of the power he had accumulated.

As Bill later assessed the situation, the family's difficulties stemmed from the fact that they had no experience in office politics, while Berlin was a master of the art.

For the family, the worst part of their predicament was not specifically that they had no real power, but that they were kept in the dark about what was happening with the company. Berlin told them only what he felt they needed to know, which was considerably less than they felt they deserved to know. If the family didn't expect to have real power, they at least expected consideration, and they weren't getting it.

The eight executive members of the thirteen-member board of directors (which was identical with the board of trustees at the time) even took to holding meetings without informing family members, who found out about the meetings only by reading the board minutes.

At meetings the family attended, they were puzzled by the ease with which they were outvoted 8–5 on measure after measure, the executives voting together with little debate and no dissent. They were outraged when they discovered the reason why: the executives were holding their own meeting ahead of time at Berlin's apartment, where they thrashed out their differences and decided on a bloc vote on all the important issues.

Ironically, it had been Randy's initial protest that tipped control of the board forever out of the hands of the family. With an 8–5 majority, the executive faction could fill any vacancy in their ranks with anyone of their choosing, regardless of the family's opinion. This meant someone chosen by Dick Berlin. Had the executive majority been only 6–5, a vacancy in the executive ranks would have left a deadlock, allowing the position to either go unfilled or be filled by someone acceptable to the family.

As it was, the executive faction, with its huge majority, could afford to ignore the family, and regularly did.

As time passed, Berlin became more arrogant toward the Hearsts. While relations were cordial on the surface, the company president often told his friends that the Hearsts "didn't know up from down," and regaled them with examples of what he considered prime Hearst lunacies. This type of talk sometimes got back to the Hearsts, who could only seethe in rage and frustration.

The Hearsts were handicapped in their opposition to Berlin by an intense amount of intrafamily bickering and disputes. Several of the wives couldn't stand one another, and the sons blamed one another for being either lazy or pompous, depending on who was criticizing whom. After John died, his children and wife felt, with considerable justification, that they were getting "pushed around," by the company and the rest of the family. Berlin gloated at the internecine quarrels, and was fond of the mot "the family is its own worst enemy."

The Hearsts grumbled among themselves that Berlin had become power-hungry; they were tired of hearing him talk about how smart he was. They were astounded when he got license plates for his limousine that read "NYC 1." "Maybe he thought he was the Mayor," commented one Hearst sardonically; but there was absolutely nothing, or so it seemed, that they could do.

One of the fish Berlin tossed the family was that they could at least pretend to have power within the corporation. Bill, especially, traded heavily on this pretense of power, and it worked. To most people outside the corporation, and in fact to many within the company—at middle-management level and below—William Randolph Hearst, Jr., was the head of the Hearst organization.

In late 1958, a researcher for *Time* magazine was assigned to find out what was happening in the Hearst Corporation. She correctly ascertained that a power struggle between Bill Hearst and the executors of W. R.'s will had been taking place. However, her conclusion was that Bill had been winning every skirmish so far and, "in other words, our dope is that the lifetime executors of the Old Man's were as dead as the Chief, only they didn't know it. Our sources say that Dick Berlin, Gorty, Carrington and the rest of the Old Guarders will have to buy the papers to see what's in 'em hereafter."

One of the researcher's chief sources had been Frank Conniff, Bill's

right-hand editorial assistant, so it would be fair to assume that her conclusion represented nothing so much as wishful thinking in the Hearst
camp.

(3)

Among the "Hearst Service"—a self-designation used by many of the
top Hearst editors, columnists and reporters—the early betting had been
on John Hearst to succeed his father as head of the organization.

"I always thought Jack was going to be the one to take over the
empire from his father," recalled Adela Rogers St. Johns. "He was
brighter, quicker to see a thing. He was the most like his father."

Bill Hearst, she felt, although he was "utterly trustworthy and
dedicated," was "not very bright," at least compared to Jack.

Miss St. Johns was far from the only person who rated Jack the most
capable of the Hearst sons. Even Dick Berlin considered Jack "the only
one with something on the ball."

Jack impressed the people he worked with. He acted deliberately, as
if he always knew exactly what he was doing. Physically, he was a com-
manding presence—a blond six-footer, built like a running back, with a
deep, resonant voice. He just looked and sounded like someone who
should be in charge.

Nonetheless, in the years before W. R. died, insofar as any of his
sons could be considered an heir apparent, it was Bill, not John. The
difficulty with John, as his father saw it, was that "he's got the ability,
but he just won't work. He's lazy."

Lazy. It was a charge that would be hurled at the middle Hearst son
all his life. His first wife, the beautiful and vivacious Dorothy Hart, left
him because she couldn't stand him staying in bed until noon every
day. No ambition. She then married a man with ambition to spare—Bill
Paley, president of Columbia Broadcasting Systems.

In his defense, Jack would argue that he wasn't lazy, he just wasn't
given anything to do. Why should he come into the office to sit around?
Jack Hearst wasn't the kind of person who would put up with make-
work projects.

There was more than a touch of bitterness in Jack's attitude toward
his father and for that matter the whole Hearst organization. In its
simplest terms, Jack felt betrayed.

Jack had never wanted to go into the publishing business. As a teen-ager, he had begun to exhibit a decided talent for drawing cartoons and artwork. His mother thought he should become an architect. Jack also had an interest in geological engineering, and he read widely on the subject. Of course, his father wanted him to join the family business— the magazines, W. R. argued, would be the perfect place in which to put his artistic talents to work. Jack didn't completely buy that argument, but his father also dangled a more tempting inducement—a salary of $100,000 a year.

It was 1928, Jack was nineteen years old and enjoyed material comforts as much as the next person. Jack took the bait. He dropped out of college and became president of the Stuyvesant Company, the Hearst organization which oversaw *Town & Country, Harper's Bazaar, Home & Field*, and *Connoisseur & International Studio* magazines. Later he moved to vice-president of International Magazine Company, which controlled the bigger magazines—*Cosmopolitan, Good Housekeeping* and others. In the fall of 1932, he became assistant to the general manager of all the Hearst newspapers.

When the financial crunch hit in late 1937, one of the first belt-tightening measures instituted was to slash the sons' high salaries down to $15,000. Here was the betrayal. Jack had dropped out of college, given up a possible career as an architect, for money. Now, suddenly, that money was gone. His father had frittered away a fortune.

And still, Jack was trapped in the family business, since $15,000 was more than he could make anywhere else.

Jack's second marriage in 1933 to Gretchen Wilson ended four years later amid much bitterness and recrimination. There was one child, John junior, known as "Bunky," born in 1934. In 1938 he married model Fanne Wade; together they had three more children: Joanne, born 1939, William Randolph Hearst II, born in 1942, and Debra, in 1950.

After the financial crisis, Jack began to withdraw from involvement with the Hearst Corporation. With his mother's backing, he began dabbling in real estate, which eventually occupied him full time.

The 1950s in many ways were good years for John Hearst. His daughter Joanne recalled that her father was usually happy, remembered especially his "infectious laugh," and guessed that he probably "had more fun than any of his brothers, except maybe George." Jack was constantly on the move, checking out real estate or vacationing, usually with his wife. Occasionally he performed some public-relations function for the Hearst foundations, such as accompanying his mother in May of 1956 to present a collection of tapestries, valued at $500,000, to the Detroit Institute of Arts.

Nominally, his position with the Hearst Corporation was "assistant general manager of the Hearst newspapers," although he spent far more time working on real estate and, in at least one case, on an oil-lease deal. He had one oil lease on the grounds of the Abilene, Texas, public golf course, while another was on the property of an orphanage. Although Jack hoped the orphanage well especially would hit so "the place will derive 12½ percent of all the oil we get out of it," neither site proved successful.

In all the real-estate deals, Millicent held a veto power that sometimes exasperated Jack. In one case, she turned thumbs down on an opportunity to buy a large tract of land near Camden, which Jack thought was a good deal. He complained good-naturedly that she would want to "buy Fort Knox for a dollar down and a dollar a month," but his mother remained adamant.

His letters about other family members often were strewn with incisive and caustic humor.

From a letter dated only "Nov. 16":

> Billy had his birthday party and his brat friends were just as bad this year as they have ever been. I had five of them in tow all afternoon and believe me, never again. What with them throwing peanuts all over the Polo Grounds and banging one another over the head with the programs, it was a real gone nightmare. Why I had to pay good money for seats for a football game I'll never know. They never saw five minutes of it and could have raised just as much havoc on a park bench.

His views in February 1956 about his brother Bill and wife:

> We saw Uncle Bill and Aunt Bootsie and Randy off at the airport night before last as they started on their round the world flight. Your mother was green with envy but I for one would not care to be on that trip. Aunt Bootsie is difficult enough at home without having to be her traveling companion for the next 30 or 40 days. It should be interesting, however, and you can follow Gullables travels in your local Hearst Sunday paper.

Discussing his son Bunky in January 1957:

> Bunky is taking this being inducted into the army as a personal affront. I wouldn't be surprised if he never spoke to Eisenhower again. He is being taken from us just as he was on the verge of doing nothing.

Then in April of the same year: "Bunky has been assigned to some outfit in Long Island City and your mother is sure he thinks he is going to live here. *But,* he is not. Of course, we all love him, but enough is too much."

On a postcard from Puerto Rico showing a lush hillside with one small shack: "Here is a picture of our new home in the Islands. The house needs a little fixing, but you know how handy Mom is with money."

If there was a darker side to Jack Hearst's life, it was his health. He was afflicted with a variety of chronic conditions, including asthma and a tendency to perspire profusely, which in turn made him highly susceptible to colds, flu and chest infections. He took a number of drugs for the ailments and apparently developed a dependency on some of them. In addition, he had a heavy drinking habit, which he sporadically battled—at one point he spent time at an alcoholic treatment farm in upstate New York.

The drugs sometimes left him tired to the point that he was unable to stay awake for more than an hour or two at a time. He complained that he didn't see a single entire game of the 1957 World Series because he kept falling asleep.

Much of the time, Jack stayed in bed the entire day, reading newspapers, conducting some business and drinking large quantities of soda water, which he bought by the five-gallon bottle. He said he needed the rest because of his health problems. His wife, though, sometimes complained that he was just lazy.

In the fall of 1958, Jack was feeling better than he had felt for some time. Some earlier marital difficulties had been resolved, and his children were doing well in school. He and Fanne took a trip to the Virgin Islands for a vacation and to look at a house in St. Thomas. They were staying at the Virgin Isle Hotel in St. Thomas on November 12. In the middle of the night, Hearst got out of bed, grabbed his stomach and pitched forward onto the floor in pain. Within moments he was dead. An autopsy determined the cause as a pancreatic attack.

(4)

David Hearst, known in family circles as "Buddy," was always the quiet one. He led a relatively simple life, was married only once, and kept his name out of the society columns. Definitely different from the rest of the family.

From an early age, Buddy displayed one prominent un-Hearstian characteristic—an appreciation of money—a noticeable lack of the care-free spending habits that afflicted his brothers. In fact, his brothers some-times called him "Rockefeller," out of amusement, admiration or envy of the fact that Buddy always managed to conserve his allowance and have a few dollars left over.

Eventually Buddy became the wealthiest of the five Hearst sons due to his simple life style, prudent investments and an inheritance from his grandmother that remained out of the clutches of his father. Phoebe left property to each of her five grandsons, but during the financial crunch, Hearst persuaded the three oldest sons to turn over their inheritances to him. The twins, David and Randy, were too young to legally relinquish their properties.

Reporters at the Los Angeles *Herald-Express*, where David was publisher during the 1950s, considered him downright cheap. One em-ployee recalled how Hearst made a couple of reporters spend several days looking for some place he could get a Johnson outboard motor at a dis-count.

"Sure, Buddy has money," a family member commented. "He's only been married once and doesn't fool around with girl friends. Do you have any idea how expensive girl friends are?"

Born in New York City, December 2, 1915, David Hearst was originally named Elbert, after one of Phoebe Hearst's uncles. Elbert wasn't pleased with the name, and he legally changed it to David when he became a teen-ager. As a youngster, Buddy was perpetually over-shadowed by his twin, Randy, who did better in school and was a better athlete. Upon entering St. George's Preparatory School at Newport, Rhode Island, David only placed in the first form, while Randy made it into the second.

After St. George's, David went on to Princeton, quit in 1936 and joined the staff of the New York *Journal* as a cub reporter. The next year he went to the Baltimore *News-Post*, where he worked in a number of positions before transferring to the Los Angeles *Herald-Express* in 1939.

In March 1938, David married seventeen-year-old Hope Chandler, a showgirl in a Manhattan nightclub. He had been dating her for almost a year, but had been ambivalent about marriage until she was featured on the cover of *Life* Magazine that December, where she was billed as "The Prettiest Girl in Paradise"—Paradise being the nightclub. The article apparently convinced Hearst, who was then twenty-two, that if he didn't marry the girl soon, someone else surely would. The couple had two children—a daughter, Millicent, born in 1939, and a son, David, born in 1944.

Beginning in 1939, David quietly advanced through a series of executive positions on the *Herald-Express*—business manager, general manager, vice-publisher and finally, in 1950, he succeeded Dr. Frank Barham as publisher.

A jovial six-footer, Hearst was an ardent golfer, took an interest in tennis and was sports-minded enough to serve on the 1956 Southern California Committee for the Olympic Games. He learned to fly, and in 1957 he qualified for the national "Mach-Busters Club" by piloting a jet F-100F Super Sabre at close to 1,000-miles-per-hour over the Mojave Desert, thus becoming one of the first nonmilitary flyers to surpass the speed of sound.

Hearst also took an active role in a number of small, direct charities —providing a bell for St. Timothy's Catholic Church, securing a headquarters for the local Boy Scout council, raising money for asthmatic and crippled children.

However, as a publisher, Hearst could most charitably be called a caretaker. Under his stewardship, the *Herald-Express* continued as it had always gone. Unfortunately, what was appropriate in the '30s and tolerable in the '40s was sadly out of date by the 1950s. The style of the paper, in the words of one reporter, was "phony Hearst." That is, big headlines, lots of crime stories, but no substance, no real muckraking or campaigning. Newsplay and story selection were dictated by sleazy and unethical criteria. It was a standing rule that no stories involving advertisers or potential advertisers could be printed without consent of the ad department. And definitely unfavorable stories about advertisers were not allowed. A businessman who was in trouble with the law or was involved in some other difficulties could be assured of kid-glove treatment from the *Herald-Express* if he took out a large ad. In one case the paper ran a laudatory profile of a car dealer who had just been indicted, on the same day as his full-page ad.

Herald-Express reporters felt that they were the poor cousins to the other Hearst paper in town, the *Examiner*. *Examiner* salaries generally ran at least 50 percent above those at the *Her-Ex*; it also provided better equipment and higher expense accounts. A former reporter described the *Herald-Express* as "such a penny-pinching operation that it was a major project to get a new typewriter ribbon."

Reporters from the *Examiner* looked down at the *Herald-Express* and its staff. Said one *Examiner* reporter, "By and large, it [the *Herald-Express*] was staffed by the absolute dregs, guys who couldn't get jobs anywhere else."

Her-Ex reporters generally viewed *Examiner* people as overpaid and underworked snobs and consoled themselves by telling one another that the *Herald-Express* was a more fun place to work in. To a large extent this was probably true. The *Her-Ex* city room was the scene of innumerable practical jokes; there were squirt-gun fights every Friday; at least one reporter took pride in growing a marijuana plant on his desk; and standard equipment for reporters and photographers covering the autumn brushfires was a station-wagon-load of beer.

As the 1950s drew to a close, profits of the *Herald-Express* dropped sharply.

It was a situation that worried Dick Berlin and the New York executives, and it provided them the opportunity to dump David and advance another Hearst who was more to their liking—George Hearst, Jr., the eldest grandson of old W. R.

It fell on Randy to break the news to his twin, that he was out as publisher. David did not take the news well, but there was nothing he could do. Berlin had made a decision, and as usual, he had the votes on the board of trustees to back him up.

After retiring as publisher at the age of forty-five, David fell into a depression and became something close to a recluse, venturing out for public functions only occasionally, seemingly content to play golf, entertain a few close friends and stay near his Beverly Hills home. The company opened an office near his home, and David went there to work when the mood struck him. He was, after all, still a vice-president of the Hearst Corporation.

(5)

"Fun-loving" and "good-natured" were adjectives that people used to describe George Hearst, when they were trying to be nice. Otherwise, they used words like "drunkard," "pathetic" or "stupid."

The eldest son of W. R. Hearst was held in low esteem by the rest of the family, who worried a great deal about his drinking and the type of women he hung around with and often married. A family joke went something to the effect: "Put George blindfolded in a room with ninety-nine debutantes and one whore and he'll go straight to the whore." His own mother said she was sure that George would die in a gutter someplace, and she just hoped it wouldn't be too embarrassing to the rest of the family.

A diabetic, and extremely overweight, George by 1951 had also become an alcoholic. Ironically, owing to his diabetic condition, which was not well controlled, he often appeared to be drunk when he wasn't, the symptoms of an insulin reaction being somewhat similar to those of intoxication. As it was, he was drunk often enough, sometimes going on benders for days or a week at a time, and afterward having no recollection of events during that period.

Friends could laugh at some of the predicaments flowing from George's boozing. There was the time he lent a friend his car while under the influence; after sobering up and discovering the vehicle gone, he reported it to the police as stolen. The cops arrested his astounded friend a few hours later in Bakersfield and clamped him in jail until the matter was eventually resolved. On another occasion, George brought home some supplies for a party that he and wife Sally were hosting that evening, but forgot the vermouth. Sally sent him back to the liquor store, and that was the last she saw of him for three days. When George finally returned home, he had the vermouth under his arm, but no explanation for what occurred in the intervening three days. It was humor etched with pathos— an unfolding tragedy, apparent to almost everyone except George Hearst.

"I used to think I was happy," George noted some twenty years later. "No one could tell me I wasn't having a good time."

In the years immediately following his father's death, George became embroiled in several disputes with wives and ex-wives, disputes that could have been the raw material for a stage comedy. It started in March

1951, when he married wife number four, Sandra Rambeau Spencer, in Juarez, Mexico. Previously there had been Blanche Wilbur, the mother of his twin children, George junior and Phoebe. He and Blanche were divorced in 1929. Then came Lorna Velie and Sally Alvarez Kirkham, with whom he split in 1949.

The marriage to Sandra Rambeau lasted but seven months, at the end of which he sought a Mexican annulment; four hours later, he married longtime friend and actress Colette Lyon. However, Sandra challenged the annulment, citing a Mexican law that required that she be given a day's notice for each 40 kilometers between her home (which was in Delano) and the Juarez courthouse. The distance—1,568 kilometers—entitled her to thirty-nine days' notice and she had only been told of the proceeding two days in advance. Sandra fought the case through the Manhattan Supreme Court, which sided with her, canceling the annulment and George's marriage to Colette. Sandra then turned around and divorced the hapless George, citing nonsupport, cruelty and abandonment, and was granted $500 a month support. George faced up to the additional alimony as best he could and married Colette again.

Meanwhile, Sally Kirkham, growing restless because George never managed to make his alimony payments to her, filed suit to break the family trust and recover money owed her. In what was to become a landmark decision, the federal district court ruled in August 1954 that the "spendthrift" provision in Hearst's will made the family trust safe from all creditors.

The litigation unnerved some of the other Hearst family members, who began to perceive George's growing list of ex-wives as a threat to the estate, and were convinced that George was an easy target for women out to make some fast bucks. In order to protect George from himself, his children—at the urging of their mother, Blanche—and Randy, got a lawyer and drew up a document in 1955 by means of which George renounced all rights to his share of future income from a trust set up by W. R. for Marion Davies, which would revert to the five sons upon her death. Instead, all rights to the "M. D. Trust" were given to his children, George junior and Phoebe. The document was written in a way that allowed the children, at their option, to take their father's money, although they would not necessarily do so. The alleged purpose of the arrangement—which George signed while sick and under threat of being entirely disinherited by his mother—was to put George's wife and all potential wives on notice that he had absolutely no money except what the family consented to give him.

It was a bitter pill for George to swallow, at what must certainly have been the low point in his life to date—his marriage to Colette on the rocks; his health poor; his own children, mother and brothers writing him off as an incompetent; and to top everything off, being virtually broke. When he wondered how his life ended up the way it had, the man he blamed was his father.

As the eldest son, George bore the brunt of his father's impossible expectations. Indulged as a child, he went to Berkeley for a year, then was hustled into the family business at age nineteen, when his father decided, in early 1924, to put him to work as business manager of the San Francisco *Examiner*. By May of that year, the Chief decided that George wasn't cutting the mustard. In a telegram to Neylan, he conceded that George would never succeed as a business manager and that a competent executive would have to replace him if the paper was to survive. In that same wire he harped once more on his constant theme—that George needed to develop a sense of responsibility—even though the son was no more irresponsible than the father had been at age nineteen or twenty.

The Chief even toyed with the idea of making George get a job in some outside company, reasoning that if he was in some business where he had no financial stake to rely on—where he would have to sink or swim like anyone else—he would do much better. That, of course, was something Hearst himself had never been forced to do—to work for someone else and comply with someone else's rules.

Hearst decided, however, that it would be better to keep George in the family business, where he could more readily be browbeaten into line. It didn't work. George was transferred to Los Angeles, then to New York, where he was president of the New York *American,* and in 1929 back to San Francisco, where he became publisher of the *Examiner.* Nicknamed "Fanny" by friends and family, George acquired a reputation for joviality, sometimes treating the entire composing room to drinks at a nearby bar. But he never caught on in the newspaper business, and resignedly put up with it, as he told friends, only because "I have to be here."

George's real interest and talent lay in the nascent field of aviation.

He learned to fly in the middle 1920s. "From then on, I wanted to fly everything that was built," George recalled, "and they were throwing together some weird contraptions in those days." He once set a speed record flying from Oakland to Los Angeles. One of his more colorful aeronautical ventures was to sponsor and fly a powerful trimotored plane, "The Spirit of San Francisco," which was often used in rescue work. The plane was entered in the ill-fated 1928 "Dole Derby"—the first civilian attempt to span the Pacific from California to Honolulu—and was lost at sea with a crew of three.

In 1928, George formed the Avion Corporation with his mother-in-law Ada Wilbur and a couple of friends, John K. "Jack" Northrop and William Kenneth Jay. The company did research on and manufactured all-wing and all-metal aircraft, the most sophisticated flying equipment of the time. The company built four models of aircraft, one of which—an all-metal craft known as the Northrop Alpha—was used by Trans World Airlines.

About this time, Hearst decided that George was taking the aviation business altogether too seriously, and he pressured him back into the newspaper field. Avion was sold in 1930 to United Aircraft and Transport Corporation, the forerunner of giant United Industries.

Hearst reined in his son again when he began building speedboats in Oakland, and when he made plans to compete for fast mail contracts across the United States.

By 1936, George was at the Los Angeles *Examiner* again, being subjected to a training program devised by his father. Bart Guild, an executive on the *Examiner*, wrote Neylan that in addition to two hours of instruction by the head of the mechanical department, George was being subjected to a four-hour crash course in the whys and wherefores of newspaper publishing. Guild could almost see his friend's sarcastic smile. But Neylan only replied: "I hope that George Hearst takes advantage of the opportunity. I know of nobody who has neglected so many opportunities as George Hearst. I know that his father is always hopeful, and far be it from me to dampen any optimism."

And so it went, Hearst forcing George into jobs for which he had little aptitude and less interest, and squelching his tentative stabs at independent activities. A friend who knew George since the 1920s, summed up the number-one son's reaction: "Finally George said, if that's the way it's going to be, the hell with it, and went out and became a drunk."

George might well have fulfilled his mother's prediction that he would die in a gutter someplace, had it not been for his sixth and last wife, Rosalie Wynn, a woman of uncommon understanding and forcefulness.

Her influence on him began when George promised to give up drinking if she would marry him. Rosalie insisted he quit before they were married, and George—against all probability, based on past performance—went on the wagon for eight months, long enough to convince his future bride that he was serious about licking his drinking problem. They were married in 1960.

Rosalie had a profound affect on George Hearst's physical and emotional health. During the course of their marriage, George lost weight, brought his drinking and diabetes under control, and began to involve himself in activities such as the Hearst Foundation Senate Youth Program. "I wouldn't even be alive today if it hadn't been for her love and concern over my well-being," George concluded after ten years of marriage to Rosalie.

Upon George's death in 1972, Millicent paid her daughter-in-law a moving compliment, thanking her for "making my son into the man I knew he could be." Unfortunately, that man came along too late to play a role in the events that engulfed the Hearst Corporation after its founder's death.

(6)

Poised, self-assured and handsome, Randy Hearst was a natural aristocrat who grew up on the premise that whatever he needed in life would just come from somewhere without undue worry on his part. More often than not, he was right.

While his twin brother, David, was quiet and even repressed, Randy was a robust, ebullient youth who quickly accepted the perquisites of wealth, while refusing to be awed or intimidated by the lavish grandeur that permeated the world according to Hearst. A childhood friend remembers the time when he and a couple of school buddies called at the Hearst Sands Point house and found their hale companion, built like a bear, sleeping off the last night's party, stretched out on satin sheets that covered a dainty circular bed. He awoke; "Can you believe this place?" he said, shaking his head. He looked at it all that way.

After graduating from the Lawrenceville School in New Jersey, where a classmate remembers that Hearst "never did a damned thing and was proud of it," Randy went on to Harvard, on what basis no one seems quite sure.

A few months into the semester, one of the most popular students, an admiral's son, decided to leave for Annapolis; the Harvard men met to see him off, lament his loss and offer their condolences. Randy got up to console the group—"Don't worry," he assured them, "you still have me." He had that kind of poise.

"Even at that age," said Seward Brisbane, a Harvard classmate of Randy and son of columnist Arthur Brisbane, "he had more poise, more confidence than almost anyone I've ever known. He reminded you of Jack Kennedy [another Harvard classmate] in that sense."

Hearst made the Harvard swimming team and broke the school 50-yard free-style record. Some said that he was of Olympic caliber, but Randy never trained. He would come to the pool badly hung over after a weekend carouse, hit the water, and relying on natural strength and energy, outswim the men who had been working themselves to death.

He went about his academic work in much the same fashion. Brisbane remembers how Randy tackled one of the tougher philosophy courses, one in which Brisbane was interested, studied hard, but still didn't find easy. "The night before the exam Randy gave a cocktail party. He was sitting there with a drink in one hand and his notes in the other, in the middle of the women and music," Brisbane recalled. "And he yells to me, 'Hey Seaweed, what about this fellow Plato?' Even at that he scored a seventy-five."

Randy lasted just one semester. On leaving Harvard in 1934, he became assistant to the editor of the Hearst-owned Atlanta *Georgian* and quickly established himself as one of the city's most eligible bachelors. He met Catherine Campbell, the daughter of Morton R. Campbell, a comptroller for the telephone company, when she was sixteen and had just made her debut. They were married two years later, on January 12, 1938, after she graduated from Washington Seminary.

The newly wed Hearsts moved to San Francisco, where Randy had a job on the *Call-Bulletin*, and the first of five daughters, Catherine, was born in 1939.

During World War II, Captain Hearst flew for the Air Transport Command, ferrying planes to England, the only Hearst son to serve in the armed forces.

Randy returned home from the war, charged with energy and ready to sink his teeth into a new challenge, an important job in the New York office. But for some reason, his father wasn't ready to give him a responsible position just yet. It may have had something to do with their flap over the will. At any rate, the father's reluctance took a lot of the ambition out of Randy. "Sure he even thought about leaving [the Hearst Corporation]," reflected his brother Bill. "So did I. But there was always the problem, where else could we make so much money? Anyway, Randy went out to the Coast and stayed there."

From 1945 to 1947 Randy was associate publisher of the Oakland *Post-Enquirer*, then became executive editor of the *Call-Bulletin* and, in 1950, took the step up to publisher of the *Call-Bulletin*, replacing Edmond Coblentz, who opted for "semiretirement" as associate publisher, following half a century with Hearst.

If Coblentz needed a model for semiretirement, or even full retirement, he had a wonderful example in Randy Hearst. Newsmen on the *Call-Bulletin* knew Hearst as a playboy who preferred golf to his office, where in fact, he was seldom seen.

Coblentz and brother Bill tried mightily to get Randy to take an active interest in the business, but for the most part their coaxing, cajoling and badgering fell on deaf ears, or at least ears that were more attuned to the pleasures of drinking, duck hunting and golfing.

Randy had also become a family man in a big way. It was ten years after their first daughter was born that the second, Gina, came along in 1949. Patricia—whose notoriety would one day surpass even that of her grandfather—was born in 1954. Anne and Vicki arrived in successive years following.

Once in a while, Bill would be heartened by indications that Randy might be settling down and taking the family business seriously. In the summer of 1957, Bill wrote to Coblentz: "Randy has suddenly taken hold and comes in every day—at least for a while. He has put his teeth into the San Simeon publicity problem (tossed at him by the boys in New York) and is really on the ball. He is off to Mexico this week (with David) on a fishing and picture-taking expedition requested by *Sports Afield*. These are the kind of things he should do, and I am hoping he will keep it up. As you know, Cobbie, when Randy gets 'hopping mad' he can move mountains, but, as we both know, he doesn't stay mad long enough. So—we shall see."

What Randy may have lacked in the way of ambition and drive was more than compensated for by his wife, Catherine, a woman of unbridled energy, who was determined that her branch of the family would live up to the traditions established by Hearst forebears. She goaded her husband to claim his rights as a Hearst son; if she had anything to do with it, he wasn't going to slip into the malaise that devoured three of his brothers. And always, she kept a jealous eye on Bill and his vivacious wife, Bootsie, who seemed to consider themselves first among equals in regard to the rest of the Hearst family. And maybe they didn't even think the rest of the family equal at all.

Catherine was painfully conscious of her lack of any formal education beyond the Georgia convent school, and determined to overcome whatever shortcomings this might present. She cultivated herself relentlessly, read voraciously, and liked to describe herself as a serious student of Greek, Roman and Egyptian history, the Hapsburg dynasty, the kings of England and the Hawaiian monarchy. She resorted to the ambitious device of writing papers on the history of France, in French, for her own benefit, and made a great show of having mastered the heavens with her Questar telescope. She was especially fond of the Pleides—"They are so small and sparkling and perfect," she would say, "I am always at peace looking at them." But in her eagerness to present the image of a well-educated person, Catherine often pushed too hard, and struck people as a bit eccentric in the way, for example, she laced her conversation with random comments on such disparate subjects as astronomy and medieval history.

Perhaps taking a cue from Phoebe Apperson Hearst, as the model of a good Hearst woman, Catherine dabbled in good works. She was a trustee of the San Francisco Museums and the Ballet, and was considered a prime mover behind the San Mateo Society for Crippled Children and Adults—an interest sparked by the fact that her eldest daughter, Catherine, had been afflicted by a childhood condition which arrested her physical development.

But the work that, for Catherine, counted most, and the one that thrust her into the public eye, was the University of California. She was appointed to the Board of Regents in March 1956, to fill a vacancy left by the death of Edward A. Dickson. Apparently a few old debts went into the making of Regent Hearst—Governor Goodwin Knight, who made the appointment, was a friend of Edmond Coblentz and enjoyed weekends at the Coblentz country manor in Sonoma; as Lieutenant Governor under Earl Warren, Knight fought alongside Regent John Francis Neylan, the long-time Hearst attorney, to impose a loyalty oath on the university's faculty, a move to which Warren had been bitterly opposed. It also could not have hurt that Phoebe Hearst and the Hearst foundations had donated heavily to the university over the years.

Catherine is remembered as a regent who regularly attended meetings and was conscientious, but did not speak much for many years. She came into her own as a regent during the turbulent '60s as part of the clique that wrested the university from Clark Kerr and the liberal activists and turned it over to straight-shooting Ronald Reagan. To those who were baffled and confused by the sudden turmoil on the campuses, Catherine Hearst was a symbol, not so much for what she did, but for who she was. As the universities heated with wave upon wave of rebellion, Catherine stood out as a representative of all that had once been holy, a staunch defender of tradition and privilege.

From all accounts, Catherine is a woman to whom things like propriety, good form, tradition and social position are frighteningly real and of utmost importance. Quite likely, there is in her a certain insecurity stemming from the knowledge that the Hearsts as a family have not quite penetrated the very top circles of society; they never climbed into quite the same class as established San Francisco aristocrats like the De Youngs and the Crockers. Indeed, despite their fortune—which ranks in the billion-dollar bracket—one seldom hears the Hearsts mentioned in the same breath with the Vanderbilts, Mellons, Guggenheims or Rockefellers, some of whom they outweigh when it comes down to strict dollars and cents. Part of the problem is that the Hearsts have never taken root; they have spread their energies between New York and San Francisco, Washington and Los Angeles; they have never entrenched themselves and cultivated the sort of long-lasting connections and marriages that make the very wealthy a class apart. Another part of the problem is that certain vagaries had long been associated with the name Hearst, most of them the doing of W. R.—his open liaison with Marion, his politics, his newspapers. Catherine's almost militant conventionality and obsession with propriety could be explained as part of her attempt—whether conscious or unconscious—to cement the family's social status as genuine aristocrats.

To Catherine, the campus turmoil was something evil and sinister, in which she saw not only a challenge to long-held assumptions and attitudes, but a real threat to the essence of her being, to the things that gave her life meaning, to the terms that defined Catherine Hearst.

In 1967 Catherine introduced a resolution calling for the dismissal of students convicted of narcotics offenses. The resolution began: "The regents of the University of California are deeply concerned by reports of rapidly increasing use of dangerous and unlawful drugs by college and university students. The often tragic consequences of the use of such drugs are chronicled in the now-familiar accounts of bizarre behavior, degradation, impairment of mental faculties, injury and death." After heated debate, the regents passed a watered-down version of her resolution, which stopped short of demanding that students be dismissed for use of "dangerous drugs and narcotics," stating only that they should be "subject to disciplinary action, including dismissal from the University."

During antiwar demonstrations at the Berkeley campus, newsmen recall seeing Catherine, trying to appear incognito in dark glasses and babushka, observing the action from behind police lines. Such personal research led her to the conclusion that "immorality and Communism on campus" were assuming alarming proportions, although she failed to convince her fellow regents that this was a major problem.

At home her favorite topic of conversation became how the university was deteriorating, a condition she attributed to permissive professors. Ronald Reagan, she felt, was doing a great job trying to save the schools.

Meanwhile, Randy was still badly adrift, seemingly unable to find anything to hold his sustained interest. Occasionally something would catch his eye, and he would plunge into a frenzy of activity for a while. The Senate Youth Program was one such project—bright high-school kids were brought to Washington for a week in February with Hearst money to watch the government in action. Randy played a major role in organizing the program in 1962, working closely with Hubert Humphrey.

By the middle 1960s, serious problems had intruded on Randy's marriage. To begin with, in temperament, he and Catherine could hardly have been more dissimilar. He was genial, easygoing and tolerant, although he had a temper that could flare quickly, but would subside just as rapidly. Catherine was more obtrusive, strident, rigid. A militant Catholic, she insisted that their five daughters be raised in the Church and educated at Catholic schools. Randy, lackadaisical about religion in general, had been raised a nominal Episcopalian, had converted to Catholicism when he married Catherine, and became a nominal Catholic. Randy was also more comfortable with power and position, and certainly never had to push as hard as his wife.

One of Randy's habits—perhaps it was more of a hobby—that irritated Catherine no end was the way he was continually buying and selling property, especially houses. There was property in Mexico, where Randy kept a boat for fishing, a condominium in Hawaii, a vacation home at a ski resort. A family friend described Randy as "the world's greatest used-car dealer." When Catherine spoke of his habit, it was with an edge of sarcasm; she supposed he was out trading an orange grove for an elephant.

The corollary to Randy's trading habit was that he liked to travel, especially to visit his properties. Catherine disliked extensive traveling— a long weekend in Hawaii was an ordeal. As for Mexico, "it's not a country, it's a disease," she once said. Catherine's interests centered around reading and shopping, church and some good-works activities.

There were other strains within the family. Catherine had difficulty relating to her daughters, who were raised by governesses and educated in boarding schools. She basically was out of touch with their generation, and would go so far as to try to engage them in conversations about medieval history.

Perhaps the forces that tugged and pulled on the members of the Randolph Hearst family were no more severe than the strains afflicting any number of ordinary American families; but then, the Hearsts were not an ordinary American family, and not many families would ever face the type of stress that would confront the Hearsts in just a few years.

(7)

Bill finally stepped out of his father's shadow and laid down his credentials as a journalist in his own right when he brought home the Pulitzer Prize for International Reporting in 1956 for interviewing Khrushchev and other Russian leaders. It was only the second time anyone connected with Hearst had won the coveted journalism award.

Bill shared the award with J. Kingsbury Smith and Frank Conniff—the two who actually did most of the work—but it was the Hearst name that got the team to Russia in the first place.

The adventure started almost as a joke when Hearst journeyed to Washington in December of 1954 for the annual Gridiron dinner, and over drinks at the National Press Club bar with Dave Sentner, chief of the Hearst newspapers Washington bureau, the idea came up of asking for a Russian visa. They fully expected the request to be turned down—after all, C. L. Sulzberger of *The New York Times* had had his visa application on file for seven years—but they thought it would make a nice little item for Hearst's column. Much to the amazement of Hearst and Sentner, the visa was quickly granted—so quickly, in fact, that Hearst was alarmed. "I'm sure not going over there alone," he said, and insisted that visas be requested for Frank Conniff, his editorial assistant, and J. Kingsbury Smith, European general manager of International News Service, who had been to Moscow in 1947 to cover the Big Four foreign ministers' conference.

Again, amazingly, the visas for Conniff and Smith came through. Then the questions and headaches began. Should they go? What were they going for? What would they do there? The project had the Hearst hierarchy and family in turmoil, with most of the arguments coming down against going. Hearst's mother was afraid the devious Russians would use a woman to compromise her son and subject him to some sort of blackmail. There was also the possibility that the Russians might arrest him on some sort of trumped-up charge. Dick Berlin, Coblentz, and some of the other executives were sure that Bill would make a fool of himself and embarrass the Hearst organization.

Hearst himself recalled what had happened during World War II when he had an opportunity to visit Russia, tagging along, as it were, with Major General Fred Anderson, head of the Eighth Air Force Bomber Command in England, for "a first-hand view of the Soviet Union." His father thwarted the scheme, reasoning that Stalin had caused the entire Polish underground leadership to quietly vanish with no one visibly upset about it. "There won't be much sympathy for you either," W. R. told his son, "if you suddenly get lost in those Russian spaces."

Stalin wasn't around anymore, but the specter of the Communists as international bogeymen was firmly entrenched in the Hearst psyche.

Nonetheless, the opportunity was too much for the journalist in Bill to pass up, and the executives were somewhat appeased by the knowledge that Smith and Conniff would be looking out for Young Bill.

J. Kingsbury Smith was considered a first-rate newsman, even by journalists outside the Hearst organization, who often commented that he was "much too good to be working for Hearst." The forty-seven-year-old Smith had been with INS since 1924 and covered D-Day and the Nuremberg executions. He was also something of an old Russia hand, having obtained a telegraphic interview with Soviet Premier Georgi Malenkov in 1953, and having succeeded in getting Joseph Stalin to reply to questions in 1949.

Conniff began his journalistic career in 1929 as a sports writer for the Washington *Post*, later became sports editor, then joined the Hearst organization, becoming one of the in-house heavyweights, both literally (he pushed the scales past 220 pounds) and figuratively—he was a sports columnist, wrote several books, and served as a war correspondent in Europe and Korea. He and Bill ran together for a while in Europe and stuck together in the postwar years. By 1955, Conniff was Bill's editorial assistant, a position that included writing most of Hearst's columns.

After numerous meetings between Hearst executives and family members, it was finally decided that the trio would just go, see what happened, and decide nothing until they got back.

Over they went on January 25, 1955; and they settled into quarters in Moscow's National Hotel. J. Edgar Hoover had personally warned Hearst to expect all manner of Communist duplicity—the telephones would be bugged, microphones would be planted in their hotel rooms, and they would be shadowed by the Soviet secret police. Hoover had suggested that the best way to foil a hidden microphone was to run a water tap while talking. Therefore, most of the trio's strategy sessions were held in Hearst's bathroom, while the tub filled with water.

Interestingly, Bill was not the first Hearst to set foot in Russia, the intrepid Phoebe having ventured to St. Petersburg and then on to Moscow some sixty years earlier, braving the horrors of the Russian railroad system and perhaps even the Tsarist police to see the Hermitage collections, the palaces and galleries. She found the Neva a fine stream, wider than the Mississippi, the palaces magnificent and the School of Mines the finest in the world, although the rest of the country—or as much as she could digest—seemed flat and uninteresting.

The first order of business for the latter-day Hearst expedition was to send out requests for interviews to all the top Russian officials. After that, it was a matter of sitting back and waiting.

Within three days, the first answer came back—they would be able to interview Foreign Minister Vyacheslav Molotov. For all the interviews the task force undertook, Smith did the real work—he mapped out the line of questioning, took complete stenographic notes, so a verbatim transcript of each interview was available, and did most of the writing.

Molotov's most significant statement during the interview concerned the United States Navy's project, which was then just beginning, to protect the evacuation of Chinese Nationalists from the Tachen Islands. There had been considerable speculation and worry that the Communist forces might attack the convoy, perhaps touching off a full-scale war. However, Molotov assured the Hearst journalists that "if Chiang Kai-shek desired to withdraw his troops from any islands, hardly anyone would prevent him from trying to do so." The message was clear that Soviet Russia favored a reduction of tension in the Formosa area.

In fact, the theme the Russians hammered at in all their interviews with the Hearst team was "peaceful coexistence," as they tried to dispel the bellicose war-mongering image that most Americans seemed to have of the Soviet leaders.

It was a message the Hearst team wasn't prepared to receive. Marshal Georgi Zhukov, first deputy minister of defense and commander of the Russian forces that captured Berlin, reiterated time and again that the Soviet Union had no aggressive intentions, and he pointed out that, if it had had such aims, there had been ample opportunities to attack Western Europe after the fall of Hitler, when European defenses were weak.

"Those people who try to frighten the Western people about Soviet intentions must have some other motive," Zhukov summarized. "Do you understand me?" Old prejudices die hard, if at all.

The team also got interviews with Svetlana Stalin, daughter of the late Soviet leader, composer Dmitri Shostakovich, the First Secretary of the Communist Party Nikita Khrushchev. Khrushchev was considered a real prize, one of the two main targets of the interview team, the other being Premier Malenkov. In the course of a three-hour conversation with the Hearst team, Khrushchev stressed again the concept of peaceful coexistence between the Soviet Union and the Western nations.

The Kremlin tried to interest the Americans in interviewing Defense Minister Nikolai Bulganin, but were curtly informed that "Hearst was not interested in minor cogs like Defense Minister Bulganin, but was concerned only with meeting the bigs." This was in keeping with the team's strategy, wherein Smith and Conniff treated Hearst as if he were a "chief of state," on a par with the Premier and Communist Party chief, and not, as they put it, "one to be fobbed off with lesser Communist powers than his own opposite number."

The team learned to its dismay on February 8 that the Russians had been trying to hand them an international news scoop. On that day, the trio was sitting in the press gallery of the Supreme Soviet—the Russian parliament—when Premier Malenkov, to the shocked surprise of the 1,300 delegates, asked that he be allowed to resign and step aside in favor of "another Comrade with greater administrative experience."

That afternoon, Khrushchev nominated Defense Minister Bulganin to take Malenkov's place, and the delegates unanimously voted in the new Prime Minister.

Back at the hotel, Hearst received a phone call from ABC commentator John MacVane, which resulted in an interview that must have sent chills up the spines of Dick Berlin and the other executives who had feared that Bill would make a fool of himself. Part of the interview:

MacVane: You certainly are there in Moscow at an exciting time. We heard a great deal about the resignation of Malenkov. You've been on the scene for the past week and you've talked with the Soviet heads of state. Did you have any inkling that the change in leadership was coming?

Hearst: Not the slightest, Johnnie.

MacVane: Was this a great surprise generally there in Moscow?

Hearst: I would say no one here (*static*) for the moment (*static*) in diplomatic circles (*static*) would even (*static*).

MacVane: I see. What has been the effect on the people of Moscow? Is there open discussion of the matter in the streets?

Hearst: If there is it's in a language I can't understand.

MacVane: I mean are they gathering together and discussing the affair, do you think?

Hearst: I purposely looked out the window a dozen times.

MacVane: Yes.

Hearst: To see whether there was any difference in the crowds that walk along the street.

MacVane: Yes.

HEARST: There's not a ripple or murmur.

MACVANE: I see. Well, what does it mean as you see it, Bill? Particularly the fact that Marshal Bulganin is an Army man and now becomes Prime Minister.

HEARST: Well, everything is full of about ten different interpretations.

MACVANE: I see. So that the diplomats and correspondents there aren't agreed whether this will mean any sudden change in the course of Soviet policy, for instance.

HEARST: No. We just left the Supreme Soviet.

MACVANE: Yes.

HEARST: It looks like they're going to keep this on and on and on (*static*) the usual propaganda lie.

MACVANE: Yes.

HEARST: How strong Socialism was getting and how neolithic Capitalism was lagging.

MACVANE: Yes.

HEARST: And you know, that's hard to take in your own language, much less in Russian.

Two days later, the trio prepared to board their homeward plane at the Leningrad airport, without having interviewed either the incoming or the outgoing premier. Although immediately after leaving the session of the Supreme Soviet, they had asked the Kremlin for an appointment with Bulganin, they felt the chances of it coming through were virtually nil.

The flight was delayed for half an hour due to engine trouble. As the group waited—Smith was playing chess with the Intourist guide who had accompanied the task force on its travels, Hearst tried to tune in a Radio Leningrad broadcast on a portable radio, and Conniff sat in a corner, forlornly rubbing an aching gout-stricken foot—a telephone call came through from the INS Moscow bureau. Premier Bulganin would see them the next day.

The task force hurried back to Moscow by night train, and talked to Bulganin, who pretty much reiterated what other Russian leaders had been telling the Hearst team for the past week. Still, it was important to interview the new leader, and that talk quite possibly made the difference in later winning the Pulitzer Prize.

Back in the United States, Bill Hearst had suddenly become a prominent "expert" on Russian affairs. His return to the United States even rated a small notice in *The New York Times*, which may have felt compelled to get something on the record in light of the big fuss the Hearst papers were making over their native son. Shortly afterward,

Hearst consulted with President Eisenhower on the status of United States-Soviet relations. Bill told the President that the current American policy of strength without provocation, "keeping our guard up and maintaining a strong retaliatory force in readiness," was the correct one. He also passed along the message that Marshal Zhukov, with whom Eisenhower had worked after World War II, had inquired about the President's health and general appearance, and especially wanted to know if Eisenhower's hair was gray or if he was balder. *The New York Times* reported that the President "smiled somewhat grimly" when Hearst relayed the inquiry.

One of the New York Hearst executives hit upon the idea of Bill, Smith and Conniff exploiting their Russian trip and getting some publicity for the Hearst newspapers by traveling around the country and giving talks at advertising luncheons, before civic groups, to city fathers, press clubs and other such organizations. The talks were a great success, with the combination of Conniff's wit, Hearst's foot-scuffing boyishness and Smith's somberness and intelligence. The roadshow was in Los Angeles when Bill walked into Romanoff's restaurant and was greeted by a friend, "Hi, Bill, where ya been lately?" It was years before Hearst talked to the guy again.

The Hearst Corporation was forced to acknowledge Bill's growing stature by naming him editor in chief of all the Hearst newspapers, a position that had been vacant since W. R.'s death in August 1951.

And, of course, the ultimate award came the next year when Hearst, Smith and Conniff shared the 1956 Pulitzer Prize for international reporting. Their interviews, in the words of the citation, provided the "first definite indication of what the policy of the new rulers of Russia would be on the great issues of war and peace."

The next few years were good ones for Bill. At last he had been able to step out of his father's shadow with an accomplishment of his own. He returned to Russia again in 1957, then in 1959 covered both Richard Nixon's visit to the Soviet Union and Khrushchev's trip to the United States. Although publicly he played the role of obeisant admirer of his father—writing for example in 1959, "For several years, I have studied intensively the career of my late father, in the hope that some of his journalistic wisdom might rub off on a less gifted son"—his family reports that Bill began thinking of himself not so much as a "less gifted son," but as something like a reincarnation of old W. R.

(8)

By the late 1950s, Millicent Hearst was approaching eighty and beginning to slow down. She didn't do quite as much traveling as she used to, her hearing was almost gone, there weren't quite as many parties as in earlier years, but she was still the glue that held the Hearst family together.

Her annual Christmas party and Thanksgiving dinner were virtually the only times the whole family would get together. Some of the parties—always elaborate productions—were memorable occasions, such as when a team of flamenco dancers performed in her apartment and all the stomping knocked down the ceiling plaster of the apartment below, which belonged to Bernard Baruch. Fortunately, Baruch was at the party.

Millicent—affectionately called "Mamalee" by the family—for many years had lived with her sister Anita, who had been married once but was widowed in the 1940s. Anita, perhaps by virtue of being the elder, had taken upon herself the role of manager of the household. Anyone who wanted to see Mamalee had to first go through Aunt Anita. When Anita said Millicent wasn't feeling well and didn't care to see anyone, no one could ever be certain whether it was really Mamalee who didn't want any visitors, or Anita who didn't want her to have any. Anita was generally perceived as a rather mean-spirited individual, always ready to complain about something or someone. Her continual dissatisfaction with the household help became something of a family joke; Bunky once said he would like to market an "Aunt Anita Doll"—wind it up and it fires the cook.

There was always an element of grandeur surrounding Mamalee, almost as if she were a queen or some sort of royalty. Granddaughter Joanne recalled that visits for tea with Mamalee were always stiffly formal occasions. "God forbid that you walk in wearing blue jeans. You had to look your best and sometimes that wasn't even good enough." Joanne can recall her grandmother rebuking her for the way she wore her hair or the dress she was wearing, but always suspected that Anita had somehow put Mamalee up to such criticism.

"Mamalee had a hearing aid, but Anita thought it didn't look good and would take it out," Joanne said. "Then Anita would whisper into Mamalee's ear and tell her what was being said. Who knows what she was telling her?"

As the matriarch of the Hearst family, Millicent felt obligated to stand up for her sons against the corporation executives, although she was not always entirely successful. She had always looked on the Hearst properties as belonging, at least in part, to her, even after her separation from W. R. Her access to the Hearst papers—she referred to *my* newspapers in casual conversation with her peers—had a great deal to do with her position as a mover and shaker in New York society. With W. R. gone, she had no intention of seeing her sons shut out of the operation of the Hearst enterprises. She had maintained cordial relations with Berlin, and pressed him again and again to give her sons positions of authority. Berlin was equally adamant that the sons did not deserve and were not capable of handling authority, although he would not say so to her face.

A corporation executive recalls that in 1960, Millicent marched into Berlin's office, banged her fist on his desk and told him, "Those boys want more responsibility and they deserve it." Berlin turned on all his considerable charm and agreed that, yes, some of the boys probably could do more—of course, they would have to work, but certainly they were more mature than they had been ten years ago. So, in a magnanimous and conciliatory gesture, he made Randy president of Hearst Consolidated. That pacified Millicent for the moment, and involved giving Randy no real authority, since Hearst Consolidated was that holding company that on paper owned several of the Hearst newspapers and *American Weekly*. In reality, all management decisions concerning Hearst Consolidated papers came from people in the Hearst Corporation. The next year, Randy was elected president of both Hearst Consolidated and Hearst Publishing Company, a subsidiary of Consolidated. Both companies were remnants from the days when W. R. was throwing his publishing properties together in various groups in order to sell bonds and stock. If nothing else, they were impressive titles. At least, Mamalee seemed impressed. A close family friend remarked that "whatever titles those boys had, she got for them."

The mother was also proud of Young Bill and his accomplishments as a journalist. She read his Sunday column avidly, and no one could convince her that her son didn't write every single word himself. She had a close relationship with her son John, being involved in various business deals with him. Even George, whom she at one point considered a lost cause, spent months at a time with her during the years he was married to Rosalie.

The sons returned their mother's devotion and were solicitous of her feelings in all matters. While filial love no doubt played a great role in their attentions, it could not have been lost on the sons that their aging mother was the wealthiest member of the Hearst family, having carefully invested the money she received from her husband over the thirty-odd years of their separation.

In order to lessen the burden of inheritance taxes, Millicent began disbursing large amounts of money to her five sons during the 1950s. At least three times during the 1950s and 1960s she distributed $1.5 million to her sons or their families—$300,000 for each of the five family branches. When her son John died, leaving no estate to speak of, Millicent set up a modest trust fund to pay his widow, Fanne, $1,000 a month.

Mamalee also owned an extensive jewelry collection, which became the subject of intense quarreling among the Hearst women. For many years, Mamalee made it a practice to give a piece of jewelry to each of the women on birthdays and Christmas. In her later years, she discontinued this routine as the jewelry she was willing to part with ran out. However, she had kept the best pieces for herself, and it was this collection that was the subject of much discussion—who would get Mamalee's jewelry when she finally passed away. As things turned out, the jewelry was divided, but Bootsie did the dividing, which left some women in the family less than happy.

The family, ever careful of their mother's health, had decided that she should not know "that something had happened" to her granddaughter Patty. From February 1974 until her death that December, Mamalee was kept blissfully ignorant of the kidnap trauma and the ordeal her son Randy was going through.

"They took away her television set and told her it was broken," said family friend Charles Gould. "It was really sad. That was all the old lady had."

When she died, Millicent left an estate valued at $2.5 million, which was divided among her three living sons—the families of George and John received nothing.

"Yes, I thought that was rather strange," said Fanne, who declined to comment further.

Chapter 4

Dominoes

(1)

IN APRIL 1955, *Advertising Age* splashed a huge story across its front page under the headline "Revitalized Hearst Organization Making Money, Adding Properties." It was a laudatory article which basically assured readers that Hearst was financially healthy and getting healthier, in spite of the declining profits of Hearst Consolidated Publications, its only publicly owned division.

The team of *Ad Age* writers decided that Bill Hearst had "hit the keynote" when he told a Chicago audience in 1952 that "We don't sell newspapers. We buy them." They found it significant that "the men who took over after Mr. Hearst's death have sold or closed no newspapers . . ." and concluded that "the newspapers are in good shape." Nothing could have been further from the truth.

Advertising Age had been granted rare access to a top Hearst official, who spoke "off the record," because there was serious consideration at the time of selling stock to the public and the corporation executives decided it would be wise to let out the word that business at Hearst was booming. In doing so, they had taken a page right out of W. R. Hearst's 1935 playbook, when he conned *Fortune* magazine into printing a lavish article that gaped with awe and incredulity at Hearst's fantastic fortune and marveled at how he had come through the Depression unscathed. At the time the *Fortune* article appeared, Hearst, in fact, was reeling on the verge of bankruptcy and was preparing a massive bond offering that he hoped would bail him out of trouble.

The years of the late 1950s and early 1960s would show how absolutely wrong the *Ad Age* article had been, as Hearst newspaper properties across the country collapsed one after another, building momentum until it seemed that the entire structure might go under, or, at the very least, giving the impression that the Hearst Corporation was, in the phrase of *Forbes* magazine, "a dying enterprise, selling off its newspapers when it can and folding them when it can't, slowly dwindling into oblivion."

The chain broke in Chicago, where the afternoon *American* was suddenly sold to its long-time rival, the *Tribune*, on October 21, 1956. It was the end of a legend. Hearst was the last practitioner of the brawling, bullying kind of journalism that gave Chicago the reputation for being "a tough newspaper town." The Hollywood image of the newspaper reporter as a hard-drinking cynic in perpetual pursuit of the all-important "scoop" was bred in Hearst's Chicago city rooms, where kick-in-the-door-style police reporting was refined to a science. Murder, scandal and adultery were the raw materials of news, routinely advertised in six-inch headlines. *Newsweek* magazine noted nostalgically in its story on the sale that "the curtain had finally rung down on the slapdash, gin-soaked kind of newspapering that inspired the play *The Front Page*."

Sale of the *American* surprised the publishing industry, as well as the general public, most of whom couldn't remember when Chicago did not have a Hearst newspaper—there had been several name changes of the Hearst papers in Chicago over the years, always some combination of "American," "Herald" or "Examiner."

Only four years earlier, in 1952, Bill Hearst had stood up before the Chicago Federated Advertising Club and assured its gathered members that "Chicago is a vigorous, forward-looking town in which we always intend to have representation. We have been publishing here for more than fifty years."

What Bill failed to add was that they had been losing there for fifty years as well. Hearst was never able to compete successfully with McCormick, proprietor of the *Chicago Tribune*, whom W. R. admired above all his competitors. Year after year he had watched McCormick win, beating his circulation, cornering the advertisers that should have been his. It was pride that kept Hearst in Chicago—pride and a fair amount of blood.

Some of the blood was literal. When Hearst decided in May 1900 that he was going to start a Chicago paper, his business manager, Solomon Carvalho, warned him that "It's a tough town. We'll have to shoot our way in."

"Take all the ammunition you need," Hearst replied.

From the time Hearst's *American* first rolled off the presses in July of that year, until the outbreak of World War I, ferocious circulation and distribution wars raged between the city's competing newspapers. The biggest box of ammunition in the Hearst arsenal was Max Annenberg, the *American*'s circulation director. He supervised a crew of thugs whose job it was to convince newsdealers and newsboys—with blackjacks and brass knuckles when necessary—to buy ever-increasing numbers of copies of the *American*. It was the dealers' and newsboys' problem to sell the papers; Annenberg's motto was "sell 'em or eat 'em." Since all the newspapers in town were using strong-arm distribution tactics, the encounters often turned bloody. From 1910 to 1912, when the circulation wars were at a peak, twenty-seven newsdealers were killed, while additional fatalities were recorded among the circulation crews of the various newspapers.

Some of the blood spilled by Hearst in Chicago was in effort, as in blood, sweat and tears. The pressure was intense, the pace fast. Not everyone could stand it. During its first thirty-seven months, the *American* had twenty-seven city editors. Small wonder that the Hearst offices quickly acquired the sobriquet "the Madhouse on Madison Street." Those who not only survived, but actually thrived in the madhouse atmosphere became local legends. Walter Howey, who achieved legendary status when Ben Hecht and Charles MacArthur used him as the real-life model for their managing editor in *The Front Page* was one of those.

In addition to his duties as an editor, over the years Howey masterminded spectacular circulation-building stunts that included giving away dollar bills inside the newspapers and planting stories with rival papers—such as the saga of an industrialist's son who was trying to lose a million dollars a year—that turned out to be promotions for serials in the Hearst paper. Another Hearst newsman who was profiled in *The Front Page*, Hildy Johnson, once was sent by his editor to give a convicted murderer $200 in payment for his death-cell memoirs—a sure-fire feature that would sell some extra papers. Johnson began talking with the man and ended up playing cards with him for hours, eventually winning the entire $200. The doomed man's last words before being electrocuted the next day were: "Don't play rummy with Hildy Johnson. I think he cheats."

It was an article of faith among the Hearst troops that Hearst reporters were just a bit more aggressive, less tactful, had more fun and were crazier than reporters for any other paper in town.

But most of the blood spilled in Chicago was financial, the dye of red ink at the bottom of ledger accounts. The *American* (called the *Herald-American* prior to 1953) had been losing money at the rate of more than $1 million a year for the past decade. Five years of trying—including shuffling editors and experiments with new features and makeup—had failed to turn the paper into a money-maker. Its circulation had plummeted in the five years following Hearst's death from 541,000 to 421,000 and was still falling. Advertising had similarly fallen off. Dick Berlin was determined to stop the hemorrhaging.

The Scripps-Howard and Knight chains expressed tentative interest in buying the *American*—Knight already owned the other afternoon paper, the *Daily News*, while Scripps-Howard wanted to get into the Chicago market, if the price was right. Berlin, however, shrewdly surmised that he could get the best price out of the *Tribune* company, which had money to spend, a strong interest in preventing Knight from gaining an afternoon monopoly, and would not particularly want the added competition from Scripps-Howard. The *Tribune* finally agreed to pay something over $11 million for the *American*'s name and good will.

The new owner kept the *American*'s staff, but changed the paper's name and logotype, and made a conscious effort to suppress anything—even an innocent story on vivisection—that might remind readers that the paper was a Hearst creation. The name of Hearst, which had burst into Chicago fifty-six years earlier with the fanfare and excitement of a fireworks display, circus and street fight rolled into one, disappeared with scarcely a ripple.

(2)

On May 9, 1958, officials of the Wire Service Guild, increasingly worried by rumors that International News Service would be sold to United Press, asked INS General Manager J. Kingsbury Smith for an explanation. Smith assured the Guild that such rumors were completely without foundation.

Two weeks later, as rumors of an INS sale persisted and increased, Ray Mann, administrative officer of the Wire Service Guild, and a representative of the Commercial Telegraphers Union, requested a meeting with INS management to clarify the situation. They met May 23 with INS personnel manager Tom Brislin, who refused to confirm or deny the rumors. At 4:22 P.M., during a recess in the session, the Dow-Jones wire began moving a three-paragraph story quoting a "high Hearst official" that a merger between INS and UP had been completed and would be announced soon.

Associated Press wires picked up the story, but Brislin still refused to confirm or deny the report, saying that only J. Kingsbury Smith could make a statement and that Smith was unavailable.

Later in the day, Bill Hearst issued a statement denying the Dow-Jones report.

Mann, meanwhile, issued a statement that said in part: "We are appalled by reports of a merger agreement between INS and UP by which more than 400 employees in our jurisdiction may be thrown out of work."

At noon, May 24, 1958, New York time, bells rang on United Press and International News Service teletypes throughout the world, indicating news of "bulletin" importance was about to move on the wires. The two wire networks simultaneously began transmitting:

NEW YORK, May 24 (UPI)—The United Press Associations and the International News Service joined forces today around the world in the creation of a single news agency named United Press International.

This is the first dispatch of the news service which will embrace the largest number of newspapers and radio clients ever served simultaneously by an independently operated news and picture agency.

Agreements covering the consolidation of services were signed by both sides on May 16 . . .

Bitter INS newsmen said it wasn't a "merger" at all. UP had simply swallowed INS—the agreement provided that all UP personnel would keep their jobs, while most INS staffers, numbering more than five hundred, were let go.

The teletypes were still clattering the merger story when two men entered the INS bureau in New York. One identified himself as being from the UP and said he would be "working around here the rest of the day." The other was from Pinkerton Security, who had been assigned "to see you guys don't steal nothing, see?" As one INS man in the office on that day later remarked, "We died with vinegar in our wounds."

Perhaps the most amazing aspect of the INS-UP combination was that it hadn't occurred years earlier. For half a century the two wire services not only had been competing against each other, but more significantly, had been fighting uphill battles against the monolithic Associated Press. Together, they might have given the giant a run for its money. United Press Associations was born in 1907 when E. W. Scripps took three regional press networks under his control and joined them as a single corporation, which he hoped would provide stern competition for the Associated Press, which had been started fifteen years earlier. Hearst started INS in 1909 as an expansion of a wire network that served just his own newspapers.

What kept both UP and INS in business against the bigger and better-financed Associated Press was the AP's policy of granting exclusive territory rights to each of its franchises. This meant that normally only one newspaper in any city could have the AP service. Other newspapers that wanted to print national news coverage had to rely on UP or INS. Of course, some clients took two or all three of the wire services. Unlike AP, which was a nonprofit membership organization, UP and INS were profit-making companies that sold their service to anyone who wished to buy.

As early as 1927, Roy Howard, who was then running UP, suggested to Hearst that the two services combine and together they could "break the AP cartel." Hearst considered the proposal seriously, but decided he would prefer to run his own show, and poured more money into INS.

Perpetually outmanned by both UP and AP, INS reporters had to rely on ingenuity, resourcefulness and colorful writing to compete with the bigger wire services. Editors appreciated the INS flair, which usually brought a human-interest angle into major stories; however they never seemed to fully trust the service's accuracy. Howard Handelman, chief of the INS Detroit bureau during the late 1930s, recalled that the publisher of a client newspaper told him forthrightly that he never carried an INS story unless it was confirmed by one of the other wires.

Some of the wariness in regard to INS accuracy may have been the legacy from a *Harper's Weekly* exposé in the fall of 1915 of INS European war coverage. The magazine revealed that a platoon of INS byliners supposedly reporting from the capitals of Europe—Frederick Werner in Berlin, Franklin P. Merrick in Paris, John C. Foster and Lawrence Elston in London, Brixton D. Allaire in Rome and Herbert Temple, "the European manager of INS"—were ghosts.

The magazine revealed that articles appearing under these bylines—coverage that INS boasted came "out of the capitals and off the battle-fields of Europe"—were actually churned out by an officeful of rewrite men in Cleveland, Ohio, armed with stacks of foreign newspapers and magazines and active imaginations.

It didn't contribute to a reputation for integrity, either, when a federal court found INS guilty in 1917 of routinely stealing news from the Associated Press.

A variation on the ghost plot was dusted off on January 30, 1948, when INS happened not to have a reporter in New Delhi to cover a big prayer and pacification meeting led by Mahatma Gandhi. An irate Hindu who blamed Gandhi for the partition of India chose that opportunity to shoot and kill the religious leader. INS learned of the assassination through its London bureau, which was a client of Reuters, the British wire service. INS-London passed along the Reuters material to New York, and with the aid of additional information purloined from AP and UP (by way of the New York *Mirror*, which subscribed to both) an INS editor set to work composing a story on the death of the revered leader. The New York editors leafed through their index-card file of overseas stringers (part-time reporters sometimes used for special assignments) and came across one for an Indian named J. B. Sahne. Nothing had been heard from Sahne for years, nor had INS used his services, as far as anyone could remember. So that day INS printers throughout the country moved a fine Gandhi story "by J. B. Sahne—International News Service Staff Correspondent." Only a few foreign correspondents who had served in India wondered if this fellow was related to the J. B. Sahne who had died a few years before.

INS reporters considered it almost a matter of pride that each of them constantly was expected, single-handedly, to cover assignments that the other wire services routinely staffed with five or six men. Bob Considine recalled that when Eisenhower went to Abilene, Kansas, in 1952 to announce his candidacy, he was the lone representative from INS, while UP covered the event with seven reporters and AP fielded a twelve-man team.

There was a special kind of *esprit de corps* among INS newsmen, a camaraderie that came from the shared experience of doing one's best to put out a professional product in spite of snubs from other reporters, who looked down on them because they were a Hearst operation, the frustration of competing against two bigger and better-financed rivals, and the disquieting impression that their own New York headquarters was frequently the cause of many problems.

At the Los Angeles bureau, there was even talk of a mass resignation when it appeared that the bureau chief was about to be fired because he had authorized a Louella Parsons column to be spiked. As Handelman remembered the incident, Evans Hoskin, the night man at the bureau, thought Parsons' column attacking the movie *Citizen Kane*, which had just been released might be libelous. Hoskin called the bureau chief, Milt Harker, at home to ask his opinion, and Harker said that if he (Hoskin) thought it was libelous, to spike the whole column. INS did not put the column on the wire, but Parsons' home newspaper, the Los Angeles *Examiner*, ran it. When editors of other newspapers saw the *Examiner*, they wondered why they had not received the column. As a result of their inquiries to New York, word came down that W. R. Hearst himself wanted to talk to Harker the next Saturday morning.

Harker normally did not work on Saturday, but of course he came in to await the phone call, which he felt sure would be his dismissal notice. The entire bureau showed up at the office that Saturday to provide moral support for their boss. When the call came through, all that anyone could hear was Harker's end of the conversation: "Yes, sir. No, sir. That's right, sir." When the conversation ended, an amazed Harker told his gathered staff that W. R. had wanted to know if the INS Washington bureau would kill a story just because it coincided with Hearst policy. Harker had told him "no." He kept his job, which also spared the staff from having to decide whether they would resign in a demonstration of solidarity.

Hearst's question was a forlorn acknowledgment that he could not impose "Hearst policy" on INS without risking the loss of numerous clients, who did not always appreciate the Hearst editorial line. As a result, INS probably received the least direct Hearst influence of any of his publishing properties. INS employees were not unaware that they enjoyed a great deal of editorial freedom compared to the Hearst newspapers. As Handelman noted, "We bent over backwards to separate ourselves from Hearst policy."

The death knell sounded for INS in 1945, when the Supreme Court upheld a lower-court ruling that forced the Associated Press to abandon its practice of granting exclusive franchises to its member newspapers. The court held that this practice was a violation of antitrust statutes, and it directed the association to amend its bylaws to allow access to its wire services for any news agency that could afford to pay for it.

INS clients began deserting in favor of the AP and new clients were harder and harder to keep and hold. The number-three wire service's thin profit margins disappeared in a flood of red ink. By 1958, INS losses were averaging $3 million a year.

Hearst got little out of the merger, except to be rid of a money-draining enterprise. Included with the INS was International News Pictures, the affiliated photo service.

Hearst was given 25 percent of the stock in the new UPI, while Scripps-Howard had 75 percent, as well as all day-to-day management functions. Over the years, Hearst's share of the company diminished to 5 percent, while Scripps-Howard gained 95 percent control.

Few were inclined even to pretend that the combination was a merger. It was a sale. The UP people stayed, and the INS people were let go, except for a few "key personnel," who were forced to swallow bitter medicine upon going to work for UPI—they had to forgo all severance and vacation pay to which they would have been entitled had they been merely laid off, and then join on a six-month probation with no seniority. The arrangement literally made some INS veterans sick, and one, William Hutchinson, the INS Washington bureau chief, died of a heart attack the day after the combination was announced. It was hard to convince his friends that the INS sale wasn't at least partly responsible.

The Guild was upset because there had been no prior notification of the arrangement that would cost hundreds of its members their jobs. A statement issued by Ray Mann, Guild administrator, attacked as "cruel and heartless the manner in which the Hearst Corporation treated its many loyal INS-INP employees."

Mann also called on the Justice Department to investigate the merger for possible antitrust violations. In fact, the department had already begun just such an investigation. At virtually the same time Mann issued his call for an investigation, Victor R. Hansen, assistant attorney general in charge of the Antitrust Division was worrying publicly that the merger "may raise a serious question under the anti-trust laws." Section 7 of the Clayton Act of 1914 took a dim view of mergers whose effect "may be substantially to lessen competition or to tend to create a monopoly." The Supreme Court, however, had ruled that Section 7 did not apply when one of the companies merging was "a corporation with resources so depleted and the probability of rehabilitation so remote that it faced the grave probability of business failure."

At the end of May, the Justice Department dropped its opposition to the merger, finding that INS was in fact a "failing corporation" under the court definition and had been losing money for the past fourteen years.

A strange little epilogue to the INS collapse was reported on June 6 in *The New York Times,* under the headline "Two News Chains Deny Plan to Kill Newspapers." The story reported a rumor that the Guild had requested the Justice Department to investigate: namely, that Scripps-Howard planned to close its newspaper in San Francisco and Hearst its paper in Pittsburgh, leaving each city to the other chain. The *Times* news item quoted a Justice Department official as saying that one of the department's first moves in its investigation of the UP-INS merger had been to ask about possible related plans. The official said the two organizations had denied, in writing, that they had discussed any suspension of newspapers.

At the time, it seemed a curious item, saying more, perhaps, about the Guild's paranoia than anything else. Events of the next few years, however, would reveal that the Guild's apprehension was fully justified.

(3)

The biggest news in San Francisco on Saturday, August 8, 1959, didn't come off the police beat; it came out of the executive offices of the two afternoon newspapers, the *Call-Bulletin* and the *News*. And it was bad news for the four hundred employees of the two papers who would be out of work Monday.

Stories inserted into the late editions of each paper announced that a merger had taken place between the 104-year-old *Call-Bulletin* and the 56-year-old *News*; beginning Monday, they would appear as a single, new entity, the *News–Call Bulletin*.

The new paper would be published by the recently formed Apex Publishing Corporation, owned 50 percent by Scripps-Howard, publisher of the *News*, and 50 percent by Hearst, publisher of the *Call-Bulletin*.

The merger gave the new newspaper a monopoly in the San Francisco afternoon field, while the Hearst-owned *Examiner* and the independent *Chronicle* competed in the morning.

The announcement stated that Scripps-Howard would run the editorial side of the newspaper, while Hearst would take care of the business aspects.

Charles Schneider, editor of the *News*, who was slated to assume the same position on the new publication, tried to put the best light possible on the subject that most concerned employees of the two papers—the new publication, he said, would retain more employees than either of the two predecessors. There would be about 550 employees on the *News–Call Bulletin*, compared to 500 on the old *Call-Bulletin* and 450 on the *News*. This still left some four hundred workers out of a job. All employees, Schneider said, would be informed of their status during the weekend by registered mail or telegram.

The merger was not exactly a surprise in the publishing industry. Rumors predicting exactly what happened had been circulating for more than a year. The previous year, the *News* had answered the rumors in an editorial, which stated: "Despite a recent rash of rumors to the contrary, the News has no plans, never had any, and does not contemplate any plans to cease publication in San Francisco." And only two weeks earlier, in the July 25 issue of *Editor and Publisher*, Roy Howard again denied the rumors that the *News* and *Call-Bulletin* would combine their operations.

The partnership with Scripps-Howard was neither as smooth-working nor as profitable as either company had hoped it would be. Although in the years since 1951 the Hearst organization had acquired a reputation as a hard-nosed, profit-oriented outfit, the performance of Apex Publishing did nothing to enhance that image. By 1962, the Scripps-Howard people wanted out of the partnership, having sadly concluded that it was a mistake to let Hearst control the pursestrings of the operation. There was also considerable friction between the Hearst and Scripps-Howard executives, stemming from the feeling of both groups that they were answerable to their own organization, but not to each other. Hearst executive Charles Gould later admitted that the *News–Call Bulletin* was losing money on the order of more than $1 million a year, though in 1961 the figure was closer to $2 million.

In June 1962, Hearst bought out Scripps-Howard's half interest in the newspaper for $1 and added $437,500 for debts owed by the *News–Call Bulletin* to two Scripps-Howard companies.

"This was an unusual experiment in newspaper publishing," commented Jack R. Howard, president of Scripps-Howard Newspapers. "A very considerable amount of money was devoted to the experiment, but it just did not pan out."

(4)

The ax fell next in Pittsburgh, where the *Sun-Telegraph* was sold to the morning *Post-Gazette* for a reported $5 million in cash on April 22, 1960.

News of the sale was broken to reporters in the city room shortly after 4 P.M. as they worked on the "blue streak," the last edition of the day. They finished the edition, then en masse tumbled across the alley to the Naples Bar, where they could drown their sorrow and wonder why Hearst management had given up on the *"Telly,"* as they fondly called the paper. Most of the reporters had been around six years earlier, when a new three-story building was put up next to the main eight-story *Sun-Telegraph* headquarters to house new presses. That certainly didn't sound like something the management of a faltering newspaper would do.

The reporters had no way of knowing that their *Telly* had been draining Hearst Corporation coffers to the tune of $3 million a year for the previous several years. The new press building, however, was not wasted. The *Post-Gazette*, a six-day-a-week morning paper, moved its entire operation into the old *Sun-Telegraph* quarters and immediately began publishing both a morning and afternoon edition, and a Sunday paper, which it called the *Post-Gazette and Sun-Telegraph*. The "Sun-Telegraph" part of the logo was printed in smaller type, which kept getting smaller and within two years had disappeared altogether.

The *Sun-Telegraph* employed nine hundred people, but only a handful of them were invited to join the *Post-Gazette* staff. Ed Bell, former assistant city editor at the *Telly*, was one of the lucky few, making the transition to night city editor on the expanded *Post-Gazette and Sun-Telegraph*.

"The city suffered for the *Telly* going out of business," said Bell, who was still at the *Post-Gazette* twenty years after Hearst abandoned Pittsburgh. "We lived the news. We covered everything."

When the *Telly* went out of business, a lot of job security in Hearst city rooms across the country also disappeared, as the anxious employees of the remaining thirteen Hearst newspapers asked each other: Who's next?

(5)

At 3 A.M. on the morning of November 7, 1960, more than one thousand employees of the Detroit *Times* were awakened by the delivery of a telegram that read:

> It is with deep regret that the management of the Detroit Times must inform you of the termination of your services on November 7, 1960. It is not necessary for you to report for further duty. Your paycheck will be available on the usual payday in the Detroit Times lobby.

More than a few of the workers were puzzled by the message, delivered at such an ungodly hour. Some thought they had been fired. Others took it as a prank. It all became clear later in the morning, when they read front-page stories in both the Detroit *News* and the *Free Press*. The *Times* had been sold to the Detroit *News* for an estimated $10 million. For that price, the *News* had gained possession of the *Times*'s plant, printing equipment and subscription lists, along with distribution rights to the

American Weekly, King Features comics and half a dozen daily columnists.

It was a bad time to be out of work and in Detroit. Unemployment in the area stood at 7.2 percent that month, and would rise steadily to hit a peak of 15.2 percent the following March. Workers in the automotive industry were used to seasonal layoffs, but being out of work was something new to most *Times* employees. Indeed, the median length of service with the paper was more than twelve years; in certain departments it was much longer—in the editorial department, 57 percent of the workers had been with the paper at least ten years, and 34 percent had been on the *Times* staff twenty years or longer.

The suddenness of the closing bewildered and embittered many employees, who felt they had been cruelly betrayed by an institution that was more than just a job. A study by the Upjohn Institute for Employment Research of Detroit *Times* workers in the six months after the closing showed that virtually all the *Times* employees had been quite content with their jobs, and the one phrase that was repeated time and time again was: "The *Times* was a good place to work in."

Management-labor relations were characterized, the study noted, by "a high degree of friendliness and good feeling."

Louis Ferman, author of the Upjohn study, noted a real sense of identification with the paper—the feeling that the *Times* was not just a place to work in, but represented a way of life that extended beyond the newspaper professionals and included file clerks, switchboard operators and maintenance workers.

According to a top management official at the *News,* the secrecy surrounding the sale had been at the insistence of the Hearst people, who were worried that *Times* employees would remove or destroy records if there was an announcement ahead of time. Originally, the sale-completion date was set for November 14, but on Sunday, November 6, it was learned in New York that *Newsweek* magazine had somehow gotten wind of the paper folding and was running a feature article in its next edition. In order to beat *Newsweek* to the punch, the sale completion time was moved up to 3:01 A.M. on Monday, November 7. Only the general manager of the *Times* was informed, and a telegram was drafted to be sent to each worker when the sale went into effect.

The *Times,* bought by Hearst in 1921 at a receivership sale, had long been a stalwart moneymaker of the chain. It started slipping into the red in the late 1940s and continued to break even, more or less, until the second half of the 1950s, when the losses quickly mounted. The bulk of the *Times*'s distribution and circulation was in the central city, meaning that the migration to the suburbs in the 1950s took a heavy toll on profits. Between 1950 and the year it was sold, the paper lost ten million dollars, while circulation plummeted from 440,000 to 373,000.

(6)

A half-page ad in *The New York Times* on October 2, 1961, explained the whole Boston situation. In large type the ad announced that the Boston *Daily Record* and the *Evening American* would be combined into one newspaper. "An All Day Newspaper Which Provides the Largest Circulation in Boston," the ad said.

In smaller type, the text of the ad began:

> Today, October 2, the morning Record–evening American combination became the Daily RECORD AMERICAN—a *single* newspaper serving the Boston community and its trading area throughout the day not only with fresh up-to-the-minute news but with the combined editorial features formerly in its separate morning and evening newspapers.
>
> This constructive, forward move clarifies for advertisers, in one giant step, the complicated Boston combination-newspaper situation.
>
> CONSIDER THE GREATER IMPORTANCE OF THIS SINGLE, EXPANDED NEWSPAPER.
>
> The Daily RECORD AMERICAN combines into a *single, expanded daily newspaper* the cream of both former newspapers' columnists, features, comics; local, national and international news coverage facilities.
>
> And, as before, the new Daily RECORD AMERICAN will continue to have by far the largest circulation of all Boston newspapers—an estimated 450,000 to 475,000 daily (more than the combined circulation of the A.M. and P.M. Globe; more than the combined circulation of the Herald and Traveler).

Compared with most other Hearst newspaper closings, the one in Boston could actually be called uneventful. It scarcely rated a three-paragraph story in *The New York Times*. But the conjunction of the Boston merger and the publication of W. A. Swanberg's biography of William Randolph Hearst the previous month, was enough to launch *The New Yorker* magazine's press critic, A. J. Liebling, on a 2,200-word verbal rampage against Hearst and his newspapers.

Liebling was outraged that Swanberg had called Hearst a genius—at least five times in the book, and twice on one page—and felt compelled to dissect the Boston *Record* for evidence that Hearst was not a genius. Liebling had picked the Boston *Daily Record* of September 30, having been attracted by an announcement therein that—as he put it—the *Record*, "a Hearst morning tabloid . . . had swallowed its evening sibling, the *American*, and would appear henceforth as both of them." It was not unfair to judge Hearst by the contents of the *Record*, Liebling decided, "because Hearst papers have changed little since his death in 1951—or, indeed, since about 1909, when the pattern hardened."

Liebling went on to disparage the *Record*'s coverage of a gambling raid by U.S. Treasury agents, and the fact that a $250 holdup was given equal prominence with foreign news accounts. After mocking the exaggerated descriptions of the stable of Hearst columnists—Bob Considine was the "Famed Global Reporter," Louella Parsons was "First Lady of Hollywood," George Sokolsky was "Dean of Political Columnists," and Walter Winchell was "America's Best-Known Reporter"—Liebling devoted the rest of his column to reminding the public that Hearst's wealth came from his father, not his newspapers, and that he was not a genius, and had barely managed, in Liebling's opinion, to stay within the legal bounds of sanity. "The most dangerous myth about him," Liebling concluded, "is that he was a genius or even a good newspaperman, because it might lead to the erroneous conclusion that he ran newspapers the right way, or that the way he ran them is the way to make money. The latter delusion might be the most dangerous of all."

If nothing else, the Liebling article demonstrated that a great deal of passion still swirled around the name of W. R. Hearst, even ten years after his death.

(7)

Carl Francis first got the news at an evening meeting held at the Sheraton West Townhouse. The top Hearst advertising executives in Los Angeles, which included Francis, were meeting with some of the New York executives. The news was a shocker. The *Examiner* was going to fold, leaving just one Hearst newspaper in town—the afternoon *Herald-Express*.

The fifty-three-year-old Francis, who held the dual positions of *Examiner* national advertising manager and manager of the Hearst Advertising Service, couldn't believe what he was hearing. Everyone had known for several years that Hearst couldn't keep both papers going in town, but it was just assumed that the *Herald-Express* would be the one to shut down. The *Examiner* was the prestige paper, the moneymaker, published seven days a week. The *Herald-Express*, as everyone who worked for the *Examiner* liked to say, was a cheap, sensational rag. Francis, who had been with the Hearst organization for twenty-eight years, was told that he would be transferred to head up advertising for the *Puck Comic Weekly* in San Francisco. He considered it a clear demotion.

When the meeting broke up, Francis started drinking at a nearby bar. Distraught and depressed, he downed drink after drink for several hours, then got into his car and started driving, fast. Shortly after midnight he was racing along Highway 101, six miles south of Ventura, when his car drifted into the wrong lane and smashed head-on into a car driven by an eighteen-year-old gas station attendant from Oxnard. Francis was killed instantly. The other driver died on the way to the hospital, never knowing that he and Francis may have been the first casualties from the closing of the Los Angeles *Examiner*.

At the time of William Randolph Hearst's death, Los Angeles was riding a wave of postwar prosperity, fueled by the booming aerospace industry. The city had grown into the nation's third-largest and was served by five daily newspapers, all competing hungrily for readers and advertising revenue. By far the strongest of the lot was the morning *Times*, owned by the Chandler family, and considered the conservative voice of the city's Republican establishment. Holding down the morning prestige slot for Hearst was the *Examiner*, whose appeal was to a slightly less affluent audience.

In the afternoon, the *Herald-Express*—with its vintage Hearst formula of big photos, large headlines, plenty of sex and crime stories—aimed at an undereducated, decidedly lower-class urban audience. Its direct competitor was the tabloid *Mirror*, started in 1948 as the Chandlers' attempt to capture some of the mass market. The fifth paper was the liberal twenty-four-hour *Daily News*—the only Democratic-leaning paper in the city—which was oriented toward a working-class constituency.

Although the *Times* was the favored advertising vehicle of the city's establishment, the two Hearst papers together outsold the combined Chandler papers and were solid enough to make the organization an editorial powerhouse in Los Angeles.

The *Daily News*, never an economically healthy operation, sank fast during the early 1950s and folded in 1954.

The *Mirror* too was never a strong paper. Despite affiliation with the *Times*, the *Mirror* was not deeply rooted in Los Angeles. Much of the staff had been hired outside—publisher Virgil Pinkley had been United Press bureau chief in Europe and had brought a number of UP staff members with him. Ed Murray, the managing editor, had been UP manager in Italy. Hearst by contrast, was entrenched, and held the pulse of the city's lower reaches through editors of the Jimmy Richardson and Agness Underwood mold. Hearst, especially with Louella Parsons, dominated entertainment coverage by means of its contacts in the Hollywood community.

By 1958, the Chandlers decided that something would have to be done about the *Mirror*. In its ten years of existence, the paper had never turned a profit, and, in fact, was losing heavily—an average of close to two million dollars per year. After studying the matter, a subcommittee of the *Times*'s board of directors concluded that the *Mirror* could not break even for at least five years, let alone show a profit. The Chandlers carefully considered their options.

As Otis Chandler viewed the situation, "If we look at the *Mirror-News*' potential profitability as marginal, the only apparent advantage in continuing publication is to act as a wedge against the Hearst papers." It was, however, an expensive wedge, especially since even the *Times* was experiencing some financial setbacks, as advertising linage during 1957 and 1958 fell for the first time since the war years. The Chandlers were sure they could use the *Mirror* to bargain some concessions out of the Hearst people.

In April 1959, Norman Chandler wrote to Hap Kern, then general manager of the Hearst newspapers, proposing that the *Examiner* "discontinue publication in the daily morning field and the *Mirror-News* do likewise in the evening field." Such an arrangement would leave the Chandlers with an exclusive morning and Sunday paper, while the Hearst organization would have an exclusive evening and Sunday paper. Edward Becker, manager of the Los Angeles Hearst newspapers, analyzed the

Chandler proposal. He took a look at how many people bought evening papers. Likewise, he looked at total advertising linage in the morning (the *Times* and the *Examiner*) and saw that it was greater than the total in the evening (*Herald-Express* and the *Mirror*). He considered that while the Chandlers had their daily and Sunday distribution system already set up, Hearst had only daily distribution in the evening—a setup they would be obligated to keep because of union contracts—and would have to add the Sunday distribution system. The current *Examiner* distributors would not be able to make a living distributing just a Sunday paper. He considered a few other factors, such as the fact that the *Examiner* was then making money ($1 million in 1959) and the *Herald-Express* was losing ($950,000 in that year). The Chandler proposal, he concluded, stacked up as a "bad deal for us."

By the next year, 1960, the Hearst executives had come around to agreeing with *Examiner* publisher Franklin Payne, who had been saying for years that the merchants of Los Angeles simply were not going to allocate enough advertising dollars to support four metropolitan newspapers. As far as the Hearst executives were concerned, there was no longer any question that at least one of the four papers would have to go. It was only a matter of whose paper, under what circumstances, and when.

The Hearst people started tentative and informal talks with the Chandlers. The Hearst organization proposed buying the *Mirror-News*. The Chandlers were not receptive to that idea, and said they might want to buy the *Herald-Express*.

In the course of the informal talks, Kern casually mentioned to Norman Chandler that Hearst might be willing to consider an exclusive morning-evening division, a Chandler paper in the mornings and Sunday and a Hearst paper in the evenings and Sunday—in other words, the same proposal the Hearst organization had rejected the year before.

Chandler was confused by this latest Hearst proposal, and Milton Day, comptroller of the Times Mirror Company, was instructed to make an analysis of what would happen if there was an exclusive morning-evening division. Day's report, which was dated November 9, 1960, concluded that such an arrangement would give an overwhelming advantage to the Times Mirror Company and, in fact, "would load the whole future circulation pattern very heavily in favor of the *Times* morning and Sunday, and probably, rather than increase competition in Los Angeles, would place the *Times* in such a dominant position that both the evening and Sunday Hearst papers would be in a very difficult competitive position."

The Chandlers reasoned that the Hearst people couldn't be serious about the exclusive morning-evening arrangement, and must be using the proposal as some sort of smokescreen. They resumed their efforts to convince the Hearst people to sell the *Herald-Express*.

Ironically, the Chandlers' offhand dismissal of the exclusive morning-evening arrangement served further to convince the Hearst executives that it was a good plan for them. A better plan, of course, would be for Hearst to buy the *Mirror-News*, but the Chandlers weren't having any of that either.

By the following March, when the Chandlers made an official offer of $5 million for the *Herald-Express*, the Hearst executives had resolved to tighten their belts and keep both of their papers going until the Chandlers came around to their senses—that is, until they decided to give up on the *Mirror* in one way or another.

The Hearst executives were firmly opposed to selling off their evening paper to the Chandlers, because it would give the Times Mirror Company a healthy paper in the morning, and an exclusive paper in the evening, which would presumably be making money. This would leave the Hearst *Examiner* squeezed into third place. From previous Hearst experience in other cities, they were convinced that a third-place paper could not survive long.

Not without some irony, at the same time, Times Mirror comptroller Day was warning Norman Chandler that a single Hearst morning paper would likely be stronger than the Chandlers had anticipated, because local merchants were in mortal fear of a Chandler monopoly and would go out of their way to give the *Examiner* advertising. He estimated the *Examiner* would pick up an additional $3 million worth of ads.

Soon after their first offer, the Chandlers submitted another proposal to buy the *Herald-Express*, this time with a complicated deferred-payment plan that hinged on the combined circulations of the evening papers at the time of sale. The second offer was estimated to be worth about $5.3 million.

Hearst officials firmly rejected both offers, and let the Chandler representative know that they were still interested in an exclusive morning-evening division of the newspaper field.

Now Norman Chandler thought he knew what the Hearst people were up to with their morning-evening proposal. They were trying to dupe the Chandlers into making some kind of illegal offer, something that would be a violation of antitrust laws, then Hearst would use the Chandler legal violation as leverage, or blackmail, to force them to sell the *Mirror*. But antitrust law was somewhat hazy in areas such as this, and Chandler just couldn't be sure he had the Hearsts figured out.

Deciding to take the bull by the horns, Norman Chandler contacted Dick Berlin directly and asked him what Hearst wanted to do in Los Angeles. If they wanted more money for the *Herald-Express*, Chandler said, *Times-Mirror* was willing to "go substantially higher." Berlin replied that Hearst was interested in acquiring the *Mirror-News* or splitting the newspaper market into exclusive morning and evening fields by means of a cross sale.

Still cautious, Chandler replied that such a plan was fine with him, but wouldn't it cause antitrust problems? Berlin promised to retain counsel to explore the antitrust problems with the Justice Department. And there matters stood, in the spring of 1961.

Why was the Hearst organization, which had rejected an exclusive morning-evening arrangement two years ago, now so eager for that same arrangement?

In the two years since the Chandlers first proposed an evening-morning division of the Los Angeles newspaper market, the Hearst corporate thinking had swung 180 degrees on the matter, primarily because the *Examiner*, which had made more than $1 million in 1959, was now losing money. In 1960, the *Examiner* lost $654,000. The *Herald-Express* in that same year lost $1,620,000. In fact, the sharp downturn in profits from 1959 to 1960 was the most drastic in the history of the Hearst Los Angeles newspapers.

As opposed to two years before, when the Chandler proposal would have meant that the Hearst organization would give up a moneymaking property, while the Chandlers gave up a losing property, it was now a case of both organizations giving up losing properties. Another consideration was that the *Herald-Express*, in terms of circulation and advertising linage, was increasing its lead over the *Mirror*, while the *Examiner* was losing ground to the *Times*.

It would become clear years later that the Hearst decision to push for exclusive morning and evening fields was a mistake, and a very large and costly one.

If the Hearst executives made one fatal error, it was that they analyzed the whole Los Angeles newspaper situation strictly as an accounting problem. They looked at total revenue and circulation figures, and considered various ways of cutting up the totals, and what would be to their best advantage. Judging from numerous memos dealing with the Los Angeles situation, never once did the Hearst people consider the possibility that the quality of their newspapers might have something to do with how many people bought them and how much advertising they carried. The *Examiner* was widely, in fact, almost unanimously considered the better of the two Los Angeles papers; but this factor was never considered in discussing which paper to close.

To be sure, the Hearst newspapers had a number of real problems that were discussed. One of the main problems was that the two Hearst papers seemed to compete hardest against each other, instead of against the Chandler papers. Publisher Payne complained frequently that the advertising staffs of each paper seemed to spend all their time trying to steal accounts from each other, instead of taking them away from the *Times*. In 1956, the two papers moved physically into the same building, in order to share production facilities. This caused immediate problems because certain press runs of the two papers, especially when color was used, overlapped.

The Hearst analysis of newspaper economics was strictly a statistical one. Figures—not people, not attitudes, not product quality—were all that seemed to matter. When asked for some moneysaving suggestions, *Examiner* publisher Franklin Payne immediately thought of eliminating the annual Christmas parties, for a savings of $3,700, and slicing one or two hundred dollars a week out of *Examiner* editor Warden Woolard's salary. He apparently never wondered whether these moves might have a negative influence on staff morale, which might in turn affect productivity.

Ironically, in spite of their emphasis on accounting and bookkeeping, the Hearst officials may have made one stupendous accounting blunder. An auditor from the federal General Accounting Office, who went over the books of both the Chandler and Hearst papers in 1963 as part of a Congressional investigation into newspaper monopolies, discovered that some shared expenses between the *Herald-Express* and the *Examiner* were being overcharged to the *Examiner*, and that the *Examiner* was being overcharged for certain services from other Hearst Corporation divisions. The result, the government auditor found, was that from 1957 to 1961 instead of showing a net loss of $2 million, the *Examiner* should have shown a net profit of $6.1 million. Although Hearst Corporation officials disputed the government audit, the report did raise the possibility that even by their own criterion—whether the *Examiner* was making or losing money—the Hearst organization may have made a mistake in closing the *Examiner*.

Throughout the summer of 1961, Berlin called Norman Chandler from time to time to tell him that the morning-evening arrangement was still under discussion with the Department of Justice. The department had definitely ruled that a cross sale would be a violation of antitrust laws. There might be other possible solutions, but it would all take time.

On October 19, 1961, Hearst attorney James McInerney wrote a letter to Attorney General Robert Kennedy, asking that the Hearst Corporation and Times Mirror be exempted from antitrust regulations because both the *Herald-Express* and the *Mirror* were "failing corporations." A couple of weeks later, a Justice Department attorney called the Hearst lawyer and told him the department could not give its approval.

McInerney then went down to Washington to talk with Lee Loevinger, an attorney in the antitrust division of the Justice Department. The problem was explained to Loevinger, and he told McInerney that the proposed deal had the appearance of a scheme by which the Chandlers and Hearst were trying to avoid "the possibility of somebody else coming in and buying the failing ventures and thus providing competition." McInerney argued that the Hearst Corporation was losing millions of dollars and urgently needed Justice Department permission to shut down. Then Loevinger mentioned that there was nothing in antitrust law to prevent a company with a subsidiary that was losing money simply to close down the subsidiary.

For McInerney, that was enough, and he reported back to Berlin that the Justice Department had approved the closing down of both money-losing subsidiaries. Loevinger later said that his comment was not meant as official department approval of anything. It was, after all, only an oral comment, and there had been no discussion about the companies' shutting down their papers simultaneously. Berlin immediately called Norman Chandler, who flew to New York to hear the report from Mc-Inerney. After being assured that simultaneous closing had the approval of the Justice Department, Chandler told Berlin that if the Times Mirror board of directors approved the plan, they would close the *Mirror* while the Hearst Corporation closed the daily *Examiner*. Times Mirror directors approved the plan on December 26. In the *Mirror*'s city room, Norman Chandler faced 175 grimly expectant staff members, and with tears in his eyes announced that "The *Mirror* is being combined with the Los Angeles *Times* . . . this is the most difficult and heart-rending statement . . . the *Mirror* was my dream." It was the last day of publication for the *Mirror*.

A mile and a half away, in the huge building at the corner of 11th and Broadway that housed the *Examiner* and the *Herald-Express*, the ending was more impersonal. Employees were told that their pay checks, normally not due for three more days, were available at the cashier's office. Inside each envelope was a brief notice signed by Randolph Hearst. "Economic circumstances have necessitated the discontinuance of publication of the Los Angeles *Examiner*," the statement read in part. Later a notice was posted on the city-room bulletin board, announcing that Saturday's edition would be the last.

Fourteen hundred employees of the two newspapers were thrown out of work, one thousand at the *Examiner* and four hundred at the *Mirror*. The two closings prompted concerned comment on the general future of newspapers in the country, and Congressman Emanuel Celler announced that his House antitrust subcommittee would investigate newspaper mergers and combinations, with special emphasis on the Los Angeles situation. Those hearings were held the next year, at which time the story of the Hearst and Chandler negotiation to split the newspaper field into morning and evening monopolies came out. Celler concluded that there had been a "technical violation of the law" but felt there was no point in prosecuting either the Hearst or Chandler organizations. The hearings ended with no recommendation for actions, although information developed during the course of the hearings was later the basis for the Newspaper Preservation Act of 1970, a law which exempted newspapers from much antitrust legislation.

(8)

A strike by members of the American Newspaper Guild Local 51 shut down the Milwaukee *Sentinel,* oldest newspaper in Wisconsin, on May 28, 1962.

Shortly after the Guild set up picket lines, *Sentinel* management informed the craft unions that the paper would cease publication until the strike was settled.

The bargaining was hard. "We felt it was the toughest negotiations we ever had," said Tony Ingrassia, a *Sentinel* sports writer, who served as the Guild's chief negotiator. The talks dragged on into the middle of June, then to the end of June, with little or no progress. The Hearst Corporation sent Thomas Brennan, an attorney from the New York office, out to Milwaukee to head up the management's bargaining team.

Management-labor relations at the *Sentinel* had always been very much an adversary situation, at least for as long as most of the *Sentinel* workers could remember. A few of the older Guild members longingly would reminisce about a time in the hazy past when management seemed much "nicer," and there was a spirit of cooperation all around. Ingrassia's answer was always "Yeah? If they were so nice, how come you guys always got such lousy contracts?"

It seemed to Ingrassia, who had joined the *Sentinel* right out of college in 1948, that since the middle '50s, the management had really begun to tighten up and economize, even going so far as to prohibit employees from taking copies of the paper home with them.

"They had someone at the door watching to make sure we weren't taking out a copy of the paper when we went home," Ingrassia recalled.

When it was time to negotiate a contract, the management team always made it clear that the *Sentinel* was a "consistent loser" and Hearst would have no qualms about shutting down the paper if the union didn't moderate its demands. Management said it again in 1962, but the Guild negotiators had been hearing the same warning for so many years that they didn't take it any more seriously than they did lawyer Brennan's admonition on the first day of the strike that "you guys better have good leather on your shoes, because you'll be walking [the picket line] for a long time."

"The Guild just read the signals all wrong," said Henry Gronkiewicz,

Sentinel business manager. "They figured we were making money because we were fixing up the building a little, trying to make it nicer."

In the middle of June, one hundred members of the International Typographical Union, who had been locked out when the strike began, applied for unemployment benefits and received them from the state, even though Wisconsin law at the time specifically denied benefits to anyone out of work because of a labor dispute. The law made no distinction between active participants in a dispute and those laid off as a result of a strike by other unions. The state unemployment compensation department director explained that the payments were made because the money was coming out of the *Sentinel*'s reserve account, and the *Sentinel* had not objected to the payments.

"We have no dispute with the typographers or any other craft," said Gronkiewicz, in explaining the unaccustomed benevolence. "Our disagreement is only with the Guild."

On June 27, the one-month anniversary of the strike, a deadlock developed in negotiations. Frustrated Guild negotiators accused Brennan of refusing to move on the issues.

"I'm moving," Brennan retorted. "I might be moving backwards and I might be moving sideways, but I'm always moving. That's what bargaining is all about." The talks broke off until July 9.

The American Newspaper Guild put its $500,000 international defense fund at the disposal of *Sentinel* members.

"Milwaukee Guildsmen will get full support from their international union, however long it takes to win this strike," vowed William J. Farson, Guild executive vice-president.

On July 19, a bargaining session was scheduled for 10 A.M. with a federal mediator, and for the first time, a state mediator was also present. The management negotiators showed up an hour late and they had a bombshell: There would be no more negotiation because the *Sentinel* had been sold to the afternoon *Journal*.

"The Guild people were in shock, and angry," recalled Gronkiewicz, who himself had only learned of the sale ten minutes earlier. "I was still in shock myself. All the negotiation for the sale, everything, was handled by the Hearst people out of New York."

Members of Local 51 suspected afterward that Hearst had been planning to sell the *Sentinel* even before the strike began. They generally have only very circumstantial evidence, but most of them are convinced nonetheless. One piece of evidence some cite is the fact that when the *Journal* interviewed *Sentinel* staffers for jobs, they called all the leaders of the Guild last, except for the strike steering committee chairman, who was one of the first editorial employees called for an interview. A night re-write man, he had become active in the Guild at the time of the strike. This indicated to some Guild members that the *Journal* had dossiers on the union leaders, which had been prepared ahead of the strike. Since this one man had only become active recently, no special file had been prepared on him, or so the reasoning went. A similar piece of evidence, which showed that the *Journal* had definitely received background information on the union leaders, was that during his *Journal* interview, one of the Guild activists was questioned about a socialist group he belonged to back in the 1930s.

Gronkiewicz, however, denied vehemently that dossiers or files were kept on any Guild leaders. "We had no files, I can assert that positively," he said.

Dick Berlin and Gerard Markuson, the general manager of the Hearst newspapers, issued a statement in which they said the *Sentinel* had suffered substantial losses over a long period.

"Prohibitive operating costs and labor demands have forced us to leave the Milwaukee newspaper field where we have been privileged to serve for 38 years," their statement added. "We greatly regret this move is necessary, but we have no alternative."

One published report said the *Sentinel*'s losses were running up to $200,000 a year. In fact, that figure was much too low. Until the year and a half before the paper was sold, losses were several million dollars a year; one year in the early 1950s, the paper lost eight million dollars. During the last eighteen months, the situation had begun to turn around, and Gronkiewicz was convinced that the paper could soon show a profit if the Guild would be "reasonable" in its demands. Losses for the last year and a half were at the annual rate of $300,000 to $500,000, Gronkiewicz said.

The *Journal* continued to publish the *Sentinel*, out of the recently modernized *Journal* headquarters, but without most of the former *Sentinel* staff members. About thirty members of the "old" *Sentinel* editorial staff were hired to help put out the "new" *Sentinel*—significantly, none of those hired was a Guild activist.

(9)

Among the printers and craftsmen employed by the New York newspapers, there was a certain body of folk wisdom, by repetition of which they reassured themselves that various newspapers—particularly the one on which they were employed—would never fold. *P.M.*, it was said, would never fold because it was owned by Marshall Field, who was the third-richest man in the country, and he wouldn't close it because it was a tax write-off. The *Sun* wouldn't close because it was owned by a trust fund set up for the New York Public Library, and one of the provisions was that it couldn't be sold or closed. The *Herald Tribune* would never be closed because it was the voice of the Republican Party. The *Journal-American* would never fold because it was the flagship of the Hearst chain, and Hearst needed a New York dateline.

And the *Mirror* would never fold because Hearst would not concede defeat to the *Daily News*.

But on October 15, 1963, Hearst did concede defeat. Rumors began circulating in the morning that the *Mirror* would close, and by mid-afternoon everyone suspected that there was some truth to it all. The official word came, not from Hearst management, but from the Guild. Wilfred Alexander, president of the Newspaper Guild of New York and shop steward for the *Mirror* unit, was given the Hearst announcement to read to the seventy-five reporters and desk men working in the editorial office. Alexander read the announcement—the Hearst Corporation was "reluctantly" ceasing publication with the October 16 issue, while "the name, good will and other intangible and physical assets of the *Mirror* have been sold to the *New York News*"—and added a few words of his own, denouncing "the callous and cold-blooded way this was kept from you."

Even Walter Winchell had not known of the closing in advance. To the radio and television people who had already swooped into the *Mirror* city room to watch the death throes of the newspaper, Winchell grumbled, "I've just been informed I go to the *Journal*. My secretary told it to me when I walked in. She said, 'I understand we're going out of business,' and I said, 'How can a paper with the second-largest circulation go out of business?'"

Some reporters reverted to wisecracks, stock in trade of newspaper humor. One typed out an obituary for the *Mirror*, thirty-nine-year-old "partner of the Hearst Corporation," dead in its home "after a long illness." Services to be held in the offices of the *Daily News*. Others were just bitter. "It was a typical Hearst closing," one rewrite man told a *New York Times* reporter. "They ring down the curtain in the middle of the third act and don't tell anybody anything."

Harsh internal debate had raged through the Hearst Corporation over whether the *Mirror* should be closed. Bill Hearst was against it, for the reason that he, personally, had the most to lose. He had worked hard for his title, editor in chief, and now that he had it, he didn't intend to see the chain sold out from under him. The *Mirror*, with the second-largest circulation in America, made Hearst a contender in the greatest newspaper market in the world. Surely, he argued in the Hearst executive councils, there was some value, albeit an uncertain one, to keeping a big metropolitan newspaper. The good will, even prestige, would offset the strict dollar loss. And there was always the possibility that the paper could be turned around financially. With new equipment and some big circulation-building promotions, it might work.

But to Berlin, it seemed a very tenuous "might," and as for putting more money into the *Mirror*, they might as well throw it down a hole. Furthermore, Berlin reminded the other executives, holding onto money-losing newspapers for prestige or political clout made the kind of good sense that nearly bankrupted the company twenty-five years earlier.

Money problems were nothing new for the *Mirror*, a racy morning tabloid, heavily loaded with columnists and still reflecting in many ways the slogan Hearst had adopted when he founded the paper in 1924: "90 percent entertainment and 10 percent news."

Although Hearst had sought to imitate the fabulously successful *Daily News*, started by Joseph Medill Patterson five years before the *Mirror*, Hearst was able to match only the *Daily New's* format; in advertising and circulation he could never catch up. Consequently, while the *Daily News* turned into a virtual gold mine for the Patterson organization, the *Mirror* was always a drag on Hearst. At one point, in 1928, Hearst even sold the paper, but he bought it back two years later, convinced that he had given up too soon in his battle against the *Daily News*.

By the middle 1930s, the *Mirror's* circulation had hit 600,000, but the *Daily News* was selling more than a million copies each day. During the years of World War II, the *Mirror* was profitable, but the profit margins declined through the 1950s, and by the end of the decade, the paper was losing money at the rate of some $2 million a year.

In 1962, Dick Berlin publicly stated that the *Mirror* could turn a profit if it sold for 7 cents instead of 5 cents. However, with other morning papers, and in particular the *Daily News*, selling for 5 cents, it was impossible for the *Mirror* to raise its price without risking a huge loss in circulation. Berlin's statement would indicate that the *Mirror*, with a circulation of about one million, was losing at a rate of more than $10,000 and less than $20,000 per day. That translated into annual losses of between $3 million and $6 million.

The 114-day New York newspaper strike that lasted from December 8, 1962, until April 1 the following spring, badly wounded the *Mirror*. Although the *Mirror* itself was not struck, the Hearst Corporation closed it in a show of publisher solidarity with the four newspapers directly affected by the strike, which included their own *Journal-American*.

The lengthy shutdown caused the *Mirror* to miss the Christmas and Easter advertising bonanzas, the two most lucrative times of year for the retail trade and, hence, the newspapers, which lived on their advertising. Not that the *Mirror* ever pulled in ads on a scale comparable to the *Daily News*; observers of the New York newspaper business had noticed that advertisers tended to patronize only one newspaper in a given category. Among the "class" morning papers they favored the *Times* over the *Herald Tribune*, while the *Daily News*, not the *Mirror*, got the bulk of the ads directed at a "mass" audience.

What advertisers the *Mirror* did have were no doubt dissuaded from spending as much money as they might have by the fact that the *Mirror* never seemed to regain the readers it had before the strike. Circulation slipped from 900,000 toward 800,000 in the fall of 1963.

Among other troubles that plagued the *Mirror* was that its equipment was antiquated and dilapidated, contributing to inefficiency in putting out the newspaper.

Perhaps the most vexing problem, and all the more aggravating because in theory it should have been the easiest to resolve, was the price of the newspaper. A price hike was long overdue. After the strike, the other morning newspapers raised their street price to a dime, but the *Daily News* remained at a nickel. As long as the *News* stayed at five cents, the Hearst executives felt that they had no choice but to keep the same

price as well. On several occasions during the summer and early fall of
1963, Dick Berlin reportedly talked to *Daily News* publisher F. M. Flynn
in an attempt to convince him that the *News* should go up to at least
seven cents, if not a dime. But Flynn, although he bemoaned the increasing costs, declined to move up the *News's* price, contending they
were doing all right at a nickel, and wanting to stay below the *Times*
and the *Herald Tribune*. Berlin thought the real reason for Flynn's staying at a nickel was that he was trying to run the *Mirror* out of business.
And unfortunately, Berlin concluded, Flynn was succeeding.

By October, when Berlin had convinced the other Hearst Corporation
directors (even a reluctant Bill Hearst finally went along with the decision) that it was time to pull the plug on the *Mirror*, the newspaper was
reportedly losing one million dollars a month.

On the *Mirror's* last day of publication, the closest thing to an official
comment came from Bunky Hearst, working there as a photographer,
who wandered into the city room in the course of the evening. Besieged
by reporters asking for his reaction, he groped for words to explain what
he felt, and finally sputtered, "What can I say? It takes everything I've
got to keep from crying. If we could have economized, we would have
done it. Most holes have a bottom, but this one did not seem to have
any."

The *Mirror* went out with spirit on its last day. After the first edition,
the drinking started in earnest, on the assumption that there would be no
further changes in the paper. But during the evening, the editors decided
to replate for a two-star, then a three-star. At 11:30 P.M., a copyreader
yelled over to Mort Ehrman, the night editor, "Hey, Mort, we got a five-
star coming up?"

"Damn right we got a five-star coming up," Ehrman shouted. The
five-star page-one banner headline, the last Ehrman would write for the
Mirror, read: "VALACHI SINGS HERE TODAY." Then, at 1:25 A.M.,
Ehrman, a member of the *Mirror* staff since 1925, put on his coat and
said farewell to the crew—"Well, gentlemen, goodnight. And before you
leave, be sure to kill the bottles."

The last press run began at 2:17 A.M., and when it was finished at
3:30, the *Mirror* was dead.

Chapter 5

Realpolitik

(1)

PERHAPS, as Dick Berlin stoutly maintained, it had been absolutely necessary to close, merge or sell all those newspapers. But others were not so sure. In fact, the wave of newspaper deaths had created a sharp division among top company management—within the organization they even used a Civil War metaphor and called the split the "blues and the grays," newspaper people against the magazine people.

"There was no rhyme or reason to those closings," said a Hearst official who had argued against many of them. "They just went one after another as Dick Berlin decided their market position was bad."

As the Hearst Corporation let go of newspaper after newspaper it created a widespread impression that the whole organization was withering away or on the verge of total collapse. It was a kind of loser image that people like Bill Hearst especially disliked, all the more so because it was not accurate. By 1960, the Hearst Corporation had pulled through a decade of financial difficulties—for the first time since it had been issued in 1948, Hearst Corporation common stock was paying dividends —and the future, if it didn't look exactly rosy, at least did not look dismal.

Dick Berlin was a magazine person. He had come up through the magazine ranks; he understood magazine advertising; he had developed a feel for the special chemistry that makes a magazine work. He loved to talk about magazine distribution, graphics, editorial content. Everything about them.

Newspapers, however, were another matter. Some people saw Berlin's attitude toward newspapers as strictly pragmatic—they were a business, and they either made money or didn't. And if they didn't, they got shut down or sold. His closest associates, however, knew that Berlin had a more deep-seated, emotional attitude about newspapers. He didn't like them. In particular, he didn't like the Hearst newspapers.

It was a curious sort of attitude, particularly for the top Hearst Corporation executive. Part of it was a reaction to his years working under old W. R. More than the other Hearst executives, Berlin had been able to see firsthand that W. R. Hearst had a blind spot in relation to money. Berlin had been there when the corporation was on the verge of bankruptcy, and he saw that it was brought there in large part because of Hearst's fondness for his newspapers. The old man never willingly sold a single paper, and some of them were bleeding him white. The losses ran into the millions. And what was more, profits from the magazines were constantly being diverted to subsidize newspaper losses. It was a painful, frustrating experience for Berlin to sit and watch the newspapers gradually eat the Hearst Corporation deeper and deeper into debt. His experience in those years undoubtedly formed the basis of his opinion later, which he expressed to colleagues when the Chicago *American* was sold, that the heyday of newspapers was over, that in the future, unless a newspaper was the biggest and best in its market, it would not be able to make a profit. Berlin very much admired the strategy of the Gannett newspaper chain, which was to buy papers in medium-sized cities where there was no competition.

There was another reason Dick Berlin disliked the Hearst papers, and it was something he only talked about obliquely. It had to do with the connotation carried by the name "Hearst." The name was tainted; it represented cheapness, sensationalism, an absence of ethics, maybe even a tendency toward fraud. Try as he might to ignore aspersions on the name of Hearst, Berlin was painfully aware that they existed, and he was probably only seeing the proverbial tip of the iceberg. He saw it when the Hearst Castle was offered to the State of California, and resistance arose on the Parks Commission, because of "a certain hostility to William Randolph Hearst," as Berlin was told. Berlin knew that journalism schools used the Hearst press as an example of yellow journalism. He recognized the aspersions when an editor at Simon and Schuster suggested to Edmond Coblentz, who edited *William Randolph Hearst, A Portrait in His Own Words*, that he not dedicate the book to the five Hearst sons, because it would make the book "look more official than it will look anyway." Coblentz didn't understand what was wrong with looking "official," even after the editor explained that magazine editors had refused to serialize the book, because, "I suspect it's the old legend that is principally involved in their reluctance to buy it." It was a "stupid legend," the editor continued, but nonetheless "anything that suggests to readers all the overtones and undertones of earlier prejudices, therefore seems to me a little unhappy."

The opprobrium aroused by the name Hearst, Berlin realized, was due entirely to the reputation of the Hearst newspapers. No one ever considered *Cosmopolitan, Good Housekeeping* or *Motor Boating* "cheap," "sensational," or any other adjective applied to the yellow press.

Berlin once remarked to a friend that he wondered what kind of reputation the Hearst organization would have if they sold all their newspapers, got out of the newspaper field entirely. The friend, not sure whether this was a course of action Berlin was seriously considering, replied that it would be "catastrophic" and unthinkable. Berlin then said, yes, he supposed so, and the subject was dropped. But in his attitude toward the newspapers, it was clear that Berlin took a coldly unsympathetic view—he tolerated them. He even exaggerated the extent of his "pragmatic" approach to the newspapers; he liked to tell friends and family members that he had a strict rule: if a newspaper lost money for three years in a row, they got rid of it. An examination of just a few Hearst papers indicates that this was not a strict rule, if it was even a guideline. The Milwaukee *Sentinel*, for example, never turned a profit from the end of World War II until it was sold in 1962. The Los Angeles *Herald-Express* lost money in eight of its last eleven years, with an uninterrupted losing streak from 1956 through 1961. But even if a "three-year" rule was not enforced, the mere fact that Berlin would boast of taking such a tough stance toward the survival of the Hearst newspapers bespoke an underlying hostility that certainly could not do the papers any good.

(2)

While the crumbling Hearst urban dailies received the most attention from outside media and, therefore, from the public in general, there was, within the Hearst organization, a great deal of simultaneous building that passed relatively unnoticed. In the early 1950s the company had substantial assets, but many properties were producing no income, and, of course, some were losing money. Berlin's general plan for dealing with the company malaise was to dispose of the nonproducing properties and reinvest the money in more promising ventures. In the first half of the decade, he turned a considerable amount of real estate into cash, including the million-acre Babicora ranch in northern Mexico and about 29,000 acres of land near Los Angeles. At the time, there might have been no way for Berlin to foresee it, but the Southern California land he disposed of at rock-bottom prices was later the site of the exclusive Westlake Village housing development. He came close to selling off the 67,000 acres of timberland in Northern California on which W. R. Hearst had built his Wyntoon estate. To the lasting good fortune of the Hearst Corporation, the highest offer for the land—$5.5 million—came from Joe Kennedy, whom Berlin had never forgiven for his attempt to buy up the stable of Hearst magazines in 1939. The Kennedy offer brought Berlin up short in his determination to quickly sell off the land. "If that son of a bitch is offering five and a half million," he fumed to his associates, "I'll bet a year's salary that land is worth three times as much."

He immediately ordered a timber cruise, and for the $35,000 it cost, learned that the lumber, if taken out all at once, was worth $25 million to $35 million. Or, the land could be scientifically logged indefinitely for an annual output of about $2 million per year, which the Hearst Corporation decided to do.

In 1953, the company added the first publishing property to its fold since W. R. died. For a reported price of almost $1 million, they bought the sixty-six-year-old *Sports Afield*, a monthly magazine with a circulation of 860,000 that ran neck-and-neck with the competition, *Field and Stream* and *Outdoor Life*. The purchase, Berlin announced at the time, was "the first of a series of acquisitions by the Hearst Corporation, and part of a long-term expansion program."

Berlin's statement implied a great deal more organization than anyone in the Hearst Corporation was aware of. There may have been some specific expansion program on the drawing board, but it was a secret to everyone except Dick Berlin.

But if he didn't have a specific program in mind, he did have some general principles regarding new acquisitions. First, and most importantly, the Hearst Corporation would not go into debt to buy new properties. Secondly, Berlin preferred specialized magazines, not the mass-circulation giants like *Saturday Evening Post*, *Look*, and *Life*, whose profit margins were paper-thin and depended on sustained and massive doses of advertising to stay in business. Newspapers, if the company was going to acquire any, would be along the lines of the Gannett model, in medium-sized cities where there was no competition.

And, finally, the corporation was in no hurry to acquire new properties; if one came on the market, it would be considered, but in no sense could the Hearst Corporation be said to be aggressively looking for new publications.

In 1955, Hearst acquired *Bride and Home* magazine. In 1958, the company bought the fifty-six-year-old *Popular Mechanics*, which its owners, the H. H. Windsor family of Chicago, had been trying to sell for nearly a year. *Popular Mechanics* was a particularly savvy purchase, as Berlin demonstrated by turning around and selling the building that was included in the sale for nearly as much as he had paid for the magazine and building together. The next year, *Science Digest* was added to the Hearst magazine division, along with Avon Publications, Inc., a publisher of paperback drugstore thrillers, which had put out 117 titles the previous year.

Heading up the magazine division was one of Berlin's protégés, who by coincidence was named Richard Emmet Deems, a tall, good-looking man, who shared many of Berlin's personal characteristics. He dressed immaculately and conservatively, and, as co-workers commented, "sells his personality rather than his product . . . engulfs his business associates in a warm wash of charm and compliments." The perfect salesman. He had joined the Hearst organization in 1939 on *Harper's Bazaar*, after working in the circulation departments of *The New Yorker* and *Esquire*. He was advertising manager for *Harper's* from 1947 to 1952, where cautious, methodical work caught Berlin's attention and he rose quickly to vice-president in charge of Hearst magazines, the top magazine division post.

Second in command to Deems on the magazines was Fred Lewis, a diminutive, colorless man, who often struck people on first meeting as being shy. In fact, Lewis was a hard-boiled troubleshooter, whose sharp eye, always trained on the books, made sure that no one was getting any money that he or she wasn't entitled to. "Fred goes through a sheaf of bills like a cost accountant," an associate said. "He doesn't let a supplier get away with a thing." One of Lewis' primary functions was to make sure the five Hearst sons didn't spend money they didn't have, by charging bills to the newspapers or other Hearst enterprises. An insider at the company confided that it was almost a full-time job for Lewis, as the Hearst heirs felt strongly that they were entitled to certain perquisites by virtue of the family name. But Berlin—through Lewis—disagreed. A friend of Berlin's recalled one day in the early 1950s, when he was with Berlin in his office and the Hearst president spotted an item in Dorothy Kilgallen's column "about the diamond necklace from Tiffany's that Bill Hearst had given his wife, Bootsie, for their anniversary." Berlin immediately summoned Lewis and ordered him to "find out how much that thing cost and how he paid for it." Lewis learned that the piece of jewelry, costing something over $10,000, had been charged to the *Journal-American*. Lewis was dispatched to compel Bill to return the necklace.

While Lewis' cost-controlling was generally effective in a bookkeeping way, the sort of thing Berlin appreciated, it did not always turn out to be profitable in the long run. To take just one example, it backfired badly when Lewis, Deems and Berlin decided that Herbert Mayes, editor of *Good Housekeeping*, was overpaid. They did not renew his contract in 1958. Mayes then tripped off to edit *McCall's* and *Redbook*; and under his charge both magazines, within four years, doubled both their circulation and their advertising revenues. *Good Housekeeping*, meanwhile, dropped behind its long-time competitors, *McCall's* and *Ladies Home Journal*.

In 1960, the Hearst Corporation picked up its only new newspaper during the Berlin years. The buy was the Albany (New York) *Knickerbocker News*, the only afternoon paper in a city where Hearst already owned the *Times-Union*, the only morning paper.

The acquisitions were all deliberate, careful and, above all, profitable. But there was one spectacular failure, not in anything the company bought, but in what it failed to buy. Shortly after the *Sports Afield* acquisition, the company was given a chance to buy the fledgling *TV Guide* for $75,000. Berlin turned up his nose at the deal, sniffing that television was "just a fad." He stuck to this position three years later, when the magazine was offered for $2 million. Shortly afterward it was sold to another publisher for $7 million, eventually garnered the largest circulation of any magazine in the country, and came to be considered the most valuable magazine property in the world.

As even Berlin's most loyal friends concede, he "had a blind spot a mile wide when it came to television." For years, Berlin refused to allow a television into his home, and he only relented in 1957 at the strong urging of his family. Once a television was installed in the house, however, Berlin was hooked. According to his nephew, Ted Harbert, Berlin was fascinated by sports coverage and spent hours watching baseball and football broadcasts. Nonetheless, he stoutly maintained that no one watched commercials. "They just get up and go to the bathroom," he would say irately when anyone tried to tell him otherwise.

But his skepticism about the future of television did not prevent Berlin from competing aggressively to get television channels for the Hearst Corporation. One of the hardest-fought battles was in Pittsburgh, where Hearst and four other applicants were in competition for Channel 4.

"Dick loved a good fight," his wife noted. "I think he would go after something just because he knew someone else wanted it."

The fight in Pittsburgh, which had been pending for several years, appeared to be over in 1954, when—in a typical Berlin move—Hearst arranged a merger of all five applicants for the station. But the merger fell apart when one of the other participants backed out.

Scheming, plotting and negotiation among the various parties continued as the FCC moved toward a hearing on the applications. The Hearst team was led by Charles McCabe, publisher of the *Mirror* and chairman of the "Radio and Television Committee of the Hearst Corporation." Although the Hearst subsidiary, WCAE Inc., which was applying for the license, was part of Hearst Consolidated, McCabe held no official position with Consolidated. It was another indication that official titles and corporate divisions, which abounded within the Hearst organization, meant very little. Behind the scenes, calling the shots, was Dick Berlin, whom McCabe kept posted on developments.

McCabe was convinced that the other four applicants were interested in the station only as a speculative investment—once they had the license to operate, they could then turn around and sell it, especially if the station was affiliated with CBS, which was then the most valuable network tie-in. McCabe felt that even a corporation controlled by Irwin Wolf and Earl Reed, the most serious competitors for the license, was "thinking only in terms of capital gains through some manipulation with CBS."

By 1955, when CBS had signed an affiliation with another Pittsburgh-area television station, the only network available was ABC. McCabe set out to disabuse the other applicants of any notions they might have harbored about quick profits from getting the television license.

From an office memorandum of a meeting between McCabe and a group of stockholders in a company called Wespen, which was competing for the license:

> Mr. McCabe explained to the Wespen group that since the Columbia network had signed an affiliation agreement with Channel 11, that Channel 4 had available only an ABC affiliation. Therefore, the proposition was not as attractive as when we previously attempted to merge the applicants. . . . If Wespen or any other applicants could come up with a proposal for merger that would be satisfactory to all applicants as well as Hearst, it would have to be understood that there would be no inflated values introduced into the proposition that would increase the capitalization, such as unneeded real estate, etc. Moreover, any former proposals which contemplated high-salary jobs for applicants or relatives of the applicants, would not be feasible on an ABC operation. It was explained that an ABC operation would have to be operated as tight as possible in order to keep the losses in the early years to a minimum. At this point several of Mr. Fink's stockholders seemed to lose interest in the entire project, particularly Mr. Cruikshank, who had the impression that any grant of an application would be worth $2 million to a recipient . . .

Some of the other applicants suggested that Hearst "buy them out," that is, pay them in order to drop their applications. Other suggestions included one that a merger be arranged, with Hearst to buy out the other stockholders afterward.

In April of 1956, an FCC hearing examiner recommended that the Reed-Wolf group, which was calling itself Television City, be granted the license. However, Irwin Wolf then died, and the examiner reconsidered the evidence in light of the new development and decided in April of 1957 that Hearst should get the license. The examiner's finding was not final, but was merely a recommendation to the full seven-member commission. The next month, Earl Reed had lunch with FCC chairman George McConnaughey, and somehow formed the impression that

McConnaughey favored Television City. On June 3 of that year the commission heard oral arguments from the license applicants; the commissioners split 3–3 between Television City and WCAE, the Hearst company.

A series of rather suspicious developments then occurred, which became the subject of a congressional investigation the following year. Since the commission was split 3–3, the vote of chairman G. C. McConnaughey was crucial to the successful applicant.

On June 11, Berlin met with FCC commissioner Richard Mack— the point of the meeting was never clearly explained. The meeting had been arranged through the office of Senator George Smathers of Florida. Berlin told McCabe that the meeting was of a purely social nature and did not involve discussion of the television license. However, at the congressional hearings, the next year, one of the committee members wondered why a social meeting had to be arranged through a Senator's office. Mack had been one of the three commission members who voted for Television City.

The next day, McCabe wrote a letter to McConnaughey, starting his letter "Dear George," and addressing it to McConnaughey at home. Although McCabe said that he decided not to send the letter, which dealt with a meeting between Hearst and the Reed-Wolf group, investigators felt the salutation and the fact that it was addressed to the commissioner at his home indicated a familiarity or perhaps an *"ex parte"* contact that was somehow unethical.

At about this same time, Reed began circulating rumors that McConnaughey was soliciting bribes for his vote on the case; amounts mentioned ranged from $50,000 to $200,000. The bribes allegedly would be paid over a period of years, in the form of legal fees. In the congressional hearings, Reed maintained that he could not remember where he had heard the rumors, and everyone else who testified traced the rumors back to Reed. If Reed had deliberately started these rumors, it was not clear exactly what he hoped to gain from them, though obviously he must have hoped, in some way, to put pressure on either Hearst or McConnaughey.

In June it was also known that McConnaughey intended to resign at the end of the month. Hearst and Reed-Wolf began discussing a merger between Television City and WCAE, convinced that if something could be worked out between the two of them, it would have certain board approval, if it got done before McConnaughey resigned. Otherwise, a new board member might have to be briefed on the background of the case, with a resulting delay of months or even years. As Hearst and Reed-Wolf viewed the situation, every day they didn't have a television station in operation was another day they were failing to earn broadcasting revenue.

The Hearst and Reed-Wolf people were not particularly amiable business partners, and their negotiation was characterized by stormy sessions that ended with one side or another walking out, ultimatums, deadlines, and charges of negotiating in bad faith. At one point in the merger discussions McCabe wired Earl Reed that he had until noon the next day to decide whether to take an option on 50 percent of WCAE Inc. stock. Reed fired back a wire protesting that he had received McCabe's telegram at 9:15 P.M. (Wednesday) and didn't have any recent financial statements on WCAE, and could not possibly be prepared for a meeting by noon Thursday. Reed concluded his wire with the icy notation: "You neglected us entirely for 2 weeks and then demanded action in 14 hours. Let me know when and where you want to meet Friday evening, if you care to do so."

Back and forth it went, and no merger was arranged by the time McConnaughey left the FCC. The day after McConnaughey resigned, he became associated in a law firm with George O. Sutton, who had been representing Television City before the FCC. The Hearst people thought something smelled fishy, but there wasn't much that could be done. Negotiation with Television City moved ahead, with an eventual agreement that Hearst would acquire 50 percent of the stock of Television City and the group would pay $50,000 to each of the other three applicants for the Channel-4 license to get them out of the picture. This arrangement was approved by the FCC on July 23, and on July 27 the channel was awarded to Television City.

The Hearst Consolidated report for 1958 noted proudly that "Television station WTAE (Pittsburgh), in which we own a half interest, went on the air on September 14, 1958. WTAE is affiliated with the ABC network. Operations to date have been most satisfactory."

The Consolidated report didn't mention that nine days after the station went on the air, the first report of an investigation for the House Special Subcommittee on Legislative Oversight was made public, and a resulting set of hearings kept the allegations of bribes, and unethical behavior by both Hearst and the Reed-Wolf group before the public eye for two months.

Berlin maintained a remarkably disingenuous attitude toward the whole affair. At the height of the publicity over the case, a close friend asked Berlin what had really happened before the FCC. Replied Berlin, "Who's on the FCC?" They changed the subject.

Within a few years, Berlin's attitude toward television had evolved to the point where he led the fight against considerable opposition on the Hearst Corporation board of directors to buy out the Reed-Wolf interest in WTAE. In 1962, the Hearst Corporation laid out $10.5 million for the Reed-Wolf half share. (On the books, Hearst Consolidated owned the first 50 percent of the station while the Hearst Corporation owned the rest). It was probably one of the most astute investments the company ever made. In 1978, the Hearst Corporation turned down an offer of more than $100 million for the station.

(3)

Dick Berlin had a philosophy about competition in the publishing business—it wasn't good for business. It was one of his bigger frustrations that competing magazine publishers frequently engaged in rate-cutting in order to lure advertisers away from each other—a practice that would force everyone to lower rates, or else run the risk of losing advertising clients to the rate-cutters. Berlin summarized his attitude in 1941 when he wrote to Hearst telling him that he had just met with the publishers of McCall, Curtis and Crowell in an effort to pound some reason into them and get them to increase their rates. In that case Berlin was successful, and the other publishers eventually did increase their rates to match the Hearst publications.

Whether it was newspapers or magazines, Berlin saw the path to greater profits in steadily increasing advertising and circulation rates. He wholeheartedly endorsed and frequently repeated the advice to Hearst publishers given by W. R. in 1948:

> Raise your rates often and raise them sufficiently . . . otherwise you will be at the head of an unsuccessful newspaper.
> Immediately after one raise of rates you should be laying the foundation for another raise.

Advertising rate raises should be continuous, and circulation rate raises should be frequent.

I think that the various papers should interchange information as to rate raises and contemplated rate raises . . . Keep in communication with your associates in other cities and what is more keep in communication with your competitors in your own city.

It helps materially if all the papers in the city make raises as a constant practice.

"Cooperation." That was Berlin's intuitive business sense talking. "Antitrust" . . . "Conspiracy to monopolize" . . . "Restraint of trade." That was the United States Department of Justice talking. Inevitably, they ended up talking to each other a lot.

In virtually every Hearst newspaper sale of the 1950s and 1960s, the U. S. Justice Department investigated for possible antitrust violations. Berlin habitually pressed close to the limits of legality, and perhaps strayed over the boundary such as in 1961 when the government charged that King Features was involved in a conspiracy to monopolize the printing of Sunday color comics. The government lawsuit was eventually settled by a consent agreement—Hearst agreed not to engage in price-fixing or attempt to prevent other parties from printing and selling comic supplements.

The economics of newspaper publishing provided a particular temptation to engage in deals that created a monopoly. It was no coincidence that in each of eleven Hearst newspaper sales, the buyer was the publisher of a paper in the same city. After several Justice Department investigations, Berlin began sending company lawyers to Washington to get department approval before closing deals that involved possible antitrust violations.

Berlin's network of Washington contacts proved extremely helpful in such situations, according to Hearst executives, who remain vague as to exactly how this help manifested itself. In one case, at least two Hearst executives claim that President Lyndon Johnson exerted pressure on the Justice Department to approve a pending Hearst deal—a joint operating agreement between the San Francisco *Examiner* and the *Chronicle*.

Although no independent verification of Johnson's role could be obtained, circumstantial evidence in the case points toward the likelihood of unusual high-level involvement.

On October 23, 1964, the Chronicle Publishing Company and Hearst agreed to form the San Francisco Newspaper Printing Company, whose stock was to be owned equally by the two parties. The new corporation would perform the mechanical, circulation, advertising, accounting, credit and collection functions for both newspapers. In other words, the two papers would merge all operations except editorial. Profits of the joint operation would be split 50–50. The agreement provided that Hearst's *News-Call Bulletin* would be suspended and the *Examiner* would become an afternoon paper. The proposed agreement was submitted to the Justice Department for approval. At this point, the Hearst-Chronicle arrangement ran into some amazingly good luck—which some claim was more than luck.

At the same time that the Hearst and Chronicle joint-operating agreement was submitted for approval, the Justice Department was in the midst of an antitrust suit against the Citizen Publishing Company of Tucson, Arizona, in which the antitrust division was attempting to show that a joint-operating agreement in effect between the Tucson *Citizen* and the Tucson *Star*—exactly the same type of agreement proposed for San Francisco—was a per se violation of antitrust law.

The prospects for the Justice Department winning the Tucson newspaper case looked good—in fact, the department did eventually win a court trial on the matter. But nonetheless, the department gave approval to the *Examiner-Chronicle* joint-operating agreement. Actually, the department said it "would not oppose" the semimerger "at this time."

Dark rumblings among the suburban newspaper publishers hinted at some kind of "fix" in the *Examiner-Chronicle* agency. In testimony before the House antitrust subcommittee of the Committee on the Judiciary on September 26, 1968, Richard W. Nowels, owner of four small weekly papers in the Menlo Park area near San Francisco, placed into the record a memo from one of his publishers who formerly worked for the San Francisco *Examiner*. The publisher, Don Wilson, said he learned from a trustworthy source that "there were many really big names involved" in the Justice Department approval of the semimerger. "Doubtless there are many skeletons involved."

The biggest of the names was apparently that of Lyndon Johnson, a long-time friend of Dick Berlin's. Berlin's nephew Ted Harbert confirmed that the Hearst Corporation president was on very friendly terms with

Johnson and said that Berlin had even let him listen in on several telephone conversations with the President. At various times Berlin had been
able to do Johnson several favors—making sure that the San Antonio
Light endorsed him when he first ran for Congress; and once he waived
an International News Service bill for Johnson's television station. This
was definitely Berlin's style. As his son Richard put it, "My father was
always ready to do a favor for anyone who might be in a position to help
the Hearst Corporation, and in turn he never hesitated to extract favors
from these same people."

As Charles Gould, publisher of the *Examiner* remembered it, William
Orrick, who later was the judge who sentenced Patty Hearst to prison,
was an assistant attorney general in the antitrust division of the Justice
Department, and—in Gould's words—"He got his hands on our proposal
and said 'No way.' I don't think it was until Bobby Kennedy or maybe
Lyndon Johnson stepped in and told him it was better to have two
papers than just one that the thing even went through." Interestingly,
Orrick resigned from the Justice Department at the end of August 1965.
On September 13, the joint-operating agreement went into effect.

The immediate effect of the joint agreement was that the two newspapers raised their advertising rates. The *Chronicle's* open line rate went
up from $1.20 per line to $2.32 per line. The *Examiner* raised its rate
from $1.03 to $1.55 per line. The real squeeze on both advertisers and
the suburban competition newspapers was in the combination advertising rate. For $2.58 per line, an advertiser could get his ad in both
newspapers. The combination rate was only 26 cents above the rate for
the *Chronicle* alone. Since no other afternoon paper was available for
$.26 per line, businesses naturally tended to advertise in both San
Francisco newspapers; indeed, they could hardly afford to do otherwise.
What amounted to a sudden doubling of advertising rates, however, did
not sit well with the major advertisers, though there was little they
could do. Lamented one head of advertising for a Bay Area department-
store chain: "After the merger we no longer had any leverage. With our
bargaining position removed, we no longer get the position in the paper
we want . . . With even two independent papers the . . . stores could
advertise heavily in one at half the price charged by the merged papers.
Now we have to take space in both papers."

Clearly, someone was following Berlin's advice to keep in touch with
the competition when it came to the matter of rates.

(4)

Hearst Consolidated Publications, Inc. The very name gave Dick Berlin a headache. As the only corporation within the Hearst organization that had ever sold stock to the public, it was required to publish annual statements of income and make other financial disclosures not required of the parent corporation or any other Hearst subsidiary. That was a nuisance. In addition, Consolidated was not doing well financially. That was an embarrassment. And, finally, if Consolidated missed four dividend payments in a row, the stockholders could kick out the Hearst directors and elect their own slate to run the company. That was a threat.

The problems with Hearst Consolidated began even before the company actually existed. Back in 1924, W. R. Hearst found himself strapped for funds, having just splurged on his San Simeon castle and St. Donat's castle in England, along with some Manhattan real estate and a few million dollars' worth of artwork. To raise cash, he grouped most of his newspaper properties together in a holding company called Hearst Publications Inc. and floated a $12 million bond issue. An easy $12 million. That was Hearst's first fling with outside financing—that is, spending other people's money—and he liked it. He liked it so much that in 1930, with the legal assistance of John Francis Neylan, he hatched a plot that would bring in a painless—or so it seemed at the time—$50 million. He took all the newspapers in Hearst Publications (which was still paying off its $12 million bonded debt) and added a few other newspapers, plus the *American Weekly* Sunday supplement and a paper mill and called the whole thing Hearst Consolidated Publications, Inc. With a barrage of publicity in his newspapers, Hearst began selling stock—nonvoting stock, called Class A 7 percent preferred—directly to the public at $25 per share. The public, which had to go no further than the nearest Hearst newspaper to buy the stock, bought two million shares between 1930 and 1935. Although the Class A was nonvoting (Hearst himself kept all the voting stock) there was a provision that allowed Class A stockholders to take over the company if four dividends in a row were ever missed.

For several years, the dividends flowed regularly, 43½ cents per share every three months. Then, hard times hit Hearst in 1938, and Consolidated passed a dividend. Stockholders were up in arms; one group filed suit against Hearst, charging that he "dominated" the board of directors and operated the company "for his own personal gain." They were especially incensed by a 1935 transaction in which Hearst sold his Baltimore, Atlanta and San Antonio papers—which were losing a total of $550,000 a year—to Consolidated for $8 million.

The stockholder plaintiffs felt Hearst had slipped into a flight of fantasy—or fraud—by valuing the money-losing papers' "circulation, press franchises, reference libraries, etc." at $6 million.

The Consolidated headaches had begun. The company weathered the lawsuits, and somehow found the cash to pay out at least one dividend per year, thus preventing the stockholders from locking up the whole Hearst hierarchy for vagrancy. By the time Hearst died in 1951, the company had missed 22 quarterly dividends, placing the stock $9.62½ per share in arrears. But the real problems were just beginning.

Consolidated profits had been dropping steadily from a high of $13.5 million in 1946 to $2.9 million in 1951. The next year was even worse—$1.6 million. And in 1954, the company showed a loss for the first time in its history, falling into the red by $340,000.

The biggest single problem within Consolidated was *American Weekly*, the pioneer Sunday supplement magazine in the country. Started in 1896 on Hearst's personally designed formula of "sex, sensation and sea serpents," the magazine boomed in the first three decades of the new century, serving its readers astounding features on archaeology, science, history and astrology, along with popular fiction, bizarre crime ("Nailed Her Father's Head to the Front Door," ran the classic headline), gaudy illustrations, and lightly clad "Zodiac" cover girls. Unfortunately, by the 1940s, *American Weekly* was looking downright old-fashioned, never having changed its typography or format. What was worse, from an advertising standpoint, the *Weekly* never adopted modern color-printing technology. While rival supplements such as *This Week*, which started in 1935, were using the rotogravure process, the Chief insisted that the *Weekly* continue to be printed on his old Hoe-Pancoast four-color presses. The *Weekly* also faced competition for advertisers' dollars from the new picture publications, such as *Life* and *Look*, which emphasized high-quality printing. The result was that advertisers, unhappy with the way their products looked in the *Weekly*, began deserting in favor of the slick rival publications. Campbell Soups pulled its advertising schedule because the *Weekly*, it complained, could not print tomato soup that looked like tomato soup. Within months after the Chief died *This Week* surpassed *American Weekly* as the largest Sunday supplement in the country.

For sentimental reasons, Berlin truly wanted to rejuvenate the *Weekly*; although it was lumped together with the newspapers, he considered it closer to a magazine, and if nothing else, Berlin prided himself on knowing how to get a magazine to produce a profit.

Following Hearst's death, two immediate changes were made—both things the Chief had stubbornly resisted. The magazine was changed from rough newsprint to slick rotogravure, and it began selling to non-Hearst newspapers.

Robert Levitt, a Hearstling since the early '30s, was installed and he brought in editor Ernest Heyn, who modernized the format with how-to articles, fashion, homemaking and beauty features. It wasn't enough, and the *Weekly* still lagged. Levitt shuffled editors; still, there was no improvement, and in 1955, Levitt was shuffled out in favor of John K. Herbert.

Nothing seemed to work. Advertising revenue was $24.7 million in 1957, declined to $23.2 million the next year, and suffered precipitous drops to $15.7 million in 1959 and $11.0 million in 1960.

The Hearst management was becoming desperate. Thinking that advertisers might be staying away from the *Weekly* because its circulation duplicated that of other Sunday supplements—it was estimated that 40 percent of the *American Weekly*'s circulation was also covered by *This Week*, *Parade* or *Family Weekly*—Hearst decided to quit selling to some twenty non-Hearst newspapers that carried the magazine. Starting in January of 1962, *American Weekly* appeared in only nine Hearst papers and the Chicago *American*, a former Hearst paper.

Losses by the *Weekly* were a carefully guarded secret at Hearst headquarters, but they apparently were substantial. In May of 1963, Hearst announced that *American Weekly* would cease publication after its September 1 issue.

The Hearst Consolidated annual reports recited the same litany of complaints each year—higher newsprint costs, higher labor costs, and bad business conditions in general. The 1952 report provided and reiterated Hearst management's business philosophy: "Our business . . . is highly competitive. In no city do we have the only newspaper. Whenever our competitive position has permitted, we have raised the selling prices of

our newspapers and our advertising rates and further increases are contemplated whenever possible." Unfortunately, the report went on to note,
"These increases in prices in many cases tend to result in temporary
losses of circulation and of advertising lineage."

It was about as clear a demonstration of the Hearst bookkeeping
philosophy of newspaper publishing as one could expect to find. The
answer to increased costs was simply to increase advertising and circulation rates, when it could be done without losing too many advertisers or
readers. It never seemed to occur to the Hearst management that improving the quality of their publications might attract more advertisers
or readers.

From the 1956 annual report: "As a result of the substantial increase
in labor costs, plus this latest newsprint increase, we are faced with the
problem of materially greater expenses in 1957. To offset these increased expenses we are continuing our efforts to increase advertising
rates and circulation prices whenever practicable."

The 1957 report: "The latest increase of $4 per ton in the cost of
newsprint . . . and the continuing demands for increases in labor scales,
including the attendant fringe benefits, both took their toll from our
profits. Our efforts to offset rising costs included the institution of
further operating efficiencies, circulation price increases, and advertising
rate increases . . ."

The 1958 report: "Union wages, including fringe benefits, continue
to mount. The battle against rising costs is never-ending."

In 1960, the company lost a whopping $6.4 million, and the annual
report raged against "the unrealistic demands of the unions for higher
wages, shorter hours, longer vacations and fringe benefits," which were
continuing "to mount without abatement." In addition, the report said,
the first three months of 1961 were worse than 1960, but "your management is still hopeful that the unfavorable trend will soon change."

It didn't change. In 1961, the company lost $8.8 million, but Berlin
by then had decided to put an end to the embarrassment. If the papers
couldn't turn a profit, at least they didn't have to announce the fact to
the entire world. He decided to call in the Hearst Consolidated stock,
and make the company completely private.

In May, the Hearst Corporation offered to buy all outstanding shares
of Hearst Consolidated at $25 per share. Since the stock was then trading
on the over-the-counter market at about $13, it seemed like a generous

offer. It was also a bargain for the company, since the corporate charter
provision that allowed the company to call in the stock required payment of $5 above par value (par value was $25) plus all back dividends.
That would have been a total of $50.56¼ per share.

In September 1964, the company exercised its option to call all outstanding stock, and the only window on the Hearst Corporation's finances
was nailed shut.

(5)

The concept behind the *World Journal Tribune* was spectacular—
merge three of New York City's daily newspapers into an afternoon giant
that would combine worldwide resources with a truckload of features
and columnists, making it, without question, the biggest and best afternoon newspaper in the country. It would give the *Times* a run for its
money and drive poor little Dorothy Schiff and her *Post* right out of
town. At least, that was the plan.

By 1964, the *Journal-American* was in the red, and Dick Berlin began
thinking about some way of salvaging the situation, without resorting to
the drastic step of shutting down the publication. He talked to *Herald
Tribune* publisher Walter Thayer about a merger between their respective
papers, but the plan fell apart when they discovered their press facilities
were incompatible. Berlin next turned his eye toward the *World-Telegram
& Sun*, the local Scripps-Howard paper. Since Bill Hearst was a pal of
Jack Howard, president of Scripps-Howard Newspapers, Berlin figured
that Bill should be the one to broach the subject of a possible merger.

Bill didn't much like the idea, and pointed out to Berlin that the joint
ownership with Scripps-Howard of the *News-Call Bulletin* "had never
worked worth a damn in San Francisco."

Bill had other reasons for being uneasy about merging the *Journal-
American* with someone else's newspaper. More than any of the other
Hearst newspapers, in fact, more than anything else Hearst owned, the
Journal-American was Bill Hearst's baby. It was the paper he had grown
up around, ever since coming to New York in 1928; it was his little
corner of the Hearst legacy, where Berlin let him act like an editor.

The *Journal-American* made Bill feel important even when he knew he wasn't. The people who ran the paper, men like Bill Curley and later Paul Schoenstein were his friends. They liked him in a very personal way, and if they knew all about his weaknesses—knew that he spent more time in the clubs around town than in the office, knew that he would be hard-pressed to write one of the columns that bore his name by himself—they still looked out for him, always. It was something of an unspoken agreement that whatever the *Journal* did, Bill got the credit. Even letters to the editor were printed as though they had been addressed to Bill personally: "Dear Mr. Hearst," was the standard salutation.

Bill reveled in the attention that the paper brought him. "There was a time when you couldn't unfold a napkin in this town without me dropping out of it," he would say years later. "I was everywhere, a part of everything. For many, many years, I would always be the youngest man on the dais. My god, I never had to pay for a meal." That was his life— baby-kisser, palm-presser, front-man for the paper. The *Journal-American* set him up; it put Bill at the center of all its promotions, stroked his ego, kept him in the news, never letting a week go by without running a photo or a flattering item. Elsa and Igor plugged his parties; they picked up items at his table in 21 and made him a stock character around Manhattan, one of the people who made New York what it was.

The little people on the *Journal*—the rank-and-file reporters and copy editors—liked Bill too. He wandered through the newsroom, so they knew who he was. Like his father, he would back them up, saving a job for someone who was fired, arranging sick pay for an old-timer who was down on his luck. The *Journal* was a paper where all the energy came, not from the top editors, but from the bottom—the reporters chasing crooks and firetrucks as they had always done. And Bill liked to feel that he was part of that energy.

It was all little enough, but it was Bill's, and he wanted to keep it, because it made him who he was, and as he wistfully recalled later, "it was so damned much fun."

And now Berlin wanted to—not exactly take it all away—but perhaps, well, Bill wasn't sure what Berlin wanted to do, but it didn't sound good. Berlin assured Bill that he wanted to keep a Hearst newspaper outlet in New York, and the best chance of doing that was by merging with one of the other newspapers in town, because the *Journal* was losing money by itself, and after all, half a newspaper would be much better than no newspaper.

Bill reluctantly went to see Jack Howard. Howard was interested.

But the merger discussions had just begun when Walter Thayer suddenly wanted to get into the deal, making it a three-way combination.

Thayer, acting on behalf of *Herald Tribune* owner John Hay "Jock" Whitney, had been trying gracefully to get rid of the *Trib* for two years. Whitney, the United States ambassador to the Court of St. James under Eisenhower, had purchased the *Trib* in 1958 from the Reid family for a reported $3.2 million as a favor to his friends in the Republican Party— the idea was to keep the paper as the voice of the liberal Eisenhower branch of the party, as distinguished from the conservative Taft branch. The *Trib*, which had been owned by the Reids since 1872, had a proud history of unprofitability—in 1922 Helen Rogers Reid threw a banquet for the newspaper executives at which she announced, "It's been a glorious year. We only lost $150,000"—and Whitney did not expect it to be a big profit maker. However, neither did he expect it to be quite as much of a drain on his pocketbook as it turned out to be. When he bought it, it was losing just over $1 million a year. Within five years, the losses had tripled. Reluctantly, Whitney instructed *Herald Tribune* president Walter Thayer to make some discreet inquiries about selling the paper.

Thayer had come up with what seemed a magnificent solution. In 1963, while the Great Strike was still in progress, he went to *New York Times* publisher Orville Dryfoos and proposed to sell the *Herald Tribune* for just the value of its physical assets—in other words, its junk value. The only catch, and it was really a modest request, was that Whitney would retain control of the editorial content of the newspaper until his death, after which, the whole thing would belong to the *Times*. Thayer also suggested that the *Trib* become an afternoon paper, so the *Times* could produce it out of their own plant. Dryfoos died in mid-1963, and the sale discussions were carried on with his successor, Arthur Ochs Sulzberger. However, the *Times* eventually turned down the offer, citing difficulties in putting out two newspapers from their one building. Thayer tried to interest several other prospective owners in buying the paper, but no one wanted it, and by the middle of 1965, he was getting desperate, as losses on the *Trib* continued to mount.

Berlin and Jack Howard, unaware of exactly how desperate Jock Whitney was to get out from under the burden of the *Herald Tribune*, welcomed him into their merger discussions, feeling that the "quality" of the *Trib* could only enhance the stature of the joint operation.

Berlin and Howard were in favor of all three publishers pooling their resources to put out one big afternoon newspaper. Whitney, however, insisted on keeping the *Herald Tribune* as a separate entity within the combination. His proposal was to have a joint company that could publish the *Herald Tribune* in the morning and a *World-Journal* in the afternoon. Berlin and Howard argued that the *Herald Tribune* would not be able to make money against the *Times* and *Daily News* in the morning. Whitney insisted that by taking advantage of combined production facilities, he could turn a profit. He also advanced the argument that without a morning paper to give them a little bit of competition, the *Times* and *Daily News* would get so big that they would threaten the afternoon paper, which was envisioned as the combine's big money-maker. Berlin and Howard were still not convinced, and began talking about dropping Whitney from the merger plans. Whitney tried another approach. He was so sure he could make money with the *Trib* in the morning, that he offered to indemnify Hearst and Scripps-Howard against any losses that the *Herald Tribune* might cause the combined operation for a period of two years. Then, if the paper still wasn't making money, he would shut it down. Berlin and Howard now liked the idea, because they figured they would be getting something for nothing.

The World Journal Tribune, Inc., was formed, with the Hearst Corporation, Whitney Communications, and Scripps-Howard as stockholders. The company was capitalized at $6.4 million, with each partner also arranging to lease *WJT* equipment they already owned at token cost. The corporation would be governed by a nine-member board of directors, each partner having three representatives. Hearst was represented by Berlin, Bill Hearst and G. O. Markuson.

The figures looked incredibly rosy. They would combine the *Journal* and *World* alone for an easy million circulation—700,000 from the *Journal* and 400,000 from the *World*—then pick up whatever they could from the *Trib*'s 300,000 readers as gravy. All of this with a staff the size of the *Journal*'s alone.

The only trouble, said Bill, was that all those businessmen had left one factor out of their calculations—"To tell you the truth, those guys never gave any consideration to labor on a single, solitary thing. There they were, about to put four thousand people out of jobs, and they never considered what that might mean. That's how business can get."

Bill, Jock Whitney and Jack Howard jointly announced the impending formation of the *World Journal Tribune* on March 21, 1966. They talked of "an amalgamation of strengths" and massive cost savings. It was a "new direction," maybe even a revolution in newspaper economics. And what was unique as far as newspaper mergers went, no one was being swallowed; each owner would remain an independent voice in the "cooperative enterprise." The *Herald Tribune* would continue to be published as a separate morning paper, although it was part of the combine, while the *Journal-American* and the *World Telegram & Sun* would be merged into a single afternoon paper. On Sunday, all three would be printed together as the *World Journal Tribune*.

Union leaders were taken aback as they contemplated some ugly arithmetic that lay behind the publishers' bright predictions. There were at least 5,700 employees working at the three papers, 2,300 of them at Hearst. At least a third, maybe more, would lose their jobs. The union chiefs were in a tough position; they were responsible, at least as much as the publishers, for determining who would go and who would stay. Thomas Laura, president of the Mailer's Union local, emerged from a huddle of the ten major labor groups and announced that as far as labor was concerned, the World Journal Tribune, Inc., would start with a clean slate—the old contracts would not apply.

With mediator Theodore Kheel in the middle of the fray, the publishers and union representatives haggled for a month over incentives for early retirement, methods of staging the mass "execution," and additional severance pay for the thousands of newspaper people who wouldn't survive.

Publication of the *World Journal* was scheduled to begin April 25. As the date approached, none of the ten unions had reached agreement with the publishers, a situation that several observers attributed primarily to Thayer and Whitney taking a curiously hard-line approach to the negotiation, and at one point breaking off talks with the ITU completely.

On Sunday, April 24, the Newspaper Publishers Association of New

York City held a meeting and informed the three owners that if they had any labor troubles, the rest of them—meaning the *Times* and the *Daily News*, since Dorothy Schiff was not a member—were not going to shut down in sympathy. After the meeting, Matt Meyer, a Scripps-Howard executive who had been named president of the WJT, put on a bold front and announced that the WJT had not asked the other publishers for a news blackout because "we think we can bring these union leaders to their senses."

As Meyer was making his announcement, Guild pickets were taking up positions in the chilly drizzle outside the *World-Telegram* building. Within the hour pickets also began to march at the *Herald Tribune* plant on West 41st Street and the *Journal-American* on South Street.

Sentiment for the strike was by no means unanimous. At the *Herald Tribune*, a group of thirty-five reporters stayed in the city room for an hour after the lines went up. Richard Reeves, one of the dissident reporters, said, "We just want our leadership to know we're not quite unanimous in demanding that the paper fold," while another called the protest sit-in "a mark of contempt for [Guild executive vice-president Thomas] Murphy . . . we feel that we're striking against our own jobs." But by 4 P.M. they were out and the doors of the *Herald Tribune* were closed, as it turned out, forever.

Needless to say, no *World Journal* appeared Monday, April 25. Negotiation with the unions continued, but without mediator Kheel, who withdrew from the bargaining, convinced that Thayer and Whitney did not want to settle.

Bargaining dragged on through the spring, with the Whitney-Thayer contingent, in the words of one participant, "throwing monkey wrenches into the works every step of the way." Whitney occasionally mentioned that he might have to close down the *Trib*, and suddenly it became clear to Berlin what the *Herald Tribune* owner was up to—he was stalling the talks, never intending to publish the *Trib*. If he could suspend operations before the two newspapers got off the ground, he would be out of his obligation to pay losses for two years, and furthermore, Scripps-Howard and Hearst would have to foot the bill for two thirds of the *Herald Tribune*'s $5 million severance-cost obligation.

Berlin and Howard were so mad at Whitney that they were determined to settle the union questions, if for no reason other than to make him pay for two years. With Hearst and Scripps outvoting Whitney's objections down the line, in the space of a few weeks they had settled with all the unions except the pressmen.

In spite of Hearst and Scripps-Howard's best attempts at a quick settlement, the pressmen proved just a bit too stubborn, and the delay in reaching agreement with them gave Whitney the opportunity to do what he apparently had been planning for some time: to close his newspaper, while laying the blame for his problems on union recalcitrance. On August 15, WJT president Matt Meyer announced that the *Herald Tribune* was dead.

With the *Herald Tribune* buried, but Whitney still part of the combine, it meant reshuffling newspaper executives and planning for a single afternoon newspaper. Long-time Hearstman Frank Conniff, who had been scheduled to be editor of the afternoon *World Journal*, was slotted for editor of the *World Journal Tribune*. James G. Bellows, editor of the *Herald Tribune*, was out of the picture completely, and left to take a job with the Los Angeles *Times*.

Not only were the newspaper executives rearranged, the owners had to reopen negotiations with the nine unions that had already made agreements, to settle the matter of further layoffs, all the while continuing negotiation with the pressmen.

There was no jubilation and precious little relief when a settlement was finally reached on September 6. The last bargaining session had gone ten hours in the Publishers Association office, and the ragged agreement that finally emerged left many small issues unresolved while the unions opted to defer bread-and-butter issues until the next contract. Neither side felt that it had won a victory, and no one was particularly happy. A weary Bertram Powers and Thomas Murphy announced that their men would begin reporting for work, while Meyer said only that the paper would be there come Monday, the twelfth.

And, to the surprise of many, 900,000 copies of the *World Journal Tribune* rolled off the presses Monday, although not without a two-hour delay and some ill feelings caused when Pressmen's Union president William J. Kennedy refused to allow Mayor John V. Lindsay to press the button that started the presses. Kennedy called Lindsay a "publisher's representative" and the press run was held up until the mayor left the building.

Monday was "a slow news day," editor Conniff explained, which accounted for four columnists on the front page. But the paper quickly sold out at the newsstands throughout the city, grabbed up by curious New Yorkers, eager for a look at the three-headed amalgamation they had been hearing about for six months. Initial reaction to the paper was favorable. The Washington *Post* pronounced the *WJT* "sober enough for the suburbs and sharp enough for the subways"—in other words, a product of "lively respectability." The Sunday paper carried *New York Magazine* and a book-review supplement, both formerly in the *Herald Tribune* and generally praised for their high quality. After the initial spurt of novelty sales, the "*Widget*," as readers quickly began calling the new hybrid creation, staked a solid hold on 700,000 daily readers and 800,000 on Sunday, easily outdistancing its only afternoon competition, the *Post*, which sold 380,000 copies daily and had no Sunday edition.

But the *Widget* had its problems—problems in production, problems in the editorial department, problems in advertising.

At the most basic level, equipment malfunctioned. Telephones were not working when the paper began publication. The presses, rated for 55,000 copies an hour, never produced over 35,000 per hour. Linotype machines broke down with alarming frequency and often did not have complete fonts of type. "On the linotype machines they have a red light to indicate a breakdown . . . that tells the machinist where the breakdown is," Powers said. "There were about seventy machines in that composing room and so many red lights were on at one time that it looked like a Christmas tree."

The problem in the newsroom was that the department never quite clicked. The people never quite meshed, never developed the rhythm and cadence of a well-adjusted machine. Part of the difficulty was undoubtably the unusually large number of older reporters, due to the use of seniority in picking the staff from among employees on the three merged papers. The average age in the newsroom was forty-seven, and about a third of the staff was over sixty. The younger reporters, who typically provide the spark and enthusiasm that is often contagious in a newsroom, were absent.

Even some of the older reporters, no doubt thankful to have their jobs, noticed that the whole operation suffered and somehow seemed off balance, because reporters in their twenties and thirties were missing.

"You know, it was funny," said Charles Rowland, education writer for the *WJT* who had held the same position for many years at the *Journal-American*. "I had never been to school in my life, entirely self-taught. And there I was, at the age of seventy-two, covering all those stories that were breaking in the schools and on the campuses in those days."

Some reporters spoke of a lack of identity with the *WJT*—reporters thought of themselves as *Tribune* men, or *Telly* men, or *J-A* reporters, but never considered themselves really part of the *World Journal Tribune*. The staff, to some extent, was split into factions from the three merged papers, and often refused to take orders from supervisors who had come from a paper other than their own.

And there was considerable doubt that Frank Conniff was the right man to lead the staff. "Frank was a nice guy," said one of his colleagues, "but to tell you the truth, he was never very able." Talk on the staff had it that he had married someone very important to the Hearsts—someone in the family or very close—and that explained the job. In fact, it was not quite so complicated. The three owners had decided that the editor would come from the Hearst organization. Conniff, for years, had been Bill Hearst's right-hand assistant, and Bill had been able to get Berlin and Markuson behind the appointment.

Rowland could remember Conniff as the months rolled on, slumped in his chair looking depressed, "absolutely no idea" what to do about his sagging operation.

In January, Conniff promoted Clay Felker, editor of the *New York* Sunday magazine, to associate editor of the daily paper, with the idea that Felker could inject some of the zip that had made the Sunday magazine a success into the *WJT*. Felker rolled up his sleeves and went to work. "You can do a lot for the *World Journal Tribune*," he said. "More interpretive writing, for one."

Unknown to its editors, however, one of the owners had already given up on the *Widget*. It was the last week in November when Meyer told the three partners it would be necessary for each of them to put up an additional $250,000 in capital to cover losses on the operation. Whitney refused.

Just three weeks before, Whitney, along with Hearst and Scripps-Howard, had answered a call for additional capital by putting in $250,000 each. At that time—the beginning of November—it had been predicted the extra contribution would take the *WJT* through to April 1 of the next year. Now, just three weeks later, the projections had been revised and more money was needed immediately.

"We looked at the situation, we looked at the costs, we looked at the projection and said, 'This newspaper can't go, it isn't going to fly,' " explained Thayer. "We [were] losing at this stage at the rate of $700,000 a month . . . in the best part of the year, October, November and December. These are supposed to be the best months."

Berlin, Markuson and the Scripps-Howard people were furious. They talked to Thayer, trying to get him to change his mind, but Thayer held firm and he had the contract between the owners to back him up. The contract provided that any stockholder had the right not to put up capital.

"Hearst and Scripps-Howard could have refused to put it up," Thayer said. "They put up the additional capital, however. This was their judgment."

Indeed, without Whitney's support, Hearst and Scripps-Howard each had to put up $375,000 to keep the *Widget* alive.

"From our judgment it was hopeless and we said so," Thayer said. "We thought they made a mistake in going ahead. Maybe they thought the paper would go. I don't know. They each have a chain of newspapers. I think there is great pride in being in New York, as far as Hearst and Scripps-Howard are concerned. I think it was a terrible pill for them to take, to have to get out of business in New York, and I think they hoped against hope that they could somehow make this paper go."

Although Whitney wasn't contributing to the *Widget*, he wasn't about to give up his stock ownership either. Since neither Hearst nor Scripps-Howard owned enough stock to make the losses deductible, it was all the more painful.

At the bottom line, the *Widget*'s problem was advertising—or, more accurately, the lack of it. The five-month delay in publication had eliminated most fall national advertising accounts, since such ad schedules are prepared months in advance. The local advertisers also stayed away from the paper—their thinking seemed to be that businessmen bought the paper only for the late stock-market reports, and the type of people who were attracted by the horoscope, advice columns and comics were not likely to have much spending money. Some people, knowledgeable about the New York advertising business, said that the *Widget* advertising salesmen were simply not as aggressive or as thorough as their counterparts on other newspapers. "They were much too willing to take 'no' for an answer," said one observer. "They also didn't seem to even contact a lot of potential advertisers. I always got the impression their attitude was that the advertisers would come to them."

Speculation on the causes of the lack of advertising could go on endlessly. But the hard fact was that the ads were not there. During March and April of 1967, the *Widget* carried 4.1 million lines of advertising, compared to 14.8 million for the *Times* and 7.3 million for the *Daily News*.

At the end of February, Whitney was finally persuaded to give up his stock in World Journal Tribune Inc., paving the way for either Hearst or Scripps-Howard to buy the other out, so if the paper wasn't going to make money, at least the one owner would be able to deduct the losses. There were still some details, however, to be worked out concerning obligations of the various owners—and former owner, in the case of Whitney—regarding severance pay in case the paper should fold. Jack Howard had the idea that maybe they could give the paper away to someone who would be willing to assume severance liabilities, but he couldn't find any takers.

Meanwhile, negotiation with all the unions was starting again.

Toward the end of April, the ITU reached agreement with the *Daily News* on a new three-year contract that would raise wages 21 percent over the three-year period. It was understood by all parties involved—the newspaper owners and the unions—that the *Daily News* contract would be the basis for ITU agreements with the other newspapers, and very likely the basis for contracts with the other nine unions.

What worried the *Widget* management, more so than simply the wage increase, was a provision that they felt was aimed directly at them. The contract stipulated that if a paper merged or folded, employees would be paid eight weeks' severance pay. If the Sunday paper was discontinued, any employee who lost his job as a result would be entitled to three weeks' severance pay.

"I do not think in the minds of men who were negotiating at the *News* that there was any great anticipation that the *News* was going to drop its Sunday or stop publication," Meyer commented.

The *Daily News* settlement triggered some quick decision-making on the part of Hearst and Scripps-Howard executives. Meyer produced figures showing that on top of planned losses, the *WJT* was going straight downhill. In January, losses were $136,000 more than the projected budget loss, in February they were $303,000, in March $349,000, and in April $422,000. "It was beginning to worry us," Meyer said, in what was certainly a droll understatement of the *Widget* management's concern.

Dick Berlin called everyone, including Whitney and Thayer, together in a meeting at his office on Sunday afternoon, April 30, to make some decision on closing the paper. It didn't take much debate to decide that the time to close the paper was right then, when severance costs would be lower than under a new contract. Berlin also wanted to know if Whitney intended to pay his share of severance costs. It took some wrangling and threatening, but eventually Whitney agreed.

News of the *WJT* closing was given to the editorial staff at 10 A.M. Friday morning, May 5, in the form of an announcement signed by Matt Meyer: "It is with a real sense of personal regret that I must tell you that the *World Journal Tribune* is permanently ceasing publication with today's issue. Your employment will terminate at that time."

Meyer attributed the decision to shut down primarily to the recent settlement at the *Daily News*. "If applied to all unions," Meyer said, "[the settlement] would add $10.5 million to present payroll costs over the contract . . . under the circumstances, it is totally impractical for the *WJT* to assume this increased burden."

There were other opinions on what caused the paper to close. Ted Kheel said the paper was doomed from the start because the owners were trying to put out a metropolitan paper "on a piggy-bank budget." An executive close to the publishers summed up the problems saying, "You can't run a horse with three men on it and nobody in front."

As far as the weary employees of the *Widget* were concerned, reporter Atra Baer probably spoke for many of them when he said: "This was a newspaper born out of trouble. It lived in trouble and it died in trouble and nobody is surprised."

Bill Hearst may not have been surprised, but that didn't make the pain of losing the last Hearst outlet in New York any easier to take.

"He wasn't just disappointed," whispered a secretary who had known

Bill for more than thirty years. "He was devastated." Some at the Manhattan Hearst headquarters went even further, claiming that in the years
after the Widget's demise, Bill was never the same person again.

A lot of it was that Bill had become the victim of his own PR. He
had almost forgotten how very little he did for himself; that Kingsbury
Smith had really won his Pulitzer; that Conniff and John Watson and
Leo Monsky were writing his column. Nobody eavesdropped in the clubs
anymore, and so he had to realize that except for his Hearstlings, nobody
had really cared. The papers that remained still carried his column, but
it wasn't the same as having it appear in New York, where the people
who counted were. And that bothered him so much that he resorted to
having it printed up each week in pamphlet form and mailing it out to
his roster of friends—they assured him that they couldn't imagine a week
without it. And when he had something really important to say, as in
1968, when his blood was up over America's failure of will in the rice
paddies of Vietnam, he had the column reprinted as a paid ad in The
New York Times. His father, dead more than fifteen years, who had commanded a legion in New York, would have wept.

(6)

The small group of men in the conference room of the Los Angeles
County Federation of Labor headquarters were grim and unsmiling. Some
of them betrayed just a hint of weary desperation in the way they
gulped coffee from Styrofoam cups and stubbed out cigarettes in the
little glass ashtrays strewn about the big walnut table. It was 10:30 A.M.,
December 15, 1967.

Sigmund Arywitz, top official of the "County Fed" left the room and
tersely informed Bob Rupert and Jerry Rollings that the Herald-Examiner
management was standing firm on its last offer. Rupert, an international
representative of the Newspaper Guild, and Rollings, Herald-Examiner
unit chairman of the Guild in Los Angeles, were disappointed, but had
almost expected as much. Intervention by the County Fed had been a last-
ditch attempt to reach a settlement before the 11 A.M. strike deadline.

Rupert and Rollings joined the group in the conference room. Almost
as if he were playing a worn record, Rupert repeated what he had said

innumerable times in the past week. The Guild would settle on the same terms as it had with the neighboring Long Beach *Independent Press-Telegram*, largest of the suburban newspapers in the Los Angeles area. Rupert had negotiated the Long Beach contract, where agreement was reached just six days earlier. "Hearst can afford to do much better and his employees cannot accept less than their Long Beach counterparts," Rupert said, putting emotion into a statement he had already recited previously without success.

William O. McCarthy, labor counsel for the *Herald-Examiner*, complimented Rupert for the "admirable manner in which the Guild has been conducting these negotiations," but insisted that the company's last offer was the best they would do. The company offer, McCarthy said, was "reasonable and equitable."

"Do you mean to tell me," Rupert demanded, "that this company cannot afford to make a similar contract to that approved by the Long Beach paper, which is smaller in circulation and has much less of an area from which to draw revenue?"

"It is not a question of what this company can or cannot afford," McCarthy replied icily. "I can assure you that this company can afford any contract it sees fit to make. I also can assure you that this company does not see fit to make such a contract as this."

Rupert stared at McCarthy, and a sinking feeling hit him in the stomach. They had come right down to the wire, and McCarthy wasn't going to budge an inch. Sitting with McCarthy that day was George Hearst, Jr., publisher of the *Herald-Examiner*. This was the first time that Hearst had appeared at any of the bargaining sessions, and he had said nothing as he sat watching, his face a stony, impassive mask.

Rupert suddenly found himself wondering what McCarthy and Hearst would do if he suddenly said that the Guild would accept the company's proposal. The meager company proposal was so low as to be almost ludicrous. *Herald-Examiner* reporters were already the lowest-paid on any major newspaper in the country, with a top minimum of $175 a week. (Top minimum is the least amount a reporter can make after a specified length of service with the paper, usually five or six years.) That was $33.50 per week less than the San Francisco Hearst paper paid. The company was demanding a settlement that would place them even further behind other metropolitan papers and even behind many suburban newspapers.

It had offered an increase of $16 a week in pay and benefits over two years. The Long Beach paper had just settled for a new top minimum of $200, and the Guild was determined to get no less at the *Herald-Examiner*.

The Guild had been preparing for a strike ever since their contract covering more than one thousand *Herex* workers had expired on November 17. But until this moment, Rupert had thought an agreement could be reached without a strike. He told Rollings to get ready to pull all Guild workers out of the *Herald-Examiner* plant at 11 A.M. Rollings left the room.

Rupert tried one more approach. The Guild might settle for less than the economic package at Long Beach, he said. They would be flexible. He just wanted to see some indication that the company was willing to move from their current position. Again, McCarthy said the company would stand on its previous proposal package.

There was nothing left to say. McCarthy leaned over and whispered something to George Sjostrum, business manager of the *Herald-Examiner*, who usually participated in the negotiation sessions. Rupert made small talk with some of the County Fed officials and representatives of the other labor unions that attended this session. Rupert mentioned that tomorrow was his birthday.

Minutes ticked by as the big hand on the wall clock climbed toward vertical. When it pointed straight up, Rupert cleared his throat and announced: "Gentlemen, American Newspaper Guild Local 69 is now on strike at the Los Angeles *Herald-Examiner*."

George Hearst, Jr., was a cold man. A man in charge of his emotions. Or, maybe, thought some, a man who had no emotions.

Handsome, with short, slicked-back hair and the trim build of a high-school athlete who still kept in shape playing polo, George Hearst was a man with a goal. He was determined to make a name for himself by ridding the *Herald-Examiner* of troublesome unions once and for all.

Even in a family where Eisenhower Republicanism was considered to be a shade too liberal, George junior stood out as a particularly hard-line conservative; it may have had something to do with the fact that he was raised by his mother, Blanche Wilbur, a hard, determined woman who successfully ran several business enterprises of her own and who left no doubt that she felt the blood on the Hearst side of the family had thinned out considerably in the generation after W. R.

Anyone who knew George junior was impressed by his ambition, his energy, his apparent command of the business. In almost every way, he was the direct opposite of his father—old friends who could always count on George senior to go out for a good time, found that young George couldn't even be coaxed out to lunch. "I'm having a sandwich here," he would reply. "I've got too damned much to do."

The corporate people held great hope that young George would turn into something close to a reincarnation of his grandfather. When he was appointed to the family position on the board of trustees after John's death, the executive bloc courted him, inviting him to their rump sessions where policy was thrashed out in the absence of the Hearst members. Young George quickly found himself more comfortable with the executives than with the Hearsts; any allegiance he may have had to the Hearst family was thin anyhow. He and his sister Phoebe were only two years old when their father and mother were divorced. His mother remarried a man named Cortlandt Hill, and George grew up with virtually no contact with his natural father.

His grandfather, however, took a strong interest in little George, perhaps hoping that he would show some of the spark and drive that was lacking in the five sons. W. R. supervised George's early education and apparently exercised a little more care than he had with his own sons. He made sure that George was not pushed too fast, and he broke him in at the executive offices of the San Francisco paper. In his final years, the old man discussed newspapers with his grandson and incidentally left no doubt as to his disappointment in his own sons.

"My grandfather was an amazing man," George would say years later. "I admired him enormously." Of his own father, young George would only say, "He had no effect on me one way or another." And about the rest of the Hearst family, he flatly refused to comment.

It was a devastating blow to the rest of the Hearst family trustees when they found out that George junior had been attending the executive bloc's rump sessions. To the other Hearsts it meant that Dick Berlin had the Great White Hope in his pocket.

In 1960, the New York executives rewarded George for his corporate loyalty by making him, at age thirty-three, the publisher of the Los Angeles *Herald-Express*, replacing David Hearst. When the *Examiner* folded in 1962, young George emerged as publisher of the renamed *Herald-Examiner*, whose gigantic afternoon circulation topped even the New York *Journal-American*'s, making it the largest paper in the Hearst chain, and indeed, the largest evening newspaper in America.

George had an unpleasant run-in with the Newspaper Guild in 1964, when he wanted to hire "combo" men—reporters who would also take pictures—for small bureau offices around the Los Angeles area. The Guild objected to this plan, on the grounds that there was no provision in the contract for "combos" and they would be taking a job away from either a reporter or a photographer. George didn't understand this argument; to him it was plain that the Guild was imposing inefficiency on him by demanding that two persons be hired where one could do the job.

The next year, Hearst personally headed the management bargaining team during contract negotiations with the Guild. He took it as a personal insult when negotiation reached an impasse and the Guild staged a two-day strike, which shut down the newspaper when pressmen refused to cross the picket lines. The bargaining experience left Hearst with deep, antagonistic feelings toward the Guild.

By 1965, other pressures were beginning to wear on publisher Hearst, the principal one being that the *Herald-Examiner*, after roaring into the black when the *Examiner* was folded in 1962, was no longer making money. Although George was still the golden boy of the corporation, he foresaw a distinct threat to his career if the paper plunged deeply into the red, as it seemed on the verge of doing. And, as George Hearst saw the situation, the main trouble with the *Herald-Examiner* was in its unions. "Featherbedding" was a word Hearst liked to use, and he could easily tick off a handful of expensive examples, such as the Guild's opposition to combo men.

His dislike for unions also had the philosophical underpinning that to his way of thinking, unions were an interference with the owner's inalienable right to manage a company as he pleased. Furthermore, it was his observation that unions were directly responsible for numerous newspaper failures in the preceding few years. What galled him was that every time a Hearst newspaper folded, everyone at the corporation complained about how the unions were killing them, but no one did anything about it.

George junior decided that if no one else was going to stand up to the unions, he would.

In 1967 he began talking with some of the executives at Hearst headquarters about his plan to permanently rid the *Herald-Examiner* of unions. He immediately obtained the support of G. O. Markuson, then general manager of the Hearst newspapers. Together, the two of them constructed an argument that won the backing of Dick Berlin, and gradually the other directors fell in behind the scheme.

George's argument was straightforward, and he assembled the figures that backed him up: if the *Herald-Examiner* succumbed to what the unions were demanding this year, and again two years from now, the costs would be so great that the newspaper would no longer be economically viable. However, by taking a hard line now, the increasing cost spiral could be reversed and, after some initial costs of fighting the strike, the paper would soon be showing a profit. And by fighting a strike he didn't mean keeping the paper shut until the unions gave in to reasonable demands. He meant publishing the newspaper without unions. The Los Angeles *Times,* he reminded them, had taken a hard line against unions once, and they had a completely union-free operation now, which, incidentally, was also a very profitable one.

The Hearst directors agreed that it seemed like a good plan.

George Hearst arranged everything. He got the replacement workers lined up, stockpiled supplies, had the department heads briefed. When the union workers walked out, the replacements walked in and took over, missing only one day of publication. Food was brought into the building by an industrial caterer, so no one had to worry about confronting the union pickets at mealtimes. Everyone worked at least sixteen hours a day. Cots and showers were provided for the production workers so they could sleep in the building.

There were a few minor foul-ups—George hadn't thought about janitorial service, and the building got filthy in a hurry. The first janitorial duties after the strike began were performed by nine members of the Malibu Polo Club, who came in to clean up the building one day, as a way of helping out their pal George. The strike was going well, and if George was at all worried, he didn't show it. On December 30, he was out playing polo at Will Rogers State Park for the Malibu Riviera team.

The striking unions got their first indication that George Hearst might be involved in something more than hard bargaining on January 4, 1968.

Sigmund Arywitz, head of the County Fed, emerged shaken from a bargaining session with the company management with the news that Hearst had insisted that his strikebreakers be accorded "superseniority," if and when there was a settlement. This meant that the company wanted to grant the strikebreakers seniority over everyone who had been on strike. It was unheard of in labor negotiations.

"This is not only completely unacceptable, but immoral and unworkable," Arywitz said, adding, "we don't intend to accept any phase of it."

George Hearst had a straightforward reason for putting forth that demand. "I can't see terminating them [the strikebreakers] and hiring back the people who tried to put you out of business," he said.

The unions clearly needed to step up their efforts to bring pressure on Hearst for a settlement. The County Federation of Labor dispatched Bill Robertson to coordinate activities among the various striking unions, who were oftentimes at odds with each other. A soft-spoken, courtly man, who could nonetheless be blunt when the situation demanded, Robertson exuded an aura of quiet toughness. He had joined the County Fed as a full-time staff member just the previous month, after working his way up through the ranks of the local Hotel, Restaurant and Bartenders Union. With himself assuming the role of strike director, Robertson smoothed over differences between the *Herald-Examiner* unions, convincing everyone of what they really already knew: they were up against a determined adversary and if they were going to win, they couldn't waste energy fighting each other. It was a matter of everyone sinking or sailing together.

January dragged into February; there were constant negotiating sessions between the various unions, groups of unions and the management, but the result of every session was the same. No progress. The lack of a settlement discouraged many of the union strikers, who had not expected to be out of work so long. The daily union newsletter, "On the Line," tried to keep everyone's spirits up with pep-talk articles, reports on how much advertising and circulation the *Herald-Examiner* was losing, and constant written abuse of the strikebreakers, who were standardly referred to as "scabs," "rats" or "hoodlums."

"On the Line" also dug up stray historical facts dealing with the irony that William Randolph Hearst had been an early champion of labor unions and reprinted his ringing editorial statements on the subject. "A business which cannot afford to pay living wages to its employees cannot exist and should not," read one. "American wages are high . . . because of the plucky fight that union men have made," proclaimed another, which comforted the strikers as little as his observation that the strikebreaker is a "very pathetic workman" who "betrays his own kind" and "finds comfort in the praise of the rich men that praise him and despise him."

Perhaps the quotations fed the outrage of the union members, but the strike was getting nowhere, and the union leaders knew it. Guild representative Rupert was convinced that if George Hearst himself were only aware of the facts in the case, a settlement could be reached quickly. Finally, in a move that was half desperation and half inspiration, he decided to contact George Hearst directly without informing the other union leaders or the *Herald-Examiner* management negotiators. He reached Hearst by phone at the publisher's club, and explained who he was and that he wanted to meet with Hearst, completely off-the-record, to talk about the strike situation. None of the other union people knew about this conversation, he assured Hearst.

Surprisingly, Hearst seemed to think such a meeting was a good idea, and he told Rupert he would give him a call at home that evening at 6 P.M. A traffic jam on the freeway delayed Rupert's arrival home that night, and it was 6:15 by the time he reached his house. To his dismay, his wife informed him that Hearst had called only minutes earlier, but left no number where he could be reached. Later in the evening, Rupert learned that a strikebreaker had been shot in front of his hotel. Upon hearing the news, he was sure that George Hearst would certainly blame the unions for the shooting and would never call back. Hearst never called back and Rupert dropped any further attempt to contact him.

The strikebreaker was Maurice Maynard, a thirty-five-year-old printer from Walnut Creek, California. He was shot in the chest on February 13 and died on February 22. George Hearst knew whom to blame. The thick headline above a front-page editorial the next day thundered: "And Now, Murder." The editorial went on to list 150 specific acts of violence allegedly committed against the paper and its interim personnel.

The police questioned dozens of union members in their investigation of the killing, but no one was ever arrested. One union official had an iron-clad alibi: he was in a coffee shop a few blocks from the newspaper with a striking pressman at the time of the shooting and had been seen there by several witnesses. When the police investigator asked what the two men had been discussing, the union leader replied evenly, "We were discussing ways to blow up the *Herald-Examiner* pressroom." The police officer laughed and put away his notebook, apparently relieved that these two, at least, still had their sense of humor.

"He thought we were kidding," the union official said later. "But that's what we were talking about. We were so damned frustrated at that point, I think we were all getting a little bit crazy."

While picketing, demonstrations, and a vociferous campaign to boycott Hearst products was carried on daily, the unions also pursued other avenues that might lead to a settlement. Robertson asked former California Governor Edmund "Pat" Brown to offer his services to mediate the strike, which Brown did. He was rebuffed by Dick Berlin, who crisply informed him that the Hearst Corporation was "very satisfied with the course of events in Los Angeles."

In the middle of March, Mayor Sam Yorty announced the appointment of a three-man mediation panel to seek a settlement of the three-month-old strike. The panel was headed by Lloyd H. Bailer of New York, a professional labor arbiter, and included a union representative, Herman Leavitt, president of the Los Angeles Joint Board of Hotel and Restaurant Workers Union, and a management man, Ralph Woolpert, director of labor relations for the Thrifty drugstore chain. Robertson immediately responded to the mayor's panel saying the striking unions were "ready to meet in good faith for meaningful negotiations" under the auspices of the mediation board. There was no immediate reaction from the *Herald-Examiner* management.

As the weeks passed, the company still remained silent on official recognition of the mayoral panel. Bailer met with George Hearst but failed to get a clear response on any acceptance of the mediation efforts.

"The role of this panel does not appear to be clear with Mr. Hearst," was Bailer's only comment. He said efforts to "explore the situation further with management" were continuing.

However, on April 18, the panel resigned in a body, saying it could get no commitment from the company to bargain.

A statement from the mayor's office was terse: "The panel quit because management won't talk with them."

Later that summer during a speech in San Francisco, the management member of the mayor's panel, Ralph Woolpert, commented that repeated

efforts by the panel to bring *Herald-Examiner* management to the bargaining table were "brushed aside, and we saw that one party didn't want
to settle."

With the failure of the mediation panel, the Joint Strike-Lockout
Council redoubled its efforts to bring economic pressure on Hearst, and
especially on George Hearst. Appeal to the rest of the labor movement
was direct, and it hammered at the theme that the issue was union-
busting and the attack was on unions everywhere.

The national AFL-CIO endorsed a nationwide boycott of all Hearst
publications and the "Dirty Dozen," the twelve biggest advertisers in the
Herald-Examiner, a roster that was headed by the giant retailers Sears,
Roebuck & Company, J. C. Penney, Inc., and the May Company. During
the summer of 1968, a four-man union "Truth Squad" toured the country,
speaking at state and national labor conventions, where they showed a
short film on the *Herald-Examiner* strike entitled "Return to Tyranny."

At midnight, September 8, the *Herald-Examiner* labor dispute achieved
the dubious distinction of becoming the longest active newspaper strike
in United States history as it entered its 268th day.

As the first anniversary of the strike approached, a sense of fatalism
settled over many of the union leaders, who more and more were talking
about taking some form of "militant action" against the *Herald-Examiner*,
The extent, duration and possible goals of such action were the subject
of heated debate among the various union officials. The ITU's national
representatives—George Duncan, Bill Williams and Tom McGrath—
seemed to be the most militant, strongly pushing what one other union
official derided as "some wild ideas about getting into the plant, busting
up the machinery and hopefully ousting the scabs."

The union leaders, including those of the ITU, eventually agreed to
a proposal advanced by Guild representative Rupert, who envisioned a
massive labor demonstration using the civil-disobedience tactics of the
civil-rights movement. "It was my hope that we could persuade labor
leaders to supply thousands of militants for this demonstration," Rupert
said.

It was a naïve, impractical hope, as Rupert discovered in meetings
with leaders of the UAW, Longshoremen, Teamsters, Building Trades,
and other unions as well as a number of political groups. The message
they gave him was clear: a sustained effort that would not stop until all

the labor activists in Los Angeles were in jail or until Hearst had agreed to arbitration, was just not going to happen.

The massive-demonstration idea was eventually abandoned, although not without bitter recriminations between the ITU and Guild leaders.

The discouraged unions were further disheartened and angered by a December 27 *Time* magazine article, which proclaimed "The Defeat of the Strikers." Though it acknowledged that the dispute was "technically a stalemate," it insisted that "actually, the strike is over—and the clear winner is George Hearst."

Angry union members who wrote *Time* to say the strike was still very much alive, received the magazine's even-toned reply: "A realistic appraisal of the situation led us to conclude that the war was lost as of the date of our story."

In fact, the war was just beginning, in the sense that the unions had recently abandoned hope of reaching a contract settlement as their primary goal. The goal now was simply to beat Hearst, even if that meant destroying the paper. The unions had come to view the dispute in the same light as George Hearst had viewed it right from the beginning: this was a struggle to the finish, and only one party was going to get up off the floor.

BOOK THREE

NEW HEARST

Chapter 1

Renaissance

(1)

"HELL, my father used to *own* this," mutters the seventy-year-old Bill Hearst, as he threads his way across Broadway, cursing the taxi drivers (who "never used to be vicious, not like this"), and sweeps his hand around the teeming circumference of Columbus Circle in midtown Manhattan. "This was his end of town once. Back in the thirties, before the crash, he and Brisbane owned every plot of land on this end of Central Park. They had great plans for the area. They were going to make this the media center of the world . . ."

In fact, Hearst senior once had great plans not just for the Circle, which he had hoped would someday be christened "Hearst Plaza," but for the whole broad corridor of mid-Manhattan that lay between 56th and 59th Streets, from Eighth Avenue, where he published his magazines, to Park Avenue, where he sometimes lived with Marion in a penthouse at his own Ritz Tower Hotel. In the early 1920s, when most of Fifth Avenue above Grand Central was still lined with aging brownstones, Brisbane had convinced Hearst that the future lay with the upper Fifties. There would be an automotive bridge across the East River at 57th Street, he predicted, and the railroads from Long Island and New Jersey would converge in a new central terminal, which would be built, he believed, along Seventh Avenue. Brisbane foresaw a commercial explosion on Manhattan's near West Side; and Hearst, who found the editor's vision compelling, decided that this piece of the island must become his stronghold.

Working, as ever, without a blueprint, William Randolph Hearst, builder, broke ground for what might have become the empire's capital city. At the intersection of 57th Street and Park Avenue, the eastern border of his zone, he began by acquiring all four corners. With the northeastern lot, he took over the Ritz, which he intended to make the world's grandest hotel—an aristocratic haven in this democratic land, and a sumptuous residence for the dignitaries who came to do business with his enterprise. "Our idea is not to make a hotel for general use," he once admonished Neylan, "but a very high-class hotel for the very best people, like Claridge's used to be in London. Anybody who was of real importance went to Claridge's. As a matter of fact, if they were not of real importance, they could not get into Claridge's . . . That is what I want the Ritz Tower to be." The other corners he gave to Marion, who held them, and who later secured her private fortune when she leased two of them as sites for the Davies and Douras Buildings.

Further west on 57th Street, in the old entertainment district that was then beginning to blossom with galleries and "smart shops," Hearst bought dozens of lots for future development. And nearby, on Sixth Avenue at 54th Street, he built the Ziegfeld Theater (an art deco pleasure palace that was designed by Joseph Urban and completed in 1926), which he then surrounded with a complement of Hearst-owned luxury hotels, the Warwick, the Lombardy, and the Devon.

Brisbane, anticipating the advent of a railroad terminal that never arrived, busily acquired the rows of ramshackle low-rent shops that then lined Seventh Avenue. ("I think Papa must have bought out every tailor on the West Side," sighs his daughter Alice, who was still waiting for the predicted boom when she and her siblings inherited the properties in 1936.)

But Hearst reserved his special attention for Columbus Circle, where, according to Bill, he meant to establish his imperial headquarters. Already he commanded the park's southern entrance with his memorial to the Hearst martyrs, the men who died on the battleship *Maine*, and he had fortified the adjacent wedge, between Central Park West and Broadway, where the Gulf and Western Building now stands, with the hulking

two-story blockhouse that housed his New York *American*. (Built in
1915, the newspaper office had steel in its roof for forty additional floors,
which its owner was sure it would someday require.) In 1923, on the
present-day site of the New York Coliseum, he added the New Cosmopolitan Theater, an Urban-designed cinematic showcase, where Marion's
mid-career classics would be presented to audiences that might include,
on a single night, an array of fans as brilliant as Scott Fitzgerald, Lillian
Gish, D. W. Griffith, Flo Ziegfeld, Sam Goldwyn, George S. Kaufman
and Irving Berlin. And beneath the ground, he laid a foundation for the
coming wave of theaters and shops and bustling Hearst offices: for even
the cavernous subway interchange that spreads through the bowels of the
district was, in a sense, the publisher's handiwork. Originally, the cross-
town lines were to be laid through the park, along 72nd Street. But
Hearst, still a powerful party boss, used his influence to bring them
thirteen blocks south, into the territory that he had marked as his own.

Bill, of course, regrets that his father never realized his dream. He is
sure that "even without Brisbane's railroads, Pop could have made the
West Side work."

"Look at it now," he grumbles. "There's garbage in the streets. Bars
on all the windows. Kids running in packs over here with knives and
those goddamned radios. Pop would never have let that happen. He
would have made this part of the city, the way the Rockefellers made
Fifth Avenue."

But in 1937, when the banks began to pressure the Institution, Bill
and his fellow executives had no choice but to surrender the theaters, the
hotels, and most of the undeveloped lots. It was discovered that many of
Hearst's mortgage loans had been obtained on the basis of false financial
statements provided by several of his enterprises. Payments on most were
overdue, and the Chief, who was by then living permanently in California,
had begun to lose interest in his scheme. So the Manhattan domain—
which "included some incredible properties, properties that might have
made the Hearsts the richest family in the country today," according to
Harry Huberth, a real-estate expert, who helped to dismantle them—was
turned over to creditors, for liquidation.

Today, just one building of the complex that was to radiate from
Hearst Plaza remains standing. It is a strange, forlorn-looking structure,
an antique, a relic, an oddly flamboyant little pile of stone that seems
almost impossible in this day when mass and austere uniformity have

become the watchwords of architecture. Nestled on the corner of 57th Street and Eighth Avenue, at the edge of Manhattan's old automotive row, it is riddled with peculiarities throughout. It is six stories tall, but has steel in the walls and roof to support twenty floors that have never been built. Its fixtures of ancient brass and mahogany are madly extravagant, perhaps irreplaceable, and the doors are so thick that every room is virtually soundproof. In the back, the greatest surprise, the building hides a gaping hole where its erstwhile proprietor had intended to install yet another in his chain of motion-picture palaces.

This building was designed by Joseph Urban in 1928, as a home for the Hearst Magazine Division, and as a companion piece to the Ziegfeld Theater. Like the theater, which was demolished more than a decade ago, it is studded with pillars that jut weirdly toward the sky, supporting nothing but the Renaissance figures that balance precariously at the top of each. The walls are of surfaced limestone, the color of California sand, and one senses immediately that the whole might be less incongruous in Berkeley or San Francisco than here, in the heart of dirty, gray Manhattan.

At first flash, too, the Hearst Magazine Building, which has long served as the corporate headquarters, appears to be the very image of decay—perhaps an appropriate shell for a company grown accustomed to trading on past glory. Yet, beyond the curious, time-worn façade of 959 Eighth Avenue, very little at Hearst remains what it was ten years ago, when the papers were collapsing, and when even the most acute observers were caught wondering whether the corporation itself was fated to survive.

(2)

Richard Berlin surrendered his grip on the Hearst Corporation in February of 1973. It was not an easy retirement, not a smooth and gracious transfer of power to a third generation of leadership.

Berlin, who was seventy-nine years old in the year he stepped down, had been left behind by the revolution that rocked the media business in the sixties. The truth was that in a day when Knight, Gannett and Newhouse were building their megachains (and when that old Hearst competitor, the Los Angeles *Times*, was becoming a national force, largely by virtue of its wire-service link with the Washington *Post*), the Hearst president had never really known what to do with his newspapers, unless to cash them in. When *Time* magazine last caught him, in 1960, he had been on his way to the "family jewel box," as the Luce writers put it, to fish out yet another property, the Pittsburgh *Sun-Telegraph*, for a quick cash conversion. Looking bull-necked and peevish, more like a collection agent than a publishing tsar, he told a reporter soon afterward: "We're not going to carry losers any more. I'd be willing to sell everything but the wife and kids if the price were right." And even where the magazines, his special pets, were concerned, Berlin had become dangerously prone to trim rather than to develop. He had no new ideas for the magazines, nor did he seem to be alive to the ideas of others. In 1967, the president of his magazine division, Dick Deems, produced a program for Hearst's first self-developed magazine since *Motor*; it was to have been a slick, pseudo-psychedelic, pop-culture monthly called *eye*. But Berlin let the embryo float for only a single issue before he panicked at the expense of creating a new property and, in the face of Deems' horrified objections, summarily condemned it to death.

Two years earlier, he had signaled his willingness to let even the eighty-year-old *Cosmopolitan* collapse, unless Deems could find a way, without expense, to make the old literary warhorse pay. When the magazine began to founder, falling some $1.5 million into the red, Berlin had talked of killing it outright, a course from which he had been deterred only by the $2.5 million in outstanding subscriptions that would have to be met. Instead, he resolved to choke it to death, by cutting the operating budget in half—to a meager $30,000 per issue—and by raising the subscription price, in order to discourage new readers, who, he reasoned, would only increase his losses. In early 1965, when Deems recruited an ebullient, fortyish career-girl–author named Helen Gurley Brown to edit the failing magazine, Berlin was hardly interested. Scanning the dummies for the racy, sex-oriented women's monthly that *Cosmo* was to become, he pronounced them tasteless and improper. But because he was losing money, and because he had no better ideas, he grudgingly allowed Deems to hire Helen Brown, the woman who, in time, would redefine the company's future.

Regarding the delicate question of succession, Berlin proved to be as sphinxlike as Hearst himself. He kept a handful of men in the hierarchy believing that he was about to resign—and that they, each of them, had been marked to succeed him. But the promised transition never arrived. John Miller, who was then the general manager of the magazines, was told repeatedly that he "was going to be president of this company some day." But others—among them Gerard Markuson, the newspaper manager, and Frank Massi, the corporation's executive vice-president—had heard the same intimations. Eventually all of them realized that Berlin would never go willingly. "Dick was a lot like the old man," one of the corporate directors remarked. "He believed he was immortal. Of course, he didn't want to let go. He used to eat, sleep, and drink Hearst. And he was cagey enough to know that as long as he kept things vague—as long as everybody believed that *he* was next in line—nobody would ever get big enough to knock him down."

So there was this final tribute to Dick Berlin's hold on the corporation: no one at Hearst dared to dethrone him, even when they saw that his mind was beginning to slip. Harry Huberth (whose uncle Martin had been one of the original Hearst trustees) remembers that in the late sixties, Berlin had become troublingly maudlin and erratic. At one point, he commissioned Huberth's firm to develop a new headquarters for Hearst, a great center where the magazines, which were scattered in offices throughout the city, could be brought together in a single imposing complex, like Bill Paley's Black Rock or the Time-Life tower in Rockefeller Center. A new building was badly needed. Even Berlin understood that the little hutch on Eighth Avenue was bad for the corporate image, because it suggested that Hearst was hidebound and static, and perhaps too precarious to afford something better. But when the time came to close the deal, he suddenly collapsed in a fit of depression. "There is a building over on Third Avenue today that was built to Dick's very exacting specifications," says Huberth. "He let us get that far. But when the day came to sign the lease, he just couldn't do it. He started carrying on about the tradition, and the old man, and how they'd be better off to stay in the old place. My God, did we have a row over that. But as far as he was concerned, the deal was off. He had decided that Mr. Hearst wouldn't have wanted him to leave Eighth Avenue, so he wasn't going to budge."

Others noticed that when the Old Chancellor grew tired, toward the end of the long days he spent in his office, he would often slip into a rambling reminiscence about the corporation—about what it owed him and about how he had saved it when the wolves were at the door. His contempt for the family would often surface: "Those people are their own worst enemies, their own worst enemies," he carried on again and again, as if to excuse the way he had bullied and constrained them for twenty years past. Sometimes, too, he would talk about "Pop," and finally his listeners came to realize that he meant not his own father, whom he had scarcely known, but Hearst, whom he had come to regard as his parent.

The bitterness he had roused was deep and lasting, and many of the Hearst trustees, family and nonfamily alike, had scores to settle with Berlin. But they continued to fear him almost beyond reason. They had allowed him to become bigger than any of them, had let him play on their jealousies and petty ambitions, and now no one among them had the will or the power to depose him. For several years, his lieutenants tried to cover his foibles. Miller and Deems, the palace guard, pushed ahead on their own authority, deferring to Berlin when he seemed to be lucid, and discreetly holding visitors at bay on the many days when he was not. But not until he was almost eighty years old, did the deterioration become too serious to ignore. He was having lapses of memory by then, failing to recognize lifelong friends. According to one story that made the Hearst rounds, Berlin, who was still running the corporation, had ordered his wife of forty years out of bed one night. "No. I'm sorry," he had muttered in embarrassment. "My mother wouldn't like it."

To the end, the trustees dealt gingerly with Berlin. They eased him out quietly, with a barely audible sigh of relief. He was allowed to retain his office, the grand executive suite, complete with formal dining facilities, where he had been attended, like a king, by cooks and waiters from the *Good Housekeeping* staff. And the press release announcing his retirement insisted that Mr. Berlin (who was discreetly said to be "in his seventies") would remain in harness as a consultant and as chairman of the board of the testamentary trust that administers the funds of the Hearst foundations.

Still physically vigorous, the "little guy from Omaha, Nebraska," would continue to report to 959 Eighth Avenue each day, to reminisce, and—when the mood was on him—to issue an unceasing stream of commands. To be sure, he had been relieved of his authority. He retained only his titles, his secretary, and all of the corporate courtesies that belong to a faded old soldier. But according to those who have known him best, Dick Berlin, whose mind is gone, believes even now that he remains the unchallenged ruler at Hearst.

(3)

There were signs that the company's internal balance had begun to shift even before Berlin's pathetic retirement. Bill insists that his friend Joe Kingsbury Smith lent the family covert assistance in breaking the stranglehold that Berlin had placed on the trustees from the day the will took effect. According to Bill's tale (which Smith concedes is essentially correct), Berlin, believing that Hearst junior's traveling companion would move with the executive bloc, offered Smith a board position in 1960. "But Joe fooled him," gloats Bill. "He was true to the family from beginning to end. We had an understanding that he'd let Dick think whatever he wanted to think. But the next time a board opening came up, we had him. It would be six to six on the new appointment—for once, Dick would have to compromise."

This was a small, but critical change. It gave the family spirit and weight, and caused it to harden in a way that had never been possible when Berlin held the power to assign them jobs, to set their salaries, to confer or withhold the little favors (like trips abroad, home mortgages, or company cars), that made their lives too easy. Of course, they had always carped about money and titles; for twenty years, the sons had used Millicent to wrest concessions from her friend, the chief executive, who was occasionally willing to respect her wishes. But now, as he aged, the Hearsts became bold, and many began to question the assumptions that made the patronage system work. They had once accepted that they were inept, and that Berlin, whatever his faults, was a fiscal genius who had saved them, first in the 1930s and then again in the decade just past, from almost certain bankruptcy. Yet now, with so much of the empire gone, they could only begin to wonder. "You know, Dick used to *tell* me he was a genius," huffed Jack Cooke, who is married to George's daughter Phoebe, the oldest of the cousins. "He must have told me a dozen times how he sold Babicora. He'd say, 'Jack, you just don't know how to handle these Mexicans. I went down there on a Monday without a dime, and I came back on Wednesday with two million bucks in my pocket.' . . . Do you understand what he did? He sold a million-acre ranch at two dollars an acre. And threw in maybe 50,000 head of cattle for free! The Mexicans recovered the sale price on the timber alone in two years . . . If there was genius in that, I sure can't see it."

Randy was outraged by the notion that Berlin had kept the Hearsts in the dark, that he had never allowed them to know the company's condition or the extent of its wealth, and so he pressed for an independent audit of the organization's books. This was a radical measure, an open challenge to Berlin's good faith. But Randy insisted. He hired an outside auditing firm, which labored through the corporate records, assessing values and checking through accounts, until it came to the startling conclusion that Hearst was not so much a working corporation as a glorified piggybank. Berlin was a packrat, a compulsive saver. He had reduced the corporate debt to zero; and then, betrayed by his dogged, Depression-era mentality, he had begun squirreling away valuable capital, amassing some $43 million in cash while the family scratched for income and the sorry, dollar-starved Hearst properties continued to shrivel and die.

For some of the Hearsts, this was too much. According to Cooke, there was a time, in the wake of the auditors' report, when "everybody was running to the probate file, looking for a loophole." Family members talked of breaking the will, or about asserting their rights as trust beneficiaries. They were forced to concede that the old man had left them no mandate to run his empire; but under the terms of the law, the trust was to be administered in their best interests, and few believed that their interests had been served by Berlin or by the executive clique that he controlled.

The family could have sued for control of their heritage. The estate was administered by the probate court, and the arguments they could have presented, had they been willing to open the company records, might well have proved compelling. But in those last years—when Berlin was tottering, ready to fall—there was still no leadership, still no real competence among the sons. For Bill, the family had little respect. They had come to think him pompous and silly and more than a few of the younger Hearsts were frankly repelled by his patronizing air. As one niece said in open disgust, "He likes to think he's the patriarch now. It's taken him many moons to get there, so he's decided to make the most of it. The way Bill sees it, everybody is incompetent but himself. Nobody can do anything but him. He's got an inflated idea of his own value, and if you want to know the truth, I think he'd like to keep everyone else in the dark while he feathers his own nest."

There was a touch of envy in their feeling toward Bill. Many suspected that he had done *too* well. His salary was high, and he had his chauffeured car, his Fifth Avenue apartment, his house on the hill at San

Simeon. He did his globe-trotting at company expense, and some of his kinsmen resented this in a special way. They hinted that the "Trio," as they called the Hearst Task Force, was a gimmick contrived to keep him happy, the payoff for some sort of deal with Berlin. Joanne Hearst was one who understood that the arrangement was a "farce." She learned this, she said, when she met the "Three Musketeers" in Hong Kong. "I was there for the Federal Trade Council," remembered Joanne. "They were in Hong Kong for some reason, I don't know what. It happened to be Bob Considine's birthday, but the poor guy was typing away in the Hilton or wherever they were staying. Everybody but Bill was working. He was working hard at the tailor's . . . being outfitted with his polo coat and his this and that. I never saw him do a stitch of work. None at all. The Task Force always worked that way. He went along for the name and the ride. He took the credit, but the rest of them did the work."

Bill's adventures on the road were a family joke, but to watch him in his New York office was still more painful. Always a heavy drinker, he had aged quickly and very badly. He had put on much weight; his eyes had become deep, almost haunted, like his father's; and he no longer seemed to care that even his imposing title, Editor in Chief of the Hearst Newspapers, was a sop, something he had been given to salvage his pride. Much of the time he seemed to be lost in a dream. In an antic mood, Bill might entertain himself by mimicking Pop, calling to his secretary in a high, hoarse voice, "Johnny, Johnny. I've got a spot on my tie from lunch. Would you please see if someone from *Good House-keeping* or one of our other very practical magazines would be kind enough to remove it." Or he might dawdle on the phone with his "darlin', sweetheart," Bootsie's young niece, a Columbia student who'd been keeping him company. Or, more seriously, he might banter about politics and crime in the streets with Jack O'Connell, the latest of his Brisbanes, who would labor to turn these random thoughts into a readable column.

But whatever he did, he was strangely remote. He was spending his days in a world of his own—as was David, who had withdrawn to his home in Beverly Hills, and, pleading ill health, had refused to be bothered with the family, or the papers, or any of the empire's muddled affairs.

The truth was that of the surviving brothers, only Randy had vitality enough to push for a change, to penetrate the malaise that had fallen over the business and the clan since his father's death. Yet even Randy had his failings. He was notorious for his lapses of interest and for his addiction to gentleman's sports (corporate demands would fall by the way when he disappeared for a week hunting duck, playing golf), not to mention the sublime decadence that allowed him to appear for dinner on some days still arrayed in rumpled silk pajamas. This was Randy, the most robust of the sons! He was a man who preferred his exile in Hillsborough to a life in New York, in the eye of the storm; a man who preached change, but dodged responsibility, and who always seemed to become worried and skittish when he came up against the hard decisions. ("That was the horror of these last five years," notes his twenty-six-year-old nephew Austin Hearst. "Randy has always hated to face decisions that he knows will affect other people's lives. That made him uncomfortable in the army, and in the company too. I guess I don't have to tell you what that meant with Patty.")

These character flaws had slowed Randy down. They had kept him from becoming his better self, the potential leader of a crippled family; and so, in 1973, when he replaced Bill as chairman of Hearst's corporate board (a 19-member panel that is distinct from, and subordinate to, the trustees), Randolph Hearst was only beginning to grasp at matters that he should have mastered years before.

But if Randy was only beginning to move, only beginning to apply his anger in ways that might change their dreary status quo, some of the younger Hearsts had no intention of waiting for his back to stiffen. Among the senior members of the cousins' generation (or the "grandchildren," as they are more often called in family circles), pressure was building toward a confrontation. They wanted a change in the family's status. They wanted a greater share of the fortune than they could ever expect to enjoy under the terms of the will.

Some of these cousins—like the twins, George and Phoebe who were born in 1925, and John's son Bunky, who came nine years later—were old enough to remember their grandfather. And what they remembered, without exception, was not the strangely mercurial tyrant who had too often taunted and badgered their fathers, but rather a frail and beneficent old man, an aging wizard who had been only too willing to share what he had. For Bunky, who lived at San Simeon after his parents' separation in 1946, the dominant memory would be of his grandfather's suit of billiard-table green—as the grandson wrote later, "Other men who wore clothes like that would have looked as though they were with the circus.

But because Grandpop was so dignified, he made the clothes look dignified too." He would remember, too, how the withered old man had beamed when the boy, at the age of fourteen, had asked for a job on one of the papers. "If you want to be a newspaperman," came the time-worn reply, "don't go to journalism school. Learn all you can while you are working. In five months you can pick up everything they can teach you in a school. Watch everything, ask questions and learn why. That is the way I did it, and I think it's the best way."

To George's children, Hearst senior was Santa Claus, nothing more nor less. "I have nothing but the best memories of him," says Phoebe. "At Christmas he would shower us with presents by the truckload—so many that my mother, who knew better, would have to make us pick one and give the rest to charity. He was very good to us. He told us many times that he wanted us to have a part in what belonged to him."

Indeed, the grandchildren could almost believe that Hearst had cared for them even more than he cared for his own five sons. There had been fewer distractions as he aged—fewer crises over Marion, fewer ugly confrontations with his wife. He had the time to coddle his young progeny, and coddle them he did. He kept them at the castle for months on end, and sometimes, when they were old enough, he talked about their future with the Institution; he promised that it would be different from what had awaited the boys. George, especially, had enjoyed his attention. Hearst had placed the boy carefully, in San Francisco, where he could monitor his progress. And, what was surely more important, he pushed him along far more slowly than he had pushed any of the sons. Phoebe was convinced that with George, her grandfather intended to avoid the mistakes that had crippled her father's generation. "He wanted George to turn out right," she insists. "Sure, I think he was looking for a little bit of himself in his grandchildren."

To the cousins, then, it seemed only an accident that they had been caught in a testamentary trap intended more for their parents than for themselves. They knew, of course, that the will was sacred writ, the document on which the whole intricate system of business and family was based. And they knew that under its terms, they, the cousins, were entitled to only the slimmest inheritance. ("The beneficiaries were given enough to survive—that was *it*," explains Phoebe.) But at the same time, some, at least, were coming to believe that the spirit of the testament was somehow less harsh than its painfully literal clauses. "Anyone who ever looked at it," remarks Jack Cooke, "would have to admit that whatever else he wanted, Mr. Hearst wanted to leave *something* for his family."

That the Hearsts were finally to have their adjustment is one of the family's more closely guarded secrets. In the last five years, there has been a shift in the fortune—a major change in the network of Hearst institutions, a change that has for the first time allowed the family to tap the profits that had long been locked into the corporate structure. In a very real sense, this reorganization represents a triumph for the Hearsts: Randy and Bill both fought to see it consummated, and the Cookes, along with a younger ally, Bill's son Willie, fought harder still to see it conducted according to their own exacting standards. And yet the family is reluctant to discuss the change that has at last brought them into their own. Perhaps they are squeamish because the maneuvers involved were precarious; in effect, what they did was to skirt, if not quite violate, the patriarch's will. What's more, wealth is always a delicate matter. Few among the very rich will talk freely about what they have. But if anything has made the subject more painful—has turned it into the one remaining taboo in a day when Marion is discussed freely, if without much interest, and when even the long-running corporate squabbles have been aired—it is surely the brutal fact of Patty. For the family finds it difficult to admit that even as Randy was trying, in vain, to persuade his daughter's captors that he possessed no special wealth, the clan had become much richer than ever before.

The Hearst trustees have taken measures to obscure this shift in the family's status. In June of 1975, they persuaded Los Angeles Superior Court Judge Neal Lake that Hearst's will and fourteen volumes of related documents, which had been part of the public record, should be sealed, because, they said, the probate file was "like a hit list for terrorists," and because the family was under "clear and present danger" of attack. More bluntly, corporate director Phoebe Cooke has explained that "We simply weren't interested in having people know where we live or what we own."

But of the story that lies concealed in the file—which remains closed, though Patty is free and her revolutionary companions are now dead or imprisoned—at least this much has now become clear:

In the will that was filed on the day of his death, William Randolph

Hearst had managed to preserve his empire only by leaving the bulk of its assets to charity. Under the terms of his testament, the voting shares of the Hearst Corporation—the 30,000 shares of Class A preferred, which paid the sons their $30,000 each year—were placed with the thirteen administrators of the family trust. But at the same time, the body of his actual wealth, represented by a large block of nonvoting common stock in the company, was vested in a separate, residual trust, which was to be administered for the benefit of two tax-exempt philanthropies, the Hearst and William Randolph Hearst Foundations.

For some eighteen years, the wealth had remained safe with the charities, which were controlled by a corps of staunch Hearst loyalists (all of them executives or family members), who took care to distribute no more than a small percentage of the annual Hearst profits, usually through programs like the William Randolph Hearst Journalism Awards or the Hearst Senate Youth Program. But in 1969, Congress saw fit to close the loophole that had allowed the press lord, like so many millionaires of his generation, to avoid the burden of inheritance taxes while keeping his estate intact. Under the omnibus Tax Reform Act of that year, no tax-exempt foundation was permitted to hold more than 5 percent of its assets in a single enterprise. Within five years, the Hearst foundations, which were "wholly owned," would be forced to divest their treasure of common stock.

Strangely enough, a stricture that might have panicked a less tightly held company proved to be a blessing in disguise for Hearst, for the ingenious tax shelter that had once saved the fortune also carried a hidden threat. Under the law governing charitable foundations, the assets of the residual trust—that is, the bulk of the corporation—eventually would have been distributed (in about the year 2000, according to actuarial tables) among the trust beneficiaries, presumably the programs that were then receiving Hearst money. According to one family member, "There had been a lot of worry about that through the years. Even though it was a long way off, we were beginning to see that the stock could wind up with just about anybody. We figured someone would get their hands on a chunk of the corporation, then come in and try to run it." Now, however, the company was suddenly free to redeem itself. Not only was there cash on hand, for Berlin's quiet hoarding had left some forty or fifty million dollars in the coffers, but there was no outstanding corporate debt. By using its tremendous reserve of cash and credit to purchase its own stock from the foundations, the corporation could eliminate the annual contribution to charity, and, incredibly, *leave the Hearst family trust in sole possession of the fortune.*

In 1974, when Patty was abducted, the maneuver was already well under way. The foundations had hired outside attorneys, to prevent an obvious conflict of interest, and the corporate officers had devised a plan under which all of the company's stock, both preferred and common, would be replaced by a single issue of new, voting, Hearst Corporation common shares.

Apparently, the scheme had almost run aground when the attorneys general of New York and California were called in to value the corporation. For purposes of the sale, the state officers set the company's worth at $210 million (although, in fact, its various assets would probably have netted close to $1 billion if sold individually), while they reckoned the value of the family's existing preferred shares at a bare $5 million—a figure dictated by the will, which pegged the redemption price of the family stock (some of which had belonged to Millicent) at $80 per share. The independent foundation attorneys argued that their clients' shares must then be worth the balance—a full $205 million. At which the corporate minions gasped that the figure was exorbitant, that the common shares could scarcely be worth $50 million, because they had no voting rights and no genuine market value.

Randy lobbied the state attorneys. The parties compromised on what the directors must concede was a bargain price, $135 million for the entire block of Hearst common stock. And so—while Hearst squeezed its foundations for the $2 million that was to have been Patty's ransom—and while company representative Charles Gould tersely informed the Symbionese Liberation Army that "neither the Hearst Corporation nor the Hearst foundations are controlled by members of the Hearst family"— the corporation was mobilizing its vast reserve, to buy its own freedom from the charitable trust.

It was no accident, of course, that the new shares issued to the family trust carry no dollar limit on the dividends they may pay. The sons, who for years had "scraped by" on their intentionally inflated salaries and the annual $30,000 allotment, saw to it that the corporate directors would be free to declare an appropriate pay-out each year. According to one of the Hearst beneficiaries, the family now divides approximately 10 percent of the company's net, which currently approaches an impressive $100 million.

Thus, each of the five Hearst families can expect to receive as much as $2 million from a trust that once recokoned its benefits only in tens of thousands.

Clearly, Bill is pleased to be making what he calls "real money" from the organization he has served for so long. "We fought pretty hard for a percentage," he has maintained in a guarded discussion of the corporate shuffle. "I think we were pretty much entitled to a piece of the action after all these years."

But at the same time, it seems clear that a younger generation was forced to carry what may well have been the critical battle in the company's ticklish recapitalization. For according to Jack Cooke, a Hearst in-law who sits on the corporate board, several of the grandchildren were shocked to find that under the deal hammered out by the eager executives, the family trust was originally intended to receive only 7 percent of the new stock issue, with the rest lying dormant in the vault, awaiting the day when the directors might decide to take the Hearst Corporation public. "They had their eye on *Times-Mirror*, and frankly, we didn't like it," says Cooke. "It wouldn't have cost us anything in the short run, because we owned all the shares that were out—we'd get all the dividends. But in the long run, they were thinking about taking the rest of the shares to Wall Street—and over there it would have been a big selling point to be able to say that the Hearsts were out of the picture, that they only held 7 percent."

The sons seemed willing to accept that arrangement, perhaps because they believed that the money was enough, that it no longer mattered who owned the business, as long as it paid an annual return that would allow them to live in comfort. But the Cookes—with strong support from Will Hearst III, who had recently been appointed to the corporate board—had no intention of losing a company that seemed to be on the threshold of prosperity. They hired attorneys and accountants of their own, and insisted that they would block the deal, that they would sue in the probate court, unless 50 percent or more of the new shares remained in the family trust.

Cooke concedes that the action "caused a lot of hard feelings." He believes that he and his wife were branded as rebels, corporate mavericks who were "rocking the boat," and threatening to capsize the arrangement that was about to make the family wealthy. But he also believes that he and Phoebe and Willie were right—that their grandfather had wanted the institution to remain a private preserve, not just for his sons, but for his family "two and three generations down the line." They knew that the family might gain in both stature and wealth if they were to throw their enterprise open to the public, like the Chandlers, the Fords, the Sulzbergers, and the rest. But their reservations were deeply rooted. The three of them feared—and still fear—that the unissued stock might prove to be a loaded gun, that a cabal of executives, who still maintain a majority on the board of trustees, might award themselves the shares as a "bonus," making the corporation their own.

Ultimately, the rebels won their point. In a watershed victory, the three compelled the Hearst directors to place not 7, but 40, percent of the new shares into the family trust; and while that block is short of an absolute majority, it is enough to guarantee that the family trustees will continue to control the organization, whatever becomes of the unissued shares.

The cousins, of course, were proud of their triumph—and they were puzzled, to say the least, by the sons' failure to support them in a fight that they felt would be decisive for the future of the family. Only when the battle was won, says Cooke, did Bill and Randy quietly offer to share the burden of legal fees, which by then had become almost staggering. "They wouldn't lift a finger to help us," notes the cousin. "But you can be sure they were happy as hell with the way things turned out."

(4)

For two full years there was a caretaker president, the jovial, gray-haired Frank Massi, who was already sixty-three years old in the year Berlin stepped down. Massi was less the media master than a faithful accountant; until Berlin named him executive vice-president, he had served for long years as the company treasurer, and several trustees have privately noted that his appointment was a holding action, a measure they took not because they wanted him, but because they were deeply uncertain about the man whose claim to the office was greatest.

This was John R. Miller. Proud, confident, and quietly driven. Vigorous at the age of fifty-nine. A Berlin protégé, a magazine man, and a relentless worker, who managed to believe much longer and harder than the rest when the fading president promised that he, John Miller, would someday rise to replace him.

Miller owed his career to Hearst. He likes to recall that he came to the company at the age of nineteen, as a clerk in the magazine division, where he worked not upstairs, among the powers, but in the basement circulation department, Room 358. There he labored in deep obscurity, entering numbers in a corporate ledger, while the editorial stars made headlines and the financial prodigies spent weekends at the ranch. His salary was $30 a week. On that he supported a wife and a son. And yet Miller enjoyed a degree of psychological independence that was rare among the Hearst personnel. For his father was the president of a paper company, a thriving firm in Virginia, and Miller, who went to school at St. Paul's in New Jersey and then to a business college in Wilmington, had already been groomed for a place in his own family's business. He had intended his position at Hearst to be temporary, a stopover on his way to Princeton. But the sheer energy of the place had caught him, and so he stayed, he married, and he decided to carve out a place of his own in the ranks of the publishing empire.

There was decidedly little drama in his rise. His career had faltered just once—in the beginning. In 1937, when he had been with the organization for almost four years, he caught the eye of Berlin, then the magazine president, who told him that playing with numbers was fine, but that "you've got to be a salesman if you want to get anywhere in this business." Berlin offered Miller a position in sales—with the proviso that he take a five-dollar cut in his weekly pay. "But I just couldn't do it," the executive recalls, with the hint of a grimace. "Those were tight days. My wife was expecting, and I'd made up my mind to live without my family's money. So I told him, no, Mr. Berlin, but thanks. I guess I'll stay put."

Miller stayed in the basement, and for a month he worried that he had grievously erred, that he had hesitated in the face of a risk, and that Berlin would never forget his weakness. His anxiety deepened when Arthur Moore, the magazines' general manager, learned that Miller had been talking with Berlin, dealing "over his head."

"He tore me apart for playing politics—the tension was incredible, almost unbearable. I genuinely believed I was through," says Miller. But the banks closed in on the company that year, and before the ax could fall on the clerk, both Moore and the entire sales unit that Miller had been asked to join disappeared.

The rest had been almost grimly regular. Berlin—who fervently believed in caution—who had only been charmed by a young man's refusal to stake five dollars a week against one shot at a blazing sales career—eased Miller into his executive clique. He made him the manager of subscription sales, and then the head of magazine circulation. Later, in 1960, when Dick Deems became president of the magazines, Berlin named Miller their general manager. The old Hearst president worked closely with the two, sometimes dealing with the men as a team, sometimes playing them one against the other, but telling them always that they counted for more than the rest, because they were responsible for the magazines, and the magazines were the company's treasure.

It is interesting that Deems is no older than Miller, and that for thirteen years he served as Miller's superior in the hierarchy. Deems may well have believed that he enjoyed a certain priority; but company lore has it that Miller was always closer to Berlin, and always closer to the president's office. "Dick thought John was a hell of a lot tougher than Deems," was the way one executive put it. "Deems is outgoing, a salesman, and Dick loved him for that. It was a little bit of himself. But he wanted something more from the guy who was going to follow him."

Miller helped to ease Berlin out. He carried the burden of persuading the president, who was no longer thinking for himself, to resign without resistance. And he might have inherited the executive office immediately if the family (and especially Randy, who threw his weight behind Massi's appointment) had been less reluctant to advance a man whose loyalties were suspect. For Miller made no secret of his respect for Richard Berlin. He regarded the old man as a patron, almost a corporate father, and to the end he remained belligerently proud to have backed him in the years when they decided to kill the foundering papers instead of spending good money to save them.

That loyalty is almost surely what kept John Miller subordinate to Massi for two years, even though, as executive vice-president, he was making the company's critical decisions. Miller affirms that he, and not Massi, negotiated the more than $100 million in loans that were used to buy out the foundations' stock. "It was the first thing I did when I took over," he has said—although, strictly speaking, he had not yet taken over in 1974, when the loans were being closed. Miller was responsible, too, for the company's initial reaction to Patty's abduction. "I ordered everyone to stay away from it," he explains. "We had editors with their tongues hanging out, trying to get a piece of that story. But I decided that nothing we could write would do us—or her—a bit of good. We simply blacked it out."

Not until March 1975, however, did the trustees choose to make John Miller president of the corporation. It was clearly a long-delayed decision. But it was also a decision that they have never, for a minute, had reason to regret.

His reign would endure for only four years, but for Hearst those years were a whole new era. It was the time of the miracle, the Great Revival, when energy long dormant became vital and when age-old properties began to yield profits that might have been almost embarrassing had the company seen fit to make them public. Revenues surged by tens of millions of dollars each year, and in 1978, when they far exceeded the half-billion-dollar mark,* Wall Street analysts began to speculate that Hearst had become the largest privately held corporation in America. Investors clamored for a piece of the action. "They literally begged us to let them in," says Miller. But the trustees held their treasure tight, while the company's net doubled, then doubled again, and then continued to rise at a rate—said to exceed 40 percent per annum—that left even Bill, who remembered his father's great wealth, shaking his head in wonder.

"I don't know how he does it," said the son in November of 1978, when he received yet another astounding quarterly report. "I don't know how. He turned a $17-million operation into $70 million a year, free and clear. And still going up . . .

"I guess John Miller is a very smart guy."

Miller was indeed a "very smart guy"; but more than that, he was a consummate businessman who had spent some forty years weighing the value of the various Hearst properties. He knew all the numbers—their linage, their revenue, and the story of their steadily falling circulation. He knew the people who ran them. And he knew, in the last analysis, that the organization was worth a great deal more than what Berlin, whom he respected, had realized.

---

* John Miller has privately maintained that if Hearst had been a publicly held corporation, its revenues would have placed it at number 348 among the *Fortune* 500. In 1977 (the time to which Miller referred), the Hoover Corporation, which held that position, reported sales of $591 million.

To hear him tell it, the task that he faced was exquisitely simple. "It was all lying right there in front of us," he has said, referring to the elements of his new Hearst empire, a media conglomerate that ranks once more with the nation's largest. "We already owned so much—and all of it was just begging to be developed. We only had to learn how to use what we had."

For his own part, Miller had already come to understand what had escaped Dick Berlin: that it was cheaper by far to refurbish than to acquire, that the risks involved were relatively small, and the dividends potentially spectacular. Ten years earlier, the executive had been deeply mired in the problems that were killing *Cosmopolitan*, which had once stood shoulder to shoulder with the great general-interest magazines— *Colliers, Life,* and the *Saturday Evening Post*—but which, like so many Hearst properties, had only grown ramshackle and shoddy in the hands of a president who would not spend money on maintenance and fine tuning. Miller had watched its editorial formula disintegrate, as it slipped from the high-toned cultural forays that were Ray Long's legacy into a kind of lurid come-on ("Four lousy husbands explain why," "A kept woman explains her life," shouted the covers) that was aimed low, at supermarket sales. Then he had seen the Berlin-ordered cuts do their work. The editorial staff was reduced, the four-color pages were dropped, and the business department was all but dismantled, while the crucial accounts, the magazine's lifeblood, continued their ebb toward quality books like *McCall's* and *Ladies Home Journal.*

Ironically, Miller himself was the enforcer who kept the magazine on its starvation budget. When Bob Atherton, who was then its editor, begged for more money to save *Cosmopolitan* the general manager refused, because, as he put it, the magazine was "going nowhere," and because he knew that Dick Berlin would never tap his reserve to support a property that couldn't survive on its own.

Perhaps there was a time when John Miller accepted that reasoning. Perhaps he believed with his boss that a property should stand on its own, or else be allowed to weaken and die. But he was also a man with a great deal of pride. He had come to believe that the magazines were somehow more worthy than the papers, that these, at least, were quality publications, almost untouched by the sordid side of the old man's genius. And so it pained him deeply to admit that one of the best magazines in his stable had become cheap, almost laughable, because the corporation would not take steps to make it better.

This more than anything prodded Miller when Helen Gurley Brown, who was bright and sure, though she had never worked for a magazine, descended on Hearst in a flurry of shocking ideas. She, the hustler-queen, had already spun two books (*Sex and the Single Girl* and its sequel, *Sex and the Office*), a pair of recordings ("Lessons in Love" and "Helen Gurley Brown at Town Hall"), and a movie title (*Sex and the Single Girl* again, for $200,000) from her primal theme, that any girl can get her man; and now, early in 1965, she offered to make her formula work for Hearst. Brown presented Miller and Deems with a twenty-page dummy for something called *Femme*, a superslick monthly that would lean its missionary pitch toward the lost and lonely, the twenty-five million single girls, who, she pointed out, were spending millions of dollars in their unrelenting prowl for available males. The executives pushed instead to give her *Cosmo*. She would have money (though never enough) and a free hand to transform the book. They would calm the unhappy Berlin, who doubted, but who had been compelled to let his top lieutenants have their way.

The new magazine was flip, warm and outrageously sassy. It was bubbling with energy, because Helen Brown bubbled; she popped and fizzed with new plans and new angles, and her spirit was contagious, so no one really cared that she was scattering old Hearst habits to the winds. Her very first issue, which came out in July 1965, confronted the world with a daring cover: it flaunted pale-pink lipstick and long blond hair on a statuesque model, stunning and cool in her low-cut Jax dress. That is Our Girl, chirped Brown, as the *Cosmo* staff marched through her office, one by one, to hear the first round of her never-ending pep talk. That is Our Girl, not as she is . . . but the way she wants to be. I want you to think about her. Worry about her. Get to be her *best friend*, said Helen. Remember, she's lonely. She's not making much money, but she works very hard. She wants to make her way up in the world, and more than anything, she wants to be *sexy*, because she knows that "a sex object is the most *wonderful* thing that a girl can be!"

They were going to make a magazine for *her*, the mousy little girl who was, eternally, just about to blossom. So absolutely everything would have to be upbeat. The writing would be nothing less than inspirational, peppered with italic and glad exclamation. ("Now, young lady, is it absolutely clear? *No bad reviews,"* she warned her film critic.) The girl would *always* get her man.

"Do you *really* think you can believe in what I'm trying to do?" she asked the editors as she concluded each briefing with an exhausted sigh.

Yes, they believed, the Hearstlings replied, nodding warily. And apparently they did, because soon the staff, largely held over from the Atherton regime, was producing a whole new *Cosmopolitan.* They went décolleté on every cover (strapping the underweight models with tape, to bring their cleavage up to snuff), and scrabbled for writers who understood that "It's Just as Easy to Love a Rich Man." The sexual reportage was startlingly frank. "What, Me? VD?" blazed one of the new banners, while others promised to tell Our Girl "How to Marry a Billionaire" and "How to Make Your Bed So *He* Will Lie in It."

The Helen Brown approach to fiction alone would have been enough to send Ray Long tottering over the brink. In an early issue, the editor ecstatically reported that "Bill Guy, our fiction editor, brought in this month a great chiller-thriller about a secretary who gets strangled (aaaaaaap!), a lovely story by Nadine Gordimer about a plain sister who wins out over a beautiful one (love that theme, don't you?) and two other fine short stories."

Betty Friedan, of course, was appalled. She declared the magazine "quite obscene and quite horrible." And Dick Berlin almost choked when *Women's Wear Daily* got hold of a report that Helen had ordered up an article on the erotic potential of breasts. "We are doing an article on how men should treat women's breasts in lovemaking," the editor had told her staff in a cheery memo. "It will either sell another 100,000 copies or stop publication of *Cosmopolitan* altogether." She went on to ask each of her female assistants, "What pleases you in terms of having your breasts caressed?" And "Any personal experiences you've had yourself or know about where somebody didn't like having her bosom caressed and then she was able to begin enjoying it?" But before the tantalizing replies could return, a sputtering Hearst president had canceled the piece.

Berlin, the staunch Catholic and family man (whose own daughter Bridgit had left the strait and narrow to become one of Andy Warhol's "Chelsea Girls"), would always have pangs of conscience about what he had allowed *Cosmo* to become. It was largely out of deference to him that Burt Reynolds was asked to cover his genitals in the famous nude foldout, another Brown brainstorm. But for John Miller, the balance sheet carried a message that could hardly be ignored. "The initial figures were stunning," he says of the reborn magazine. "Much better than anything we had ever dreamed possible." In the first year alone, the Helen Brown revival raised circulation by 15 percent and advertising revenue by half. Those new readers stayed with the magazine (though some of the old ones drifted away, complaining that *Cosmo* was sex-obsessed). The ad linage multiplied, and by the middle seventies, when Miller began his stewardship at Hearst, the new *Cosmopolitan*—just one of twenty Hearst glossies—was adding as much as $30 million each year to the corporate coffers.

That has become the paradigm at Hearst, the model for a long-term program that John Miller calls "the reacquisition of our own properties." Both Miller and his hand-picked successor, a forty-three-year-old Texan named Frank Bennack, have begun—only begun, in spite of the in-credible gains of the last five years—to tap the vast pool of unused potential that has accumulated since the patriarch's death.

Sometimes they have simply rerun the pattern, taking a property that is worn out or performing below potential, and then gutting it, finding new talent, and rebuilding the whole from the inside out. According to Miller, Hearst pulled a "clean sweep" on its three FM radio stations in Baltimore, Pittsburgh and Milwaukee. "They were nothing, they were on hold," he says. "But we reprogrammed the group all at once, and every one of them turned out to be a gold mine." And again, they have done much the same with Avon Books, the paperback company that Berlin had acquired in 1959. Even while he was still with the magazines, Miller had been pained by the Avon formula, the wholehearted devotion to dime-store Gothic that made the division a perennial embarrassment. He likes to recall that one day, in the middle sixties, he took an armload of "that pulp" to Fred Lewis, who ran the book program for Hearst, and dumped the whole stack on his desk, telling Lewis that if they had to publish garbage to make money, they should just get out of the business.

Lewis told Miller to do better if he could. And that marked the advent of Peter Mayer, the brash and free-spending editor who put Avon in a league with giants like Pocket Books, Bantam, Fawcett and Dell. For Miller recognized the thirty-year-old Mayer, who had been hired by Avon's Frank Taylor to explore the potential of an educational line, for the broad-ranging talent that he was—and to meet Lewis' challenge, he was willing to gamble. He pushed the young editor ahead, to the positions of editor in chief and then publisher, assuring him all the while that Hearst wanted profits, but that it also expected quality and range, a respectable product from all its divisions.

Still, Avon only simmered while Berlin held the purse strings. Through the sixties its list held steady at perhaps a dozen titles a month, and while many of those titles had become more respectable—for Mayer was building long-term reprint relationships with solid authors like Daphne Du-Maurier and Elie Wiesel—a good many more fell into the old categories, the grimly reliable Westerns, Gothics and formula thrillers.

Not until 1972, when power had finally begun its shift toward Miller, was Mayer free to vent the energy that would make his company a major contender. In an almost explosive twelve-month period, he stretched his list to a full twenty-eight titles per month, and he opened new lines— Camelot, Flare, Equinox and Bard—that took the company beyond the mass market, into a wider, more permanent field, where the editors and not the sales representatives would decide what worked and what didn't. Avon would do juveniles, art, and humor. It would carry a list of distinguished authors—Saul Bellow, Thornton Wilder, Heinrich Böll, Gabriel García Marquez—and it would take the radical step of publishing originals, with no hard-cover record, because, as Mayer put it, his company was "suspicious of old attitudes, methods, even goals . . . We're trying everything all at once and are still looking for more new directions."

Perhaps the most radical step of all involved the way that Peter Mayer spent Hearst money. It was late in 1972 that the publisher pried loose the towering sum of $1 million for the rights to a single book, the transactional bible, *I'm OK—You're OK*—and then came back only a few days later to demand another Hearst million for a slim little volume called *Jonathan Livingston Seagull*.

Amazingly, John Miller delivered the cash, though he can still remember Berlin, too old to resist, gasping in exasperation: "John, John. You spent a million dollars on a goddamned seagull!" But still more amazingly, the investments paid off, just as surely as the money they had spent on *Cosmo*. Figures at Avon showed revenues up by 147 percent in 1973. From November of 1972, the company was overwhelmed with new business, and for three full months, from January through March of the next year, its rickety distribution system virtually broke down under the weight of new orders. *I'm OK—You're OK* topped four million copies, while the seagull alone returned some $5 million in sales.

"Business was just too big. It was embarrassing for us," said Mayer. But for Miller the only embarrassment was that it had taken Hearst so long to discover that it could build its stature, that it could find profit not just in cheap mass, where it had always excelled, but in quality and even in good reputation.

This last, in fact, has become crucial to Miller and his cohorts. For in their hurried drive to reclaim the company, they have discovered that Hearst does best where it enjoys good credit, where it has earned the good will of its media consumers. And they are quickly learning to make that credit pay great dividends. Miller might laugh at the title *Good Housekeeping*: "Isn't that the last thing on earth you'd name a magazine!" he chuckles. But he is shrewd enough to understand that the homely title has magic for the five million women who buy the magazine (a recent survey showed that an astonishing 78 percent of its readers feel *complete confidence* in the products it advertises—this compared to a 63 percent rating for the competing *Ladies Home Journal* and a miserable 42 percent for *TV Guide*), and that the magic can be parlayed into millions of dollars. "We build on what we've got in the bank," he explains. "If we understand that women have confidence in *Good Housekeeping*, we look for ways to develop and use that feeling. We'll put the title on a series of books, the *Good Housekeeping Gardening Encyclopedia*, for instance, and sell them through the same (Hearst-owned) distribution network. Or we'll use *Good Housekeeping* to float a trial balloon—say a one-shot issue like "Country Living," "Needlecraft," or "Beauty Book." If it flies, we'll do it again. Maybe go quarterly. If we still like it, well, we've got a new magazine, risk-free."

In much the same way, the eighty-year-old *Motor*, Hearst's first magazine, has become the platform for a thriving series of auto repair books, while *Popular Mechanics* supports a direct mail *Do-It-Yourself-Encyclopedia* that Miller likes to call the "biggest continuity service in the world." *House Beautiful* has spawned *Colonial Homes*, a magazine-in-embryo that may soon take its place in the monthly stable. From *Cosmopolitan* comes *Company*—a wholly owned British counterpart, edited by Maggie Goodman—along with a spate of licensed editions that spread the Brown gospel through some fourteen countries around the world.

*   *   *

Thus all of these things—adjustment, conciliation, imagination and unremitting effort—have combined to make the seventies a watershed decade for Hearst.

The television stations are all ABC now; they have the top network in three prime markets witth a lucrative AM-FM tie-in for each. The hundred-million-dollar debt, legacy of the stock deal, has been painlessly cleared. The magazines are healthy and fertile, like so many fat geese, laying their golden eggs each quarter, and spawning a new generation of homey, remunerative periodicals for Hearst.

The Publishers' Periodical Service Bureau, once on the rocks because of its dubious, high-pressure sales techniques, has been cleaned up. For a half-dozen years the division has been peddling some 3,300,000 subscriptions annually without resort to the sleight-of-hand that had made Hearst salesmen the terror of wary consumers.

The executives have proved themselves sharp and conscientious. ("It has to make you feel good knowing that you've got guys like Miller and Bennack on your side," says Jack Cooke, who is convinced that the new regime can be trusted.) And best of all, the corporation is not only wealthy, but private. There are no public stockholders to be considered, no troublesome reports to be filed with the SEC. Major decisions are reached quietly, almost without breaking the flow of a smooth-running business day. A handful of phone calls to the nineteen directors is usually enough to obtain unanimous consent for a last-minute bid on a newspaper (as when Hearst dropped into the battle for the Wilmington *News and Journal* with an offer that fell between the $55 million bid by the Washington *Post* and the $60 million tendered by successful Gannett), or an authorization for the agents out stalking a hard-cover publishing outlet (like Arbor House in New York, which Hearst acquired in 1979).

Peace and prosperity have finally arrived. The struggle between family and executives is over, and the deep-seated doubts about corporate survival have at last been dispelled. The strategists talk once more, not about empire, but about expanding their massive media network to challenge the giants, the Times Mirror Company and Time, Inc.

But even in the face of unquestioned success, of profits that leave Wall Street observers agog, there remains a certain uneasiness at Hearst. For the powers know they have yet to contend with that lingering problem—the newspaper chain they had all but destroyed.

Chapter 2

The Monarch

(1)

ONCE THEY WERE A POWER, but now the Hearst papers are a weary little chain, thirteen dailies in twelve cities that would like to leave their reputation behind. Their combined circulation is 1.5 million, barely more than the *Wall Street Journal*, and fewer by far than the *Daily News*. Their revenues are approximately $300 million, perhaps a third of the total Hearst income. As for their status—that is, at best, uncertain. For, despite the heady talk of revival ("Hearst is a *newspaper* company . . . we don't sell papers, we buy them," says Frank Bennack, rehearsing a line that Bill has worn thin), the group has yet to produce on its dazzling promises, has yet to spawn a single great journal, has yet to overcome the devils with which it has grappled for thirty years past.

This time it was Randy who believed there was some easy way, some quick fix that would change the papers and undo the damage that years of neglect and mismanagement had wrought. For whole decades he had been willing to let them go—to laugh at their foibles or to write them off as a hopeless loss. When Cobbie, his own friend Cobbie, had told him he was "heartsick" to see what the papers had become, Randy had only been sympathetic. He agreed that the newspaper chain was a sham, one more blight on the family name, but he did nothing at all to stem the decay that was consuming the dailies one by one. He never had the leverage to contend with Berlin. He never had the will to challenge Bill, even though he had become far more liberal than his brother, and had come to see that his front-page columns—which were usually nothing more than a pompous, meandering rehash of his father's ancient philosophy—were bringing the chain little credit.

Even the *Examiner*, which he might have controlled, he allowed to become one of the country's least respected papers. While Randy golfed his life away, the Monarch grew pinched and gray, and turned into a kind of doddering old matron that felt more threatened than exhilarated by the surge of energy that passed through its beat, the San Francisco Bay area, in the sixties and seventies. Its reporters—whose average age was forty-five—still worked the police blotters in a day when the best journalists, the out-of-towners from New York and Los Angeles, were busy in the Haight and Berkeley caucuses, searching for the roots of a rebellion that the *Examiner* could only abhor. For its editors would have no truck with new journalism, or personal journalism, or even the wild antics that turned the *Chronicle*, its Siamese twin, into what its chief, Scott Newhall, called an "underground newspaper for adults." Let the *Chronicle* chase the fads—let it send its reporters into People's Park to be roughed up by the police and splash its pages with the whole gamut of trendy gimmickry, from pop art and op art to folk music, wife-swapping, and the developing oddities of suburban California.

For its own part, Randy's *Examiner* preferred to sit home and harden its arteries. The paper had no use for the "New Left ringleaders"; it pitched instead for what it called "the non-militant, unoppressed, well-adjusted, studious, middle-class majority." And like that silent majority (which was epitomized by the good regent, Catherine Hearst), it believed that the forces of change should be stopped. The *Examiner* played straight man to the revolution. It wagged its finger at the "campus outlaws," warning that they must be "recognized for what they really are and treated as such"—even though its own bankrupt pages could offer the public little more than a world of old cheesecake photos (typical fare: chesty girl in hot pants pumps gas above a leering caption, "It's tough to keep your eye on the prices at the pump . . .") and tired Hearst writers, like the warhorse Bob Considine, who, in 1973, could still spend a column on a portrait of three "great Americans," Douglas MacArthur, Franklin Roosevelt and Bill Hearst.

Randy had allowed it all to happen. He, the newspaper's president, had only looked on while its circulation slipped, lower and lower, until it commanded fewer than 150,000 readers to the *Chronicle's* towering 500,000. He watched its prestige virtually disintegrate. (As *Chronicle* columnist Herb Caen put it, "I knew the paper was through when I saw the police haul an *Examiner* truck away for illegal parking. Twenty years ago, they'd have had the commissioner fired.") And Randy listened without really hearing when his own daughter, the adolescent Patty, told him that no one under eighty would read the paper, for reasons that she, at least, could understand.

Until 1970. The year in which Randolph Hearst became very ill in a way that was somehow more than physical.

According to one of his top news executives, Randy became mired in a personal crisis that year. It began when his ulcer erupted in the middle of an outing, a fishing expedition in the Gulf of California, near La Paz. He had been flown to Los Angeles in acute pain, and had almost died before the doctors there could stem his attack. The convalescence was prolonged—he found that he would never again be as robust, as capable of absorbing self-abuse as he had always been in the years of his youth. For a time he wallowed in an ugly depression; and then, in the middle of his recuperation, he began to talk seriously about how he had been wrong to let so many things—the paper, the business, the family—slide into such sad disorder. "Really," says a friend who could understand his remorse, "it was a predictable thing, almost normal for a man like Randy. He spent the good years playing. Why not? He had the money to do it. Now he was ready to shoulder his burdens." Ready to shoulder his burdens, at the age of fifty-five.

When he returned to his work, Randolph Hearst seemed to be a man reborn. He came riding back on a tide of new energy, sparked by his raw determination to involve himself, to find out what was wrong with the *Examiner* and, goddammit, to fix the thing once and for all. His spates of enthusiasm could be downright staggering; his daughters would see him explode from his bed at 5:30 A.M., rush to the city for a day at the paper, and then stay long into the night because he had wired himself to some scheme that couldn't be dropped. The new Randy was talking about a new *Examiner*. He was juggling headlines; playing with layouts; cornering anyone who would give him an opinion about what had become of the paper and why. Civil-rights people told him to open his staff? Fine. Of course. He couldn't agree more. He lent his wholehearted support to Lynn Ludlow, an outstanding reporter, who was commissioned to begin an aggressive program of minority hiring. Ghetto activists felt that the paper had neglected their interests? Yes, perhaps. But he, Randolph Hearst, would visit the ghettos and barrios (Patty called this his "Little Brown Brothers thing"), to find out what they were doing and to see for himself what the *Examiner* had ignored.

As always, when the spirit was on him, he was good. Randy flashed anger, and things got done. Randy flashed charm, and the paper made friends. But—as always—the spirit began to flicker before the job was half begun.

At the outset, the *Examiner* had been swept by a wave of hope because someone who mattered, a ruling don, had finally discovered the paper and its problems, and was giving it the kind of attention that could save it. Reporters and deskmen thrived on their contact with Randy. They liked him and respected him, and they were delighted to find that he could talk about papers as glibly as the best of them. Randy had worked a beat, he knew the code. He could banter about grinding out leads and making up pages, and even about what made the dailies in Detroit, St. Louis or Louisville click in a way that the *Examiner* didn't.

But it was only a matter of months before the *Examiner* people began to sense that Randy would never really master the paper. They saw that his attention span was disturbingly short; he would wrestle with a problem for only so long before he frowned and turned away with an oath, "Oh, screw it." Everything depended on Randy's mood. "If he's in a good mood, you get everything. If he's in a bad mood, you get nothing." That was the rule. And soon it became only too clear that the Editor (as he had taken to calling himself) was avoiding the deep decisions, the choices that would determine the *Examiner's* fate. Randy might listen to the endless round of staff complaints; but, as one reporter put it, "If he moved to correct the paper's deficiencies or improve morale, the movement seemed glacial." He might make a show of running things, he might take a hand in daily decisions; but in the end he continued to rely on the very executives—like his publisher, Charles Gould, an old Hearst PR

man, or his executive editor, Tom Eastham, another Hearst lifer from
the old *Call-Bulletin*—who had done the most to make the paper what
it was.

In the words of one despairing staff writer: "Randy was always this
much a Hearst: just when you thought he was ready to turn things
around, to get away from the spotty news coverage and stone-age editorials, he would hesitate. It would happen every time. He'd get defensive and start to tell you that, after all, the paper had never really
been that bad, that it had always been fighting for the 'little guy,' like
Pop."

(2)

It was sheer terror, the awful mingling of liability and fear, that
brought the *Examiner* reeling out of its long malaise.

On the first night, of course, there was only the thrill of an explosive
story, a story that erupted at 10 P.M. on a deadly dull Tuesday (intended
lead: Mayor Alioto reconciled with wife), when Charles Gould, the
publisher, a Hearst family friend, called the city desk to stammer, mis-
takenly, that Randy's "youngest daughter" Patty had been kidnapped in
Berkeley an hour before. "Jesus Christ, Charles, Jesus Christ," moaned
the night city editor Dave Dietz, who had never worked the desk before
and who knew how little prepared he was for news that would break his
paper wide open. Dietz had exactly two reporters—two reporters to cover
the night side of an area that spanned both sides of the bay. He had no
permanent staff in Berkeley; just weeks before, the beat had been dropped
when the news executives decided that the campus was too quiet to rate
full-time coverage. In Oakland, his bureau was shut tight, because its
work day ended when the courthouse closed.

And so he had only a scratch team of journalists to pound through
the night, trying to pin down what had happened to Patty—how she had
been abducted, when, where and why. Dietz worked the phone at a frantic
pace, collecting his editors, a rewrite man and a handful of reporters to
trace the few leads he had managed to cull from Gould. In Berkeley he
connected with Carol Pogash—twenty-eight, very bright, a straightforward investigator—who seldom worked the East Bay, where she lived,
but who found her way to police headquarters, and there spent a weary six

hours scrambling for the pieces of a story that was more than sensational. The police were reticent; they wanted time. But Pogash got the stunning facts: that Randy's middle daughter, age nineteen, had been yanked screaming from a student apartment on Benvenue; that there was a gang involved, they had several cars; that Patricia had been stuffed in a trunk; and that, yes, shots had been fired, at least five, from a .38-caliber Browning automatic. On top of that, Carol reported, there had been a second abduction. A lab worker, Peter Benenson, had been held by a man and two women who stole his car, an old Chevy convertible. The car had turned up; it was the kidnap vehicle. The FBI was in on the case already. And Patty's live-in lover, Steven Weed, twenty-six, was lying in Berkeley's Herrick Hospital, beaten badly, possibly shot.

While Pogash prodded the police for more, Dietz dispatched another reporter, Jim Woods, to Herrick. But Woods was held at bay by the police, who said that Weed wasn't ready for the press. And there things might have stuck for the night if Dietz hadn't pulled a Hearstian coup. For on his staff, the editor had a young Hearst cousin, the twenty-six-year-old Jay Bosworth, a city-side reporter who was married to Patty's sister Gina. Another man might have paused, but Dietz apparently felt no qualms. He assigned Bosworth to cover the hospital. The reporter went, together with his wife. And all through the early morning hours, the two sat with Weed (who, it turned out, had been kicked and beaten, but not shot), shuddering at the terrible question—where was she right now?—while they patched together an exclusive for the paper.

By midmorning, much of the *Examiner* staff was in action. Eastham and Gould had appeared in the city room, and Randy had called, just once, to warn that they'd damned well better be careful, they'd better not do anything that could get Patty hurt. A gang of reporters was working the girl's neighborhood for more detail, more comment; and at about 11:00 A.M., right on deadline, the East Bay bureau chief Don Martinez phoned in a report, on deep background from a source in police intelligence, that the authorities had already made a connection with a "mysterious" revolutionary group, the Symbionese Liberation Army.

But it was Bosworth who brought the story home. When no one else could get to Weed, the only witness who really mattered, he, the Hearst in-law, had managed to see him, to grill him, and to make him recall the minutes of horror that would bring the next day's paper alive. From Weed, Jay learned that the raid had been a "commando-like" operation, that the kidnappers moved with military precision, "very purposeful and intent," glancing always at their watches, as if the action were timed. He discovered, too, that three days before, the apartment had been scouted by a couple—a white woman and a black man—who came with a dubious tale about renting the unit. He got solid descriptions of the pair, and of the three abductors, one woman and two men, who conducted the raid.

But even more than that, Jay Bosworth found his way to the heart of the terror. He coaxed Steve to tell him what it had been like—how it felt to lie helpless while Patricia was taken. He pressed his questions where an ordinary reporter, from routine delicacy, might have held back. And so, on Wednesday, when other media would have only the bare police bulletins, the *Examiner* would describe how Weed, who was bound on the floor with a next-door neighbor, had heard a voice say, "We've got to get rid of them, they've seen us," and then a metallic click. It would report that in that instant, he felt he had "nothing to lose," so he shoved himself to his feet, bellowing in panic, to run into the night through a patio door.

Briefly, very briefly, the story had hung up. Some time in the predawn hours, the Berkeley police, leery of crank calls and fake ransom demands, had requested an embargo on kidnap news, and the *Examiner* complied, though the newspeople who had worked all night were almost frantic to run their stories. Jerry Belcher, the twenty-year veteran who had anchored the main story from a rewrite desk, said that all of them, the reporters and editors alike, shared a "sucked out, empty feeling" when the first edition ran with the mayor's wife in the headline. But at 10:30 A.M., KGO radio broke the news—just a step ahead of William Knowland, the old Hearst adversary, who had warned police that he would smash the embargo, because he was getting dozens of city-desk calls, and because, he said, everybody but the readers of his Oakland *Tribune* already seemed to know what had happened.

The *Examiner* people were jubilant. (So much so that Gould called Knowland to thank him, to assure him that he had done the right thing.) In their two-star edition, the main press run, they were free to cut loose with a spectacular front page, a fast-breaking triumph in the old Hearst style. The paper erupted in a long lead story—seventy-eight machine-gun paragraphs written by Belcher—together with three sidebars, six photos (morgue shots of Patty and Weed; newsphotos of Benenson, the kidnap neighborhood, and the Benvenue apartment), and a map that traced the kidnap scenario. The story was fraught with deadly tension: "She was half-dressed, naked from the waist up . . . She screamed, 'Please let me go!' " ran paragraph two of the startling lead. It was loaded with brutal fact—with minutes counted, with shots numbered, with spilled groceries described in painstaking detail; and it was mean with the kind of suppressed rage that *Examiner* writers had learned how to handle. Already it had the SLA. Even then, on the first day, the paper was offering a tentative link to Nancy Ling Perry, who was wanted in connection with the slaying of Oakland school superintendent Marcus Foster. It had Patty's voice, and Weed's reaction—and best of all, it had these things before anyone else.

Largely thanks to the news embargo, the *Examiner*, a beat-hungry afternoon daily, had come in not just ahead of the *Chronicle*, but ahead of all the world. Reports that went over the wires that day drew heavily on what the Hearst legmen had learned the night before. The Monarch of the Dailies owned the story, and owned it not for the obvious reason —because Patricia was Randy's daughter—but because the paper, under pressure, had finally pulled out the stops and performed.

Surprisingly, that energy stayed with the paper all through the months when the girl was a fugitive and the story kept looming larger and larger. To Gould, it was downright alarming, the way his people had seized on the thing and kept working it, inside and out, as if they had some special call, some quasi-divine mandate, to unlock the riddle of Patty/Tania. "It was a Woodward and Bernstein complex," he grumbles. "We went way overboard. Every copy boy in the building thought he'd be the one to get Patty Hearst."

The publisher, who would never understand that drive, who thought of it as a craving for "personal glory," did what he could to contain it. In the early days, he holed up in his office, to work the paper's Patty hot line himself. There he sat, day after day—calmly, like the businessman he was—sorting through the deluge of raw leads, the anonymous tips and outrageous demands, that he was loath to turn loose on his eager staff. With each of the callers he was ruthlessly systematic. Before he would listen to some tantalizing offer, one more mad scheme to produce Patty for a price, Gould would insist on hearing her voice, or on knowing what she had called her dog, or on having the pet name (Mamalee) she had used for Millicent. And when each caller in turn failed these stern tests, the publisher quickly hung up, because he,

Charles Gould, could not send reporters (who were paid solid Guild wages) to chase after every crank in the state.

Only once did Charles Gould waver. One of the callers—his name was Henry Winston and he was a fight promoter, a razor-sharp black who lived in Oakland—said, no, he couldn't answer Gould's twenty questions. But he was smart enough to know that until they reached the right people, the right *kind* of people, the Hearsts weren't going to get Patty back. He said that he didn't know the SLA, but he knew the kind of people who did. He had connections who could find the abductors and could squeeze them, but it was going to cost money, $10,000—and if Gould didn't think it was worth the price, he should check with Patty's cousin Willie, because Willie was Winston's bosom friend.

Charlie Gould must have been tired that day, because he did check with Willie (who had been an *Examiner* reporter since 1972), and when Willie, who liked to think himself streetwise, said, "Yeah, Henry talks a lot of bullshit but he's all right," the publisher said fine, they were playing with good money, but they might as well see what this one could do. Gould—who is very straitlaced, very conservative, and was never seen in those days without an American flag pinned to his lapel—took $5,000 and a reporter named Ed Montgomery to the Hotel Leamington, an aging landmark in downtown Oakland. There the two sat in the bar, waiting for Winston. They fidgeted uneasily, and apparently they looked enough like old Hearstlings on a caper to intrigue one lone woman, who kept edging closer to the pair, until finally Gould whispered, "Shhhh . . . It's Charlie Bates in drag." Eventually, though, Winston appeared; and like everyone else he did have contacts, but nothing hard. He wanted time to put out feelers. He outlined a wild scheme that involved, among other things, buying cocaine for Huey Newton. It was all too familiar, all too utterly predictable; but Gould, resigned, shook his head and handed over the cash they had brought. He never again heard from Henry Winston.

In his way, Gould was probably right. Too much of the energy unleashed by the story was burned off in a mad rush just to find her, to close the case by bringing Patty home, the way Emil Gauvreau, with his legions of Hearst gumshoes, had once tried to bring the Lindbergh baby home as the ultimate publicity stunt for the *Mirror*. They still had old-timers like Eastham, the ex-Marine executive editor, who thought it would end with a quick cash drop and a blaze of glory. Two months into the kidnap, when Gould had already been burned, Tom Eastham was still working the hot line. He wanted to bring Patty in. He wanted the scoop, and he wanted it so badly that he managed to make himself believe when one of the callers, more violent than the rest, screamed in his ear that he had the motherfucking Hearst girl right there, and that Eastham could have her for $250. *Two hundred and fifty dollars!* After a ransom demand that had ranged into the hundreds of millions. But the editor was so hungry to find her that he took the money, almost half of it his own, to a drop in Berkeley, where he left it in a shoebox, by a gray Volkswagen van. He honked his horn twice, the signal that was supposed to produce Patty. Of course, nothing happened. He returned to the paper. But, astonishingly, when he got a second call, more vile than the first, from a voice that told him, "Now we are mad, you son-of-a-bitch. I told you to leave the *cover off* the goddamned box. My partner is real mad; he says this is gonna cost you another $500"—he repeated the whole charade again!

Montgomery was another old-timer who found himself jarred to life by the kidnap. There was nothing Woodward-and-Bernstein about him; if anything, he was Hildy Johnson, a tough-talking, beat-hardened *Front Page* reporter who had been good, very good, in his day. Montgomery was one of the few Hearst reporters who remembered the old man's whims. "During my salad days," he would recall, "they'd assign me to get him crabs down at the wharf. I'd go down there and pick out a dozen or two live ones—they had to be live. Then we'd photograph them while they dropped them into the pot. I'd go down to the wharf about four, then run them out to the airport. By eight o'clock, they had fresh crab dinners at San Simeon." But when he wasn't running crabs, he had been busy with the police and the FBI, developing contacts, picking up leads that he turned into a string of spectacular stories. Monty once solved a double murder by breaking into a suspect's home and digging up the bodies that had been buried under the basement floor. In another case, he used a planted dictaphone to unravel a case of gangland extortion. In 1950, he won a Pulitzer Prize—Hearst's first—by exposing a tax-extortion scheme in Nevada that eventually cost seventeen IRS agents their jobs.

And now Patty became his last hurrah.

There was something almost pathetic about the way Montgomery pursued the girl, with whom he had sometimes picked blackberries at San Simeon, where he stayed as a guest of the family. Too many of his connections had dried up and died. The FBI would tell him only what they were telling the rest of the press, which was little. And he could do nothing at all with the radical community, because, in his later years, he had done too many harsh stories about revolutionary leaders like Angela Davis and Huey Newton. ("I couldn't get into the middle of it," he grumbled. "It would have been like rubbing salt in their asses after some of the stuff I'd written.") So Montgomery, the old newshound Montgomery, picked up whatever loose ends he could find. At one point, a psychic, one of a dozen who were haunting the paper, announced that she saw Patty near a body of water and a tower. Assuming that the tower was on power grid, Montgomery got charts from all the utilities and regional maps that marked every lake in the state. For weeks he pored over the material, looking for conjunctions, correlating data, and venturing out to check remote cabins that seemed to fit the hazy vibrations.

Montgomery never found the SLA hideout, nor did he have much luck when he tapped his gangland friend, Mickey Cohen, for help in cracking the underground network. Not that Cohen didn't try. Much later in the saga, during Patty's lost year, the gambler (who said that he had always liked old man Hearst, because he ordered his editors "not to keep calling me a 'hoodlum' so much") called Montgomery to report that his men had been passing out hundred-dollar bills in Watts, and it looked as if they finally had something hot. "Yeah, yeah, tell Randy to get down here," said Cohen. "We've gotta set this thing up fast."

Monty sent Randy and Catherine to Los Angeles. They went with their lawyer, James Martin McInnis, and there they met with Mickey Cohen, who told them he had solid information about a gang of black men who were holding a white girl captive in Cleveland. No, he wasn't sure it was Patty. But DeFreeze was from Cleveland, so there was a connection. And besides, he, Cohen, had worked out a plan. They would fly Catherine to Cleveland with a squad of enforcers, some of the young black heavies who collected his bets. There they would put Catherine in an ambulance, dressed as a nurse. The enforcers would infiltrate the house, one at a time. And when they had the enemy outnumbered, they'd grab the girl and go. "Once we get her in the ambulance," figured Cohen, "Cathy can check her out. She oughta know her own daughter. If it's Patty—we got her and we can take her any place you want. And if it's not . . . hell, we'll drive around the block, open the door, and kick her in the ass!"

That was the *Examiner*, Hearst's *Examiner*, a paper that kept getting older but never grew up. The year was 1974, and there it was, still playing cops and robbers—still stuffing hundred-dollar bills in a shoebox and fingering gangster pals for tips—though none of the old tricks, the cheap movie stunts, could ever work their magic again.

But even then, a new, more vital force seemed to be feeding on the story. Much of this energy flowed from Carol Pogash, who was young and aggressive, and who had also been caught up in the kidnap dynamic. Even before the first night, when she kept her vigil with the Berkeley police, Pogash had been pursuing the SLA. For she had originally been assigned to the Foster killing, the bizarre assassination that had opened the SLA's reign of terror; and after she had banged together her first stories—the traditional who, what, where, when—she found herself bothered by the hard question. Why had they done it?

The reporter had begun trailing the radical band. She worked hard to follow their thinking, and for weeks on end she traipsed around Berkeley, using friends and friends of friends to move in as close as she could to the group. Eventually she began to form a picture. She learned that the SLA were renegades, a motley collection of rebels who had fallen away from the rest of the movement. No one in the mainstream left would defend them; some activists told her they were actually Fascist provocateurs, and others maintained that they were just loners, "completely out of touch with Third World politics." Through a confidential source who knew some of the group, she discovered an early link, via Foster's alleged killer, Joe Remiro, with the Vietnam Veterans Against the War—though when she put this in a story, her editors, fearing a libel suit, killed it. Later she even produced a name. In January 1974, when the SLA safehouse in Concord was burned down, Pogash had spent hours sifting through the wreckage until she had enough evidence to identify Nancy Ling Perry as a member of the group.

Pogash had done what Montgomery never could. She had gotten inside the SLA, had come so close that she could almost feel them (on some nights the fear kept her out of her own home); and now, after the kidnap, she was frankly desperate to use what she knew. In the first few weeks, she fought endlessly with Eastham, and with his city editor, Larry Dum. She insisted that the paper pursue not the girl, but the story. That was their business. That was their job. They could go back to her sources and work them harder. They would get names and faces. Identify the abductors. Find out where they came from, how they thought, and exactly what they wanted. The *Examiner* might belong to Hearst, she argued, but it was a newspaper first, or it was nothing at all. So just this once, let it stay with the story, let it open the thing up and exhaust it, as it had never exhausted anything before.

Pogash, who believed that she knew the kidnappers better than anyone else in the business, was to be bitterly disappointed, bitterly frustrated by the editors' reaction to her pleas. She learned very quickly that the *Examiner* was not to stalk the SLA, but, on the contrary, was to treat the group as gently as possible. Gould himself set up the guidelines for covering the guerrillas; he established at the outset that his paper would never lead on kidnap news, and that it would follow its competitors—on whom he privately urged similar restraint—only with caution. It would not seek the names of SLA members; indeed, when Montgomery used an FBI contact to identify Donald DeFreeze, the paper suppressed the news for weeks, until finally the flamboyant Marilyn Baker duplicated the scoop and flashed it, with great fanfare, over KQED-TV. Moreover, the reporters were not to jeopardize Patty by approaching contacts in the radical underground. Randy himself, through Larry Dum, ordered Pogash simply to forget that the SLA existed.

"I felt shitty, just terrible," said Pogash, who had to watch, helpless, while the drama unfolded without her. Of course, she understood the guidelines. "I realized that Randy was a father first and a businessman second," she explained. But like so many of the younger staff, who were beginning to sense what the paper could do, she found it agonizingly hard to let go.

In all that hell of clamoring voices, the harshest were the ones that held Randy and his paper to blame for everything that had happened. This sordid theme had been swelling since the first rambling tape, on which Donald DeFreeze, basso profundo, revolutionary Gothic, had claimed that Patty was "arrested" to atone "for the crimes that her mother and father have, by their actions, committed against we, the American people and oppressed peoples of the world." To understand that charge, rumbled Cinque, "We must first understand who the Hearsts are, who they serve and represent. Randolph A. Hearst is the corporate chairman of the fascist media empire of the ultra-right Hearst corporation, which is one of the largest propaganda institutions of this oppressive military dictatorship of the militarily armed corporate state that we now live under in this nation."

The rhetoric was insane; no one condoned it. But the harsh chord it struck would never stop ringing. When Randy called on radical activists —from the Black Teachers Caucus, the United Farm Workers, the American Indian Movement—to ask for their help with People in Need, they only snapped back that he had never helped them. His paper, they said, had shut them out. It had ignored their causes and cheered when their leaders were packed off to prison; now they would prefer not to touch Hearst money. Even when Cecil Williams of Glide Church forged a reluctant coalition of groups to monitor PIN, this peoples' commission exacted a price. There were long, stormy sessions in the Hilton Hotel, where they battered at Randy for hours on end. "It was incredible to see him sitting there," said Williams. "His eyes darting from one speaker to the next, the look on his face saying 'I didn't know any of this existed.'"

Finally his daughter had picked up the chant. In her Tania tape, the long manifesto of April 3, she taunted her father for trying to pretend that he, in his way, had served the people. "You, a corporate liar," she spat, "will say that you don't know what I am talking about, but I ask you to prove it. Tell the poor and oppressed of this nation what the corporate state is about to do, warn black and poor people that they are about to be murdered down to the last man, woman and child. If you're so interested in people, why don't you tell them what the energy crisis is? Tell them how it's nothing more than a manufactured strategy, a way of hiding industry's real intentions. Tell the people that the energy crisis is nothing more than a means to get public approval for a massive program to build nuclear power plants all over this nation. Tell the people that the entire corporate state is . . ."

And so it had gone, on and on. Tell the people, tell the truth. Use the paper to make up for your lies. This was the message that Tania hammered—until finally Randy had come to believe not that the words were literally true, but that somehow his indifference, reflected in the *Examiner*, had allowed this angry tide to rise.

In the first few months, his response to the abuse had been crude and obvious. Randy used the paper as his father might have done, in a rough attempt to barter for help. The *Examiner* became his bargaining chip. It still had influence with people who counted; this he offered to allies and friends, to those who joined in his Patty campaign.

AIM was among the first of the groups to learn this lesson. Local Indian leaders had been leery of the food giveaway; they withheld their endorsement from PIN because they didn't know Randy and because they were reluctant to handle what they called "blood money." But Russell Means and Dennis Banks, who were then on trial for their role in the Wounded Knee siege, hinted that, yes, perhaps they could help, if they could meet with Randy, face to face. So Randy called the federal judge in Minnesota. He interrupted the trial and flew the pair to San Francisco, where the three of them apparently reached an understanding. The Movement would sponsor People in Need. ("The SLA are a punk organization; they are a one-shot organization," Means told the press soon afterward.) Randy, for his part, would send an *Examiner* man to cover their trial, and then another to report on poverty among the reservation Sioux, because, as he told his reporter, he had suddenly seen that the Indians "were getting screwed."

It was much the same with Wilbur "Popeye" Jackson, a prison organizer who, by 1974, had spent nineteen of his forty-four years behind bars. Jackson was head of the United Prisoners Union; he was a public supporter of the SLA, and a sometime friend to Camilla Hall and Patricia Soltysik. But he had also proved willing to mobilize his people behind the food ransom. Jackson's energy helped stem the chaos; when the program was collapsing, he tongue-lashed the ragged coalition into line. And for this service, Randy was glad to reward him. When Jackson was threatened with parole revocation (after having been picked up with a packet of heroin, possibly planted, in his car), the *Examiner* editor, on April 7—two weeks before the parole hearing—ordered up an enthusiastic story on his work at reforming black ex-cons. The plug was followed by an editorial urging that Jackson be allowed to go free. He was more valuable on the streets than in jail, said the paper, though it never added that the man was especially valuable to Randolph Hearst.

Only much later did Randy's very convictions seem to soften and change. Shock after shock, in endless series, finally took their toll. In the wake of the Tania tape, he slipped into a black depression, and for nine days in April he could no nothing but hide himself, with his wife Catherine, in La Paz, at the home of their friend Desi Arnaz. He was pathetically dispirited when he waved off the press. "We came here to recharge our batteries and refuel our energies," he quipped without humor, "to await the next explicit and exotic torture the SLA might dish out."

That new horror came on the fifteenth, when the two were wrenched from their retreat, and back to Hillsborough, by news of Patty's participation in the robbery of the Hibernia Bank. Only nine days later they were slapped by the tape in which Tania addressed her father as "Adolph" (a blow at which he physically shuddered). And then, in mid-May, they were paralyzed by the holocaust in Watts.

Through all of this, Randy was rarely seen at the paper, or at his other favorite haunt, the Pacific Union Club, where too many well-meaning friends offered their sympathy. But late in the year, when Tania's trail grew cold and the days were empty, he began to grope his way back. That fall, he sold the family's Hillsborough home, and took an apartment—a Nob Hill penthouse—where Catherine could have privacy and he could be closer to the paper. His work, he said, kept him from thinking. When he returned to the *Examiner* he was heavy with conscience, very subdued, and anxious, if not quite eager, to lose himself in the business of running the paper.

Pride is an indomitable trait among the Hearsts. Randy refused to concede that he had changed his views to accommodate his daughter and her outlaw companions. Stubborn to the end, he continued to insist that he had always been "liberal." He might be a little more so now, he said, "but if I hadn't felt that way before, the change would have been in the opposite direction."

Perhaps that much was true (though his commitments were so fleeting that their political cast hardly mattered). But it was also true that he took Patty seriously. He said that he had to respect her beliefs; he could only assume that her conversion was genuine, and that someday Patricia would surface, as he put it, to lead a political life, "like Jane Fonda." And more than this, he had come to see the paper as a way of reaching her. His daughter had repudiated his corporate life, and she had been doubly cruel toward the way he managed his piece of the Hearst "propaganda machine." She accused it, and him, of callous disregard for the people. Now he would have to confront that charge.

In January, Randy pushed Gould aside. He did this as gently as he could, quietly placing his hidebound friend in charge of the Hearst Foundation (where Gould would grumble that he had no real power, because his decisions were tightly controlled by the trustees). But he left no doubt that he wanted a free hand to run his paper. There would be no new publisher; Randy himself absorbed the position, and from his new pinnacle of authority (for he was Editor-Publisher-President now), he began searching for ways to tap and channel the vitality that still flickered in the paper's lower ranks. For almost three years he had been told by his younger aides—by Willie, who was twenty-six that year, and by Larry Kramer, twenty-eight, a reporter and management trainee from Harvard— that he had to throw the *Examiner* wide open. They had tried to convince him that it was a wide-open city, a city where literally anything goes, and that the paper, to survive, would have to go with it. Finally, Randy had glimpsed that truth. "I don't think we or anyone else," he admitted, "have really been covering the needs of the majority of the people in San Francisco."

The first steps were faltering, but they were very creditable, very real, and they did much to put the *Examiner* in touch with the restless, multi-colored region it covered. Randy did his best to rattle the chain of command. He told his senior editors that he wanted more range and more depth, articles with a cutting edge, and a dash of sympathy for the angry outsiders who were banging on the door, trying to get in. Occasionally, the pieces actually appeared. The paper ran a strong, consumer-oriented series that asked whether P G & E, the hitherto sacred utility, really needed new rate hikes. Suddenly discovering its Chicano readers, the *Examiner* sent a team into the fields with Cesar Chavez, and it carried reports—aggressive, investigative pieces—about vigilante posses that had been trying to intimidate farm-union organizers in the San Joaquin Valley.

On the inside, there was to be more rock news, more entertainment, for he had finally been convinced that these things mattered in a libertine town like San Francisco. And the Op-Ed page, which had often run a tired hash of columns off the wire, would have to make room for opposing views. It was fine, wholly acceptable, if Larry Hatfield, a junior reporter, wanted to use his new column to endorse the idea of a prisoners' union. (If Tom Eastham didn't like the idea, he could apply his weight on the *left-hand* side, the regular editorial page.) It was fine, too, if Willie filled his own slot, a column called Other Voices, with writers who might have been more at home in an alternative paper like the *Bay Guardian.* Some readers—and editors—might be pained to see Paul Jacobs, antiwar activist, blast the Pentagon's drug experiments from Willie's platform, in the very heart of the Hearst *Examiner.* Randy himself called Jacobs a "horse's ass." But he saw that he needed the pressure valve; he had to be able to say that no responsible voice would ever again be shut out of the paper.

A pang of resentment shot through the ranks when Randy sent Will, along with Larry Dum and Bob Hayes—a black sports writer who was helping to train black writers for the paper—on a "major recruiting mission," a grand expedition to the East, where they worked their way through a half dozen cities, searching for minority journalists and top-notch investigators, the kind of people who could spark the *Examiner*. "They didn't exactly cripple *The New York Times*," huffed Ed Montgomery. In fact, the intrepid recruiters signed just one new reporter, Raul Ramirez, a twenty-eight-year-old Cuban émigré who came (with much coaxing and the added enticement of a special salary arrangement) from the Washington *Post*. But even this lonely coup was important, for the slight, long-haired, dark-eyed Ramirez was at least as good as Montgomery in his prime. He had already made his mark with one prize-winning series on migrant workers in Michigan—for this he had gone to live in their shacks—and then another outstanding piece on the heroin rings of Miami. He knew how to feel his way into a story. He could do this as well as Montgomery, whom he was ultimately supposed to replace; and yet he had something more, a simple awareness that solving murders would never be enough.

Randy went out of his way to accommodate Ramirez, and the reporter, in turn, was convinced that the publisher was sincere about reforming the *Examiner*, though he sometimes wondered if the older man really knew what he was doing. Too often, thought Ramirez, Randy was "just repeating what his critics had told him without understanding what any of it meant." But he was delighted to find that Hearst gave him his head and encouraged him to sink his teeth into stories that counted, even when important people might be hurt. In April of 1975, Randy himself asked Ramirez to begin a major investigation of corruption in Chinatown, centering on the allegedly false murder conviction of Richard Lee, a young Chinese gang member who was doing a life term in prison for the death of a rival, Poole Leong. The story was complex. It involved what appeared to be reams of false testimony, solicited by officers who needed a "good" verdict to disarm political pressure, and it had ramifications that reached back to the police hierarchy, to city hall, and to the office of the Republican Attorney General Evelle Younger, who had been calling, perhaps too loudly, for more gang convictions. With Patty still at large, headed for an inevitable collision with the law, it took a fair amount of courage to assign this story. The backlash could be severe. But the publisher had become interested in the case when his nephew, Will, brought Lee's brother William to his office, along with a free-lance journalist, Lowell Bergman, who had already begun probing the circumstances around Lee's conviction. Bergman, Willie and William Lee had convinced Randy that the *Examiner* must at least look into Richard Lee's claims, namely that two key witnesses who testified against him had been coerced by the police, and that another witness—who could prove his innocence—had kept himself hidden throughout the trial, out of fear of gang reprisals. So Randy told Ramirez to take up the case (reasoning, says the journalist, "that I was Cuban, so I'd probably get along just fine with the Chinese"); and with that he raised his paper to a higher power.

And yet, it was precisely here that Randy Hearst stopped.

It could be that he was only tired. The year had left him nervous and drawn. His laugh, that weak, involuntary giggle, had become hollow, and much of the time he seemed to be out of touch with the flow of life around him. His friends thought he often behaved like an automaton. He was always saying yes. Nodding without conviction. Agreeing to everything, any reckless scheme (like the adventure with Cohen, or an equally incredible plot to fly Patty into exile in Cuba), as long as it somehow led back to Patricia.

His stomach was beginning to rebel again. He wasn't drinking much, but his complexion was yellow. Randy was chronically ill, and sooner or later this would probably have brought him up short, even if he hadn't come to see that he had reached the limit of his competence and his courage.

Apparently he knew this. Despite all of his past bravado (for Randy, always Randy, had been the one to confront the old man), he seemed to understand that he shared the flaws of his family. His vision was clouded; he could only react, never really lead. And the critical decisions still came much too hard. There were people on the paper who had to be pushed aside. But Randy, their friend, was unwilling to face the trauma of dismissing them. In fact, he had come to a terminus. He had done as much as a Hearst could do, and he seemed to be at least dimly aware that the only way he could still help the paper was to leave it, because he was, after all, the final barrier to its progress.

It was Frank Bennack, then manager of the Hearst newspaper chain, who suggested that Reg Murphy, the editor of the Atlanta *Constitution*, should be the one to press the *Examiner* beyond its rough beginning. Bennack believed that Murphy, a business-minded newsman and a new Southern liberal, had what he likes to call "class." He could put a professional edge on the paper—he could consummate the changes Randy had begun (for Murphy was known to be a ruthless manager), and, not incidentally, he could keep the *Examiner* from falling into the hands of Young Turks like Willie and Kramer, who seemed to be rising fast as Randy faded.

Randy agreed, not least of all because he assumed that Murphy, who had been kidnapped and held for ransom in the same month as Patty, would be fair—perhaps even delicate—in dealing with his daughter.

Indeed, only Murphy was reluctant. The editor was ready to leave Atlanta: he was tempted by the pulse of a world city, and by a great deal of money—for Bennack, who was desperately in need of newspaper talent, had reportedly offered him a salary in excess of $125,000 per year. But Murphy had grave reservations about working for Hearst. The stigma still lay heavy on the papers, and he feared, with some right, that the family would never allow him a free hand.

Not until he had met with Randy, who insisted that he would surrender complete command, the positions of editor and publisher both, did Murphy finally concede. On August 30, he took over the *Examiner*. Some two weeks later, Patty reappeared.

(3)

He's had four years now to wrestle with the *Examiner*, and still it's hard to tell who is winning, Reg Murphy, the soft-spoken, hard-headed publisher from Atlanta—or the stubborn little paper that seems to resist everything he does to make it improve. The effort is beginning to tell on the man. He no longer looks boyish, which he did when he came to San Francisco. Instead, his hair is starting to gray (a little too early, at age forty-six), and the deep, worried lines that run through his forehead have become more pronounced. On the worst mornings, in fact, he looks downright haggard, his face dark and drawn, and when you ask him, "Reg Murphy, how's the *Examiner*?" he's more than likely to tell you the truth: "I wish the hell I *knew!*"

In his best moods, of course, he'll tell you that he's proud of his paper, and rightly so, because it has been doing some amazing things these days. Twice, in fact, the *Examiner* has been named the Outstanding Newspaper in California—no mean honor in a competition that pits it against the Sacramento *Bee*, which is extremely sharp, and the Los Angeles *Times*, which is overwhelming, not to mention the Point Reyes *Light*, a tough little contender that ran away with a Pulitzer Prize this year. The paper has done that, and it has performed downright nobly in some bad situations. In November 1978, for instance, one of its photographers, Greg Robinson, died in Guyana; he was snapping pictures, peering ahead through the viewfinder of his camera, when Jim Jones's thugs unloaded their rifles into his face. An *Examiner* reporter, Tim Reiterman, was with Robinson that day. He was wounded in the attack, but he continued to write dispatches from a hospital bed, a service that touched Murphy deeply, because the editor has great admiration for courage. (A quality he possesses, though not in quite the abundance he would like. His heroes are his old mentors, Jack Tarver and Ralph McGill, who, he has written, "Never flinched in facing the hard questions." Observes one Murphy friend: "Reg is pretty good. He might flinch, but he usually won't turn tail and run.")

There was another bad situation, a dangerous shoal, when Patricia Hearst, the boss's daughter, was arrested, almost on the *Examiner*'s doorstep. A nervous sensation had run through the staff; there was a feeling that even with Randy gone, they would never be able to drop their inhibitions, or to cover the story fairly and fully, and with all of the considerable ability at their command. On the day of the arrest—it was Thursday, September 18, Murphy's eighteenth day with Hearst—Carol Pogash had been bold enough to confront him. "Okay, you're the editor," the reporter had said. "What do you intend to do about her?" And the question had stopped him cold for a minute. He had managed to reply with a platitude, telling Pogash "We're going to be honest. We're going to treat her like we're working for somebody else." But even as he said it, he realized that platitudes would never be enough. This was the challenge for himself and for the paper. The staff was watching for a tangible sign: either he was going to insulate the news from the Hearsts or he wasn't, and the way he reacted now would tell. So Murphy tried to tackle the problem head on. He added four extra pages to the paper that day, to give his people some working space. Then he scrapped the routine assignments, announcing that as far as he was concerned, there was only one story in San Francisco worth having, and he wanted everybody out of the building, on top of it, covering Patty with no holds barred.

"Listen, we played it straight," says Murphy, grinning and clenching his fist in the air, remembering that indelible image of Tania, rebel queen of the SLA. "It just about *killed* my relationship with the family. But I had to tell Randy when I saw him that night—I guess it was in the car, on the way to the jail—that this was sensational news, the biggest ever, and there just wasn't any way to get around it." So the *Examiner* reported Patty as she was. It dared to flash a shocking lead photo, an enormous, top-left, four-column cut that showed Patricia Hearst—vibrant, smiling and boldly defiant—as she marched into court to face her arraignment. (Randy found this outrageous. He later told Murphy that stock art would have been more "appropriate.") The paper told how she clenched her fist in the courtroom; how she saluted her "comrades" in the spectator's gallery; how she stood "chewing gum, openmouthed," apparently bored, while U.S. Magistrate Owen Woodruff read the list of nineteen felony charges—ranging from kidnap and bank robbery to assault with intent to commit murder—that the government attorneys had brought against her. And, of course, those details bothered the Hearsts. "You knew they hated it. You could feel them cringing at every word," says one reporter who helped to write the stories. But Murphy saw his integrity hanging in the balance. He sensed that both he and the paper were lost unless they could print Catherine's hare-brained remarks (as when she warned reporters to call her daughter's arrest "a rescue, not a capture"), unless they could report the embarrassing facts, that Tania had been armed with a loaded revolver, that she was calling herself an "urban guerrilla," that her only public statement was a "message to the people," a little rhetorical flourish that ran: "I'm smiling, I feel free and strong, and I send greetings and love to all the sisters and brothers out there."

Even through the trial, the *Examiner* stayed honest, which must be listed as a major triumph, because sometimes, at least, the pressure was intense. Randy complained incessantly about the trial coverage. He thought it was insensitive and unduly sensational. He couldn't understand why his daughter had to be in the headline every day, and why the reporter, Steve Cook, couldn't be more sympathetic. (Though Cook, in fact, was openly sympathetic. He only worried that he had been too kind, and he fretted later that his articles had failed to convey the two things that finally damned Patricia: first, that she lied about the Olmec monkey, claiming that she had kept it only as an artifact, not as a token of Willie Wolfe's love; and, second, that she was dull and without expression on the stand, leaving the jury to wonder who had been brainwashed, the smiling Tania, or the zombielike creature who faced them in court.)

When the paper ran excerpts from the famed Tobin tape—with Patty giggling, "I'll be able to tell you all kinds of stories you wouldn't believe, man . . . my politics are different from way back then and so this creates all kinds of problems for me in terms of a defense"—Randy finally erupted. Was it deliberate, he wanted to know? Did they really want to see her convicted? But his anger made no sense, because the jury had been sequestered, and the transcript had already been printed by others. So it was only the old Hearst syndrome at work. The family was still trying to manipulate the news, to blur the images they found unpleasant. Murphy pointed this out, refusing to soften his coverage, and Randy conceded, though his rapport with the editor dwindled to nothing.

There have been other victories, some major, some minor, and Murphy loves to recall them, because he savors the bittersweet taste of power. He will tell you how it hurt him to purge his staff, wincing at the way he gathered twenty of his editors together in the first week, and worked to gain their confidence, assuring them all that he was at their mercy, that he didn't know as much as they did about the paper or the city, but that he wanted to learn and to get to know them, and that sooner or later he would "make the rounds to work with them all." Maybe he meant this last thing when he said it. He isn't really sure. But when he did start to learn about the *Examiner*, he saw, all too quickly, that these very people were the core of the problem. These old Hearst hands, with their memories, their instincts and their political reactions (which had become second nature—without even thinking, they edited the paper to please the front office, to protect the family), could never be retooled, not even if he had the patience to attempt it, which clearly he didn't have. So instead of working with them one by one, Murphy summoned the veterans into his office. He marched them, one at a time, through the wood-paneled lobby of the executive suite, past the portrait of the Chief that peered down from the wall, and into his white, windowless sanctum. There he began to chat about retirement plans. In his warm, Southern way, he advised the Hearstlings that they would do well to think about leaving on their own—and he admits that, all in all, "it was pretty horrible, about the worst thing I've ever done." But when he had pushed aside some forty employees (among them Tom Eastham, who was banished to Washington, to finish his career as a staff correspondent, and Ed Montgomery, who packed up his Pulitzer and retired to a house-trailer in the Napa Valley), the publisher had room for some "first-class talent."

The phrase is a telling one; for Murphy is dazzled by talent and class, and fascinated by the way these treasures flow toward him, as they have done in the years since he became notorious. He reads it as a lesson in the power of the media. The kidnap in Atlanta gave him celebrity. (He groans: "I couldn't step out the door without some dear, sweet lady telling me she remembered exactly where she was when she heard the news . . .") And his connection with Hearst raised him to stardom. It brought "an incredible amount of publicity . . . and suddenly everybody in the business was knocking on my door, looking for a job."

All of which pleased and flattered him mightily, so he took them in, filling the paper with a new class of people. "Murphy's people," the Hearst veterans called them. The phrase mingled fear and resentment and respect, for the old staff, the ones who remained, knew they were being subordinated to a new corps of loyalists, the editor's personal elite. This indignity bore most heavily on Will Hearst and Larry Kramer, the two who had virtually taken over the paper. They had been spending their days in Randy's office, advising the publisher, setting policy, plotting to reassign personnel. Now, however, they found themselves back in reporters' slots. Kramer was sent out to cover the schools, while Will was placed, without ceremony, on general assignment. And as their star descended, the outsiders arrived. Dave Halvorsen, from the Chicago *Tribune*, became the managing editor; he and Murphy prowled through the newsroom each afternoon, looking over shoulders, quizzing the reporters, and putting their personal stamp on every page. Rosalie Wright, from *Womensport*, took charge of the life-style sections, and when Murphy's wife, Virginia, left him, returning to Georgia, Rosalie and the editor became steady companions. From Atlanta, Murphy recruited Art Harris—a "damned good writer," who was hired to sharpen the paper's prose—along with columnist Paul Hemphill, the Jimmy Breslin of the South, who proved to be the one disappointment: after staying with the paper for a grim six months, he left, partly because he was drinking too much, partly because he found San Francisco a cold, bitchy town, and not least of all because he wanted more money than Hearst would pay him.

Murphy admits that he, like Paul Hemphill, has had trouble striking his roots in this town. He says that "in a way" he misses the South, misses the sense of commitment he had felt when he was working for McGill and worrying less about profits than about "doing what was right." Even now Reg Murphy, the new Hearst star, may rock with nostalgia when he tells you how it was in Atlanta, in the sixties, when his paper fought hard for black peoples' rights. "You don't have any *idea* what it was like," he says. "You just couldn't report in the South back then. I don't know how many times I had some goon call me up, mad about a story, to tell me the FBI 'was gonna have to fish my body out of some creek in the morning.'" He has tales about the way he was pinned in a phone booth by an angry white mob, kids who pounded the glass while he reported back to what they called his "nigger-loving paper." In the little town of Crawford, he recalls, they turned their only lunch counter into a private club, so they wouldn't have to serve him, the *Constitution* man. And though he doesn't dwell on it, you have to remember the kidnap, when this same Reg Murphy stared at a loaded revolver for two days, trying to talk folksy sense with an angry, red-necked Georgian, who intended to "straighten out the liberal, lying press"— beginning with one nervous editor from Atlanta.

But, knowing that he once had that kind of courage, you also have to wonder, where did it go just three years ago, when Raul Ramirez and Lowell Bergman ran into trouble on their Chinatown series—when they printed an article, based on a witness's sworn affidavit, claiming that two San Francisco police officers and an assistant DA had suborned testimony against Richard Lee, and then the witness, under heavy police pressure, later recanted, exposing the reporters and the paper to a thirty-million-dollar libel suit. Murphy was bold enough in the beginning. He assured the reporters that he stood behind the article, and he told them not to worry, that it was part of the business, that it "happens every day." He sent the pair over to Ted Kleines, the local Hearst attorney, to talk about getting their defense together; and it all seemed routine—until Ramirez was stunned some weeks later to receive a call from the lawyer, informing him that Bergman would be dropped from their case. They were going to treat Lowell as a source, not a partner. He wouldn't be entitled to Hearst counsel, said Kleines—even though Randy had originally assigned the article, and Willie had brought Bergman to Ramirez, introducing him as a partner, and had talked about ways to compensate the outsider without breaking Guild rules.

When Ramirez first appealed this decision to Murphy, the editor told him, yes, absolutely, Bergman should have corporate counsel. But by the next day, already, his position had changed. He now told the reporter that he sympathized with Lowell, but that he would have to support "company policy."

The shift left Ramirez feeling physically shaken, and unable to stop thinking: if they can do this to Bergman, will they do it to me? The reporter sensed that Hearst might be dumping Bergman—trying somehow to pin the liability on him. Or the attorneys might only be trying to clean up their case. ("Maybe they could stomach me," he muses. "But Lowell wasn't part of the club. Here he was, a Jew, and a left-leaning Jew, and the way they saw it, probably a Communist, because he studied philosophy with Herbert Marcuse. So maybe they just didn't *want* to defend him.") But as a journalist, he thought that the issue was clear. Bergman had been a working partner, so Hearst owed him protection. He argued this position before the *Examiner*'s executive committee, a group that included Randy, Murphy and Halvorsen. But the executives reacted exactly as Dick Berlin might have done. They told Ramirez that Hearst had no *legal* obligation to Bergman. They would not defend him, nor would they help their own reporter to pay outside counsel, which he had come to believe that he needed, because he was no longer certain of Kleines's support.

Murphy—who admires Jack Tarver, the *Constitution*'s president, for the way he "held the soapbox steady when no man on earth would have done it"—refused even to offer Ramirez the minimal assurance that Kleines would take the case to trial rather than settle the suit, as he had done in a number of cases before. Instead, he hewed close to the corporate line—or perhaps, as Ramirez says, he stayed well behind it.

"That was the strangest part," recalls the reporter. "In the middle of this tangle, Willie, who was back in New York, called me up. He said that the corporation wanted to find a compromise. They were willing to send a New York attorney to take over the whole case, which I thought was wonderful. I didn't want to fight with them." But two days later, the publisher—in a warm, confidential mood—pulled the reporter aside, to let him know that he, Reg Murphy, was ready to go "way out on a limb." He had just put together a proposal, he said, to have a New York attorney come out "once in a while to check Kleines's work."

Ramirez, confused and bitter—and unable to understand why Murphy would try to bargain down the company position—declined the offer. His sympathizers on the paper, of whom there were many, formed a Bergman-Ramirez defense committee, to raise funds for the reporter's counsel, and to inform the "management," which meant Reg Murphy, that they all felt threatened by the way the corporation had dealt with the affair. There was dark talk about company reprisals. Several committee members thought that their stories were being shoved to the back of the paper. Others were cornered by editors and privately warned that they were ruining their careers.

So at least some of the staff still wonder about Murphy. Does he know what he's paid for making the transition, for moving up in the corporate world? Apparently it was a Faustian bargain, this deal with Hearst. No one can fault him for having made it; but it's sad for him, being an editor and a good one, to realize that his courage has its limits, and that as he finds them, he's going to flinch sometimes, and that the newspaper people are going to notice. They'll forget the good things he did here, and they'll never even know what he did in Atlanta. They'll think of him the way newspeople always think of publishers: as a businessman and a reactionary; as the one who applies the pressure (real or imagined) to kill the good story; as the one who keeps them on the night desk, who fights with the union, who won't spend money on the out-of-town bureau they'd like to head. But then you have to remember, there's always a price. And the paper is better. And, as Murphy will tell you, if you press him too hard about some of these changes: "Ralph McGill did some crummy things, too, you know . . ."

Chapter 3

The Phoenix

WHEN THE SUBJECT of the Los Angeles *Herald-Examiner* came up at the quarterly meeting of the Hearst Corporation board of directors on December 9, 1969, the board's reaction, in the words of one member, was "one of disappointment, if not despair." Indeed, in the two years that George Hearst, Jr.—who did not attend the meeting—had been fighting the printing-trades unions of Los Angeles, the newspaper had failed miserably in living up to prestrike expectations.

But no one was sure exactly what should be done, so it was decided to just let things go on a bit longer and see what happened.

When George junior read the board minutes, he was not at all pleased with what he believed to be inaccurate implications about the way he had run the Herald Examiner, so he fired off a letter to Bill Hearst, who was chairman of the board, and in it he challenged a statement in the minutes that the paper's loss in advertising revenue was due to a loss in circulation.

The major effect on advertising revenues, George maintained, was produced by the illegal activities of striking employees, who were destroying advertisers' property and threatening them with violence and secondary picketing.

George also pointed out that the paper, although it was losing money, was showing a trend toward losing less, and that a new commercial printing plant the *Herald-Examiner* had started in the Orange County suburb of Buena Park was expected to be very profitable.

His conclusion was hopeful. He was sure he had clarified the picture and that the paper could look forward to a bright and profitable future in spite of the lingering Nixon recession.

However, a bright and profitable future was not in the cards for the *Herald-Examiner*. Although the Hearst Corporation has refused to release figures on the financial condition of the Los Angeles newspaper, discussions with various company officials indicate that the paper continued to lose money and that losses in the early 1970s were heavier than in the first two years of the strike.

"This [the strike] was our Vietnam war," one company official mused years later. "After a couple of years we realized that it wasn't working out the way we had hoped, but by that time we had put so much money into the strike already, that everyone felt we should just keep going a bit longer."

From the beginning, George Hearst suffered from a public-relations problem. Although he tried to portray the unions as the unreasonable party, the general perception was of Hearst as the intransigent, stemming from his refusal to accept any arbitration and his reluctance to meet with the mayor's blue-ribbon panel. As a result, the *Herald-Examiner* strike quickly became a "cause" among the liberal establishment of Los Angeles. Boycotting the *Herald-Examiner* suddenly became fashionable and involved much less of a personal hardship than, for instance, giving up grapes or lettuce, since the liberal element of the city had never been enthusiastic about the paper anyway. But the boycott, carried on in vociferous style, undoubtedly spread to those who might have been readers of the paper, had it not been for the negative publicity. The political aspect of the strike was something the Hearst management, both in Los Angeles and New York, apparently never fully understood.

"We used to go around and stick chewing gum into the coin slots on *Herald-Examiner* boxes," recalled Craig Buck, a television writer who had been a high-school student during the late 1960s. "Then someone told us that chewing gum was easy to remove with turpentine, so we started using liquid solder."

George Hearst may have called it vandalism, but Buck and his fellow students looked on their action as a form of social commitment. The emotions ran deep and didn't disappear when the picket lines finally came down. "To me the *Herald-Examiner* will always be a scab newspaper," Buck said, more than a dozen years later.

Similarly, otherwise law-abiding employees of the *Herald-Examiner*, who felt that George Hearst's strike-breaking actions were a threat to their livelihood, had no compunctions about using guerrilla warfare against merchants who persisted in advertising in the newspaper.

"Here's what we'd do," explained one union activist. "We'd have a couple of guys in the back of a pickup truck with wrist rockets. Do you know what a wrist rocket is? It's like a powerful slingshot with an arm brace. So in the middle of the night, we'd drive past a shopping mall where there was a May Company store, for example, and the guys in back would fire ¾-inch bolts with the wrist rockets. We could knock out every window in the store in thirty seconds. Then we'd drive over to another store and do the same thing. One time we hit more than three hundred windows in a single night."

The favored method of dealing with movie houses that continued to advertise in the *Herald-Examiner* was to lob stink bombs, filled with butyric acid, into the theaters. Butyric acid has a powerful stench that has been described as a combination of spoiled butter, excrement and sweat. Needless to say, one dose of "Smell Number 5," as the union guerrillas called it, would put a theater out of business for the evening, and would usually prompt the owner to consider cutting down on his *Herald-Examiner* advertising schedule.

Throughout the early 1970s, George junior continued to boldly predict that the financial situation at the newspaper would soon improve, but advertising revenue and circulation continued to drop. In order to stem its losses, the *Herald-Examiner* management began squeezing its employees for savings. The number of paid holidays was cut from eight to six per year. Paid sick leave was eliminated for the first three consecutive days of an illness. Payments started on the fourth day of a sickness, meaning, in effect, that there was no sick pay except for major illnesses or accidents such as heart attacks or strokes.

The company management seemed to have a knack for making employees feel unappreciated and unimportant. In 1973, in a move to clamp down on white-collar workers who were suspected of sneaking home early, the management began requiring reporters, copy editors, and advertising salesmen to punch in and out on a time clock—a stern reminder that they were hourly wage earners and nothing more. Wages, meanwhile, continued to slip lower and lower in relation to the cost of living and the prevailing rates of pay at other newspapers.

Even staunchly loyal employees, such as sports editor Bud Furillo, became disgruntled with the deteriorating working conditions, and company rules that seemed arbitrary or capricious. Furillo was particularly hurt when the newspaper refused to promote his son from copyboy to sports writer. When Furillo asked George Hearst why his son had repeatedly been passed over for promotion, Hearst acknowledged that the young man was qualified, but said he "didn't approve of nepotism." At that, Furillo could only gasp in amazement, "George, how in the hell do you think you got where you are? On your ability?" Furillo left the newspaper shortly afterward.

In 1974, the striking unions officially threw in the towel when the Joint Strike-Lockout Council suspended activities "due to all the International Unions having stopped making strike payments to the members," as Robertson succinctly put the matter in a formal letter to the Los Angeles County Federation of Labor. In other words, the unions had run out of money, having spent more than $6 million in the preceding six years. Robertson thanked the other unions for their "long and continued support" and noted that the "*Herald-Examiner* has suffered a tremendous loss in advertising revenue. They reached the point where they were the lowest daily newspaper in the state of California in total advertising linage." That was the only consolation the unions could draw from the outcome of their long battle with the Hearst Corporation.

But George Hearst had nothing to gloat over either. *MORE* journalism review put the *Herald-Examiner* on its list of the "Ten Worst Newspapers in the Country"—a distinction that other news organizations seemed to point to with relish whenever they had occasion to mention the Los Angeles Hearst paper.

There was a great deal of talk about improving the paper, of rebuilding now that the strike was "over." Managing editor Don Goodenow could wax enthusiastic whenever he was interviewing new reporters about how the *Herex* was going to open bureaus across the country, and there was golden opportunity for ambitious young reporters to get in on the ground floor, and the pay would be going up soon. The reporters, many of them straight out of journalism school and eager to make their mark on a big-city daily, took the managing editor's words at face value.

For the new reporters the disillusionment came quickly. They discovered that the city editor ruled the newsroom like a classroom full of delinquent second-graders. Reporters sat at their desks, lined up in straight rows, and waited until the city editor handed them an assignment, which as often as not consisted of rewriting a press release or a story that had come in on the Associated Press wire. It was not unusual for a reporter to spend more than half of the day just sitting at his or her desk, reading the newspaper. Reading anything else was discouraged. The city editor once reprimanded a reporter for reading a paperback book, which turned out to be a dictionary.

An occasional diversion was provided when the city editor, who frequently appeared at work intoxicated, would inadvertently set fire to his wastebasket as he flicked off the ash from an ever-present cigar. But it was no laughing matter to the dispirited reporters that the *Herald-Examiner* did no investigative reporting. Its coverage emphasized "hard news," which usually meant fires, accidents, police stories (from the police point of view) and press conferences. It was a measure of the low morale among reporters that an opportunity to cover an overturned truck on the freeway—a story that would be worth about six paragraphs at most—was considered a welcome chance to get out of the office.

Reporters who tried to exhibit enterprise soon discovered that their stories would never get printed. In one case, the police-beat reporter (who worked out of an office at the downtown police headquarters, out from under the direct supervision of the city editor), acting on a telephone tip, found that a sixteen-year-old girl who had been accidentally shot in the stomach, lay in the emergency room of a local hospital for two hours and bled to death, because the hospital, in violation of its emergency-service contract with the county, did not have a surgeon on duty. The story was confirmed through the paramedics who had brought the girl to the hospital and by sheriff's deputies who had investigated the shooting. The city editor simply refused even to consider the story, because, as he mentioned vaguely, George Hearst, Jr., was on the board of trustees of the hospital. After a few such experiences, reporters gave up trying to get investigative pieces into print.

Widespread discontent made the reporters receptive to the efforts of a group of *Herald-Examiner* truck drivers who were trying to form an independent union (independent out of necessity, since the established Los Angeles unions still considered *Herald-Examiner* workers "scabs," although due to a high turnover, the vast majority had never seen a picket line around the building).

Little by little, the editorial and other white-collar employees began signing union authorization cards. By the fall of 1975, Employees for Better Working Conditions had collected enough authorization cards to petition the National Labor Relations Board to hold a representation election.

George Hearst was more amused than alarmed by the nascent union movement. Even the union name—Employees for Better Working Conditions—sounded like an outfit run by amateurs. It wasn't the sort of thing to worry a man who had beaten the toughest printing-trades unions in the business. But just to gauge the union strength, Hearst had each of the department heads estimate how many of their employees would be likely to vote for and against the union. The survey showed that easily three-quarters of the employees were against the union.

The election, held on December 5, 1975, under the supervision of the NLRB, showed, among other things, the inaccuracy of Hearst's polling methods. The union won handily, by a margin of 2 to 1.

Winning a representation election and actually getting a contract were two entirely separate matters, however. The Herald-Examiner management simply refused to acknowledge the existence of the union. It took until March 6, 1977, for the union—which by then had affiliated with the International Pressmen's Union—to secure a contract. The signing on that date marked the first time that a newspaper had been organized wall-to-wall by one union under one collective-bargaining agreement.

(2)

The years he had spent fighting the Los Angeles printing-trades unions had not been good ones for George Hearst, Jr. The fact that, after ten years, the Herald-Examiner was again solidly union was only the least of his problems, if it could be considered a problem at all. Of far greater importance was what had happened to the publisher's private life and career during those ten years: he had been through a bitter divorce, which ended with his first wife's suicide, and his father came to the verge of suing him, in a dispute involving some $300,000, a threat that was only ended by the elder George Hearst's death. Meanwhile, relations with other members of the Hearst family had deteriorated and were certainly not helped when George became the only member of the Hearst family to vote against providing ransom money when Patty was kidnapped. And his career, which seemed in glorious ascendancy prior to the strike, was first stopped dead on the tracks by the *Herald-Examiner's* lackluster financial performance, and then derailed when a magazine exposed how he was personally making a profit from the money-losing newspaper through his ownership of companies that provided security guards, plant maintenance, truck rentals and other services.

In 1968, George Hearst's wife of eighteen years discovered that he had been having an affair with another woman, and she decided that it was the last straw for a marriage that had been faltering for some time. She filed for divorce that year, charging that she had been neglected and specifically mentioned the inordinate amount of time her husband spent playing polo. A newspaper account of the divorce case called Mrs. Hearst a "Polo Widow." It was probably an intentional irony, this reference to George's polo playing, because that was how he met Pat Bell, a strikingly beautiful woman, who worked for an advertising agency and was, according to some accounts, something of a polo groupie.

Although a divorce settlement was reached in 1969, animosity continued to percolate through the case of *Hearst v. Hearst.* Soon Mary Hearst was back in court, claiming that George had carted off a houseful of furniture that rightfully belonged to her. The matter ended on December 4, when Mary killed herself, four days after George and Pat were married in a quiet ceremony at the Hearsts' Brentwood home.

Mary Hearst's funeral was an uneasy reunion for the George Hearst family. Several family members were outraged that Pat appeared at the funeral, dressed in mourning for a woman to whose death, they thought, she had contributed. After the service there was an unpleasant confrontation between Blanche and Rosalie, George junior's mother and his father's sixth wife, respectively. Blanche said that George senior had never amounted to anything and had never been much of a father to Junior. Whereupon Rosalie, feeling compelled to defend her husband in front of the assembled family, replied that Blanche and the children seemed to have managed quite well on the money that George had supplied them. There were a few more words exchanged, and the encounter ended when Rosalie, no match for Blanche, left the room in tears.

The confrontation was a gauge of some tremendous tensions that simmered between George senior and his son—hostility that George senior said his first wife had caused by poisoning their son's attitude toward him.

Some of the hostility between father and son was almost petty in its origin—Junior often complained that his father had once promised to buy him a watch, but had failed to keep his promise. Some was more substantial—George junior's daughter, Bunny, had run away from home after the divorce to live with Rosalie and George senior, which, if nothing else, complicated relations between the three generations.

But the most severe source of antagonism involved money, specifically, the Marion Davies trust fund.

The "M. D. Trust," as the Hearst family called it, consisted of Hearst Corporation B stock and had been set up by William Randolph Hearst, Sr., for his friend Marion Davies to provide $150,000 a year income. After her death in 1961, as provided in the Hearst will, the stock was divided among the five sons. (The portion of John, who had died by then, was divided among his four surviving children.) Each of the five shares was worth $600,000 and provided $30,000 income per year.

A special case existed for George senior. In 1955, when he was sick and in debt, he had signed over all future rights to the M. D. Trust to his son and daughter, in exchange for $110,000 to pay off his debts and medical bills. The document allowed son George and daughter Phoebe to take either the income or the principal of the trust at any time.

It was an action that George senior regretted for the rest of his life, and by the early 1970s, he decided to do something about it.

"We know my son and daughter will not attempt to take this income as long as you are living," George wrote his mother in May of 1971, "but I have been told they will exercise this right at your demise. At the time they try to take this income, I shall go to court and fight it. . . . Several attorneys have told me that no one, in their right mind, would sell a $600,000 trust with an income of $30,000 a year for $110,000."

George wanted his share of the M. D. trust to go to Rosalie when he died, because, as he told his mother, "Outside of you, she is the only one who has ever done anything for me." His own son and daughter, he regretfully concluded, "have no respect or love for me."

Millicent agreed with George that it had been a mistake to sign the trust document, and urged him to go to court before she died in order to have it nullified. Unfortunately, George Hearst died before his mother, in January 1972, leaving the matter of the M. D. trust unsettled. His widow, Rosalie, not wishing to become involved in a court fight, eventually made an out-of-court settlement with George junior and Phoebe, whereby she received $3,000 per year from each of them.

At her husband's funeral, Rosalie, in what she thought was a grand conciliatory gesture, gave George junior an expensive watch set with diamonds, saying "I hope this will make up for the watch your father never gave you." It may be that George didn't like diamonds: his only response was to cut off his stepmother's free subscription to the *Herald-Examiner*. It had become necessary to tighten up on costs, he explained to her. Rosalie didn't understand how her one subscription was going to affect the newspaper's profitability. "I felt like Marion Davies," she moaned.

After Patty was kidnapped, George alienated Randy by voting against providing corporation or foundation funds for her ransom, on the grounds that it would set a bad precedent and possibly encourage other kidnappings of Hearst family members. George felt that he had been vindicated in some way when Patty announced that she had joined the SLA. Ever afterward, he liked to call her "Cousin Tania."

The roof fell in on George when the February 1977 issue of *Los Angeles* magazine ran a story by investigative journalist Bob Gottlieb that detailed how Hearst, along with the *Herald-Examiner*'s business manager George Sjostrom and lawyer Philip Battaglia, had organized their own company to do business with the *Herald-Examiner*. Gottlieb laid out how the three men had formed a company called Southern California Contractors Incorporated back in 1969. The company had then entered into extensive business dealings with the *Herald-Examiner*. Divisions of SCCI leased trucks to the newspaper, provided construction and repair service for the building, provided the guard service, rented uniforms for the production workers, and did accounting and auditing work.

George later admitted that he had been "self-dealing." But he insisted that there had been "full disclosure" to the corporation, and so there had been no violation of his trust as publisher.

What bothered the New York Hearst executives was not so much the fact that George was self-dealing—they had known about his extracurricular activities all along—but that the secretive nature of SCCI (which

operated under numerous assumed names), looked sleazy and was therefore bad for the corporate image. It seemed like a symptom of poor communications that the New York Hearst office was flooded with copies of
the article, many of them sent anonymously, and, most disturbingly,
stamped with the postage meter of the *Herald-Examiner*.

There had been on-and-off efforts by some of the New York executives to have George removed from the helm of the *Herald-Examiner*
since about 1974, but George had always resisted, and there was a reluctance to throw out a member of the Hearst family. But now, the pressure
for George's removal was greater than ever, and when George couldn't be
persuaded to step down, the matter went to a vote before the corporate
board of directors. George was removed.

"It was the hardest thing I ever had to do in my life," said one
Hearst family member on the board. "But I voted against George for the
good of the company."

George was given a luxurious office in the Occidental Center, next
door to the *Herald-Examiner*, from which he took responsibility "for the
over-all management of Hearst real-estate interests," according to the
corporation's press release.

His replacement as publisher of the *Herald-Examiner* was Frank Dale,
a former publisher of the Cincinnati *Enquirer*. Dale had been active in
Cincinnati civic affairs and, among other things, was part owner of the
Cincinnati Reds baseball franchise and the Cincinnati Bengals football
team. He had also been active in Ohio Republican party activities, serving
as Republican state chairman in the 1968 presidential election. In 1972, he
joined the other local business leaders to form an Ohio branch of the
Committee to Reelect the President, and served as chairman of the group.
In late 1973, the United States Senate confirmed him as a presidential
envoy to the United Nations and international organizations at Geneva,
Switzerland; in that capacity he held the rank of ambassador. When the
Republicans were edged out of office in 1976, Dale found himself out
of a job. After casting about a bit, he signed on as vice-president of the
Hearst Corporation and publisher of the *Herald-Examiner*.

Dale's arrival at the *Herald-Examiner* was a bit inauspicious; the
security guards refused to let him into the building because he didn't
have a proper pass. His first act as publisher was to replace the door
guards with a less menacing receptionist.

The rank-and-file workers' reaction to Dale was one of cautious optimism, summed up by the frequently heard comment: "Well, you know he's got to be pretty smart if he was the head of CREEP and isn't in jail."

Dale moved through the *Herald-Examiner* with the expansive enthusiasm and slickness of a car salesman, introducing himself to the staff and pledging a new era of management. He immediately took reporters and ad salesmen off the time clock, which had become a hated symbol of the newspaper's callous management. He got the *Herald-Examiner* sign and thermometer-clock fixed and working. He had plants put into the building lobby, along with comfortable furniture. He called his whole program "Operation Upward Bound"; he had the building plastered with "Upward Bound" posters and made the round of local talk shows, to let the town know that a new and improved *Herald-Examiner* would soon be on the newsstands.

Dale immediately brought in some new management personnel to head up the advertising and business departments. Dave Feldman, general manager of the Hearst Albany paper, came aboard as head of sales, calling his new job "the challenge of a lifetime." Theodore Grassl, lately of the Minneapolis *Star* and *Tribune*, was recruited to be general manager. Grassl took the job only after scrutinizing the *Herald-Examiner* books for the past several years and somehow convincing himself that the paper's decline had bottomed out. "If I had been asked for my opinion on what to do with the paper back in 1974, I would have recommended closing it down," he said. "Now, I think we have a chance to survive, but it's going to be a struggle."

The most pressing problem was the editorial department. Dale set out to find an editor of national stature, someone who would be more than just top quality, someone who would also bring attention to the *Herald-Examiner*'s rebuilding program. He found his man in James G. Bellows, former editor of the New York *Herald Tribune*, an executive at the Los Angeles *Times*, and, most recently, the editor of the Washington *Star*, in which capacity he was credited with pumping new life into that dilapidated competitor of the *Post*.

With Bellows' arrival on January 3, 1978, the editorial staff took it as an article of faith that this man was going to improve the newspaper. The only question was: did he intend to improve it by getting rid of the present staff? It was not an idle fear, especially since, within days of his arrival, Bellows had let it slip out that he felt there wasn't one person on the existing staff really worth keeping. "I wouldn't be unhappy if they all walked out tomorrow," he said.

The staff paranoia deepened as Bellows assembled his own crew of editors, most of them from "back East," which was virtually alien country to the Californians. They included Don Forst, a managing editor at *Newsday*, the big suburban newspaper of Long Island, who had worked with Bellows at the *Herald Tribune* and would be his right-hand man in Los Angeles; Mary Ann Dolan, brought in from the Washington *Star* to head up entertainment coverage; Frank Lalli, former managing editor of *New West* magazine, recruited for what was probably the toughest job on the paper: metropolitan editor, with day-to-day responsibility for local news coverage; Tom Plate, former *New York* magazine senior editor, who was put in charge of the editorial page; and Dick Adler, a former *New West* editor who created a gossip column called "Page 2," a clone of the "Ear" column that Bellows had successfully implemented at the *Star*.

New reporters also came predominantly from the East Coast, bringing with them a certain alien manner that the old staff interpreted with suspicion as New York cockiness. The *Herex* veterans quickly realized, too, that the "post-Bellows" staff was getting the choice assignments, best hours and favored treatment in general.

It was more than paranoia. As Bellows' new editors arrived, those they displaced were shuffled off into retirement, demoted, or fired outright. Then, with the Bellows team in place, the bloodletting reached the rank and file. By summer, nearly thirty reporters and editors, including virtually the entire entertainment section, had been fired.

There could be no disputing that under Bellows, the *Herald-Examiner* improved dramatically. The paper's appearance was immediately cleaned up, as the jumble of type faces and headline styles that copy editors referred to as "circus layout" was replaced by a format that used only two basic headline styles and more white space. The masthead was also redesigned, and throughout the paper, touches of modern graphics techniques became standard fare.

Bellows' vision was that of a lively, bouncy, "fun newspaper," with an orientation toward "people" stories—in short, a paper that would stand apart from the stuffy and well-established *Times*. He instituted a daily interview column called "Q & A," featuring a celebrity or someone who was momentarily prominent in the news, and put it on page one. The first interviewee was singer Bob Dylan. "Page 2" printed saucy, irreverent tidbits on personalities from the world of entertainment, politics, and the media—exactly the type of readers that Bellows wanted to attract. The gossip column's favorite target was the Los Angeles *Times* and its publisher Otis Chandler, a tactical ploy that, if nothing else, increased *Herald-Examiner* readership among the *Times*'s employees.

The coverage of "hard news" also reflected the quest for a different approach, the search for an unusual angle to a story, and, always, the quest for names. When Bing Crosby's grandson was killed in a motorcycle accident, following a chase by police after a traffic violation, the assistant city editor on duty that weekend marked the story for use in the "Area Briefs" column.

When Forst saw the item on the local wire service, he asked who was covering the story.

"No one," the assistant c.e. replied. "I'm just going to use the wire copy in the 'Briefs.'"

"What are you talking about? This is a big story," Forst said in amazement.

"A big story?" said the assistant c.e. "This wouldn't be a story at all if it wasn't Crosby's grandson. The kid himself is a nobody."

"That's not the point," Forst explained, somewhat impatiently. "The name is what counts. Believe me, this is a good story."

Forst then instructed the night assistant city editor, who was just coming on duty, to get the staff working on the story. The reporters interviewed people who had been at a party with young Crosby the night before, pumped the police for details on the chase and put together a major piece.

The next day, Forst confronted the reluctant assistant c.e., thumped a copy of the *Herald-Examiner* and said triumphantly, "I told you it was a good story. Look at this. It made page one."

Of course, since Forst had been the ranking editor the previous night, he had responsibility for deciding which stories went on page one. That was the news, as Bellows and Forst chose to see it.

The Bellows-Forst theory of journalism drew attention, probably more favorable attention than the *Herald-Examiner* had ever received in its history. A story about Bubbles, the two-ton hippopotamus that escaped from nearby Lion Country Safari, was kept on page one for two weeks. School children were invited to send in suggestions on how to get the reluctant hippo out of a small lake where she had taken refuge. The paper received more than eleven hundred letters. One example: "I would get 1,000 elephants and have them drain the lake."

The new Bellows team made great strides in its first six months, and there was promise of even more improvements in the months ahead, explicit in Bellows' oft-repeated statement that "We've come inches, but we still have miles to go." Expectations were high—higher than anyone, even Bellows, could possibly meet. The first few months, the staff (those who had not been fired) worked at 150 percent capacity, putting in incredible overtime, fueled by the exhilaration of being part of what had to be the greatest newspaper revitalization project in the history of modern American journalism. But as the first year drew to a close, the high was wearing off and the staff morale began to sink. It didn't help matters when early the next year, Forst—who had personally recruited many members of the new staff—accepted an offer to become editor of the Hearst newspaper in Boston. Did this mean, reporters asked each other, that the *Herald-Examiner* could not be revived? Before he left for the East Coast, Forst tried to reassure worried staffers that the *Herald-Examiner* had a great future, and that he was leaving only because he couldn't resist the opportunity to take charge of his own newspaper.

When another year had passed and the *Herald-Examiner* employees still found themselves working long hours for low wages (the pay scale was the lowest of all Hearst newspapers; for example, an experienced reporter at the *Herald-Examiner* earned $283 per week, compared to $480 per week at the San Francisco *Examiner*) many were inclined to agree with reporter Tim Carlson, who grumbled to a local television reporter that "this is supposed to be the flagship of the Hearst chain, but we're being treated like a tramp steamer."

Only the top Hearst executives knew—or perhaps they were as much in the dark as everyone else—exactly what kind of freight the *Herald-Examiner* was expected to haul.

Chapter 4

Bildungsroman

(1)

HE WAS the off-shoot, the scion, the golden boy in a family that had almost stopped hoping for a strong and serviceable heir. Raised by a status-hungry mother (so vivacious! so hard!) and by a father who taught him the value of his name. Caught up in the whirl at an early age. Washington. New York. Los Angeles. And San Simeon, always San Simeon, where he spent his summers roaming the ranch (he would sleep, with his brother, Austin, in a tent near the castle) and learning what it could mean to be a Hearst: "As a kid I would go to San Simeon and groove on the whole vision. I really admired my grandfather. What a mover! I decided you had to have money to do these things, and I realized the money came from the papers."

To Diana Vreeland, a great family friend, he was "a divinely attractive child, almost a god." Blond and blue-eyed with an aquiline nose, he seemed to be Phoebe's boy Willie reborn. He was willful and bright. Dreadfully spoiled. And, yes, he was blessed with that special Hearst charm—the poise tempered with a common touch, the muted voice (engaging, almost seductive) that says "Love us . . . we're rich, but we're not so bad."

Born in 1949 and educated in prep schools, Willie Hearst went to Harvard because a barrier had to be broken there. His grandfather (as well as Randy, his uncle), had been forced to leave the school; but still worse, no Hearst male had yet earned a degree, and so it was doubly important that Will, who was to be different, receive his diploma from the great university. In Cambridge, he lived at Waverly House, on what is called the Gold Coast. When his parents came to install him there, the aristocratic house fellows were mildly shocked to learn that the elder William Randolph Hearst was only "a modest, somewhat bewildered man," with a wife "whose manners were exceedingly worldly." Perhaps that impression stood behind the fact that Willie was not asked to join either of the two elite social clubs, the Porcellian or A.D. This was a snub, though he may not have noticed; for he was excluded not just from family prejudice, but also because his well-born peers found him "diffident." According to a friend who knew Harvard society, there was something too casual, too common about him. "Something that the heirs of Emerson, Hale and Cotton Mather found threatening and slightly déclassé."

So William Randolph Hearst III settled for the less prestigious Owl Club, and fell in with a circle of less particular scions, among them Dickie Rockefeller, Stuart Johnson and Tim Lordin. In his way he became a child of the sixties. He dabbled, though never seriously, in radical politics; like almost everyone else at Harvard, he complained about the school's "worn-out" codes, and flaunted his contempt for "bourgeois values." In a purely private rebellion, he chose to major in mathematics, not English or history, because, he told friends, he was "completely fed up with the corporate bullshit." The rest of his family could do what it pleased, but Willie Hearst didn't intend to wind up like his father, stuck in a dead-end position on the papers with a title and money, and nothing to do.

Willie was headed for an outside job. He talked about making a life of his own, without the money, the way no Hearst had done for a hundred years. But late in his senior year, when all the decisions were suddenly real, the family instincts grabbed him. A month before he graduated, in the spring of 1972, the rebellious Will Hearst asked his father for a job on the San Francisco *Examiner*.

When he came to the *Examiner* that fall, Will was exploding with enthusiasm, gleaming with potential, but he wanted to do everything all at once, without bothering to learn the rules of the game. "My God, he was fantastic when the charm was on," said one reporter who watched him work. "Willie had the touch when it came to people. But he also had the attention span of a flea." As headstrong as his namesake, and nearly as erratic, he tried to take the paper by storm. It was never enough to work one job or two, to grab hold of a thing and to master it completely. No, Willie Hearst was in a hurry, Willie intended to do it all. He hopped from the copy desk to sports, to advertising. "And before you knew it," gasped another observer, "there he was at the city desk, trying to send people out on stories. . . . It got so bad that you sent someone else to sharpen your pencils. If you got up to do it yourself, you might come back and find out that Willie wanted your desk too!"

There was a great deal of talk about "delayed adolescence." The younger staff muttered that Will would have been a "rim-rat," a copy-desk hack, if his name had been anything other than Hearst. At least a few of the older reporters thought that he was much like the rest of his family, that he was effete and shallow, and that he was using the paper as a place in which to grow up before he moved to his nest in the corporate heights.

This last judgment had an edge of truth. For he *was* "doing time." It was an ancient Hearst custom; each of the cousins, like each of the sons, had gone through this ritual of learning the business—though none had bothered to learn it well. But it was also true that Willie had more than his share of the family's best traits. Much more than the rest, he had a vast reserve of talent and pride; and when he brought these gifts to bear on a problem, he could be more effective than any of his grandfather's weak-willed sons. This, indeed, was the real danger with Will. He sensed that he was better than the others, that he was born to govern. His parents had let him feel his status; they had already advanced him to the corporate board (amid grumbling by the other directors that he was still too young, much too unstable), and they assured him that he would have a management post, in spite of John Miller, who insisted that the family must earn their jobs in a head-to-head fight with outside talent. Once Bill and Bootsie had their heir, they had pushed him, and trained him (spoon-feeding the boy from the family's Blue Bible, the *Speeches and Writings of William Randolph Hearst*), and left him with the flickering notion that he might indeed be as grand as his name.

* * *

Lynn Ludlow, forty-five, cynical and blunt, remembers the way he watched Will at the *Examiner*. He sat at a desk facing the Hearst heir (in a long white city room, where only the most well-guarded thoughts remain private), and he wondered exactly how long it would take. Sooner or later, Ludlow mused, he's going to be an asshole, just like the rest. He pondered the notion with professional detachment, a reporter coming to terms with a fact. That's how it happens, he thought, that's how the rich become what they are. He was surprised to see how simple it was. A few people using him, trying to get a free ride or put something over with his influence. That kind of thing is going to happen. It's happening here, thought Ludlow. There were people on the paper who fed his self-regard. Some of them did this in a calculated way. They understood that Will would go far, that Will, the director, could help their careers and make the company hear their complaints. And because of this, they backed him up when he had difficult assignments. They cultivated and stroked him, and allowed him to believe that he was able to do what was really still beyond his range.

But he's smart enough to see what they're doing, thought Ludlow. It's going to make him defensive and bitter, and then he'll be an asshole, just like the rest. This was part of the natural order, the education of Willie Hearst. The process was governed by implacable forces. Ambition. Self-aggrandizement. Human weakness. Nothing could stop them, certainly not he. And why should he, what did he care? He might as well try to get his share.

Ludlow was no special friend to Will, but in his own wary way he liked Hearst III—and he was beginning to sense that they needed each other. He was about to undertake a major story, a broad investigation of agribusiness in California's Westlands Water District. This was the reporter's hobbyhorse; he understood that corporate growers were using cheap federal water—tax-subsidized water provided by the Congress for small family farmers—to irrigate their vast, dusty tracts in the San Joaquin Valley. The law was being violated on a massive scale. The National Reclamation Act had specified a 160-acre limit for subsidized farms, but bureaucrats in Sacramento and Washington had helped the big growers to subvert this provision, to turn a program for family farmers into a two-billion-dollar windfall for themselves. Though Ludlow had been trying to report this for years, Tom Eastham had managed to block the story. When Murphy came, he had tried again; the assignment had finally gone through; but still, he was feeling uneasy about the project. No one was sure how far Murphy would go. The subject was intricate. The investigation would take money and time—at least three months, an eternity by newspaper standards. And it would probably win no friends for the paper. But things might be easier if he were working with Willie.

Ludlow explained later:

> In the first place, I thought it would do me some good to have him with me. He'd be a good liaison with the front office. Cut down the pressure . . . And besides that, he would probably open a lot of doors. When you have William Randolph Hearst III along—let's face it—you can get to people who wouldn't give you the time of day. But I thought it would be good for Willie too. For one thing, it would give him a chance to do something real, a good piece of investigative work. I don't know how many of these kids have been sent off to a newspaper for "editorial experience," and then spent three or four years sitting in the press room down at the police station. For another, it might be an investment in the future of the paper, of all the papers. You could see that he was going to count for something with the Hearsts. It seemed like a good idea for him to find out now what a newspaper can do.

They were an odd couple, an impossible pair. Hearst & Ludlow, Ludlow & Hearst. A condescending reporter and a twenty-six-year-old heir, one every bit as mulish as the other, and neither one sure of his partner's respect. There was always a certain antagonism between them, and this more than anything sealed their pact. Ludlow felt that Will was inept; he never believed that he would finish the project, but he wanted to bring Willie down a peg and show him what it meant to do real work. Will responded with sullen anger. He knew that he was being patronized and exploited, but he was caught in a challenge and couldn't back down. He would have to show that he could produce, if only because Lynn Ludlow doubted.

The series which the two would eventually produce was called "The Paper Farmers." It appeared in January 1976, and it ran to eight installments, almost 12,000 words. The first article, "The $2 Billion Giveaway," hammered out a scathing indictment of the "government-agribusiness complex" that had taken control of the 572,000-acre Westlands Water District on the western edge of Fresno and Kings Counties. "Paper farmers, absentee landowners and several big corporations," the pair reported, "reap most of the benefits from a federal irrigation project that was supposed to redistribute huge landholdings into family farms."

They established that the district's great landowners, in the 1950s and 1960s, had signed agreements binding them to sell off their holdings in 160-acre parcels (the limit mandated by the seventy-four-year-old National Reclamation Act) in return for ten years of federal water at a reduced price. They also established that by 1976, as many as 600 owner-operated farms of 160 acres or less should have appeared in the district; but to date, they wrote, there were only two. Big companies—among them Standard Oil and Southern Pacific—continued to hold land that was arable—and tremendously profitable—only because it was flooded with cheap water; the people who worked that land, many of them immigrant field hands from Mexico, still held nothing, not even the shacks in which they lived.

This was possible, Hearst and Ludlow would write, because the United States government, and specifically the Bureau of Reclamation in the Department of the Interior, had permitted the holders to redistribute this land not to small farmers, but—through purely technical compliance with the 160-acre limit—to themselves and to other corporate owners. The holders of the valley were paper farmers. "Like the fowls of the air, neither do they reap, nor do they sow, nor gather into barns," they said. "Instead they have front money, inside connections, an interest in tax shelters, and the direct aid of the Bureau of Reclamation."

The series was an impressive achievement, the most complex and ambitious piece of work the *Examiner* had accomplished at least since Montgomery had passed his prime. David Littlejohn, Dean of Berkeley's School of Journalism, would declare it the "most extensive piece of investigative reporting done in the Bay Area for years." Reg Murphy would package the articles in a forty-page pamphlet, and offer them up as an example of what his new *Examiner* could do. He even submitted "The Paper Farmers" for a Pulitzer Prize. This may have been a gesture, grand obeisance to Willie's involvement, for even Reg Murphy will stroke the Hearsts sometimes. But the series was good enough to stand without the name, and it did win a lesser award, $2,000 from the Scripps-Howard chain—which Lynn Ludlow divided only with regret, because he thought that Will Hearst owed him a fee ("about a thousand dollars would have done nicely," he says) for turning him into what he calls "one demon reporter."

That transformation had caught Ludlow by surprise.

In the beginning, he had really expected nothing. He had taken Will on "as a favor—or worse," and he was sure that within three weeks, maybe four, he would be working alone because Willie, he believed, was like most rich kids and had no stamina, no stomach for the daily grind of reporting. But then, what the hell, Ludlow had thought, why not push him a little and see what he'll do. So, more as an experiment than anything else, he had prodded judiciously at Willie's pride. He hinted at the outset that maybe Will shouldn't do the piece after all, because maybe, when you think it over, the Hearsts are involved. "What do you mean?" Willie had bristled. Ludlow said maybe it's a conflict of interest, maybe the company holds reclamation land, and with you a director—

Will snapped back, "I don't care if it does," and he insisted that he was doing the series. But Ludlow refused to let him begin until he had dredged through the Sunical records, to make sure that the Hearst Corporation was clean—which this time it was, although Will's cousin Jack Cooke, a Hearst land manager, was on friendly terms with some of the worst suspected offenders.

The barb had mobilized Will. It provoked a flash of righteous anger, and this was more than Ludlow had expected; so he decided to prod his partner again. In what he admits was a calculated move, he sent Willie to Berkeley, to talk with Paul Taylor, chairman emeritus of the University of California economics department, an eighty-year-old radical scholar who had been crusading for land reform since the thirties and who frankly despised the big owners (among them the Hearsts, with their 300,000 acres) because they stood between the good earth and the people. Taylor will make him or break him, thought Ludlow. He'll make him feel the weight of the crime (for to Ludlow it was a crime, the rape of the small farmer; he had grown up on a sugar-beet farm in Montana, and so he knew how it worked between the land and the farmers). Or else he'll provoke the other reaction. He'll make him defensive. He'll back him into the corporate camp, and then he'll be a director, not a reporter, but at least he'll know where he really belongs.

They met in a tiny, paper-crammed office, Room 380 in Barrows Hall. On the one side, Paul Taylor (who was crippled and half-blind, but still writing) raged that land monopolists had "torn the law to ribbons." On the other hand, Will Hearst III listened. And wondered. And was finally bedazzled by the passion and brilliance of this man—a onetime campaigner for Upton Sinclair, a lonely crusader for the homestead tradition—who opposed the very social system that allowed estates like San Simeon, Babicora and Wyntoon to exist. Taylor put Will in touch with a truth. He told the Hearst heir that there was no way to divorce the way land was held from the way rural people lived. Small farms create people with dignity, he said. Big farms and ranches create a class of rootless laborers, people doomed to poverty and discontent. He had learned this for himself, Taylor insisted; he had actually seen migrant workers starve in San Luis Obispo County. In 1937, when he was working with the California Emergency Relief Administration, he had seen pea-pickers starve in the Hearsts' own county, because they had flocked in—without homes, without cash—to harvest a crop that was ruined by a couple of weeks of wet weather.

Taylor's convictions touched something deep in Will Hearst. Ludlow is sure of it. "It was uncanny," he says. "When Willie came back from meeting Taylor, he wasn't just interested. He was outraged. Literally on fire. To tell you the truth, I think he connected with something in his grandfather. He saw himself fighting the same kind of populist battle the old man used to fight. And he wasn't bothered at all by the fact that these people, the ones who bottled up the land, belonged to what you'd have to call his own class."

From Paul Taylor, Willie learned to feel rage and guilt. These things pushed him into the project, and once he was committed, he worked in a way that brought back an echo of the long-dead past. For three months he campaigned like the other Will Hearst, the one who had used this same *Examiner* to beat back the interests—the traction trust, the water monopoly, and the same, rapacious Southern Pacific. But in a sense he was better, this second Willie, because he dug much deeper and worked much more carefully than the first ever had done. He mastered the rudiments of agricultural economics and law. (The reading was endless. Guided by Taylor, he and Ludlow trudged through an eighteen-page bibliography on the acreage limitation alone.) Then he plunged into the inevitable drudgery of index cards and photocopies, the dreary searches through land-title records and corporate offerings that had to be done as he and his partner charted out plots, traced ownership behind fronts, and gathered evidence that the Westlands District could indeed support the intensive crops that would make the promised small farms work.

Will even had his moments of genius. Working on his own, he managed to uncover a pair of tax-shelter schemes that let unidentified investors—secret shareholders of corporations registered in Curaçao, in the Netherlands Antilles—cash in on tax advantages that had been designed for resident farmers. "He had personal connections with one or two of the law firms that were doing the work, and he managed to tap them," says Ludlow. "He really knows the corporate angle. He pinned down things I still don't completely understand."

But according to Lynn Ludlow—the old Hearst hand—Will Hearst, muckraker, was actually born in the office of Russell Giffen, the Cotton King of Southern California, who had reaped millions from federally subsidized irrigation and then plowed more than a few thousand of those dollars into lobbying to protect his windfall.

Giffen liked to claim that he hadn't granted an interview since 1947. But he agreed to see Ludlow and Hearst, because, as he told Will when the two walked into his Fresno office, "Your grandfather really knew how to write an editorial." Ludlow stood confirmed as to the value of the name. But Willie made a mark of his own when he cornered Giffen into a quote that rocked the district for months.

"Here we were," marvels the reporter, "talking with a man who had spent thousands—maybe millions—of dollars defending the notion that the 160-acre limitation was ridiculous, that nobody could scratch out a living on that kind of land. Well, naturally, he carried on for a long time about how he had built up his own empire one acre at a time. 'I was flat busted in 1920, and look at me now.' That sort of thing.

"So finally, Willie, all polish and charm, leaned over and said, 'Tell me Mr. Giffen, if you had to do it all over again today. If you were a young man starting out with nothing to go on but yourself and one of these tracts, could you do it?'

"Giffen couldn't resist. He popped out: 'You're damned right I could!' before he knew what hit him."

In the wake of his work on "The Paper Farmers," a sense of uneasiness began to creep up on Will. He was pleased with the acclaim that the piece brought in, and he was even more gratified than alarmed when the powers that be tried to blackguard him. Vaughn Walker, an attorney for Standard Oil of California, said the articles were riddled with "misstatements of law, factual inaccuracies, internal inconsistencies and puerile investigative journalism." Ralph Brodie, director of the Westlands District, accused Ludlow and Hearst of "inaccuracies, distortions, and lies." But those were marks of distinction, thought Will. The pair had drawn blood. Paul Taylor would be proud.

But the experience had also left him feeling exposed. Will couldn't help but wonder how his friends regarded his work. Of course, he was a charmer, he had hundreds of friends. But they were media people—many of them backbiters and notorious talkers. So he had to wonder, how many would try to diminish his credit? How many would claim that, really, it was Lynn who had carried the load? How many would say that he was along for the ride, that he had leaned on his name, that the editors would never have bothered with the piece if Ludlow hadn't been wily enough to recruit him? He had been plagued by all of these doubts before. Indeed, he had sworn, when he was a student at Harvard, that he would change his name if he ever became a writer, because otherwise no one would take him at face value. Now the uncertainty came oozing back, mingling with all his other worries, to make him more petulant and moody than usual.

Willie married that year. His wife was a California girl, the beautiful, dark-haired Nan Peletz. The daughter of Cy Peletz, a well-established San Mateo construction entrepreneur, Nan had already made a name for herself as an architect of great flair and promise. Bootsie thought it was a dazzling match. She said it was grand that her daughter-in-law was Jewish, because she'd probably stiffen Willie's spine ("and God knows, darling, the family needs some blood"). But at least some of Will's friends sensed that he felt threatened by Nan, who seemed to be so much brighter than he. "You could see that it gnawed at him," said one. "She had so much class, so much talent. He was sort of afraid that he'd never keep up."

Nan's very brilliance seemed to keep him off balance, and nothing could reduce the tension that crackled between Will and Reg Murphy. The two watched each other with a wary eye. The editor had already been warned in New York that Willie could destroy the paper's equilibrium. He'd been told this by Bennack, who said that Will must be kept in line, brought along slowly, because it looked like he was trying to run the paper. The brass thought that Randy had let him get too big, had relied too heavily on his judgment in the last year, and they were sure that he wouldn't be ready to shoulder that kind of burden for another ten years. So Murphy had started to reel him in. He edged Will away from the editors' desks, and assigned him to the general-reporting pool. Later, he told the Hearst heir—very carefully, choosing his words with caution—that, name or no name, the company was never going to take him seriously until he came downstairs to the business office and spent some time learning the numbers. But Willie—who had no respect for Murphy's opinions, who was telling friends outside the *Examiner* that the editor was "about half as good as his reputation"—said that he preferred to stay in the newsroom. He would work as a reporter if he couldn't edit the paper. But he didn't intend to come inside, to be swallowed by the hierarchy like his father and uncles.

Suddenly he knew that he had been caught in the trap. He had taken his place in the corporation, he had agreed to play a game he abhorred, because his parents had said that the family needed him badly. These were the facts of life for the Hearsts: they had to have their future trustees; trustees had to serve on the corporate board; and to sit on the board, you had to work for the corporation. Will had thought, fine, he would go that route. But he intended to play it fast and hard. He wanted to move as his grandfather had moved. He wanted to take a paper by storm—shaking it, remaking it, turning it around with the sheer force of his editorial brilliance. And now he saw how wrong he had been. The business had become too big for that. This new corporation dwarfed the Hearsts, and with millions hanging in the balance each day, the system would control them more than they controlled the system. Of course, they would always have their perks and soft jobs. (And Miller with his pieties—"No one at Hearst," John Miller would intone, "must ever forget that this organization is run for the *benefit* of the family.") But those sharp outsiders—the Millers and Bennacks and Murphys and Berlins—would always be there to dominate the Hearsts, and Willie was too proud, he wanted something better.

(2)

So Willie Hearst quit.

In October of 1976, he resigned from the board of directors and left the *Examiner* to work with his friend Jann Wenner—the thirtyish, baby-faced *Rolling Stone* publisher—on a new magazine, an earth-minded monthly for the counterculture.

Will had met Wenner at a party and had liked him immediately, and he had soon become involved in the initial planning of the new enterprise. In fact, he had already helped to name the magazine. According to Wenner, he and Will Hearst had been roaming through the hills of San Simeon—contemplating nature in all of its Hearst-owned glory and worrying about how to spend Jann's mounting profits. Jann already had the idea for a "great magazine." (Jann always had ideas. He had one idea for an ecology reporter called *Earth Times*, which folded after a few issues, and another for a film review that was, alas, stillborn. Once he even had an idea for a new daily newspaper in San Francisco, a project that reportedly cost him a half-million dollars before it definitively failed to happen.) This new magazine would be part of the same great movement that had given birth to *Rolling Stone*. It would tap the New Consciousness, said Jann. It would blaze new trails for the Green Revolution, and ride high on the cresting wave of sympathy foɪ the planet. Not like *Sports Afield*, he added. "No offense, Will. But we don't wanna tell some rube how to go out and shoot a deer every fall." No, he rambled on, "We want to get hold of the Big Picture, the Whole Relationship, so to speak. But it's gotta have a name."

"Right," said Will.

They worried their way across the estate, cursing the sleazy jokers at *New West*, who were calling his creature Rolling Hills, and the in-house wits ("filthy, light-headed crowd"), who had already settled on *Natural Acts*. This is serious, said Wenner. ("Right," said Will.) It has to be something cosmic and real, a title worthy of the Straight-Arrow genius.

Finally, the two wanderers stopped on the ridge of a hill, one of the wind-whipped, sun-kissed peaks of the Santa Lucia range. "We were just sitting there—outside," says Wenner, with a pregnant pause. "And then, Zap!"

"Outside," said Will. "Call it *Outside*."

Wenner hired Will to edit *Outside*. He gave him the title of Managing Editor because, he says, he liked Will's ideas. "I thought he had the right stuff," contends Jann. "I tested him just like anybody else. I told him I wanted to see his ideas, to put it in writing. Hey, the guy was loaded with ideas."

But much of the magazine staff, the old *Rolling Stone* clique, believed that Will Hearst had been hired for his name. They knew that Jann was in love with celebrity and that advertisers would like the name

Hearst on the masthead, a bit above that of business manager Jack Ford. Some even thought there was money involved. Jann was looking for security, they said. A bailout by Hearst if things went bad. That was fine. Business was business. But they couldn't understand why he had to put Will in the key editorial position, and a delegation of editors actually told Jann that it just wouldn't work, that he'd have to hire someone to backstop Willie (for they knew he couldn't edit—their friends on the *Examiner* had told them that much) if he was going to insist on making him ME. "Jann saw the light," said one of the group. He allowed them to lure the abrasive, driving Terry McDonell from *San Francisco* magazine. McDonell was called the "senior editor." He was to rank just below Willie on the masthead. But the staff had decided that he was in charge. When Wenner tried to chisel $500 from McDonell's salary, they even offered to pass the hat. Said one editor, "It was that important. The magazine was at stake."

The first few months were hard on Will. He had to stand fast, for he was much too proud to yield his position, though the junior editors, his supposed subordinates, were bent on showing him how little he knew about running a magazine. "We were awfully rough," says one of them now. "I hate to admit it, but we treated him badly. He just didn't know how to edit, and we weren't about to see the whole thing go down. When he passed along a piece that wasn't right, one of us would just take it and do it all over again." In fact, the staff was edging him aside, fencing him off. They were letting him feel their lack of regard, and they could tell that they had reached him when they saw how he drank at their after-work sessions, where he downed the drinks one after another, "on an assembly line basis," to kill his nerves, which were very bad. "He felt out-classed." That was their judgment. They knew he was in 'way over his head, and that he felt outclassed—and yet it amazed them to see how he refused to let go. They had thought that McDonell would steamroller Will, that the Hearst heir would buckle in their first head-to-head fight. But Willie held his ground, even when he could see that he was badly outmatched. He had heard how his grandfather's editors fought for position—for the old man relished this sort of situation; he often put two men in one job to watch them struggle. And he was willing to win his territory the same way.

The worst confrontations between Will and McDonell (and those months saw many loud, angry, pyrotechnic displays) boiled up over the business of story assignments. Willie approached the problem like a Hearst. When he wanted a story on running, or sailing, or climbing a mountain, he did what his people always did: he picked up the phone to tap his connections, he called whoever was best in the field and simply asked them to write. But McDonell howled that Will was missing the magazine's point. *Outside*, he said, was supposed to be different. It was supposed to be working at a deeper level, looking for relationships, the hidden bond between man and nature—and to do that they had to have writers, not jocks. So McDonell assigned stories of his own. He recruited writers to "experience" the outdoors (sending one, Tim Cahill, over the top of Pikes Peak in a balloon, while Annie Leibovitz trailed behind, snapping pictures, and another, Michael Rogers, to the island of Kauai, where he wrote a meditation on the theme from Thoreau: "What is the use of having a house if you haven't got a tolerable planet to put it on?").

Most of the McDonell stories worked well. They gave the magazine its special tone: not easy and hip like *Rolling Stone*, but dazzlingly literate and almost high-minded in its reverence for the wonders of Great Mother Earth. "We believe that one cannot enjoy the outdoors without understanding it," read the editors' manifesto, "and that to understand it is to be committed to its preservation. The idea is at once as simple and as complex as nature itself. And it is where *Outside* begins." To Wenner the words might be just cant, the formula for another publishing scheme. ("It all seemed so right. I mean, the *Whole Earth Catalog* was *hot*," he would explain.) But McDonell seemed to have found an enduring theme. He seemed to understand that America had a strong tradition of fine outdoor writing: all of the best—Hawthorne, Melville, Emerson, Hemingway, Faulkner—had shaped their work around the natural mysteries. And now he wanted to rediscover that vein. He wanted his writers to revive the tradition, to bring it back in a new dimension, adding something uniquely their own, the daring and the hedonism and the pervasive environmental awareness of the seventies' generation.

Before that vision, Willie, who was overwhelmed, could only give ground. He gave it grudgingly, yielding no more than an inch at a time; and he often insisted on asserting his rights. (It was Will who chose the May cover photo, a grinning portrait of his brother Austin in waders, lofting up a trout that was obviously too long out of the freezer. "Our darkest hour," groans one insider.) But as he came to understand that

McDonell's ideas were much stronger, much sounder than his own, he had no choice but to surrender his place.

By tacit agreement, Terry McDonell was allowed in effect to become *Outside*'s managing editor. No titles were changed. Dignity was salvaged. But it was quietly assumed that Will would function primarily as the magazine's publisher, which all parties thought was both convenient and useful, since Donald Welsh, who formally held that position, had moved with the rest of the *Rolling Stone* tribe to Wenner's new headquarters in Manhattan.

Strangely enough, though, this was less a defeat than a realization. For Will had been born a publisher's son, and although he wanted to edit, although he wanted to shine with his grandfather's brilliance, he had inherited only the other talents. His genius was personal. Like his father, he knew how to win friends and to hold them. Like his father, too, he was filled with spirit, with an enthusiasm that sometimes seemed almost naïve, and this more than anything he gave to *Outside*. "Will was in love with it," says editor Mike Moore, who joined the staff later, when the contest was settled. "Terry might have been the nuts and bolts man—he knew a lot more. But Willie was the soul of the magazine." Will made his peace with McDonell. The two became bosom friends, a working unit, and together they seemed to possess the *esprit* and the vision to create a truly great institution.

Which they might have done, had Wenner not decided to kill the magazine.

Wenner lost his nerve.

Pacing the floor of his antiseptic white office (on Fifth Avenue at 57th Street, prime midtown space—empty wine bottles litter the executive desk and Warhol's pop Mao glares down from the back wall), he rattles on about *Outside*, the Frankenstein monster, the killer magazine that threatened to devour his little rock empire. "It was a nerve-wracking thing from the first day," he says. "We did everything on the wing, be-cause, you know, when you're young, you gamble, right?" He says it was his instinct against the world. He launched the magazine without marketing studies, because he knew it was right. And then he ran head-on into "all that bullshit."

"The overhead was horrible, it was ugly," says Jann—the Harvard

Business School Jann, still wearing Oxford shirts and gray wool slacks—
as he writhes in agony at the very thought of his dollars draining away.
"I brought *Rolling Stone* to New York so we could get things together.
Get everybody in one place. And then bang, there we were, strung out
over three thousand miles again." The magazine, which stayed in San
Francisco, was sucking the life out of all his best people. "There was too
much cross-over, nobody could focus." And he was "duped," he says, by
the early reports—he printed up 'way too many newsstand copies. Then
a mailing went bad. "We dropped 200,000 copies in the mail in the
middle of a postal slowdown. Screwed over by the goddamned government." So he decided to do the reasonable thing, "and, uh, cut losses—
you know—*contain* the thing before it went too far."

But the harder truth was that Wenner had panicked. He lost his
nerve after only five issues, when the magazine was only starting to move;
and Will Hearst, who had learned something about publishing rhythms
from masters like Dick Deems and John Miller, knew that once Jann
started to buckle, once he started slashing the budget, the debacle would
come in four or five months. Willie understood that New York was the
enemy. (His father had told him what killed the Hearst papers—it was
that business mentality, the fear of risk that had sapped their strength at
critical moments.) So he fought desperately to hold Jann at bay. When
Wenner ordered the first cuts, in the January issue—demanding that thirty
pages be dropped, right on deadline—Willie warned his friend not to be
suicidal. In a weary telephone marathon that dragged on for hours (and
then for weeks, for Will remained welded to his phone until the very
end), he argued that they were only now coming to the critical point, the
time when they had to overwhelm their readers. Already they were winning a solid audience. The circulation stood at over 200,000. (And the
advertisers loved them, all those young males.) Now they had to hold
them, to shore up their confidence. They had to give them a spectacular
product, "not an issue that would blow away in the first good breeze."

But when Jann insisted on cuts, Will made them, and later he reduced
the staff on his own initiative, thinking that he could save the magazine
by appeasing Wenner, by trimming expenses before Jann really moved
in. The firings, especially, left him deeply depressed. At the end of one
black Friday, when he had terminated ten people, some of them friends,
Will sat in his office, trembling, alone, until an editor came in to ask, was

he all right? "Yeah, just great," said Will, without looking up. "I was just thinking how great it is to be the most hated man in the world today." But, of course, he was wrong. There was fear and loathing aplenty for Wenner. For much of the staff felt that Jann had welshed on a firm commitment. He had agreed to put out a high-class magazine, and he had known that to do that, he might have to lose money for as long as five years. But then he had squandered his capital, they thought. He had spent too much on the move to New York, and so he was trying to make *Outside* the goat.

For Will, however, there was a growing feeling of respect. He seemed to sharpen as the mood went bad. When the magazine's fate hung in the balance, he made it his business to take the heat; he badgered Jann for more money and more time, and sometimes he refused to trim people they needed, even though Wenner had ordered them cut. If nothing else, this had sealed Will's bond with the staff. The after-work sessions found him drinking less and commiserating more. At one point, he even talked with some of the editors who had ridden him the hardest about getting out to start something on their own. "We were like a little band of Green Berets," says Tim Cahill, who thought that Will, more than anyone, kept the magazine going. "We'd get a little drunk after a bad day, and decide we could take Haiti single-handed if we wanted to. But we were more than half serious about starting all over, this time without Jann. It wouldn't surprise me to see Will do it yet."

The end came in July. Wenner decided to bring *Outside* to New York, where he could monitor expenses. (By October, he would sell it to Larry Burke, a Chicago-based competitor who later merged the magazine with his own *Mariah*.) And most of the staff, by agreement among themselves, resigned. Terry McDonell flew to Manhattan for one day, to turn over the magazine's editorial material. In San Francisco, Will, who was the last to leave the office, the old *Rolling Stone* quarters, called Michael Rogers to talk about their dream gone bad. "I'd been wondering whether I was right to quit," Will told Rogers. "Whether I was losing nerve, throwing something really good away.

"Then Jann called and started carrying on about all the sleazy little sons-of-bitches he had fired trying to collect unemployment from *his* magazine.

"I knew I was right."

(3)

The coterie of *Outside* editors dispersed. Tim Cahill returned to *Rolling Stone*, while Michael Rogers got down to work on his book, a second novel, which he was writing for Simon and Schuster. Mike Moore became an editor at *Esquire*. Terry McDonell drifted off to Denver, where he was soon caught up in another scheme, a regional magazine for the Rocky Mountains.

But for Willie, there was nowhere to go—except home.

According to John Miller,* Will came to New York that summer, begging permission to rejoin the fold. Of course, the Hearst president was delighted to comply, because he believes that the grandchildren belong to the business as much as the business belongs to them. But he sternly insisted that Willie do penance for his fling with Wenner. He was firm about this. The heir had shaken the system by taking family talent, that precious commodity, out of the company's grasp. Now he was certainly welcome to return. But his first job would be a humble one, because, said Miller, most of the papers were already overstaffed. Besides, he thought that Will "had a lot to learn."

Will took what he was given, a newly created position on the Los Angeles *Herald-Examiner*, where he was called the Assistant Managing Editor in Charge of Graphics. His primary duty was to choose pictures for local stories, a task that had been handled by the copy desk, quite routinely, until Willie arrived. Sometimes, too, he would help to find subjects for the "Q & A," a Bellows-inspired celebrity interview that runs down the left-hand side of the paper's front page. And if Frank Lalli happened to need illustrations for a story, he might assign Will to find them. But the editor understood that this could be risky. As often as not, the story would sit, while William Randolph Hearst III—who was bored with the work and who knew very well that he was only doing time —enjoyed long lunches and presumably pondered weightier matters. One incident, especially, left a marked impression on the *Herex* staff. A reporter had invested much time and effort in a three-part series on prostitution in Hollywood. Lalli sent the story to Will for art. It sat for

---

* Who, strangely enough, was toying with the idea of buying *Outside*. Before Wenner sold the magazine to Burke, Miller dispatched an auditor to survey the property. Reportedly, the Hearst agent found the accounts too tangled, and declared an accurate assessment of value impossible.

one week, then two, then three, and then four. Finally, the Los Angeles *Times* ran a superb Sunday feature on the subject—leaving the unhappy Lalli no choice but to kill the series.

By April, Will was raised once more to the board of directors, where, four times each year, he would sit in judgment on the progress of editors like Lalli and Bellows.

In October, he was named special assistant to publisher Frank Dale. And with that, he left the world of working journalists—a world that had taught him a handful of lessons, among them the hard one, that he would never belong—to be groomed, like his father, for a responsible position in the family business.

Chapter 5

Prodigal Daughter

(1)

AT TWO O'CLOCK on a Sunday afternoon—it is a crisp fall day in early December 1978—the den of Virginia Blight's Hillsborough home is abuzz with a little clutch of Patty people. There are fifteen or twenty of them (on easy terms with their hostess, they drop in and out throughout the afternoon), and few introductions are necessary, because this is not the first time they have come together to worry about Patricia—to agonize over what has happened to her, and to ask themselves whether even now there isn't something more they can do for her.

Some of this band of devotees have come because they shared a place in Patty's incredible saga. Charles Gould, the aging and haunted director of the Hearst Foundation, weathered the ordeal shoulder-by-shoulder with his friend the girl's father, from the first fatal phone call from the Berkeley police. Ted Dumke, the boyish Episcopal priest (full, round face, always very earnest) ministered to Patty in the San Mateo jail, and later organized the crusade that is fighting for her release. Others—like committee members Preston and "Winkie" Kelsey, or the Moskowitz couple (whose own son had been kidnapped a few years earlier), or one rather less familiar visitor, a silver-maned psychologist and mind-control expert from nearby Stanford—had no place in the drama of kidnap and capture. But they have plainly been touched by Patty's plight, and are no less committed than the rest to stand by her now, through the grinding aftermath of the trauma.

The Hearsts are not in evidence today, but their names run through the conversation with the ease of long acquaintance. Talk drifts from Randy's health, which has not been good, to Catherine's new home (she is back in Hillsborough now, among her own, after a long and bitter sojourn in the city). Someone wonders how "the girls"—Anne and Vicki —are doing in school. Are they "up" this weekend? Will they stop by? How does Gina like her job on the Los Angeles paper? Of course, there is also a great deal of talk about Patty, the stolen daughter, who is now in the Federal Correctional Facility at Pleasanton, serving her twenty-second month in prison for—as these people like to put it—"the crime of being kidnapped." It starts with friendly chatter. One knot of women is fretting over Patty's work in the prison kitchen; they agree that it's probably best for her to keep busy, but eight hours is *such* a long time, and besides, mixing batter for three hundred convicts isn't *really* cooking. In another group someone sagely observes that Patty is a great admirer of her great-grandmother Phoebe—"You know, Phoebe had that same love of art that Patty has. Patty thinks she was a remarkable woman, such a ball of energy . . . I really believe that Patty has the potential—if she comes through this, she's going to be another Phoebe Hearst."

Before long, though, the talk becomes more serious, betraying traces of the bewilderment and anger that are never far below the surface. Dumke kindles a flame when he erupts into a monologue about his latest enthusiasm. It is something called the "Stockholm Syndrome," the phenomenon of endearment between kidnapper and victim, which shocked Europe in 1971, when thirty-two-year-old Erik Olsson forced four hostages (three of them women) into the vault of a Swedish bank at gunpoint, and, to the astonishment of authorities, wound up the friend and lover of his prisoners by the time he was rooted out six days later. Dumke is sure that Patty was a victim of the syndrome. She was no different from the Swedish women, who coaxed their reluctant captor into making love inside the vault and kissed him goodbye—before a live television audience—when the siege was ended. Or from Barbara Jane Mackle, who confessed to having a "certain feeling" for Steven Krist, even though (or because?) he buried her alive for four days in Florida. Or, for that matter, from Reg Murphy, who, according to Dumke, went to *extraordinary* lengths in helping his own kidnappers to collect their ransom. "It's happening every day," says Patty's priest, beginning to wax rhetorical. "But nobody wants to see it. It's something ugly, something people would rather ignore. I've been trying to get *Time* to do something about it for months, but the press just doesn't care. They want to laugh. *Time* treated the Amenti girl (an Italian kidnap collaborator) like comic opera."

Mention of "the press" sends an involuntary shiver through the little group of Patty's friends. There is muted grumbling about media sins, a flash of bitter reflection over the papers and magazines and networks that "turned on Patricia," paving her way to prison with pictures of her first clenched-fist ride to the San Francisco courthouse and stories of the Tobin tapes, and then hounded her for "cheap publicity" once they had her safely locked inside. Charlie Gould—a lifelong Hearstling who kept his own *Examiner* well in line through most of the ordeal—seizes the opportunity to expound his pet media theory:

> You have to understand that the SLA didn't just capture Patricia Hearst. They captured the American press, and no one else has ever been able to do that. From the beginning they were dictating to all the papers in the country, forcing them to print whatever revolutionary garbage they put out.
>
> I can tell you that I felt unclean from the first day we started publishing the crap that came pouring out of those madmen. A lot of professional newsmen felt that way.
>
> When it was all over, they wanted to make somebody pay—and by then, the only victim who was left was Patty Hearst.

Gould believes that the press has played out its hostility and begun to swing back toward what he calls a "responsible" position. Plainly, his notion of responsibility involves open sympathy for Patricia, perhaps even tinged by a healthy dose of remorse. He points to the raft of pro-Patty editorials that have been photocopied and stacked for distribution on the nearby billiard table as a sign of changing opinion. ("Why has she been sent to jail?" writes the Chicago *Tribune*'s Andrew Greeley in one of the favorite clips. "The answer is easy. The liberal vultures in the mass media demand blood—raw human flesh—and the American judicial system, which could not convict Bobby Seale or Angela Davis, throws Miss Hearst to the vultures, placating such self-styled liberals as the *Village Voice*, which described her jail sentence as one of the best things to happen in 1977.") But others are less sure. Someone has just spotted another columnist's anti-Patty quip in an out-of-town paper—"Why won't they quit?" she wonders. And everyone knows that the committee can seldom get the coverage it deserves, especially from Reg Murphy's "New Examiner."

There is more grumbling, and general agreement that "equal justice" does not exist for the rich. With all the zeal of a persecuted minority, they repeat Ronald Reagan's question—"Is Patty Hearst in prison because her family has money?"—and assure themselves that if her name was anything but "Hearst" (or Rockefeller, or Ford, or Getty, one presumes), she would be here today.

Finally, after endless fussing with the slide projector and the screen drawn down across the paneled wall of Mrs. Blight's den, the mood is right for the main event. After all, the cult has gathered for a reason this Sunday afternoon. There is to be a service of sorts conducted by a special guest who has come up from San Diego for the occasion.

The visitor, an intense young man named Wes Davis, enjoys a certain celebrity among Patty's people. Those who have been with the Hearsts from the beginning remember him as Catherine's favorite mind-control expert, the self-styled counterinsurgency consultant who made Bay Area headlines in April of 1974, when he predicted, "two weeks *before* the event," that Patricia Hearst would renounce her family and enlist in the ranks of the SLA. It was Wes Davis who initiated the Hearsts into the mysteries of *teng-feng*, the gentle Chinese art of washing brains. Davis was a fanatic on the subject. He had studied it obsessively for eight years, working sometimes with the government and sometimes outside of it. He had lavished minute attention on Morris Wills and other American servicemen whose minds had been altered by the Chinese in Korea, and later had gone to Vietnam, where he detected the same techniques at work in villages that had been liberated by the NLF. In the troubled spring of 1974, Davis had cornered Randy and Catherine, and explained to them that their daughter's conversion had all the earmarks of the thought-reform process that had placed the Communist yoke on the Orient. She had fallen victim to a calculated psycho-political device by which anyone—from John Wayne to Patty Hearst—could be broken down and molded like putty, turned into anything or anybody at her captors' whim.

Davis has since moved on to other cases and other causes. Already he has begun to mold his own thinking around the latest sensation, the nine hundred Kool-Aid corpses in the jungle of Guyana; he is sure that these dead are the latest crop of *teng-feng* victims. But for the edification of the true believers—the tiny handful in Mrs. Blight's den, who are still groping for some final, marketable proof of Patty's innocence—he has agreed to rehearse his rendition of the Patty saga once more.

There is some final tinkering with the slide carousel, and then the congregation is quiet, filled with rapt attention as Davis winds into the incantation that will fill them with a new sense of outrage at the impossible ugliness of it all. "The events of the last couple of weeks in Guyana," he intones, as they begin their descent,

> may be our last chance to prove what has happened to Patty. We know that Patty Hearst was the victim of a very clear-cut, highly refined Pavlovian process, a process that was invented in the Soviet Union, and perfected in Communist China, and through the literature and the agents of those countries has been scattered throughout the free world. People have found it hard to accept the import and the effectiveness of the process. But I think that Guyana gives us one more shot at bringing it out into the open . . .

It must be the grandest conspiracy theory of them all. There are portrait slides of Marx and Lenin. Pages torn from the Communist Manifesto. A nutshell course in Hegel. The revolutions of 1848, and then a detour through the Paris Commune, as the plot, ever thickening, works its way toward the Pavlovian Connection. The screen flashes one of Pavlov's dogs, a pathetic, salivating creature with tubes hanging out of its gullet and gut. Davis pauses to describe the dog in terms that won't be lost on his audience. "It was all done in precise steps," he assures them. "The dog was captured, held in terror of its life, removed from its usual habitat, deprived of food and sleep, subjected to alien stimuli. Once the old habit patterns were obliterated, it was a simple matter to replace them with new behavior." Then on to Stalin and Solzhenitsyn. Hitler. Goebbels. Mao. Criticism/self-criticism. The terrifying "Flood Formula": seven steps that are guaranteed to reduce the strongest individual to a quivering mass of psychic jelly in five to seven days.

The crowd is awed by Davis' well-oiled pitch. By the time he flashes a slide of Angela Davis and launches into a horror story about the Berkeley faculty, which he assures them is rife with incendiaries and subversives, they are responding like a churchful of mortified Baptists. But Charlie Gould seems a little uneasy.

"Wes . . . Excuse me, Wes," he interrupts. "But, ah, Wes, what about Patricia?"

(2)

Ted Dumke is learning how to handle the media. At ten o'clock in the morning, his telephone is already alive with calls from news-bureau and magazine people, who sense that something is about to break and have discovered that his is the surest pipeline for Patty news. The pardon has been hung up in the Justice Department for months now, but rumors that the President is ready to rule are becoming more persistent. The latest talk has it that Patty will be home for Christmas—and gossip Herb Caen has already been wondering *whose* home that means, since word is out that Randy and Catherine have finally separated.

Dumke is cautious. Wary of forcing the President's hand with an ill-timed prophecy, he reminds his media friends that Jimmy Carter is preoccupied with loose ends in Guyana and a tottering Shah in Iran. (Only lately Griffin Bell has announced that the Hearst clemency application will be handled "in the regular course of business." The Attorney General expressly doubted that the President would reach a decision before Christmas; but he couldn't resist adding the tantalizing observation, "Anything is possible.") Nonetheless, the harried Patty coordinator has developed enough aplomb in doing televison spots in New York and radio hookups nationwide that he remembers to be upbeat. "The White House switchboard tells us that mail is running 10 to 1 in favor of commutation," he volunteers, hoping for a plug that will be just firm enough to nudge the President along.

It is a strange and hectic time for the urgent young priest, who has turned the Committee for the Release of Patricia Hearst into something close to a full-time ministry. Apparently he has been finding out that the Word has a new meaning these days: for him at any rate, it has less to do with homilies from Scripture than with high-pressure PR and constant cajolery in behalf of his friend. He is moving in the fast lane now. His life has become a welter of calls and meetings; there are briefings with contacts from *Newsweek* and *Time,* and long-drawn-out sessions with community leaders who might be able to do the cause some good. Most of the encounters end with a plea: "I really wish you'd do me a favor and write the President." In fact, one suspects that only Ted Dumke could have inspired the worried lines that conclude the committee's manifesto—"Your letters to Judge Orrick, President Jimmy Carter or your own Congressman can make a difference. Act now! The time is short . . ."

With a bare two weeks remaining before Christmas (they are secretly optimistic, already arranging a party for their heroine's return), the time is very short indeed. But the days are never so crowded that Reverend Dumke will not pause to talk about the woman who has managed to stand his life on end.

There is awe in Dumke's voice, a kind of high Gothic reverence usually reserved for the supernatural, as he remembers snatches of the tale of his own involvement with Patricia. He likes to recall that he found his way to the girl in the Time of Great Confusion. It was in the fall of 1975, when there really was no Patty, but only a sullen and angry guerrilla named Tania (or, sometimes, mysteriously, Pearl), who was sulking away the hours in an 8-by-10 cell, maximum security, in the San Mateo County jail. The family, desperate to get at their prodigal daughter, was kept on the outside by county officials who were determined that the rules would be enforced.

But Ted Dumke—an old friend who happened to be a deacon of the Episcopal Church—was able to penetrate the walls of the prison by claiming clerical privilege. "I was appalled," he gasps, recalling the Awful Vision, his first sight of the woman he had known two years before, as a seminarian in Berkeley. "She was thin and frail, and her hair was very strange—lackluster and frizzed out in a very odd sort of way. It must have been from their diet. They never ate anything but rice and beans. I could hardly recognize her. What really frightened me, though, were the holes in her mind. You know, the psychologists said that her IQ had dropped from 130 to something like 90. But you didn't need an IQ test to see that she had blank spots a mile wide. She could be very aware, very friendly. We'd be talking about old times, and then Steve's name would come up. 'Steve?' she'd ask. 'How do you know Steve?' . . . I'd been introduced to her through Steve."

Then there was the Moment of Pathos, the first real sign that Patty was responding to the day-long sessions with her friend, who drove from Sacramento every Wednesday for months to be with her. "She told me that she'd been trying to pray, but couldn't," says Dumke. " 'They even took that away from me,' that's what she said." Ted was reluctant to discuss religion: "I didn't want to be accused of taking advantage of her, and I knew the press would try to make something of it." But Patty insisted on hearing something about the Episcopal faith. She said she needed support, but she had always felt "hemmed in" by her mother's strict Catholicism. So Dumke schooled her in Anglican doctrine, and by May she was ready to be received into the Church.

That was shortly before the Second Kidnapping, a crime that fills the initiates with almost as much rage as the first one. Patty was in San Diego at the time, assigned to a medical facility where she was recovering from the lung collapse that had come in the wake of the trial. As Dumke tells the story, Judge Carter had been at a cocktail party, complaining about the expense of keeping her in San Diego, when a doctor told him, "Oh, a collapsed lung . . . She should be out in five days."

"So the old fool ordered the federal marshals to pack her up and take her to Pleasanton, just like that, without so much as an examination. They told her they were going to wrap her in a blanket and carry her out if she wouldn't cooperate . . . Can you imagine! By the time I got to her at Pleasanton, she was curled on a cot, sobbing into a piece of toilet paper. I said, 'Patty, there's some Kleenex over here.' She told me, 'They didn't say I could use it,' and she started mumbling that they had taken her clothes away and hadn't left her anything. Her clothes were hanging right there in the closet, in plain view."

There is time for a great deal more. Warming to his subject, Dumke speaks with holy wrath of the Great Betrayal (Weed's book) and the Big Lie (the maddening contention that Patty is favored because of her wealth). He fairly rocks with indignation as he rambles through the list of her persecutions, from the day she was torn from the Berkeley apartment to the final indignity, the rat in her bed at Pleasanton on the morning the Harrises pleaded guilty. His sense of bitterness is extraordinary, almost without limit. He believes that the FBI was incompetent from beginning to end. "Why were the Hearsts never told about this," he asks, waving a copy of the famous SLA memo, the one that marked Patty Hearst as a victim at the next full moon and fell into the hands of the bureau a month before the kidnapping. There was treachery in Browning's office: Dumke knows that certain defense memoranda wound up on the prosecutor's desk before the trial. And there was also treachery in New York. "The Hearst Corporation never did a damned thing for Patty, and she knows it," he raves. "If she ever sits down and puts it all on paper, those bastards in New York will probably try to get the rights and make some money on it. But they won't get it—not over her dead body."

Special contempt is reserved for William H. Orrick, the judge who sentenced Patty to seven years, and who even now—Dumke is convinced—retains the power to release her. Dumke will never forgive Orrick for having kept Patricia in prison. In fact, he claims that it would suit him "just fine" if the Harrises got out before Patty, as it seems that they very well might, since their mandatory release date is set a year before her own: "It would be poetic justice. Maybe they'd go out and kidnap Orrick's wife."

Dumke insists that the public response to his committee's appeal for Patty's freedom has been nothing less than terrific. He repeats that the President's mail has been running 10 to 1 in her favor, and he shakes his head in wonder as he makes the same observation that he's been handing to the press all fall, "It's bigger than we ever thought. The idea is to generate grass-roots support for a commutation or a pardon. It's totally grass roots, that's the amazing thing about it." He is impressed by the thought that the committee's first mailing—which went out to the nine thousand believers who had cared enough to send Patty good wishes since her arrest—turned up more than a dozen organizations with Free Patty drives of their own. (The most vigorous of the scratch committees was run from Chico by Vonnie Eastham, a woman who had devoted almost twenty years of her life to the study of Phoebe Hearst's philanthropic career. Before she succumbed to cancer, Vonnie would sometimes call Patty to talk about her great-grandmother. "They say she used to come out of a coma and tell someone to write the President," says Dumke.)

But as of the middle of December, the figures seem to be ambiguous, at best. A straw vote in the National Enquirer is running heavily pro-Patty; but the Gallup poll is evenly divided, and a recent Field poll in California shows that a solid 48 percent of the public in her native state believe that Patty Hearst should serve her seven-year term to the bitter end. Dumke is reluctant to deal in numbers, but when pressed, he concedes that his petition drive, which has been in full swing since early June, has put "about 10,000" names on the President's desk. The figure is not impressive.

Perhaps there is also room for doubt when he contends that the family has kept their millions clear of the pardon effort. Well aware that the issue is a sensitive one, he insists that Randy has not provided money for computer time and printing costs ("he thinks we're a bunch of nuts"), and that the Hearst papers always provide "the worst coverage." But there have been rumblings that Hearst attorney George Martinez has helped the "grassroots" effort along by wresting endorsements from key political leaders. And Father Dumke knows that the attorney, with whom the Patty people are closely in touch, has been well paid for his work on the formal appeal for executive clemency, a massive document that was presented to pardon attorney John Stanish on September 25.

In fact, though Dumke doesn't mention this, there is a sharp professional edge to the clemency appeal on which Patty's future will ultimately depend. It is tight, slick, and obviously expensive—undoubtedly the most imposing such application the President has ever faced, though he has reviewed some five hundred petitions (most composed by the prisoners themselves—some written out on paper bags) since taking office. Hundreds of pages in length, it marshals affidavits by the dozen and evidence by the pound. It steps carefully around the wilder accusations that float freely among Patty's friends, and it confines its appeal to the points that are likely to carry weight with the staff at the Justice Department. Patty has been "exhaustively debriefed" by the fifteen attorneys and enforcement agents who made stops at her cell in the wake of her conviction; she has been prevented by the "mark of her experiences, both at the hands of the SLA and after . . . from ever leading what by any standards can be considered a normal life"; she has won the confidence of the jury that condemned her, six of whom now believe that the time she has served is enough. Above all, the appeal prods judiciously at the one argument on which it must finally stand or fall, the argument that ordinary justice can fail in the special case. In the cautious language of a seasoned attorney, it begins:

> Although this application for clemency does not concern itself with guilt or innocence, I would like to respectfully point out that the state of our law at the present time seems ill-equipped to deal with a kidnap victim, caused by the application of numerous terrorist and criminal acts upon her to participate in conduct found by a jury to attach criminal culpability. Our conviction is that the system of justice has failed under these circumstances.

Father Ted Dumke would certainly agree that the system of justice has failed Patty Hearst. Indeed, he seems willing to go a step beyond that. As far as he is concerned, America itself has failed her, by refusing to understand that she is not just free from guilt, but filled with a higher innocence, the innocence of a martyr who has suffered something in the place of the rest. For now he is worried about his friend. There are dangers lurking in prison, and the odds in favor of clemency are troublingly slim. But for the future, he has no doubts at all. "One thing you have to understand," he says, with an air of prophecy that seems almost Biblical in its force. "She has seen it all. She's known Prince Philip and she's known Cinque. When she gets out of there—in another five years— she's going to be a great lady. Another Phoebe Hearst."

(3)

Saturday, January 20, is a routine day at the federal correctional facility for women in Pleasanton—although for at least one of the prisoners, it is to be one of the last in what has proved to be a monstrously long string of routine days. This is Patty Hearst's last Saturday of uncertainty, and very nearly the last Saturday she will spend inside the wire-topped storm fence that surrounds the 40-acre grounds of the penitentiary. In Washington, the wheels of justice are turning in her favor. But the government, impassive, has chosen to deliberate in silence. Patty has no way of knowing that an upper-level civil servant named Benjamin Civiletti has been favorably impressed with Martinez's well-packaged arguments in her behalf, and will recommend that she receive a Presidential commutation (only the fourth of Carter's term) before the next week is out. So for the moment, at least, it is business as usual at Pleasanton.

The afternoon, which is sunny and warm once the late-hanging fog burns off, finds Patty sitting in court with the little knot of visitors who have come to share her day. They seem to be the usual crowd: a handful of loyal retainers—Trish Tobin, Bernie Shaw, George Martinez and, very briefly, Randy Hearst—thrown together with a couple of writers (obligatory company since the beginning of Dumke's media blitz), and a lady friend of the attorney who is apparently along for the ride. As always, the group is huddled around a low, round table in Patricia's salon, the prison's busy visitors lounge. The hostess is clearly not pleased with the accommodations. "This is it, this is all there is," she says with a sour grimace at the noisy roomful of prisoners and guests. But the setting for her thrice-weekly at-home is hardly as uncongenial as it might be. The lounge is plastic, but clean, and bears an uncanny resemblance to the suburban recreation centers where less favored individuals endured their first dances and teen-age flings. The furniture is bright and uncomfortable, and the vending machines are well stocked with the all-American carbohydrate repertoire, from Coke and potato chips, down to an amazing assortment of synthetic burritos.

Somehow it seems natural to find her here, to see her curled in a vivid orange chair, gossiping with Tobin about the country club and Crystal Springs, chattering about things that only they would understand. The two carry on about how they used to feel sorry for girls who had their own pools. "I mean, what a drag," insists Patty. "Who'd want to swim at home, with none of their friends around? I'd much rather go to the club." Or how sad it is that Trish's brother Joe, Patty's old beau, has to pay for his own club membership now. "Thank God," sighs Tobin, "they have this wonderful, chauvinistic habit of letting women stay on their parents' tab until they get married."

Trish is frantic, green with envy, to hear from her friend that the government has installed handball courts in the Lompoc prison. "Geez," she gasps. "Geez, I wish I had a handball court!" She is bouncy and bright—much brighter than Patty, in a mindless sort of way—and nothing can stop her torrent of words. She says that she comes to Pleasanton about once a month. She misses Patty, and she loves to talk with her, and she really loves Stanford, which she missed *so much* when she wasn't enrolled (because the FBI thought it was too dangerous, she might be a target of the SLA). She breezes on about skiing and school. She skis for at least a month every year, and she really prefers Europe because it's cheaper, you know, in the long run, than Sun Valley, and she gets *so* tired of "snow-bunnie chic," all those people carting around $5,000 worth of equipment when they can't even handle themselves on the slopes. Trish Tobin says she's in law school now. Of course, she was accepted everywhere she applied. But Harvard seemed like a drag to her. Yale was all right, but really she's just a California girl, so it had to be Stanford. "Gawd, I never worked so hard in my life," breathes Patty's aimless might-have-been. "I'd like to do something really weird, like maybe be an attorney for SRI [the Stanford Research Institute] or something. I was in neurophysiology before. I think it would be really fun to do something off the wall, like the law and genetic research or something . . ."

Suddenly Patty interrupts with a long-drawn groan, a girlish expression of total disgust. A familiar figure, obviously an attorney, has just hustled in through the visiting room door. "Oh, Gawd. That means we're going to have to put up with the pencil-neck geeks." Tobin wrinkles her freckled nose, as Patty explains: "Oh, you know, the Manson girls. They're sickening. Everybody calls them that—or the 'cone-heads.' They always wear those ridiculous hats."

The dark-haired Sandra Good soon follows, flooding the room with an alien presence as she settles into a earnest discussion with the lawyer. She is wearing a brilliant-blue dress, old and quilted, and a blue knit cap. According to Patty, she always wear blue, while the other "geek," Squeaky Fromme, prefers red. But she, Patty Hearst, has "no use for either one."

"Did I tell you what that Lynette Fromme did the other day?" she asks Tobin.

Tobin's eyes go suddenly wide.

"Well, *I* was in my room reading," huffs Patty, sounding catty and indignant, like a Hillsborough matron, "when *she* comes storming in and says, 'I hear you're trying to find out about me. If there's anything you want to find out about me, you can ask me.' . . . I guess somebody told her I was reading *Helter Skelter*."

Titters from Trish.

"I told her, in the first place, I have better things to do than worry about you. And in the second place, I think you're revolting. So you can just get out of here. *Shoo!*"

Tobin is ecstatic.

"She was really mad. But just then I got a call—it was Dad—so she stormed back out."

With the sixth sense of a long-time prisoner, Patty may well suspect that the end is at hand, for there seems to be an almost wicked candor about her today. She is not exactly voluble, but her tongue is sharp, and her guard is lower than it should be. For months she has been handing out stock interviews to selected members of the press—thoroughly screened representatives of *People*, the Washington *Post*, the New York *Post*, *Look* magazine, and others have been shuttled to the prison and granted a calculated glimpse at the new Patricia Hearst, a strong, thoughtful, well-mannered young lady who clearly does not seem to belong on the inside of a federal prison. Yet on this final Saturday, the new Patricia Hearst reveals an edge that hasn't appeared in the published interviews. Her resentment is close to the surface this afternoon—so close, that one can only believe that she intends to have it seen and recorded.

When the chatter finally lags, she begins her appeal with a well-worn sermon on the horrors of Pleasanton. She moves quickly to squelch any notion that she is doing easy time, or that the medium-security facility—"Unpleasanton" she calls it, sharing a bitter laugh with Tobin—is any better than vile dungeons like Folsom or San Quentin. "People think because it looks like a campus, it is one. But I don't see anybody lining up to spend their time here," says Patty. She is at pains to point out that the place is "for real . . . just like in the movies. There are only two federal prisons for women in the country, this one and another one on the East Coast. That means we get everything. I mean, you name it. That woman right there is doing seven years for murdering her two kids. Just the other day a woman got stabbed in the bathroom, and another one had her jaw broken in the elevator."

Clearly, the prison is *not* just like in the movies. There are no walls and no armed guards. In place of the concrete bunkers of cinematic legend, there is a little cluster of buildings, brown and angular, set in the middle of a tract of greening acreage on which the three hundred inmates can ramble at will. The common buildings seem to be airy and well maintained; they stand in sharp contrast to nearby Santa Rita, the ramshackle, substandard dump that passes muster as the Alameda County jail. And even the cells are said to be bearable. They are dormlike rooms that measure a comfortable 9 by 12 feet. They have no bars and the inmates have ready access to telephones, an amenity that Jimmy Cagney and Paul Muni never enjoyed.

If anything, Pleasanton is a self-consciously humane prison, probably the best that the whole miserable system has to offer. But Patty seems determined to see it otherwise. She dismisses the soft edges as "cosmetics," a thin veneer of decency applied by federal officials in a calculated attempt to cover the essential ugliness of the place. "They keep it pretty because it's supposed to be a showcase," she says. "They're always bringing tours through, trying to convince people how wonderful it is. But what nobody ever hears about are some of the mind games they play in here. They call it 'programming.' That's the word they use. They give you a task to perform and then put as many obstacles in your way as they can, just to see if you can overcome them. They'll tell you that you can apply for a pass, and when you do all the work they turn around and say you can't have one. They say someone is outside waiting to pick you up. But when you get there, no one's around."

Patty likes to contend that no one who has been spared the ordeal of serving time can hope to understand the horror of life in prison. "You just can't know the things that go on in here," she insists. Yet she seems to have little use for the ones who might understand, the women who share the nightmare with her. She remains deliberately aloof from her fellow inmates—with aristocratic disdain, she explains that most are "stupid" and "petty" (not to mention guilty, which *she* most certainly is not), and writes them off with the grim observation, "I live for visiting days. That's it. The rest don't even exist." She freely confesses that she has no friends at Pleasanton. Asked whether she has met any good people at all in the twelve months she has served there, she wrinkles her nose and sniffs—"Maybe one." The only prisoner who impressed her, apparently, was an older woman, a widow doing time for robbery. "She worked for nine years in a bank," says Patty. "She was making $600 a month and a man in the same job was making $2,000. So she just embezzled the difference." (Tobin, a law student, asks why she didn't just pay the money back. Patty has to explain that she spent it putting four kids through college, and adds that she thinks the woman had a "pretty clear right" to the loot. Martinez looks pained, but doesn't bother to contradict.)

At the same time, Patty has no illusions about the feelings the other women have come to harbor toward her. She knows the contempt is mutual, and she is convinced that more than a few of her cohorts watch her every move, ready to pounce on the least sign of favor or special privilege. Apparently, the rat in her bed was only the best publicized sign of tensions that have been rising steadily since she returned to the prison in May. She says that in mid-December there was a serious threat of a prisonwide strike when the facility was swept by a rumor that Patricia Hearst had been allowed to go home for Christmas. According to Patty, "It was just really stupid. The warden and all the assistants had to come in at six in the morning because everybody thought I was gone. There I was, laying in my room. *I'm* not allowed to go on furlough at all. When

I went in to work, my supervisor just looked, you know, like 'What are you doing here?' Really, it's nothing but boredom. Nobody has anything better to do than to watch what I'm doing."

And even now, yet another incident has been threatening to bubble over into a full-scale crisis. Word that she is planning to hold an Indian wedding ceremony—inside Pleasanton if she isn't released by her private deadline, February 14—has been causing repercussions not just here, but in other prisons and in the Indian community as well. The dozen Indian women at Pleasanton have told her that she'll have the ceremony "over their dead bodies," and only this morning Archie Lame Deer, a burly, braided medicine man from AIM, flew up from Santa Barbara to investigate rumblings of discontent that have been reaching the movement. At an earlier interview arranged by Martinez, Lame Deer told Patty that the Indians were angry because they knew that two Indian men in Folsom had spent five years fighting, without success, for the right to marry their women in a tribal ceremony. The medicine man was clearly concerned by the volatile situation, but Patty seemed more bored than worried by the whole affair. She assured him that it was "all really stupid." The ceremony had been called off because the warden wouldn't allow it; and besides, she sighed, "The whole thing was just typical. I can't make a move without someone turning it into a federal crime."

Thoroughly convinced of her martyrdom, Patty seems to leap at a chance to prove that she has been treated cruelly by officials, by the press, by the world at large. She claims that, unlike her, the Harrises were pampered while waiting for their trial. "*They* were sending out for breakfast while I ate garbage." And she points out bitterly that other prisoners may enjoy an occasional furlough, but she is on central monitoring and is forbidden to leave the grounds. (But she fails to mention that she also enjoys favors. Officials have been providing a special room, the warden's conference chamber, for her press interviews; and at least one counselor has been receiving cookies and fudge, gifts from the family, which he slips to Patty, against prison rules.) She says, too, that she knows she's been exploited by virtually everyone who has come into contact with her since the day she was abducted. The indictment is a sweeping one, and seems all but overwhelming in its implications for the friends, like Dumke, who have upended their lives to help her. But she is little inclined to qualify it. She likes to claim that her dog Arrow was attack-trained on Judge Orrick's picture. She thinks of Steve Weed as a gold digger who invaded her privacy "for a few lousy dollars." Though she has never bothered to read his book, she is sure that it was a "finger down the throat," and it doesn't surprise her at all to hear that Charlie Bates "is getting his too now," working with ABC on a video melodrama that is tentatively entitled "Get Patty Hearst."

Patty believes she has been sinned against in a special way by "writers" —she maintains that "they are all out to make a buck off someone," and says that she could never work on one of the family's papers because she "can't stand reporters." She refuses to read the San Francisco *Examiner*, largely because she feels that publisher Reg Murphy exploited her just like the rest of the press at a time when he should have been offering badly needed support. She carries a special grudge for Lacey Fosburgh, *The New York Times* correspondent who described her in a portrait for the paper's Sunday magazine as "the ultimate reactive person . . . someone without strong inner principles or values" who "slips readily into situations where she is dependent on stronger, more dominant personalities." (In Patty's version, "She only met me once and I was suffering from food poisoning at the time. She couldn't write that I was gay and frivolous, so she wrote that I was a wimp.") And all afternoon she has been mulling over ways to deal with Shana Alexander, the television journalist who has just weighed in with Patty book number 9. Since legal action is probably out of the question—Martinez has explained that, like it or not, she is a certified public person now—she supposes she will settle for sending the author a token of her esteem, probably a saucer inscribed with the legend "CAT."

It seems to be Patty's conviction that if there is a lesson in all this, it is simply that she must learn to exploit herself. She says that she has already begun working on a book of her own, a memoir that will "set the record straight," and, not incidentally, help her to cash in on herself for a change. The last several months have also found her scheming to get something back from the press, which is, she believes, largely responsible for her conviction and seven-year sentence. She has been keeping a list of media favorites (*People* is "in" for the photos of her and Bernie in November; *US* is "out" because it is owned by *The New York Times*; the *Times* is decidedly "out" because of Fosburgh; Ken Turan of the Washington *Post*, is "in," because he called her a "Victorian heroine" and compared her to Harriet Beecher Stowe; *Look* is very "in," because the editors have agreed to hire Turan for a Patty-portrait in their upcoming inaugural issue), and makes it abundantly clear that when the ordeal is over, she intends to play the role of celebrity for whatever it might be worth.

There is probably some sort of justice in this. Patty has paid a heavy price for the crime of being kidnapped—she likes to point out that she's spent the last five years, a fifth of her life, as "somebody's prisoner," and she knows that however soon her term may end, her future will never belong to her alone. She is right when she says that "everything's changed." She will always have to cope with things like "making reservations in a different name when I go to restaurants, always looking around me when I go anyplace, being careful of who's next to me when I go through a crowd." Perhaps, then, she is also right in deciding to exploit her celebrity. If she is going to belong to the public, and find herself marked as the living reminder of a madness that flourished long ago, then she might as well sell herself dear. That much, at least, is the American way.

Perhaps, too, her decision to take control of her image has brought her closer than she knows to the one great vein that has run through her family's past. It was her cousin Willie who observed that "the Hearsts *are* PR." He was probably thinking then of his father, a man who made a career out of a name, not to mention his grandfather, the legend who taught his family—and taught the nation too—that reality is whatever makes the front page of the daily paper. But Patty too has begun to show the instincts of a Hearst. Even when she voices contempt for the press, she is not afraid to use it—and in this she is startlingly close to the secret that lurked inside of the enigma that was William Randolph Hearst.

For now Patty may insist that she will never work for the family. With something approaching open scorn, she says "I talked to my father about it once. He said I'd have to start somewhere at $400 a month. I told him to forget it—I might consider it if they paid me $1,200 a month and threw in an expense account. I could make that anywhere." But one senses that she is posturing—letting off steam in a way that she knows will get back to her kinsmen and the corporate people, making it clear that they are not yet forgiven for collectively letting her down. Patty is too much a Hearst to remain forever aloof from the family's great enterprise. She is shrewd enough to know that the name belongs to her now. (Stanford psychologist Philip Zimbardo believes that she has redefined her family's whole past, stealing the notoriety from even her illustrious grand-father.) She knows that the name is her power, and anyone who has heard her talk of negotiating a deal with *Look*, or snubbing the writers from *US*, or discussing her television future with Barbara Walters (who paid a more or less clandestine visit to the prison only a week before) must realize that she is fast learning how to use it. The name will keep her close to the media. And eventually she will discover that she is what the press has been calling her—Patty Hearst, the "newspaper heiress," the one who must, almost certainly, take her father's place in the great mandala of corporate life.

Chapter 6

Generations

(1)

IN THE BEGINNING they were a proud and restless clan. The first ancestors that anyone could remember were Scots, lowland people who spelled their name "Hyrst" (it was a Saxon word, meaning a thicket or a cluster of trees), and stood firm in the ranks of the Presbyterian Church. The Hyrsts were rigid nonconformists, many of them Covenanters—militants bound by oath to uphold their faith as the sole legitimate religion of Scotland and, later, of the whole of the British Isles. The Covenanters had resisted the Catholic revival in 1581, imposing a confession of loyalty to their Church on the Scottish King James IV. Some twenty years later they thwarted Charles I and his Archbishop, William Laud, when those two inveterate schemers tried to bring the Anglican liturgy north to the wilds of Scotland; and in 1643, they eagerly joined the great Parliamentary rebellion, only to be crushed by Cromwell, who could never countenance their demand that he inflict their singularly uncompromising beliefs on all of England, Ireland and Wales.

When the monarchy was restored in 1660, the new king, Charles II, had his way; under his aegis, the bishops came at last to Scotland. But the Covenanters resisted again. There were open-air assemblies, more oaths—secret and unlawful—and finally, in 1665, open rebellion. Later generations would remember the years that followed as "the killing time," when angry northern guerrillas fought a long and bloody war with the king's and bishops' men. The killing lasted until 1679, the year in which the Duke of Monmouth, illegitimate son of Charles II, met the defenders of the Kirk at Bothwell Bridge on the Clyde.

Monmouth broke the Scots in decisive battle, and for the next ten years, the Presbyterians lay under royal ban. For the tired or the timid, that decade was a time of weary submission. But for stalwarts like the sworn man of the Kirk, John Hurst (as the name was spelled by then), it was time to leave for a better land.

Two centuries later, an almost unlettered descendant who bore the proud title of Senator George Hearst would labor to explain what he knew of this first kinsman to set foot in the New World. The best he could do was to write:

> The great grandfather of all the Hearsts came here in 1680. I do not know where he landed. In this country he owned ten acres and nine slaves. He was a Scotchman, that is, I take it for granted he was Scotch, because all the race were Scotch. My father's cousins are all Scotch.

Had George remembered better, he might have known that "the great grandfather of all the Hearsts"—sternly religious and probably marked for extinction in Scotland because of his role in the holy wars—chose the colony of Virginia as his refuge. He landed in Isle of Wight County, and though it has never been clear whether he brought a yeoman's wealth with him on his hasty passage across the ocean, it is very certain that John Hurst prospered in America: when he died in 1727, he left a substantial estate to be divided among a thriving family, two daughters and five restless sons.

The Hurst men—James, John, William, Philip and Walter—might well have remained in Virginia. They could have expanded and developed their father's estate, growing tobacco, perhaps even working their way into the ranks of planter society, the three or four hundred families who were then entrenching themselves as the first New World aristocracy. But something refused to let them rest in Isle of Wight County. There may have been pressure from the wave of settlers coming south to the Tidewater country from Pennsylvania, or possibly a conflict with the established families, most of whom were Anglican and much too adamantly Royalist for the comfort of the rebellious Hursts. It may also have been nothing more than the urge to move again that pushed all five of the sons, in the wake of their father's death, onto the trails that led south, into neighboring North Carolina.

It was the second son, John, who settled in Bertie County and there began calling himself "Hearst." And it was his son John who in 1776 hit the pioneer trail again, taking with him eleven children and a second wife. Perhaps the third John Hearst was looking for nothing more than peace (which, in that year of revolution, meant distance from the ringing of liberty bells and the thunder of coming war) when he began his trek into South Carolina. At any rate, he seemed to have no destination in mind when he started south and inland, but was content to stop when he reached an unsettled tract on the western edge of the colony, where he took a patent on land from the royal government. There, in what later became Abbeville County, the Hearsts entrenched for a generation. Three of John Hearst's daughters are said to have married three brothers in the county, all of them Presbyterian clergymen. George Hearst, his fifth son, had four children there, and it was his eldest son William in whom the pioneering spirit was rekindled.

This time the flame was lit by talk of the Louisiana Territory, 800,000 square miles of land—some of it lightly civilized by the itinerant French, but most of it uncharted and unspoiled—which Jefferson had lately slickered from the hard-pressed Napoleon for $15 million. William set out in 1808, five years after the purchase, knowing no better than his grandfather before him just where he intended to settle. According to family tradition, the fifth-generation wanderer first went north and west through Kentucky, following the trail that Daniel Boone's party had blazed in 1803. He crossed the Mississippi by ferry at St. Louis, a trading town that could then boast some five thousand hearty souls, and there fell in with the steady stream of wagon traffic that was headed southwest along what would later be known as the "Old Springfield Road" (and still later, Route 66).

William ambled along with the oxen and horses until he reached a settlement called Biglow at the southern edge of Franklin County, where he decided to sink his roots along the Meramec River, in the hills of the Ozark Plateau. He cleared the rich bottom land of sycamore and maple, and within a year was growing wheat and corn for his own sustenance. Soon afterward he was driving horses and cattle to market, then buying more land to expand his holding, and then, finally, purchasing slaves to help him work it.

He was a solitary, enterprising man, this William Hearst. He had multiplied his talents in Biblical fashion (though he was said to be more worldly than pious, the Presbyterianism at last wearing thin), and for the better part of his life he had managed to make his way on his own. By 1817, however, he believed that he was ready to take a wife. That year he married Elizabeth Collins, the daughter of Jacob Collins, a neighboring farmer who had come into the country when it was first opened by Boone in 1803.

It was a testament to the man's deep-seated uneasiness that in the year of his marriage, William—apparently still searching for his terminus —packed up his gear and all the Collinses, and ventured a final migration, south and west again, into Texas. The ragtag band of relatives stayed for a year. But the land was hostile, and Hearst's energy too diluted by age (he was then over fifty) to sustain them. When their livestock died of cholera, the Hearst-Collins party was driven back to the relative comfort and quiet of Franklin County.

There, in 1820 or 1821 (later generations were never sure which), the first child, George, the future miner, father to the press lord, was born to the Missouri Hearsts.

(2)

At this writing, there are thirty-two living descendants of George Hearst and his wife, Phoebe Elizabeth Apperson. (See chart.)

Five direct descendants—William Randolph Hearst, Jr.; Randolph Hearst; David Hearst; John Hearst, Jr.; and George Hearst, Jr.—serve as administrators of the family trust. The same five serve as directors of the Hearst Corporation, along with two additional Hearst progeny, Phoebe Cooke and William Randolph Hearst III.

In addition to the surviving sons—all of whom still hold managerial positions in the corporation—nine family members work in some capacity for the Hearst organization. George junior serves as president of the Sunical land division, while his sister Phoebe works as an unpaid adviser to the Hearst Foundation in San Francisco. Will Hearst is an executive assistant on the Los Angeles *Herald-Examiner*. His brother Austin is busy surveying Hearst trees on the Pejepscot property in Maine—a project that was devised, says his cousin Jack Cooke, to lure him into the business.

Bunky Hearst, the sports-fishing editor for *Motor Boating* magazine, takes pictures and writes articles about fishing adventures aboard his 25-foot Bertram motor launch. Catherine Hearst, Randy's eldest daughter, answers the telephone, part time, in the corporation's Beverly Hills office. Gina Bosworth works as a copy editor for the *Herald-Examiner.* David junior works with the *Herex* computers. George III is a company accountant (working in San Francisco, with his eye on a job in the New York headquarters). His brother Steve, the feistiest of the young Hearsts, who says he "intends to play the name for all it's worth," is an advertising clerk on the Los Angeles paper.

Debra Gallagher, Joanne Lawrence and Billy Hearst (William Randolph Hearst II) all draw on the trust without holding corporate positions. Debra, who was once an aspiring actress, now lives in Southampton, where she is quietly and happily married. Joanne is a lady of leisure in Majorca. Billy, who finds being a Hearst an intolerable burden, lives under an assumed name in Marin County, California. He is heavily into est and is trying hard to become a screenwriter (his organic pineapple farm having failed some years ago).

Anne and Vicki have quit college. Anne, who is not employed, owns a home in Beverly Hills. Vicki lives nearby with her mother, and would like to become a Los Angeles County sheriff or a television technician. Catherine is happy with neither idea.

Together they are a most unremarkable brood, these copy editors and fishermen and children of leisure, who trace their roots to the pioneers. No more than a handful of them have managed to hold their family pride intact; Phoebe Cooke is one of the few who will state without hesitation, "I think we Hearsts have a fine tradition to uphold. I have always believed that my name sets me apart—it puts me under an obligation. I would never do anything to tarnish it." Among the rest, however, there is only a feeling of indifference or defeat, and a nagging fear that the bloodline has finally played itself out. "What's *wrong* with these kids?" wonders one of the older cousins, a man who is frankly bewildered by the young Hearsts' failure to take an interest in their heritage. "Why can't they see what they've got? With a little bit of effort, these kids coming up could be running one of the greatest fortunes in the world." Rosalie Hearst—George's last wife—is even more blunt. "I blame the parents," she says. "They raised their children with no real sense of where things come from. It's just plain missing. You can call these kids heirs if you want to. But most of them couldn't find their way to the corporate headquarters to pick up a check."

Rosalie has stories to prove her point. She recalls, for instance, that she has argued with Catherine for hours on end, pleading in vain that unless her daughters become involved with the company, "they're going to lose the whole thing."

"Well, I suppose so," Catherine would reply. "But these children are Hearsts. They really ought to pay them more. . . ."

So, apparently, the family has come to this: with their trust arrangement finally secure, most of them are happy to collect their dividends and to let the challenge of the business pass them by. Only one or two have shown some sign of the restless urges that once made the Hearsts an extraordinary clan.

Willie, for his part, has a future with the papers. He, at least, is contending with the old conundrum, how to make something worthwhile from the remnant of a chain that has never been good, never been respected.

And now, of course, there is Patty.

Five years ago, she was as ordinary and aimless as most of her kin. But a twist of fate has transformed her into something more. Because she was vulnerable—and, indeed, because her name was Hearst—she was swept into a chain of events that made her, in turn, a victim, a fighter, a comrade, a traitor, a captive, a survivor, and a media event. And now that she has finally won her freedom, only one question remains to be answered. What does she intend to make of herself?

To date, the indications have all been grim.

Her wedding to San Francisco police officer Bernard Shaw—which took place on April 1, 1979, in the chapel at the Naval Base on Treasure Island—was less a celebration than a display of spite. Patty herself has called it a "triumph over everyone." Certainly it was a victory over the press, for she sold the picture rights to *Look* magazine for $50,000—and left the rest of the media crowd (among them a team of reporters and photographers from her family's *Examiner*) shivering in the wind outside the church. Inside the chapel, the wedding service spoke of wrath and reprisal. "Oh Lord, thou God of vengeance, thou God of vengeance, shine forth," intoned Father Ted Dumke, the presiding priest, as he read Patricia's favorite bit of scripture, the 94th Psalm. "Can wicked rulers be allied with thee, who frame mischief by statute? They band together against the life of the righteous and condemn the innocent to death."

The guest list included four hundred dear friends, among them Trish Tobin, Paul McCloskey, Sam Hayakawa, Kathryn Crosby, and Janey Jimenez—along with Frank Bennack and John Miller, on whom Randy insisted. There were, however, some pointed omissions. Cousins Jack and Phoebe Cooke were not invited: they had joined the ranks of the unrighteous two years before, when they opposed Patty's effort to take a job with the Hearst Foundation while she was free on bail. ("With her legal status unresolved," said the Cookes, "we just didn't feel it would have been appropriate.") Editor Reg Murphy was not asked to the nuptials, that particular grudge never having been settled. Nor, for that matter, was Tania's former soul mate. Wendy Yoshimura. Questioned by an *Examiner* reporter, Wendy said that she probably wouldn't have come in any case. "Patty seems so remote to me," she added. "She's a media person. She's THE Patty Hearst."

After the wedding, Mr. and Mrs. Shaw honeymooned in Panama as the personal guests of General Omar Torrijos, the military strongman who had once closed his country's National University, because, he said, it was a breeding ground for "urban guerillas."

By that fall, Patricia Hearst Shaw was hard at work "exploiting herself." On a whirlwind trip to New York—with husband Bernie and George Martinez in tow—she signed an $800,000 contract with Doubleday, to write a memoir that will, presumably, tell all.

NOTES*

BOOK ONE: THE LEGACY

1. "FORGET HIS FAULTS . . ."

page 23
"For the NICEST": William Randolph Hearst, *Newspaper Principles*, p. 16.

page 24
"You're all working": *Time*, August 27, 1951.

page 24
"He was gone": *Life,* August 19, 1951.

page 24
"There would be no break": San Francisco *Examiner*, August 15, 1951.

page 25
"Forget his faults": Letter, J. F. Neylan to Millicent Hearst, August 15, 1951, Bancroft Library.†

page 25
"There were those": San Francisco *Examiner*, August 17, 1951.

page 27
"Song of the River": Reprinted in the San Francisco *Examiner*, August 13, 1978.

page 28
"Now Roy stop": Telegram, W. R. Hearst to Roy Howard, November 19, 1932, Bancroft Library.

page 28
"The world has lost": New York *Journal-American*, August 14, 1951.

---

* All quotations that are not cited here have been drawn from the authors' personal interviews.

† All material from the Bancroft collections is quoted by permission of The Bancroft Library.

page 28
"Stood in stunned silence": New York *Mirror*, August 15, 1951.
page 29
"How could one": San Francisco *Examiner*, August 15, 1951.
page 29
"Eyewitness to almost": Los Angeles *Herald-Express*, August 15, 1951.
page 29
"Decades ahead": San Francisco *Examiner*, August 16, 1951.

page 29
"Had often misused": *Time*, August 20, 1951.
page 29
"To demonstrate that": *The New Yorker*, September 8, 1951.
page 29
"Wicked old reactionary": London *News-Chronicle*, August 15, 1951.
page 30
"His papers bred": *Christian Century*, August 29, 1951.

2. THE LEGEND

page 31
"The crowning absurdity": Quoted in Cora Older, *William Randolph Hearst: American*, p. 61.
page 31
"So detestable": Letter, W. R. Hearst to George Hearst, January 25, 1886, Bancroft Library.
page 31
"Was the very worst": George Hearst, *Recollections of George Hearst* (New York: Hearst Corp., 1972), p. 34.
page 31
"I have begun": Quoted in Cora Older, p. 62.
page 32
"THE LARGEST": San Francisco *Examiner*, March 12, 1887.
page 32
"The *Call* is crazy": Letter, W. R. Hearst to George Hearst, no date, Bancroft Library.
page 32
"The great and good people": Quoted in Cora Older, p. 80.
page 33
"To root out": Quoted in W. A. Swanberg, *Pulitzer*, p. 11.
page 33
"I am getting so": Letter, W. R. Hearst to Phoebe Hearst, no date, Bancroft Library.
page 33
"There is a great deal": *Ibid.*, August 17, 1891, Bancroft Library.

page 34
"Man of Mystery": Lincoln Steffens, "Hearst, the Man of Mystery," *The American Magazine*, November 1906.
page 35
"Mr. Hearst has waged": *Ibid.*
page 36
"Calamity of calamities": Mark Twain, unpublished notebook, January 24, 1906, Mark Twain Collection, University of California, Berkeley.
page 37
"These Hearst newspapers": *World's Work*, October 1906.
page 38
"At first Mr. Hearst's": James Creelman, "The Real Mr. Hearst," *Pearsons Magazine*, September 1906.
page 38
"I don't like": Quoted in W. A. Swanberg, *Citizen Hearst*, p. 254.
page 39
"Mr. Hearst does not": *Fortune*, October 1935.
page 40
Written agreement: See memorandum on Wyntoon, no date, Bancroft Library.
page 42
"Despite all the uproar": Charles Beard, introduction to Ferdinand Lundberg, *Imperial Hearst* (New York: Modern Library, 1937), p. vii.

page 42
"Wonderful opportunity": Letter, W. R. Hearst to J. F. Neylan, October 29, 1929, Bancroft Library.
page 43
"IN THE AUTUMN": Quoted in A. J. Liebling, "Of Yesteryear—II," *The New Yorker*, November 14, 1953.
page 43
"America's banking system": Letter, W. R. Hearst to J. F. Neylan, March 10, 1933, Bancroft Library.

page 43
"The idea of Mr. Hearst": Adela Rogers St. Johns, *The Honeycomb*, p. 484.
page 43
"The miserable little wretch": Letter, J. F. Neylan to W. R. Hearst, April 4, 1945, Bancroft Library.
page 44
"Any man in his late seventies": *Ibid.*

3. THE FAMILY

page 47
"Bicycle girls": Program, *The Girl From Paris*, Lincoln Center Library.
page 47
"George Leslie did not have": New York *Morning Telegraph*, March 16, 1908.
page 48
"When he asked me": Adela Rogers St. Johns, pp. 131–32.
page 49
"A debauchee . . .": *Congressional Record*, Vol. 29, Part 1, 54th Congress, 2nd Session, p. 592.
page 55
"An occasional cuff": Letter, J. F. Neylan to Millicent Hearst, October 29, 1919, Bancroft Library.
page 55
"Manly" character: *Ibid.*
page 55
"No . . . Mr. Hearst will not": New York *Evening Mail*, November 3, 1909.
page 57
"I'll take the string": Elsa Maxwell, *RSVP*, p. 128.
page 57
"I was awfully angry": *Ibid.*, p. 129.
page 57
"It cast a pall": *Ibid.*, p. 130.
page 58
"I want you to accomplish": Quoted in W. R. Hearst, *William Randolph Hearst: A Portrait in His Own Words*, p. 74.

page 59
"You have had a good time": *Ibid.*, p. 79.
page 59
"Holding a milk bottle": James Creelman, *Pearsons Magazine*, September 1906.
page 61
"From what I can gather": John Hearst, unpublished memoir.
page 61
Well, "they had a good mother": Quoted in Cora Older, p. 498.
page 62
"Why don't you close up": *Ibid.*, p. 504.
page 62
"It takes a good mind": Quoted in Hearst, *Portrait*, p. 72.
page 62
"People who are divorced": Adela Rogers St. Johns, p. 143.
page 63
"I am responsible": Letter, Bill Hearst to W. R. Hearst, July 15, 1937, Bancroft Library.
page 64
"I'll tell you what": Quoted in Cora Older, p. 494.
page 65
"New York is about": Letter, W. R. Hearst to Bill Hearst, April 17, 1940, Bancroft Library.
page 65
"W. R. Hearst, Jr., spoke": Letter, W. R. Hearst to Hearst editors and

publishers, January 7, 1948, Bancroft Library.
page 66
"In the event": Letter, J. F. Neylan to W. R. Hearst, December 22, 1933, Bancroft Library.
page 66
"Of course, anybody is": Letter, W. R. Hearst to J. F. Neylan, December 23, 1933, Bancroft Library.
page 66
"By some wealthy Red": Letter,

Frej Hagelberg to J. F. Neylan, February 28, 1944, Bancroft Library.
page 66
"The chances of liquidating": J. F. Neylan, memorandum, no date, Bancroft Library.
page 68
"Retention of control": *Ibid.*
page 69
"They be no issue": W. R. Hearst, Last Will and Testament, Article 14, p. 53.

4. THE WOMAN

page 70
"There were blazing": Marion Davies, *The Times We Had*, p. 252.
page 71
"They turned on me": Fred Guiles, *Marion Davies: A Biography*, p. 6.
page 71
"Why should you care": *Ibid.*, p. 9.
page 71
"David said to me": Marion Davies, p. 250.
page 71
"You're not wanted": Fred Guiles, p. 9.
page 72
"I asked him when": John Tebbel, *The Life and Good Times of William Randolph Hearst*, p. 351.
page 72
"Please tell Mrs. Hearst": Fred Guiles, p. 17.
page 72
"I'd like to see you": *Ibid.*, p. 46.
page 73
"A wolf": Marion Davies, p. 9.
page 73
"Desperate Desmond . . . Lonesome George": Telegrams, W. R. Hearst to Marion Davies, May 8, 1918; July 25, 1919.
page 73
"Marion, I'm going": Fred Guiles, p. 80.
page 75
"There were few dry eyes": New York *American*, May 6, 1918.

page 75
"Oh, the night is blue": Reprinted in Marion Davies, p. 241.
page 76
"May I help": *Ibid.*, p. 14.
page 77
"Well, George and Blanche": *Ibid.*, p. 44.
page 78
"Most of the family": *Ibid.*, p. 44.
page 78
"I shall be glad": Letter, Bill Hearst to E. D. Coblentz, January 16, 1953, Bancroft Library.
page 79
"Go see Doctor": Fred Guiles, p. 137.
page 79
"Read all about": Marion Davies, p. 26.
page 81
"About fifty of us": Charles Chaplin, *My Autobiography*, p. 309.
page 81
"A. B. was a big crook": Marion Davies, p. 198.
page 81
"A little bit vicious": *Ibid.*, p. 202.
page 81
"The great, wonderful": *Ibid,,* p. 199.
page 83
"Sometimes I would get": *Ibid.*, p. 86.
page 84
"They weren't smart": *Ibid.*, p. 202.

page 84
"Please stay": Fred Guiles, p. 316.
page 85
"Let me get you": Marion Davies, p. 240.
page 85
"We'll come back": Fred Guiles, p. 329.
page 86
"Young man": W. A. Swanberg, *Citizen Hearst*, p. 515.
page 86
"How could one man": *The New Yorker*, February 1, 1941.
page 87
"He took great pride": San Francisco *Examiner*, August 15, 1951.

page 89
"This so-called agreement": *Time*, September 3, 1951.
page 90
"My loyal friend": W. R. Hearst, Last Will and Testament, Codicil 1, Item 1, p. 1.
page 91
"Editorial consultant": *Time*, November 5, 1951.
page 92
"Despite numerous stories": *The New York Times*, October 31, 1951.
page 92
"Thank God": Fred Guiles, p. 337.

BOOK TWO: THE DARK YEARS

1. "IMAGINE ME . . ."

page 107
"An office reign of terror": Herbert Mayes, quoted in W. A. Swanberg, *Citizen Hearst*, p. 430.
page 114
"I want some more salary": Letter, W. R. Hearst to Richard Berlin, September 6, 1940, Bancroft Library.

page 114
"Thoroughly sympathetic": Letter, Richard Berlin to W. R. Hearst, September 9, 1940, Bancroft Library.
page 114
"Was holding the empire": Albert Bermel, "The Future of the Hearst Empire," *Harper's Magazine*, January 1962.

2. YOUNG BILL

page 122
"A tenacious optimist": New York *Journal-American*, May 23, 1950.
page 122
Joseph Pulitzer II; Benjamin Reese, Oral History, Columbia University, p. 86.
page 123
"Another one of those": Eugene Meyer, Oral History, Columbia University, p. A44.
page 125
"Inasmuch as these shows": *Editor and Publisher*, March 17, 1945.

page 126
"Those closest to": *Time*, August 27, 1951.
page 127
"Telling the American people": San Francisco *Examiner*, August 16, 1951.
page 127
"That were known": Quoted in Fred Cook, *The Nightmare Decade*, p. 149.
page 129
"The Johnny-come-lately": *American Mercury*, May 1953.

page 129
"It seemed that the": *Daily Worker,*
February 27, 1935.
page 131
"A man who seemed": Joseph
McCarthy, Waldorf Astoria testi-
monial speech, February 13, 1953.
page 131
"Unmitigated liar": Fred Cook, p.
189.
page 132
"The most nefarious": *The New
York Times,* July 18, 1950.
page 132
"The Tydings Committee's": New
York *Journal-American,* July 19,
1950.
page 133
"The first job": *Newsweek,* October
8, 1951.
page 133
"Some of the worst bums": New
York *World-Telegram,* February 15,
1940.
page 134
"We are nagging": Letter, W. R.
Hearst to E. D. Coblentz, January
10, 1940, Bancroft Library.
page 134
"Somewhere between": New York
Journal-American, November 22,
1953.
page 135
"The Real Danger": San Francisco
Examiner, May 15, 1950.
page 135
"Still Too Many": San Francisco
Examiner, November 30, 1954.
page 135
"Only Pinks in Washington": San
Francisco *Examiner,* September 23,
1952.
page 136
"Rich parlor pinks": Igor Cassini,
I'd Do It All Over Again, p. 113.
page 136
"Like veins of marble": New York
Journal-American, February 1, 1953.
page 137
"I don't know when": San Francisco
Examiner, September 25, 1952.

page 137
"It is nothing": San Francisco *Ex-
aminer,* September 25, 1952.
page 137
"Walter really must think": Drew
Pearson, *Diaries,* p. 124.
page 137
"Whatever doubts": Bob Thomas,
Winchell, pp. 226–27.
page 137
"I don't kiss": Herman Klurfeld,
Winchell: His Life and Times, p.
134.
page 138
According to Winchell: Walter
Winchell, *Winchell Exclusive,* p.
253.
page 138
"When the McCarthy Red": *Ibid.,*
pp. 253–54.
page 139
"When I exposed": *Ibid.,* p. 255.
page 139
"Long before McCarthy": *Time,*
January 7, 1952.
page 140
"A *Journal-American* editor": Her-
man Klurfeld, p. 163.
page 140
"Why don't you come": Walter
Winchell, p. 291.
page 140
"Those who are discreet": James
Wechsler, *Age of Suspicion,* p. 256.
page 141
"Please edit Winchell": Quoted in
Current Biography, entry on Walter
Winchell, 1943.
page 142
"Not as satisfactory": Hearst Con-
solidated Publications, Inc., Annual
Report, 1953.
page 143
"Only one thing is certain": *For-
tune,* October 1935.
page 144
"Poorly educated, non-intellectual":
Oliver Pilat, *Pegler: Angry Man of
the Press,* p. 1.
page 144
"Odd that honesty": Quoted in
Louis Nizer, *My Life in Court,* p.
111.

page 144
"Never-to-be-adequately damned":
New York *World-Telegram*, February 15, 1940.
page 145
"If genius is": Oliver Pilat, p. 190.
page 145
"The courageous Westbrook Pegler": *Editor and Publisher*, December 2, 1950.
page 145
"Malicious and untruthful": *Time*, June 6, 1949.
page 145
"Pegler and Winchell—at the time":
Walter Winchell, p. 254.
page 145
"Though he was a giant": New York *Journal-American*, November 29, 1949.
page 146
"Well all I know": Trial transcript, *Reynolds v. Pegler*.
page 146
"Do you think Damon Runyon":
Ibid.
page 147
"Renegade Republican": Oliver Pilat, p. 242.

page 147
"The Central Intelligence Agency":
Ibid., p. 242.
page 148
"Even enemies read": *Ibid.*, p. 221.
page 148
"My Hearst employers": Walter Winchell, p. 291.
page 148
"Walter Winchell . . . never said":
Time, March 21, 1955.
page 148
"That double-cross cast": Walter Winchell, p. 292.
page 149
"Those papers and people who have been doing well": *Newsweek*, October 8, 1951.
page 150
"Have you heard the latest": William Manchester, *The Glory and the Dream*, Vol. 2, p. 879.
page 150
"So the 'Get-McCarthy' lobby": San Francisco *Examiner*, December 4, 1954.
page 150
"Threw away the Commies": New York *Journal-American*, October 24, 1954.

3. DYNASTY MANQUÉ

page 153
"The other day"; Julia Morgan, oral history, p. 57, Bancroft Library.
page 154
"If you are free": Quoted in Ken Murray, *The Golden Days of San Simeon*, p. 23.
page 155
"Will not Clark Gable": Letter, W. R. Hearst to Louella Parsons, no date, Bancroft Library.
page 158
"There was, frankly": Newton Drury, oral history, p. 282, Bancroft Library.
page 165
"Billy had his birthday": Letter,

John Hearst to Joanne Hearst, dated only "Nov. 11," private collection.
page 165
"We saw Uncle Bill": *Ibid.*, undated, private collection.
page 166
"Bunky is taking": *Ibid.*
page 166
"Bunky has been": *Ibid.*
page 166
"Here is a picture": Postcard, John Hearst to Joanne Hearst, undated, private collection.
page 172
"From then on": Quoted in a biographical sketch of George Hearst prepared by the Los Angeles *Herald-Examiner*, October 1969.

page 173
"I hope that George": Letter, John F. Neylan to Bart Guild, March 3, 1936, Bancroft Library.
page 174
"I wouldn't even be": Letter, George Hearst, Sr., to Millicent Hearst, May 21, 1971, private collection.
page 176
"Randy has suddenly": Letter, Bill Hearst to E. J. Coblentz, June 17, 1957, Bancroft Library.
page 180
"It's not a country": Quoted in Steven Weed, *My Search for Patty Hearst*, p. 85.
page 181
"A first-hand view": William Randolph Hearst, Jr., *Ask Me Anything: Our Adventures With Khrushchev*, p. 6.
page 181
"There won't be much": *Ibid.*

page 183
"If Chiang Kai-shek": *Ibid.*, p. 32.
page 183
"Those people who try": San Francisco *Examiner*, February 9, 1955.
page 184
"That Hearst was not interested": William Randolph Hearst, Jr., p. 36.
page 184
"Another Comrade with greater": Quoted in Konrad Kellen, *Khrushchev, A Political Portrait*, p. 133.
page 184
"MacVane: You certainly are": Quoted in *The New Yorker*, February 9, 1955.
page 186
"Keeping our guard up": *The New York Times*, February 20, 1955.
page 186
"Smiled somewhat grimly": *Ibid.*
page 186
"For several years": William Randolph Hearst, Jr., p. 4.

4. DOMINOES

page 190
"Revitalized Hearst": *Advertising Age*, April 4, 1955.
page 191
"A dying enterprise": *Forbes*, December 1, 1967.
page 191
"The curtain": *Newsweek*, October 29, 1956.
page 191
"Chicago is a vigorous": *Editor and Publisher*, March 22, 1952.
page 192
"It's a tough town": Quoted in George Murray, *Madhouse on Madison Street*, p. 3.
page 192
"Sell 'em": *Ibid.*, p. 43.
page 193
"Don't play rummy": *Ibid.*, p. 298.
page 194
"We are appalled": Memorandum, November 1959, files of The Newspaper Guild.

page 194
"NEW YORK, May 24 (UPI)": *Guild Reporter*, June 13, 1958.
page 195
"Working around here": Quoted in Bob Considine, *It's All News to Me*, p. 81.
page 195
"We died": *Ibid.*, p. 82.
page 196
"Out of the capitals": George Murray, p. 160.
page 199
"Cruel and Heartless": Press release, May 24, 1958, files of The Newspaper Guild.
page 199
"May raise a serious": *The New York Times*, May 25, 1958.
page 200
"Despite a recent rash": Quoted in *Editor and Publisher*, June 9, 1962.
page 201
"This was an unusual": *Ibid.*

page 202
"It is with deep": Quoted in Louis A. Ferman, *Death of a Newspaper: The Story of the Detroit Times*, p. 10.
page 203
"The *Times* was a good": *Ibid.*, p. 15.
page 203
"High degree": *Ibid.*, p. 10.
page 204
"An All Day": *The New York Times*, October 2, 1961.
page 205
"Because Hearst papers": A. J. Liebling, "A Look At The Record," *The New Yorker*, October 14, 1961.
page 207
"If we look": Hearings before the Subcommittee on Antitrust and Monopoly of the Committee on the Judiciary United States Senate, re: The Failing Newspaper Act, 90th Congress, 2nd Session, Part 5, p. 2456.
page 207
Examiner "discontinue": *Ibid.*, p. 2477.
page 208
"Bad deal for us": *Ibid.*, p. 2481.
page 208
"Would load": *Ibid.*, p. 2457.

page 210
"Go substantially": *Ibid.*
page 212
"The possibility of somebody": Quoted in Robert Gottlieb and Irene Wolt, *Thinking Big*, p. 351.
page 213
"The *Mirror* is being": *Newsweek*, January 12, 1962.
page 213
"Economic circumstances": *Ibid.*
page 215
"We have no dispute": *Editor and Publisher*, June 23, 1962.
page 215
"Milwaukee Guildsmen": *Ibid.*
page 216
"Prohibitive operating": *Ibid.*, July 21, 1962.
page 217
"The name, good will": *The New York Times*, October 16, 1963.
page 217
"The callous and cold-blooded": *Ibid.*
page 217
"I've just been informed": *Ibid.*
page 218
"90 percent entertainment": *Ibid.*
page 220
"What can I say?": *Ibid.*
page 220
"Damn right": *Ibid.*

5. REALPOLITIK

page 223
"A certain hostility": Newton Drury, oral history, p. 282, Bancroft Library.
page 223
"Look more official": Letter, Joseph Barnes to E. D. Coblentz, April 9, 1952, Bancroft Library.
page 223
"I suspect": *Ibid.*, January 31, 1952.
page 224
"The first of a series": *Newsweek*, April 20, 1953.
page 225
"Sells his personality": quoted in Albert Bermel, "The Future of the Hearst Empire," *Harper's Magazine*, January 1962.
page 226
"Fred goes through": *Ibid.*
page 228
"Thinking only in terms": Hearings before House Committee on Interstate and Foreign Commerce, 85th Congress, Volume 16, p. 5167.
page 228
"Mr. McCabe explained": *Ibid.*, p. 5169.
page 228
"Buy them out": *Ibid.*, p. 5167.

page 230
"You neglected": *Ibid.*, p. 5149.
page 230
"Television station WTAE": Hearst Consolidated Publications annual report, 1958.
page 231
"Raise your rates": Memorandum, W. R. Hearst to "All Editors and Publishers," August 3, 1948, Bancroft Library.
page 233
"There were many": Hearings before Antitrust Subcommittee of the Committee on the Judiciary, House of Representatives, 90th Congress re: Newspaper Preservation Act, p. 325.
page 234
"After the merger": Quoted in William L. Rivers and David M. Rubin, *A Region's Press: Anatomy of Newspapers in the San Francisco Bay Area*, p. 34.
page 236
"Sex, sensation and sea serpents": Quoted in *Printers' Ink*, April 4, 1958.
page 237
"Our business": Hearst Consolidated Publications annual report, 1952.
page 238
"As a result": *Ibid.*, 1956.
page 238
"The latest increase": *Ibid.*, 1957.
page 238
"Union wages": *Ibid.*, 1958.
page 238
"The unrealistic": *Ibid.*, 1960.
page 241
"It's been a glorious": Quoted in *American Heritage*, October 1967.
page 243
"Amalgamation of strengths": *The New York Times*, March 22, 1966.
page 244
"We think we can bring": *Ibid*, April 25, 1966.
page 244
"We just want": *Ibid.*
page 246
"Sober enough": *Time*, September 23, 1966.

page 246
"On the linotype": Hearings of the Senate subcommittee on antitrust and monopoly of Committee on the Judiciary, 90th Congress, 2nd Session, Part 6, p. 2734.
page 247
"You can do a lot": *Newsweek*, January 16, 1967.
page 248
"We looked at the situation": Senate hearings, *loc. cit.*, p. 2790.
page 248
"Hearst and Scripps-Howard": *Ibid.*, page 2791.
page 248
"From our judgment": *Ibid.*
page 249
"I do not think": *Ibid.*, p. 2728.
page 250
"It was beginning": *Ibid.*
page 250
"It is with a real sense": G. Merlis, "Why our Newspaper Died," *National Review*, May 30, 1967.
page 250
"If applied": *Ibid.*
page 250
"This was a paper born": *The New York Times*, May 6, 1967.
page 252
"Do you mean to tell': Memorandum, December 1967, files of the Los Angeles County Federation of Labor.
page 257
"This is not only": Quoted in unpublished monograph "Structure of a Strike," p. 7, files of the Newspaper Guild.
page 257
"A business which": Quoted in "On The Line," February 1, 1968, Special Collections Department, University of California, Los Angeles.
page 258
"And Now, Murder": Los Angeles *Herald-Examiner*, February 23, 1968.
page 259
"Ready to meet": Quoted in monograph "Structure of a Strike," p. 10, files of the Newspaper Guild.

page 259
"The role of . . . panel": *Ibid.*, p. 12.
page 259
"The panel quit": *Ibid.*, p. 13.
page 260
"Brushed aside": San Francisco *Chronicle*, about July 2, 1968. Attached to letter from Sigmond Arywitz to Ralph Woolpert, July 15, 1968, files of the Los Angeles County Federation of Labor.
page 260
"Some wild ideas": memorandum, undated, from files of the Los Angeles County Federation of Labor.
page 260
"It was my hope": *Ibid.*
page 261
"The defeat": *Time*, December 27, 1968.
page 261
"A realistic appraisal": Letter, Marilyn Miller to Claude L. McCue, April 15, 1969, from files of the Los Angeles County Federation of Labor.

BOOK THREE: NEW HEARST

1. RENAISSANCE

page 266
"Our idea is not": Letter, W. R. Hearst to J. F. Neylan, June 15, 1932, Bancroft Library.
page 269
"Family jewel box": *Time*, May 9, 1960.
page 275
"Other men who wore": *Reader's Digest*, May 1960.
page 277
"Like a hit list": Los Angeles *Times*, March 7, 1977.
page 279
"Neither the Hearst Corporation": *Ibid.*, February 23, 1974.
page 285
"Four lousy husbands": *Life*, November 19, 1965.
page 286
"Now young lady": *Ramparts*, March 1973.
page 287
"Do you *really*": *Life*, November 19, 1965.
page 287
"Bill Guy, our fiction editor": *Cosmopolitan*, July 1965.
page 287
"Quite obscene": *Life*, November 19, 1965.
page 287
"We are doing": *Ramparts*, March 1973.
page 289
"Suspicious of old attitudes": *Publishers' Weekly*, February 18, 1974.
page 290
"Business was just too big": *Ibid.*

2. THE MONARCH

page 293
'Underground newspaper for adults': William L. Rivers and David M. Rubin, *A Region's Press*, p. 37.
page 294
"Great Americans": San Francisco *Examiner*, January 23, 1974.
page 295
"Little Brown Brothers thing": Steven Weed, *My Search for Patty Hearst*, p. 22.
page 295
"If he's in a good mood": *Ibid.*, p. 161.

page 295
"If he moved": Don West and Jerry Belcher, *Patty/Tania*, p. 41.
page 296
"Youngest daughter": *Ibid.*, p. 30.
page 297
"Commando-like" operation": San Francisco *Examiner*, February 5, 1974.
page 298
"Sucked out, empty": Don West and Jerry Belcher, p. 32.
page 299
"She was half-dressed": San Francisco *Examiner*, February 4, 1974.
page 303
"Completely out of touch": *Ibid.*, January 21, 1974.
page 304
"I felt shitty": West and Belcher, p. 143.
page 304
"Arrested . . . for the crimes": San Francisco *Examiner*, February 13, 1974.
page 305
"It was incredible": Paul Avery and Vin McLellan, *Voices of Guns*, p. 245.

page 305
"You, a corporate liar": San Francisco *Examiner*, April 4, 1974.
page 306
"Blood money": Paul Avery and Vin McLellan, p. 245.
page 306
"We came here": *Ibid.*, p. 329.
page 307
"Liberal . . . but if I hadn't": *Ibid.*, p. 416.
page 307
"Like Jane Fonda": Mickey Cohen, *Mickey Cohen, In My Own Words.*
page 308
"I don't think we": *Time*, February 10, 1975.
page 308
"Horse's ass": Steven Weed, p. 126.
page 313
"Comrades" in the spectator's gallery:: San Francisco *Examiner*, September 19, 1975.
page 313
"Urban guerrilla": *Ibid.*
page 314
"I'll be able to tell you": *Ibid.*, February 25, 1976.

3. THE PHOENIX

page 322
"Due to all": Letter, William Robertson to J. J. Rodriguez, April 12, 1974, from files of the Los Angeles County Federation of Labor.
page 326
"We know": Letter, George Hearst,

Sr., to Millicent Hearst, May 21, 1971, private collection.
page 330
"I wouldn't be unhappy": Quoted in Bob Gottlieb, "The Remaking (Finally!) of the *Herald-Examiner*," *Los Angeles Magazine*, May 1978.

4. *BILDUNGSROMAN*

page 333
"As a kid I would go": *Time*, February 10, 1975.
page 335
Speeches and Writings: W. R. Hearst, *Selections From the*

Speeches and Writings of William Randolph Hearst.
page 337
"The $2 Billion Giveaway": San Francisco *Examiner*, January 11, 1976.

page 337
"Paper farmers, absentee landowners": *Ibid.*
page 338
"Like the fowls of the air": *Ibid.*
page 338
"Most extensive piece": "The Paper Farmers," San Francisco *Examiner*, 1976.

page 341
"Misstatements of law": *Ibid.*
page 346
"What is the use": *Outside*, August 1977.
page 346
"We believe": *Ibid.*

5. PRODIGAL DAUGHTER

page 354
"The answer is easy": Chicago *Tribune*, June 22, 1978.
page 357
"In the regular course of business": *The New York Times*, December 17, 1978.
page 361
"Mark of her experiences": Hearst clemency petition, as submitted in support of motion to vacate, set aside, or correct sentence, *U.S. v.* *Hearst*, No. CR-74-364 WHO, U.S. District Court [N.D., Cal.] August 2, 1978.
page 368
"Ultimate reactive person": *The New York Times*, April 3, 1977.
page 368
"Victorian heroine": Washington *Post*, September 10, 1978.
page 369
"Everything's changed": *Look*, February 19, 1979.

6. GENERATIONS

page 372
"The great-grandfather of all the Hearsts": George Hearst, *Recollections of George Hearst* (New York: Hearst Corp., 1972), p. 5.
page 376
"Triumph over everyone": *Look*, April 30, 1979.

page 376
"O Lord, thou God of vengeance": *Ibid.*
page 377
"Patty seems so remote": San Francisco *Examiner*, April 2, 1979.

BIBLIOGRAPHY

Alexander, Shana, *Anyone's Daughter*. New York: Viking Press, 1979.

Anderson, Jack, and May, Roland, *McCarthy: The Man, the Senator, the "ism."* Boston: Beacon Press, 1952.

Avery, Paul, and McLellan, Vin, *Voices of Guns*. New York: Putnam, 1977.

Baker, Marilyn, *Exclusive! The Inside Story of Patricia Hearst and the SLA*. New York: Macmillan, 1974.

Black, Winifred (Sweet), *The Life and Personality of Phoebe Apperson Hearst*. San Francisco: privately printed, 1928.

Bronson, William, and Watkins, T. H., *Homestake: The Centennial History*. San Francisco: Homestake Mining Co., 1977.

Brown, Helen Gurley, *Sex and the Office*. New York: B. Geis Associates, 1964.

———, *Sex and the Single Girl*. New York: B. Geis Associates, 1962.

Brown, Henry, *Fifth Avenue Old and New, 1824–1924*. New York: Fifth Avenue Association, 1924.

California, University of, *The Centennial Record*. Berkeley, University of California, 1967.

Carlisle, Rodney, *Hearst and the New Deal: The Progressive as Reactionary*. New York: Garland, 1979.

Carlson, Oliver, and Bates, Ernest, *Hearst, Lord of San Simeon*. New York: Viking Press, 1936.

Cassini, Igor, *I'd Do It All Over Again*. New York: Putnam, 1977.

Caute, David, *The Great Fear: The Anticommunist Purge Under Truman and Eisenhower*. New York: Simon and Schuster, 1978.

Chaplin, Charles, *My Autobiography*. New York: Simon and Schuster, 1964.

Coblentz, Edmond, *Newsmen Speak: Journalists on Their Craft*. Berkeley: University of California Press, 1954.

Cohen, Mickey, *Mickey Cohen: In My Own Words*. Englewood Cliffs, N.J.: Prentice-Hall, 1975.

Cohn, Roy, *McCarthy*. New York: New American Library, 1968.

Collier, Peter, and Horowitz, David, *The Rockefellers*. New York: Holt, Rinehart & Winston, 1976.

Considine, Bob, *It's All News to Me: A Reporter's Deposition*. New York: Meredith Press, 1967.

Cook, Fred, *The Nightmare Decade: The Life and Times of Senator Joe McCarthy*. New York: Random House, 1975.

Davies, Marion, *The Times We Had*, eds. Pamela Pfau and Kenneth Marx. Indianapolis: Bobbs-Merrill, 1975.

Ferman, Louis, *The Death of a Newspaper: The Story of the Detroit Times*. Kalamazoo, Mich.: W. F. Upjohn Institute, 1963.

Fielder, Mildred, *The Treasure of Homestake Gold*. Aberdeen, S.D.: North Plains Press, 1970.

Fifty Years on Fifth, 1907–1957. New York: Fifth Avenue Association, 1957.

Findley, Tim, and Payne, Leslie, *The Life and Death of the SLA*. New York: Ballantine, 1976.

Frankland, Mark, *Khrushchev*. Harmondsworth, G.B.: Penguin, 1966.

Gottlieb, Robert, and Wolt, Irene, *Thinking Big: The Story of the Los Angeles Times and Its Publishers and Their Influence on Southern California*. New York: Putnam, 1977.

Griffith, Robert, *The Politics of Fear*. Lexington, Ky.: University of Kentucky Press, 1970.

Guiles, Fred, *Marion Davies: A Biography*. New York: McGraw-Hill, 1972.

Halberstam, David, *The Powers That Be*. New York: Knopf, 1979.

Hart, James, *A Companion to California*. New York: Oxford University Press, 1978.

Healy, Paul, *Cissy: The Biography of Eleanor M. "Cissy" Patterson*. Garden City, N.Y.: Doubleday, 1966.

Hearst, Patricia, *The Trial of Patty Hearst*. San Francisco: Great Fidelity Press, 1976.

Hearst, William Randolph, *Newspaper Principles*. New York: Hearst Corp., 1972.

――――, *Selections From the Writings and Speeches of William Randolph Hearst*, ed. E. F. Tomkins. San Francisco: privately printed, 1948.

――――, *William Randolph Hearst: A Portrait in His Own Words*, ed. Edmond Coblentz. New York: Simon and Schuster, 1952.

Hearst, William Randolph, Jr., *Ask Me Anything: Our Adventures With Khrushchev*. New York: McGraw-Hill, 1960.

Herndon, Booton, *Praised and Damned: The Story of Fulton Lewis, Jr.* New York: Duell, Sloan & Pearce, 1954.

Hofstadter, Richard, *The Age of Reform: From Bryan to FDR*. New York: Knopf, 1955.

Huxley, Aldous, *After Many a Summer Dies the Swan*. New York: Harper, 1939.

Israel, Lee, *Kilgallen*. New York: Delacorte, 1979.

Jimenez, Janey, *My Prisoner*. Kansas City, Kan.: Sheed, Andrews & McNeel, 1977.

Kael, Pauline, *The Citizen Kane Book*. Boston: Little, Brown, 1971.

Kellen, Konrad. *Khrushchev: A Political Portrait*. New York: Praeger, 1961.

Kempton, Murray, *America Comes of Middle Age*. Boston: Little, Brown, 1963.

———, *Part of Our Time*. New York: Simon and Schuster, 1955.

Klurfeld, Herman, *Winchell: His Life and Times*. New York: Praeger, 1976.

Lewis, Oscar, *Fabulous San Simeon*. San Francisco: California Historical Society, 1958.

Liebling, A. J., *The Press*. New York: Ballantine, 1964.

McKelway, St. Clair, *Gossip: The Life and Times of Walter Winchell*. New York: Viking Press, 1940.

McPhaul, John, *Deadlines and Monkeyshines: The Fabled World of Chicago Journalism*. Englewood Cliffs, N.J.: Prentice-Hall, 1962.

Manchester, William, *The Glory and the Dream: A Narrative History of America, 1932–1972*. Boston: Little, Brown, 1973, 1974.

Marcosson, Isaac, *Anaconda*. New York: Dodd, Mead, 1957.

Martin, Harold, *Ralph McGill, Reporter*. Boston: Little, Brown, 1973.

Matthews, J. B., *Odyssey of a Fellow Traveler*. New York: Mount Vernon, 1938.

Maxwell, Elsa, *R.S.V.P.: Elsa Maxwell's Own Story*. Boston: Little, Brown, 1954.

Metz, Robert, *CBS: Reflections in a Bloodshot Eye*. Chicago: Playboy, 1975.

Mott, Frank Luther, *American Journalism, a History, 1690–1960*, 3rd ed. New York: Macmillan, 1962.

Murphy, Reg, and Gulliver, Hal, *The Southern Strategy*. New York: Scribner, 1971.

Murray, George, *The Madhouse on Madison Street*. Chicago: Follet Publishing, 1965.

Murray, Ken, *The Golden Days of San Simeon*. Garden City, N.Y.: Doubleday, 1971.

Nixon, Richard, *Six Crises*. Garden City, N.Y.: Doubleday, 1972.

Nizer, Louis, *My Life in Court*. Garden City, N.Y.: Doubleday, 1961.

Older, Cora, *William Randolph Hearst: American*. New York: Appleton-Century, 1936.

Older, Cora and Fremont, *George Hearst: California Pioneer*. Los Angeles: Westernlore, 1966.

O'Loughlin, Edward, *Hearst and His Enemies*. New York: Arno, 1970.

Parkman, Francis, *The Oregon Trail*. New York: Washington Square, 1967.

Pearson, Drew, *Diaries: 1949–1959*, ed. Tyler Abell. New York: Holt, Rinehart & Winston, 1974.

Peterson, Theodore, *Magazines in the Twentieth Century*. Urbana, Ill.: University of Illinois Press, 1964.

Pilat, Oliver, *Pegler: Angry Man of the Press*. Boston: Beacon Press, 1963.

Potter, Jeffrey, *Men, Money & Magic: The Story of Dorothy Schiff*. New York: Coward, McCann & Geoghegan, 1976.

Richardson, James, *For the Life of Me: Memoirs of a City Editor*. New York: Putnam, 1954.

Rivers, William L., and Rubin, David M., *A Region's Press: Anatomy of Newspapers in the San Francisco Bay Area*. Berkeley: Institute of Governmental Studies, 1971.

Roosevelt, Elliot, *An Untold Story: The Roosevelts of Hyde Park*. New York: Putnam, 1973.

Rovere, Richard, *Senator Joe McCarthy*. New York: Harcourt, Brace, 1959.

St. Johns, Adela Rogers, *The Honeycomb*. Garden City, N.Y.: Doubleday, 1969.

Santayana, George, *Persons and Places*. New York: Scribner, 1944–1953.

Sobol, Louis, *The Longest Street: A Memoir*. New York: Crown, 1968.

Soltysik, Fred, *In Search of a Sister*. New York: Bantam, 1976.

Swanberg, W. A., *Citizen Hearst*. New York: Scribner, 1961.

———, *Pulitzer*. New York: Scribner, 1967.

Talese, Gay, *The Kingdom and the Power*. New York: World, 1969.

Tebbel, John, *The Life and Good Times of William Randolph Hearst*. New York: Dutton, 1952.

Thomas, Bob, *Winchell*. Garden City, N.Y.: Doubleday, 1971.

Underwood, Agness, *Newspaperwoman*. New York: Harper, 1949.

Wechsler, James, *Age of Suspicion*. New York: Random House, 1953.

———, *Reflections of an Angry Middle-Aged Editor*. New York: Random House, 1960.

Weed, Steven, *My Search for Patty Hearst*. New York: Crown, 1976.

Weiner, Ed, *Let's Go to Press: A Biography of Walter Winchell*. New York: Putnam, 1955.

West, Don, and Belcher, Jerry, *Patty/Tania*. New York: Pyramid Books, 1975.

Winchell, Walter, *Winchell Exclusive*. Englewood Cliffs, N.J.: Prentice-Hall, 1975.

Winkler, John, *William Randolph Hearst: A New Appraisal*. New York: Hastings House, 1955.

———, *W. R. Hearst: An American Phenomenon*. London: Jonathan Cape, 1928.

Wood, James, *Magazines in the United States*. New York: Ronald Press, 1971.

Working Press of the Nation. Chicago: National Research Bureau, 1945–

INDEX

(The abbreviation WRH stands for William Randolph Hearst, Sr.)